Excel 97 One Step at a Time

Excel 97
One Step at a Time

Alan Neibauer

IDG Books Worldwide, Inc.

An International Data Group Company

FOSTER CITY, CA · CHICAGO, IL · INDIANAPOLIS, IN · SOUTHLAKE, TX

Excel 97 One Step at a Time

Published by
IDG Books Worldwide, Inc.
An International Data Group Company
919 E. Hillsdale Blvd., Suite 400
Foster City, CA 94404
www.idgbooks.com (IDG Books Worldwide Web site)

Library of Congress Catalog Card No.: 97-076685

ISBN: 0-7645-3139-5

Printed in the United States of America

10 9 8 7 6 5 4 3 2 1

1E/SV/RR/ZX/FC

Distributed in the United States by IDG Books Worldwide, Inc.

Distributed by Macmillan Canada for Canada; by Transworld Publishers Limited in the United Kingdom; by IDG Norge Books for Norway; by IDG Sweden Books for Sweden; by Woodslane Pty. Ltd. for Australia; by Woodslane Enterprises Ltd. for New Zealand; by Longman Singapore Publishers Ltd. for Singapore, Malaysia, Thailand, and Indonesia; by Simron Pty. Ltd. for South Africa; by Toppan Company Ltd. for Japan; by Distribuidora Cuspide for Argentina; by Livraria Cultura for Brazil; by Ediciencia S.A. for Ecuador; by Addison-Wesley Publishing Company for Korea; by Ediciones ZETA S.C.R. Ltda. for Peru; by WS Computer Publishing Corporation, Inc., for the Philippines; by Unalis Corporation for Taiwan; by Contemporanea de Ediciones for Venezuela; by Computer Book & Magazine Store for Puerto Rico; by Express Computer Distributors for the Caribbean and West Indies. Authorized Sales Agent: Anthony Rudkin Associates for the Middle East and North Africa.

For general information on IDG Books Worldwide's books in the U.S., please call our Consumer Customer Service department at 800-762-2974. For reseller information, including discounts and premium sales, please call our Reseller Customer Service department at 800-434-3422.

For information on where to purchase IDG Books Worldwide's books outside the U.S., please contact our International Sales department at 415-655-3200 or fax 415-655-3295.

For information on foreign language translations, please contact our Foreign & Subsidiary Rights department at 415-655-3021 or fax 415-655-3281.

For sales inquiries and special prices for bulk quantities, please contact our Sales department at 415-655-3200 or write to the address above.

For information on using IDG Books Worldwide's books in the classroom or for ordering examination copies, please contact our Educational Sales department at 800-434-2086 or fax 817-251-8174.

For press review copies, author interviews, or other publicity information, please contact our Public Relations department at 415-655-3000 or fax 415-655-3299.

For authorization to photocopy items for corporate, personal, or educational use, please contact Copyright Clearance Center, 222 Rosewood Drive, Danvers, MA 01923, or fax 508-750-4470.

™ The IDG Books Worldwide logo is a trademark under exclusive license to IDG Books Worldwide, Inc., from International Data Group, Inc.

ABOUT IDG BOOKS WORLDWIDE

Welcome to the world of IDG Books Worldwide.

IDG Books Worldwide, Inc., is a subsidiary of International Data Group, the world's largest publisher of computer-related information and the leading global provider of information services on information technology. IDG was founded more than 25 years ago and now employs more than 8,500 people worldwide. IDG publishes more than 275 computer publications in over 75 countries (see listing below). More than 60 million people read one or more IDG publications each month.

Launched in 1990, IDG Books Worldwide is today the #1 publisher of best-selling computer books in the United States. We are proud to have received eight awards from the Computer Press Association in recognition of editorial excellence and three from *Computer Currents'* First Annual Readers' Choice Awards. Our best-selling *...For Dummies®* series has more than 30 million copies in print with translations in 30 languages. IDG Books Worldwide, through a joint venture with IDG's Hi-Tech Beijing, became the first U.S. publisher to publish a computer book in the People's Republic of China. In record time, IDG Books Worldwide has become the first choice for millions of readers around the world who want to learn how to better manage their businesses.

Our mission is simple: Every one of our books is designed to bring extra value and skill-building instructions to the reader. Our books are written by experts who understand and care about our readers. The knowledge base of our editorial staff comes from years of experience in publishing, education, and journalism — experience we use to produce books for the '90s. In short, we care about books, so we attract the best people. We devote special attention to details such as audience, interior design, use of icons, and illustrations. And because we use an efficient process of authoring, editing, and desktop publishing our books electronically, we can spend more time ensuring superior content and spend less time on the technicalities of making books.

You can count on our commitment to deliver high-quality books at competitive prices on topics you want to read about. At IDG Books Worldwide, we continue in the IDG tradition of delivering quality for more than 25 years. You'll find no better book on a subject than one from IDG Books Worldwide.

John Kilcullen
CEO
IDG Books Worldwide, Inc.

Steven Berkowitz
President and Publisher
IDG Books Worldwide, Inc.

*Eighth Annual
Computer Press
Awards ≥1992*

*Ninth Annual
Computer Press
Awards ≥1993*

*Tenth Annual
Computer Press
Awards ≥1994*

*Eleventh Annual
Computer Press
Awards ≥1995*

IDG Books Worldwide, Inc., is a subsidiary of International Data Group, the world's largest publisher of computer-related information and the leading global provider of information services on information technology. International Data Group publishes over 275 computer publications in over 75 countries. Sixty million people read one or more International Data Group publications each month. International Data Group's publications include: **ARGENTINA:** Buyer's Guide, Computerworld Argentina, PC World Argentina; **AUSTRALIA:** Australian Macworld, Australian PC World, Australian Reseller News, Computerworld, IT Casebook, Network World, Publish, Webmaster; **AUSTRIA:** Computerwelt Osterreich, Networks Austria, PC Tip Austria; **BANGLADESH:** PC World Bangladesh; **BELARUS:** PC World Belarus; **BELGIUM:** Data News; **BRAZIL:** Annuário de Informática, Computerworld, Connections, Macworld, PC Player, PC World, Publish, Reseller News, Supergamepower; **BULGARIA:** Computerworld Bulgaria, Network World Bulgaria, PC & MacWorld Bulgaria; **CANADA:** CIO Canada, Client/Server World, ComputerWorld Canada, InfoWorld Canada, NetworkWorld Canada, WebWorld; **CHILE:** Computerworld Chile, PC World Chile; **COLOMBIA:** Computerworld Colombia, PC World Colombia; **COSTA RICA:** PC World Centro America; **THE CZECH AND SLOVAK REPUBLICS:** Computerworld Czechoslovakia, Macworld Czech Republic, PC World Czechoslovakia; **DENMARK:** Communications World Danmark, Computerworld Danmark, Macworld Danmark, PC World Danmark, Techworld Denmark; **DOMINICAN REPUBLIC:** PC World Republica Dominicana; **ECUADOR:** PC World Ecuador; **EGYPT:** Computerworld Middle East, PC World Middle East; **EL SALVADOR:** PC World Centro America; **FINLAND:** MikroPC, Tietoverkko, Tietoviikko; **FRANCE:** Distributique, Hebdo, Info PC, Le Monde Informatique, Macworld, Reseaux & Telecoms, WebMaster France; **GERMANY:** Computer Partner, Computerwoche, Computerwoche Extra, Computerwoche FOCUS, Global Online, Macwelt, PC Welt; **GREECE:** Amiga Computing, GamePro Greece, Multimedia World; **GUATEMALA:** PC World Centro America; **HONDURAS:** PC World Centro America; **HONG KONG:** Computerworld Hong Kong, PC World Hong Kong, Publish in Asia; **HUNGARY:** ABCD CD-ROM, Computerworld Szamitastechnika, Internetto online Magazine, PC World Hungary, PC-X Magazin Hungary; **ICELAND:** Tolvuheimur PC World Island; **INDIA:** Information Communications World, Information Systems Computerworld, PC World India, Publish in Asia; **INDONESIA:** InfoKomputer PC World, Komputek Computerworld, Publish in Asia; **IRELAND:** ComputerScope, PC Live!; **ISRAEL:** Macworld Israel, People & Computers/Computerworld; **ITALY:** Computerworld Italia, Macworld Italia, Networking Italia, PC World Italia; **JAPAN:** DTP World, Macworld Japan, Nikkei Personal Computing, OS/2 World Japan, SunWorld Japan, Windows NT World, Windows World Japan; **KENYA:** PC World East African; **KOREA:** Hi-Tech Information, Macworld Korea, PC World Korea; **MACEDONIA:** PC World Macedonia; **MALAYSIA:** Computerworld Malaysia, PC World Malaysia, Publish in Asia; **MALTA:** PC World Malta; **MEXICO:** Computerworld Mexico, PC World Mexico; **MYANMAR:** PC World Myanmar; **NETHERLANDS:** Computer! Totaal, LAN Internetworking Magazine, LAN World Buyers Guide, Macworld Netherlands, Net, WebWereld; **NEW ZEALAND:** Absolute Beginners Guide and Plain & Simple Series, Computer Buyer, Computer Industry Directory, Computerworld New Zealand, MTB, Network World, PC World New Zealand; **NICARAGUA:** PC World Centro America; **NORWAY:** Computerworld Norge, CW Rapport, Datamagasinet, Financial Rapport, Kursguide Norge, Macworld Norge, Multimediaworld Norge, PC World Ekspress Norge, PC World Nettverk, PC World Norge, PC World ProduktGuide Norge, PC World Norge; **PAKISTAN:** Computerworld Pakistan; **PANAMA:** PC World Panama; **PEOPLE'S REPUBLIC OF CHINA:** China Computer Users, China Computerworld, China InfoWorld, China Telecom World Weekly, Computer & Communication, Electronic Design China, Electronics Today, Electronics Weekly, Game Software, PC World China, Popular Computer Week, Software Weekly, Software World, Telecom World; **PERU:** Computerworld Peru, PC World Profesional Peru, PC World SoHo Peru; **PHILIPPINES:** Click!, Computerworld Philippines, PC World Philippines, Publish in Asia; **POLAND:** Computerworld Poland, Computerworld Special Report Poland, Cyber, Macworld Poland, Networld Poland, PC World Komputer; **PORTUGAL:** Cerebro/PC World, Computerworld/Correio Informático, Dealer World Portugal, Mac*In/PC*In Portugal, Multimedia World; **PUERTO RICO:** PC World Puerto Rico; **ROMANIA:** Computerworld Romania, PC World-Romania, Telecom Romania; **RUSSIA:** Computerworld Russia, Mir PK, Publish, Seti; **SINGAPORE:** Computerworld Singapore, PC World Singapore, Publish in Asia; **SLOVENIA:** Monitor; **SOUTH AFRICA:** Computing SA, Network World SA, Software World SA; **SPAIN:** Communicaciones World España, Computerworld España, Dealer World España, Macworld España, PC World España; **SRI LANKA:** Infolink PC World; **SWEDEN:** CAP&Design, Computer Sweden, Corporate Computing Sweden, Internetworld Sweden, it.branschen, Macworld Sweden, MaxiData Sweden, MikroDatorn, Nätverk & Kommunikation, PC World Sweden, PCaktiv, Windows World Sweden; **SWITZERLAND:** Computerworld Schweiz, Macworld Schweiz, PCtip; **TAIWAN:** Computerworld Taiwan, Macworld Taiwan, NEW ViSiON/Publish, PC World Taiwan, Windows World Taiwan; **THAILAND:** Publish in Asia, Thai Computerworld; **TURKEY:** Computerworld Turkiye, Macworld Turkiye, Network World Turkiye, PC World Turkiye; **UKRAINE:** Computerworld Kiev, Multimedia World Ukraine, PC World Ukraine; **UNITED KINGDOM:** Acorn User UK, Amiga Action UK, Amiga Computing UK, Apple Talk UK, Computing, Macworld, Parents and Computers UK, PC Advisor, PC Home, PSX Pro, The WEB; **UNITED STATES:** Cable in the Classroom, CIO Magazine, Computerworld, DOS World, Federal Computer Week, GamePro Magazine, InfoWorld, I-Way, Macworld, Network World, PC Games, PC World, Publish, Video Event, THE WEB Magazine, and WebMaster; online webzines: JavaWorld, NetscapeWorld, and SunWorld Online; **URUGUAY:** InfoWorld Uruguay; **VENEZUELA:** Computerworld Venezuela, PC World Venezuela; and **VIETNAM:** PC World Vietnam. 3/24/97

CREDITS

Acquisitions Editors
Ellen Camm
Juliana Aldous

Development Editors
Deborah Craig
Stefan Grünwedel

Technical Editor
Bookmakers

Copy Editors
Deborah Craig
Larisa North

Production Coordinator
Tom Debolski

Book Designer
Seventeenth Street Studios

Graphics and Production Specialists
Ritchie Durdin
Shannon Miller
Maureen Moore
Dina F Quan
Trevor Wilson
Elsie Yim

Quality Control Specialists
Mick Arellano
Mark Schumann

Proofreader
Nancy Reinhardt

Indexer
Richard T. Evans

ABOUT THE AUTHOR

Alan Neibauer is the author of popular books on computer software, a corporate trainer, and a consultant to companies both large and small. A graduate of the Wharton School, University of Pennsylvania with a master's degree in Public Administration, he also has a B.S. in Communications from Temple University. He served as Chair of Computer Management Information Systems of Holy Family College in Philadelphia, and has developed software for the health care industry. When not writing, Neibauer enjoys practicing Tae Kwon Do by the New Jersey shoreline with his wife, Barbara.

WELCOME TO ONE STEP AT A TIME!

TRY OUT THE

INTERACTIVE TUTORIALS

ON YOUR CD!

The book you are holding is very special. It's just the tool you need for learning software quickly and easily. More than a book, it offers a *unique learning experience*. Along with our text, the dynamic *One Step at a Time On-Demand* software included on the bonus CD-ROM in this book coaches you through the tutorials at *your own pace*. You'll never feel lost!

See examples of how to accomplish specific tasks. Listen to clear explanations of how to solve your problems.

Use the *One Step at a Time On-Demand* software in three ways:

- **Demo mode** shows you how to perform a task in movie-style fashion — in sound and color! Just sit back and watch the *One Step* software demonstrate the correct sequence of steps on-screen. Seeing is understanding!

- **Teacher mode** simulates the software environment so you can practice completing a task without worrying about making a mistake. The *One Step* software guides you every step of the way. Trying is learning!

- **Concurrent mode** allows you to work in the actual software environment while still getting assistance from the friendly *One Step* helper. Doing is succeeding!

Our goal is for you to learn the features of a software application by guiding you painlessly through valuable and helpful tutorials. Our *One Step at a Time On-Demand* software — combined with the step-by-step tutorials in our One Step at a Time series — will make your learning experience fast-paced and fun.

See it. Try it. Do it.

To Barbara, Alan, Charlene, Harvey, Elaine, Gail, Mark, Steve, Marie, Nate, Anita, Vince, Martie, Nicholas, Marilyn, Stanley, Paul, Vicky, Shirley, and in memory of Sid for keeping a song in my heart and sand between my toes

PREFACE

Welcome to *Excel 97 One Step at a Time,* part of a unique and exciting series from IDG Books Worldwide. Our goal with this series is to give quick, hands-on training, with help at every step as you're learning the features of Excel 97.

Excel 97 One Step at a Time has been designed to support your learning in the following ways:

- Lessons are paced to include small, manageable chunks of information so you never feel you're in over your head.

- You learn Excel 97 by doing. Each lesson is divided into a number of short exercises, presented in easy-to-follow steps, and with plenty of illustrations to help.

- At the start of each lesson, you learn which files you need to do the lesson, and how much time to set aside to complete it.

- A CD-ROM with sample files accompanies this book. It includes all the exercises you'll need to complete the lessons, and completed projects that you can compare your results against. This CD-ROM also features our exclusive *One Step at a Time On-Demand* interactive tutorial, which coaches you through the exercises in the book while you work on your computer at your own pace.

Who Should Read This Book

Excel 97 One Step at a Time is for people who have only a basic knowledge of computers but who are new to Microsoft Excel 97. You will also find this book useful if you have already started using Excel but want to learn more about it. This book assumes that you know how to turn on your computer and use the mouse and keyboard to interact with Windows 95. The exercises include completely detailed procedures so you'll feel comfortable working through these lessons.

How This Book Is Organized

Excel 97 One Step at a Time has a very simple structure. The **Jump Start** takes you through a step-by-step tour of essential Excel techniques and typical features. Don't try to memorize the techniques that you're experimenting with — just follow the steps to get a sense of how Excel works. You'll get more information about the techniques and features in the lessons to come.

Part I: Meet Microsoft Excel introduces you to this wonderful program, while giving you all the skills you need to start creating worksheets. Lesson 1 teaches you the fundamentals of using Excel. Lesson 2 describes how to open and edit worksheets.

Part II: Essential Excel Techniques shows you how to automate your work with Excel, rearrange and format your work, and use multiple worksheets and windows.

Part III: Key Excel Features demonstrates how to prevent and correct errors using special Excel techniques, how to use functions to perform calculations, and how to connect to the World Wide Web and link information between projects.

Part IV: Organizing and Customizing Excel shows you how to create attractive printouts, find and sort information, and customize Excel to suit the way you like to work.

Part V: Excel Graphics illustrates how to add eye-catching graphics, create charts and maps, insert special effects with WordArt, and create your own custom artwork.

Finally, four appendixes cover installing Excel 97, practice projects, answers to the bonus questions in the *Skills Challenge* exercises, and using the CD-ROM supplied with the book.

How to Use This Book

This series is designed for the way people in the real world learn. Every lesson has a consistent structure so you can quickly become comfortable using all the following elements:

- **Stopwatch:** It is best if you can complete each lesson without interruption, so look for the stopwatch symbol at the beginning of each lesson. This stopwatch tells you approximately how much time to set aside to work through the lesson.

- **Goals:** The goals of each lesson are clearly identified, so you can anticipate which skills you will acquire.

- **Get Ready:** Here you find out which files you need to complete the steps in the lessons, and you see an illustration of the worksheet you will create after completing the exercises.

- **Visual Bonus:** This is a one- or two-page illustration with labels to help you understand a special procedure or element of Excel more clearly.

- **Skills Challenge:** Every lesson ends with a comprehensive Skills Challenge exercise incorporating the skills you've learned in the individual exercises. The steps in the Skills Challenge are less explicit than those in the exercises, so you have a chance to practice and reinforce your Excel skills.

- **Bonus Questions:** Sprinkled throughout the Skills Challenge exercise are bonus questions. Check Appendix C for the answers to these questions to see if you got them right.

- **Troubleshooting:** Near the end of each lesson is a list of useful tips and tricks to avoid the traps and pitfalls that many new Excel users experience. Look over the troubleshooting tips even if you don't have problems, so you can avoid potential problems in the future.

- **Wrap Up:** Here you get an overview of the skills you learned, as well as a brief preview of the next lesson.

The One Step at a Time CD-ROM

The CD-ROM that accompanies this book includes the exclusive *One Step at a Time On-Demand* interactive tutorial. This software coaches you through the exercises in the book while you work on your computer at your own pace. You can use the software on its own, or concurrently with the book.

Conventions Used in This Book

Using this book is easy. It follows just a few simple conventions you should know about:

- Instructions to choose a command from a menu are shown this way:

  Select File ➢ Open.

  In this example, *Select* means to click the menu name, File is the name of the menu and Open is the name of the command to select from within the menu.

- In the exercises, information that you should actually type is shown in **boldface**.

- Most exercises and Skill Challenges let you start a project with a file copied from the CD-ROM that accompanies this book. Simply locate the workbook that corresponds to the lesson you're working on. To find a workbook that you need to complete a Skills Challenge, look in the Exercise directory of your computer (or the CD-ROM). It will be named "Workout" followed by the lesson number, as in "Workout 5."

- You can check your work at any time by opening a file that contains the completed workbook from the exercise or Skills Challenge. You'll find these workbooks in the Solution folder. The solutions to lesson exercises have the word "Solution" at the end. For example, in Lesson 2 you'll create a workbook called "Price Calculation." The completed workbook is called "Price Calculation Solution." The solutions to Skills Challenges are called "Solution" followed by the lesson number. For example, the Skills Challenge solution for Lesson 5 is entitled "Solution 5."

I've tried to make it easy for you to use this book by including several easy-to-understand features. For example:

The text that follows this icon contains a special tip intended to give you some "inside information" that can save you time or frustration.

The text that follows this icon explains a special note about the subject. Notes tend to be a bit more technically oriented than the rest of the text, but the information they contain is important if you want to know "why" rather than simply "what."

Feedback

Please feel free to let us know what you think about this book and whether you have any suggestions for improvements. You can send your questions and comments to me and the rest of the *Excel 97 One Step at a Time* team on the IDG Books Worldwide Web site at www.idgbooks.com.

You're now ready to begin. Start with the Jump Start for an interesting look at Excel 97, and then learn Excel on your own and in your own time, in the lessons that follow.

ACKNOWLEDGMENTS

I want to thank all of those at IDG Books who are responsible for developing this new and exciting series, and for making it such a pleasure to work on.

My appreciation goes to **Ellen Camm** for bringing me on board, to **Stefan Grünwedel** for guiding me through the development process, and to my agent **Claire Horne.** I want especially to thank **Deborah Craig** for her wonderful editing and organizational skills, and for ironing out the many rough edges of my work. Special thanks also to technical editors **Susan Glinert** and **Roy Stevens,** and to **Denise Santoro, Jennifer Rowe, Larisa North,** and **Anne Friedman** for working on the manuscript at various critical stages. For their skillful production work in such a short amount of time, many thanks go to **Tom Debolski** and **Ritchie Durdin.**

Special thanks to **Tom McCaffrey, Marilyn Russell,** and everyone at **Real Help Communications, Inc.** (www.realhelpcom.com) for creating the several thousand sound files required for the CD-ROMs in this series, under very aggressive deadlines.

I could not have completed this, or any other book, without the support, love, and understanding of **Barbara,** my bride of over 30 years. She is, in my humble opinion, the greatest there is.

CONTENTS AT A GLANCE

CONTENTS

Jump Start

GOALS

In this Jump Start, you'll learn the following:

- Typing text and numbers into worksheets
- Using AutoFill to complete a series
- Using AutoSum to insert totals
- Formatting numbers
- Formatting text
- Rotating text
- Saving and printing worksheets

Entering Text and Numbers

GET READY

There are a lot of programs that you use just because you have to. Excel is a program that you'll use because it saves you time, and can even be fun. In this Jump Start section you'll learn many of the basics of Excel to complete a spreadsheet — but don't be fooled by the word *basics*. You'll use some powerful techniques that make Excel a breeze to use, and one of the most popular spreadsheet programs of all times.

As you work through this Jump Start, don't worry about remembering all of the steps and techniques that you'll perform. There will be plenty of time to learn them in the lessons that follow. For now, take your time and work through the jump start step by step, enjoying the wonderful features that you'll soon be mastering.

When you're done with this Jump Start, you will have created the spreadsheet shown here.

To start this Jump Start, turn on your computer and have the Windows 95 desktop on your screen. Now enjoy the ride!

ENTERING DATA AND MAKING CALCULATIONS

Using Excel to create spreadsheets is really easy. You just start the program, and enter information where you want it to appear. You can enter numbers, text, and dates into the spreadsheet, and even have Excel complete a series of entries for you. When you need to perform a mathematical calculation, you enter a formula. As you'll learn, it is formulas that give Excel its real kick.

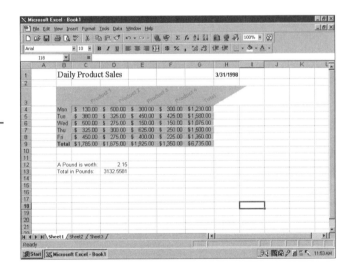

Entering Text and Numbers

Start from the very beginning. You'll launch Excel and begin entering a spreadsheet. Most spreadsheets have *labels* that describe the information either below them or to their right. You'll enter just two labels and then later have Excel complete the rest for you.

You can launch Excel in several ways. In this warm-up, you'll start Excel from the Windows 95 taskbar. You can also start Excel, however, by double-clicking on any Excel file, and you may have a shortcut for starting Excel on your Windows 95 desktop.

Entering Text and Numbers

1 Click the Start menu on the Windows 95 taskbar.

2 Point to the word Programs.

3 In the menu that appears, click Microsoft Excel. (Unless you're told otherwise, *click* always means click with the left mouse button.)

You've now opened Excel. So far, we've been calling Excel a spreadsheet program. The term *spreadsheet,* however, is a generic term for information organized in rows and columns. In Excel, spreadsheets are called *worksheets.* An Excel file is really called a *workbook,* and it contains one or more worksheets. So what you see on the screen is actually a worksheet window.

You'll see the menu bar, two toolbars, and the rows and columns of the worksheet window. The first toolbar, just under the menu bar, is called the Standard toolbar. The toolbar under that is called the Formatting toolbar. Don't worry if you don't know what all of the buttons on the toolbars are for. When you point to a button, Excel displays its name in a ScreenTip, a small box just below the mouse pointer. The bar just above the column letters, the one that contains the equal sign, is called the *formula bar.* (You'll get a more detailed tour of the Excel window in Lesson 1.)

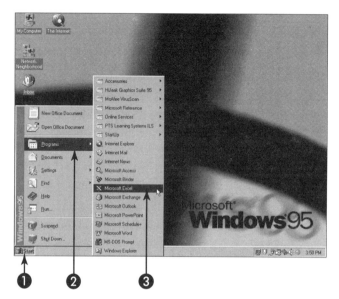

NOTE *The intersection of a numbered row and lettered column is called a cell. The cell in the upper-left corner of the worksheet is cell A1, the one to its right is cell B1, and the cell below it is A2. The cell that is ready to accept information is called the active cell, and it is surrounded by the thick frame.*

4 Click cell B1. This activates the cell so you can enter information into it.

5 Type this: **Daily Product Sales**.

When you start typing, two buttons appear in the formula bar, to the left of the equal sign. The one with the check mark is called the *Enter* button; the one with the X is called the *Cancel* button.

6 Click the Enter button.

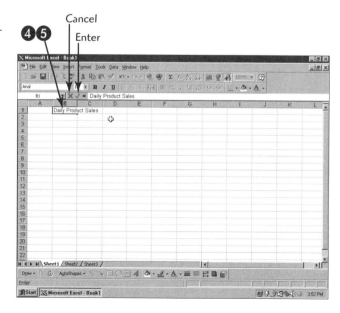

Cancel

Enter

Completing a Series Automatically

Excel runs long text entries into adjacent blank cells. If you later enter something in a cell that contains this spillover text, the extra text will disappear, but it won't be lost. When you click a cell, its full contents appears in the formula bar, to the right of the equal sign. You won't have this problem when entering numbers, as you'll soon learn.

7 Click cell H1.

8 Press Ctrl+;. (That means to hold down the Ctrl key and press the semicolon.) Excel inserts the current date.

9 Press the Enter key to accept the entry in the cell and move to the next row.

10 Click cell B4.

11 Type **Mon**.

*When instructed to type information such as this, do not type the final period. For example, in Step 11, you should type **Mon**, without the period, which just ends the sentence. If you type the period, some of the features will not work as described.*

12 Click cell C3.

13 Type **Product 1**.

14 Now enter the numbers shown in the illustration at right into the remaining cells.

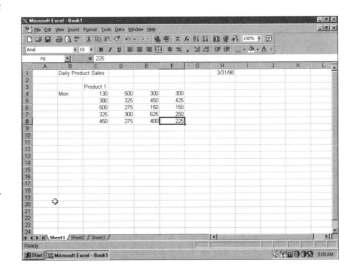

Completing a Series Automatically

Excel is full of time-saving features, most starting with the word *Auto*, as in AutoFill, AutoSum, and AutoComplete. AutoFill saves you from having to enter a series of repeating labels yourself. If you want to enter the months from January to December, for example, you just

Completing a Series Automatically

tell Excel where you want to start (with January) and Excel does the rest. You'll use AutoFill now to complete two different types of series:

① Click cell C3.

② Point to the small black square in the lower-right corner of cell C3 — this is called the *fill* handle — so the pointer appears as a black plus sign.

> *The shape of the mouse pointer depends on where you are pointing. When you point to the active cell, the mouse pointer can have three different shapes — and each performs a different function. The black plus sign appears when you're pointing to the fill handle. An arrow appears when you're pointing to the cell border; dragging when you see this pointer moves the cell. A white plus sign appears when you point in the cell; dragging when you see this pointer selects one or more cells.*

③ Drag from cell C3 straight across to cell F3.

④ Release the mouse button.

Excel fills in the series for you, from Product 1 to Product 4. Don't worry if this is not what happened. If you stopped before cell F3, just drag the fill handle to the right some more. If you moved Product 1 to another cell by mistake, or dragged the fill handle too far, just click the Undo button and try again. (The Undo button is the little curved arrow pointing to the left in the Standard toolbar.) If you just selected the cells so they appear black, click cell C3 and try again.

⑤ Click cell G3.

⑥ Type **Total**.

⑦ Click cell B4.

⑧ Point to the fill handle of cell B4 (so the pointer appears as a black plus sign) and drag down to cell B8.

⑨ Release the mouse button.

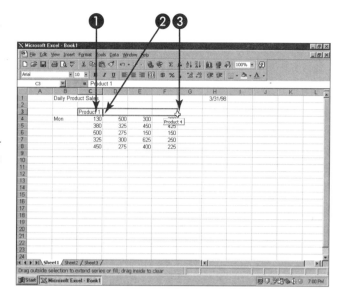

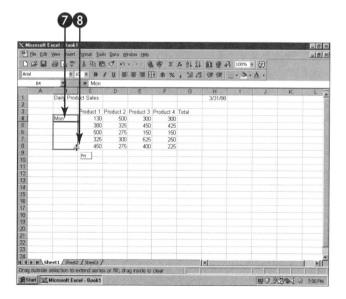

Calculating Totals

Excel completes the series from Mon to Fri for the days of the week.

⑩ Click cell B9.

⑪ Type **Total**.

Your worksheet should now resemble the illustration shown at right. If it doesn't, take a moment to enter the correct information into the cells. Just click the cell that you need to change and type. Whatever was in the cell will be erased when you start typing.

Calculating Totals

Although you can use all types of calculations in a worksheet, the most common is to total a row or column of numbers. In fact, totaling a series of numbers is so common that Excel supplies a special button for it in the toolbar — the AutoSum button. That's the button with the Greek sigma character (Σ) on the first toolbar. Try it out now:

❶ Click cell C9.

❷ Click the AutoSum button.

NOTE

Excel guesses what numbers you want totaled and surrounds them in a moving border, a frame that appears to be blinking. The notation =SUM(C4:C8) in cell C9 means that Excel will calculate the sum of the values in cells C4 through C8. This is a special calculation called a function. A function is a special predefined formula that takes values you supply to it, performs an operation on them, and returns another value. You'll learn much more about functions in Lesson 8.

❸ Click the Enter button in the formula bar. Excel inserts the total of the values in cell C9.

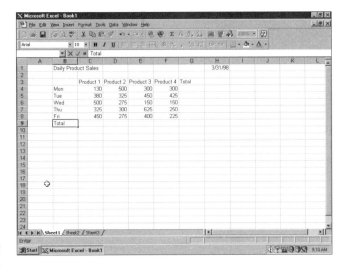

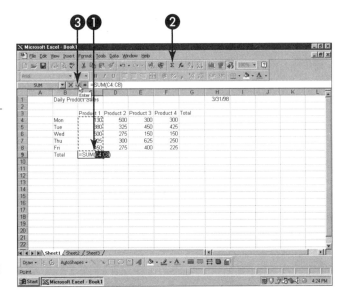

4 Click cell G4.

5 Click the AutoSum button.

This time, Excel assumes you want to total the values in the row.

6 Click the Enter button.

Now that you entered one total in a row and one in a column, you don't have to duplicate your effort for the other totals. Remember, the fill handle completes a series for you, so use it to complete the totals in the remaining rows and columns.

7 Point to the fill handle of cell G4 so the pointer appears as a black plus sign.

8 Drag the handle down to cell G8.

9 Release the mouse button.

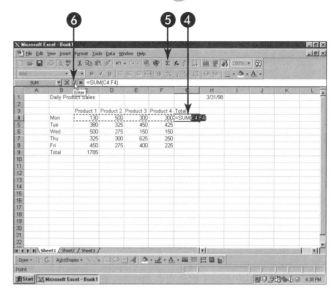

NOTE *When you use the fill handle to copy a formula, Excel copies it using a relative reference — that is, a reference that changes when you move or copy it. For example, the formula in cell G4 totals the values cells C4 through F4. However, the copied formula in cell G5 totals the values in cells C5 through F5, the formula in G6 totals the cells C6 through F6, and so on. References that don't change when you move or copy them are called absolute references; you'll learn more about them in Lesson 7.*

10 Click cell C9.

11 Point to the fill handle of cell C9 so the pointer appears as a black plus sign.

12 Drag the handle across to cell G9 and then release the mouse button.

Excel copies the total formula to the other cells in the row, again using a relative reference. Each of the formulas totals the values above it.

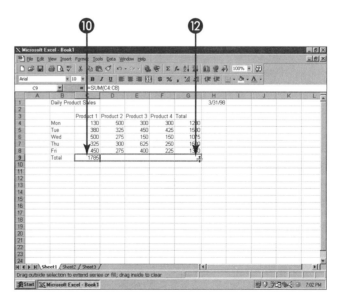

Entering Formulas

Entering Formulas

The AutoSum button is quick and convenient, but it only calculates a total. When you want to perform other types of math you can use other functions that Excel provides, or type a formula. A formula performs math using numbers or the values in other cells. In fact, you'll use a formula now to convert the grand total of your sales (that's in cell G9) to another type of currency:

1 Click cell B12.

2 Type this: **A Pound is worth:**

3 Click cell D12.

4 Type **2.40**.

5 Press Enter.

Excel removed the trailing zero from the number you just typed, displaying it as simply 2.4. Don't worry, it still has the same value, and you'll learn how to format the cell later if you want to display the zero.

6 Click cell B13.

7 Type this: **Total in Pounds:**

8 Click cell D13.

9 Type this: **=G9/D12**.

10 Press Enter.

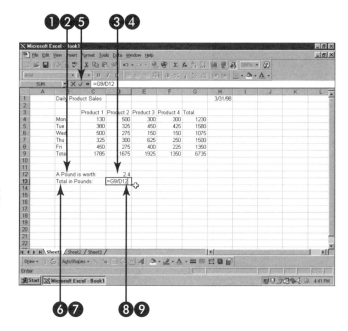

> This formula divides whatever is in cell G9 by the value in cell D12. It performs the calculation and shows the result in the cell. You must start all formulas with the = sign, which tells Excel to use the cell reference that follows as a value, not as a label.

One of the best features of Excel is *automatic recalculation*. This means that if you change a value that is referenced in a function (such as SUM) or a formula, the results are recalculated for you automatically. Check it out:

⑪ Click cell D12.

⑫ Type **2.15**.

⑬ Press Enter.

Excel automatically recalculates the result of the formula in cell D13, adjusting it to reflect the change you made in cell D12.

Your worksheet should appear as shown to the right. If cell D13 contains an ERR message or anything other then the value shown, click the cell and enter the formula again. Don't forget to start the formula with the equal sign.

FORMATTING WORKSHEETS

Now that your worksheet contains the correct information, you're ready to format its appearance. Formatting makes the worksheet look attractive, both on screen and in print. You can format the cells yourself, or you can have Excel do it for you with the AutoFormat feature. You'll use both techniques in this jump start.

Using the Formatting Toolbar

For complete control over the format of your worksheet, apply the formats yourself. The quickest way to format cells is to use the Formatting toolbar. Try it out now:

❶ Click cell B1.

❷ Pull down the Font list in the second toolbar — click the down arrow next to the leftmost box on the Formatting toolbar (it will most likely say Arial).

❸ Scroll through the list of fonts and click Times New Roman.

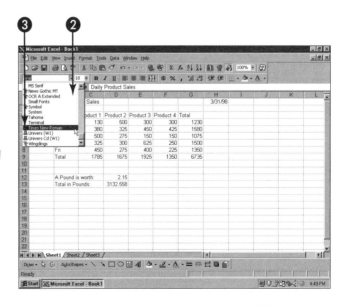

Using the Formatting Toolbar

4 Pull down the Font Size list in the Formatting toolbar — click the down arrow next to the second box from the left on the Formatting toolbar.

5 Click 16.

6 Click cell H1.

7 Click the Bold tool in the Formatting toolbar — the button with the letter B.

NOTE

When you apply a format to a selected cell, the format affects all of the characters in the cell. You can also format individual characters. If you want to boldface a word, for example, click the Bold button before and after typing the word. To change the format of a cell that you already entered, click the cell to activate it, and then choose a format. To format selected characters within the cell, double-click the cell, drag over the characters you want to format, and then choose the format. You'll learn more about formatting cells in Lesson 5.

8 Point to the cell C4 so the mouse appears as a white plus sign.

9 Drag over and down to cell G9. This is called *selecting* cells. When you select cells, the group of cells becomes surrounded by a thick border. All of the cells, except the active cell, become black and their contents white.

10 Click the Currency Style tool on the Formatting toolbar — the tool with the dollar sign. Excel adds the dollar sign and two decimal places to each of the selected numbers.

11 Point to cell B4 so the mouse pointer appears as a white plus sign.

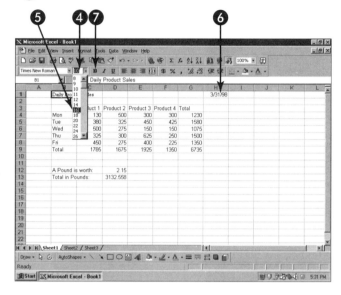

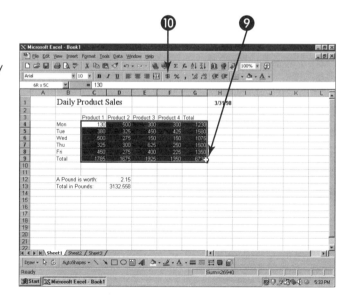

Using the Formatting Dialog Boxes

⑫ Drag from B4 down to B9.

⑬ Click the Align Right button — two buttons to the left of the Currency button. The labels shift to the right side of their cells.

⑭ Point to cell C3 so the mouse pointer appears as a white plus sign.

⑮ Drag from C3 to G3.

⑯ Click the Center tool — the button to the left of Align Right. The labels are centered in their cells.

Using the Formatting Dialog Boxes

In addition to using the toolbars to format cells, you can use a number of dialog boxes. The Format Cells dialog box lets you apply any number of formats to selected cells at one time. The AutoFormat dialog box lets you format an entire worksheet with just one click, selecting from a list of predefined formats that Excel has created for you:

❶ Point to cell B3 so the mouse pointer appears as a white plus sign.

❷ Drag to cell G9.

❸ Select Format ➤ AutoFormat. Excel displays the dialog box shown in the illustration at right.

❹ Scroll the Table Format list until you see 3D Effects 2.

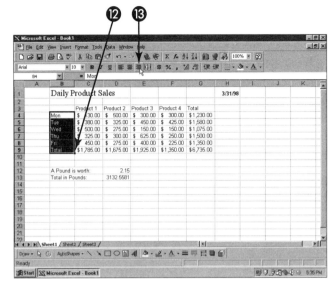

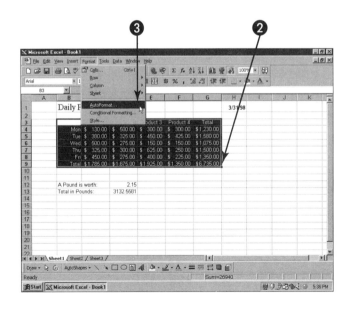

Saving Worksheets

⑤ Click 3D Effects 2. The Sample panel shows how the style affects a worksheet.

⑥ Click OK.

⑦ Click elsewhere in the worksheet to deselect the selected cells.

⑧ Point to cell C3 so the mouse pointer appears as a white plus sign.

⑨ Drag across to cell G3.

⑩ Select Format ➤ Cells.

⑪ Click the Alignment Tab. Excel displays the dialog box shown to the right.

⑫ Double-click the Degrees box.

⑬ Type **30**.

⑭ Click the Font tab.

⑮ Pull down the Color list, and click a color that you like.

⑯ Click OK, and then click to deselect the selected cells.

Your completed worksheet should look like the one shown at the beginning of this Jump Start. If it doesn't, go back through the steps carefully, comparing your worksheet with the illustrations.

MAKING YOUR WORK PERMANENT

Fame may be fleeting, but you don't want your worksheet to be. Save your worksheet onto a disk, and print copies of your worksheet, for a more lasting record of your work.

Saving Worksheets

You should get into the habit of saving your work at regular intervals so all will not be lost if your computer glitches into the netherworld. Waiting until the worksheet is completed may not be good enough — unless you want to take the chance of redoing the entire thing. Saving is easy, and just takes a few seconds, so don't be shy about it.

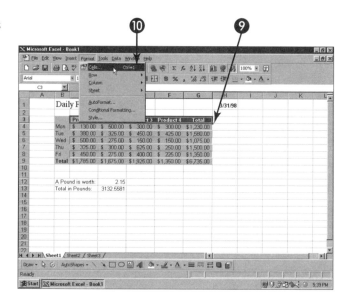

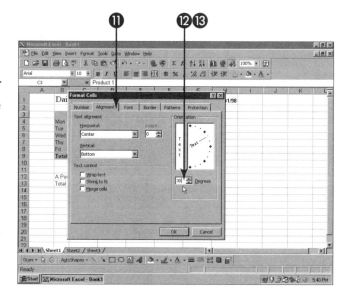

Printing Worksheets

1. Select File ➢ Save.

2. In the File Name text box, type **Daily Sales**.

3. Click the arrow next to the Save In list box.

4. Click the (C:) drive.

5. Click the Create New Folder button (the third button to the right of the Save In list box).

6. Type **My Worksheets** in the Name text box.

7. Click OK.

8. Double-click My Worksheets in the list of folders.

9. Click Save.

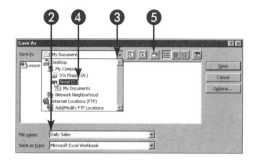

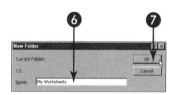

Printing Worksheets

It's nice to look at your worksheet on screen — in living color — but you'll probably need to distribute copies of it as well. If you have a color printer, your worksheet will look just as it does on screen, with all of the colors, shadings, and other effects, such as the three-dimensional appearance. If you don't have a color printer, Excel will convert colors to shades of gray, so you'll still get the same professional effect.

Turn on your printer, make sure it is loaded with paper, and then do this:

- Click the Print button in the Standard toolbar (it has an icon of a little printer on it).

After Excel sends the worksheet to the printer, you'll see a dotted line down one of the columns. The dotted line shows where the page ends.

Wrap Up

If your worksheet does not print correctly, Excel may not be set up to use the correct printer. In this case, select File ➤ Print to see the Print dialog box. Pull down the list next to the Name list box, and click your printer. If your printer is not in the list, it has not yet been set up to work with Windows 95. Check the documentation that came with your printer, or jump ahead to Lesson 10 to learn how to add the printer to Windows 95.

Print button   End of page indicator

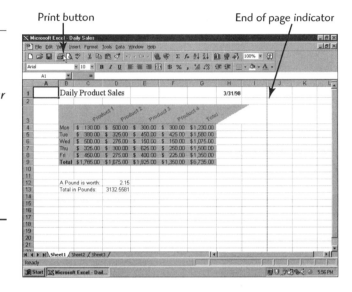

WRAP UP

Congratulate yourself. You zipped through this Jump Start at a good pace, and used these Excel features:

- Typing labels and numbers
- Entering formulas
- Using AutoSum and AutoFormat
- Using recalculation
- Formatting text and numbers
- Rotating text
- Saving and printing worksheets

Because this brief Jump Start packed a lot of power, you also got a pretty good look at what Excel can do. In the lessons that follow, you'll work more with these and other Excel features, creating worksheets of all types. In Lesson 1, for example, you'll get a good look at creating worksheets, and entering text, numbers, dates, and formulas. You'll also learn how to use the Favorites folder to access workbooks quickly and easily. Hang on, you're ready to begin.

PART I

Meet Microsoft Excel

This part introduces you to the concepts of creating worksheets with Excel 97. It includes the following lessons:

- Lesson 1: Getting Started
- Lesson 2: Working with Worksheets

Getting Started

60 MINUTES

GOALS

This lesson describes the Excel window and explains how to create basic spreadsheets. You'll learn about the following features:

- Typing text and numbers
- Entering formulas
- Pointing to cells
- Using automatic recalculation
- Printing worksheets
- Saving workbooks
- Starting new workbooks

Get Ready

GET READY

Learning and using Excel is easy and fun. All you need to get started is some basic knowledge of Windows 95. You need to know how to start your computer, how to navigate through Windows dialog boxes, and how to use the mouse. If you have that much under your belt, you're ready to start. (If not, you might want to consult a good beginning book on Windows 95.)

TRY OUT THE
INTERACTIVE TUTORIALS
ON YOUR CD!

You should also have copied the exercise files from the CD that comes with this book. These are the practice exercises and sample files that you'll be using in this lesson:

File Name	Location
Sales Prices	Exercise directory
Sales Prices Worksheet	Solution directory
Workout 1	Exercise directory
Solution 1	Solution directory

NOTE

Create the worksheet yourself, without opening the workbook from the Exercise directory. Use the files in the CD only if you get stuck and need additional help. You'll find a copy of this worksheet, minus the formulas, under the name Sales Prices, in the Exercise folder of the CD.

When you complete this lesson, you'll have all of the basic skills needed to create worksheets. You'll have created the worksheet, including formulas, shown in the accompanying illustration.

INTRODUCING EXCEL

An Excel worksheet looks like a table with information arranged in rows and columns. You use Excel to keep financial records, budgets, balance sheets, projections, forecasts, tax records, and all of the other information that keeps the fiscal world afloat. It's also great for business forms of all types, eye-catching onscreen and printed reports, lists and databases, even charts and maps.

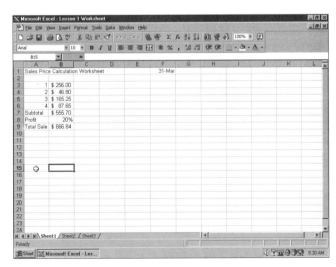

THE WONDERS OF RECALCULATION

Suppose you prepare an estimate for an important client based on the current rate you pay your employees and the prevailing cost of raw materials. After the client accepts the estimate, your employees ask for a raise, and your supplier notifies you of a price increase. How do you measure the impact of these changes, once you're over the headache? It's easy with Excel. If your spreadsheet was created with the proper formulas, as was the one shown here, you just type the new pay rate and new price. Excel instantly adjusts the subtotals, totals, and profit figures in the spreadsheet to reflect the new numbers.

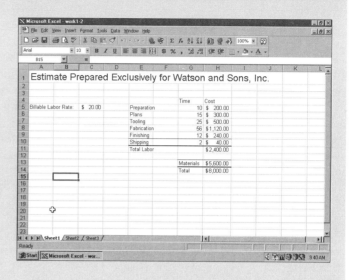

But the real power of a worksheet is a feature called *automatic recalculation*. If you design your worksheet correctly, as you'll learn how to do here, it will automatically change the results of formulas and other calculations when you change the data. You just enter the values you want and Excel does the rest. In the business world, this is called a "what-if" scenario, and it lets Excel help you analyze data and make decisions.

Starting Excel

The simplest way to start Excel is by using the Windows 95 Start button:

❶ Click the Start button on the Windows 95 taskbar. Windows displays the Start menu.

❷ Point to the word Programs on the menu. (You don't have to click it; pointing with the mouse is enough.) You'll see a list of programs installed on your computer. Look for Microsoft Excel.

Starting Excel

③ Click Microsoft Excel. Excel starts, and you'll see the screen shown below.

■ Getting Familiar with the Excel Window

There's a lot to look at here. But if you are familiar with any Windows program, you should already feel somewhat comfortable in Excel.

An Excel file is called a *workbook*. So when you save your work in Excel, you're saving a workbook. Once you've saved a workbook, you can open it again, bringing it back onto the screen. A workbook consists of one or more pages, called *worksheets* (or *sheets*, for short). By default, each new workbook that you open contains three worksheets, but you can add and delete sheets as needed. When you save or open a workbook, you save or open all of the worksheets at one time. You can use the various sheets of a workbook to store related information. For example, suppose you create 12 monthly budgets for the current year. Rather than store each budget in a separate file, create each one on a separate worksheet within the same workbook. You can then perform calculations on the worksheets, such as determining quarterly, semiannual, or annual totals.

- The *title bar* shows the name of the program you're using — Microsoft Excel. If the workbook window is maximized, it also contains the name of the workbook. The first workbook you open during a Microsoft Excel session is called Book1, the second Book2, and so on. Of course, you can name your project anything you like when you save it. On the left end of the title bar is the Control box, which you use to close Excel and change its window size. On the right are the standard Minimize, Restore, and Close buttons.

- The *menu bar* leads to all of the commands and options that you need. Click a menu option to pull down its choices, and then select from the menu that appears.

- Two toolbars appear to get you started. The *Standard toolbar* contains common features that you'll need to work with most projects, such as saving and printing. You use the *Formatting toolbar* to control the way your project looks. There are other toolbars that you can display, as you'll learn in Lesson 12.

Title bar
Menu bar
Standard toolbar
Formatting toolbar   Name box

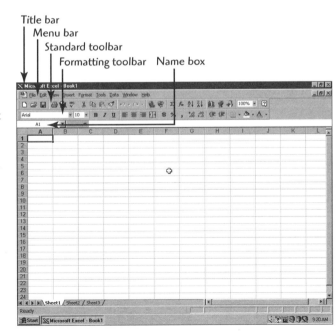

- The *formula bar* is where you can enter and edit information, and get help from Excel in creating formulas. On the left end of the formula bar is the *name box*. This tells you where you are working in Excel (that is, which cell is the active cell), and lets you move quickly around the spreadsheet.

- The *worksheet window* is where Excel's magic really happens. The worksheet contains all of the text, numbers, and formulas that make up whatever you are doing, such as a budget, earning projection, or client list.

- To the right and below the worksheet are the vertical and horizontal *scroll bars,* the standard Windows controls that let you move around the worksheet.

- Below the worksheet window is the *status bar,* where Microsoft Excel tells you information about the worksheet and displays certain indicators, such as CAPS when you have the Caps Lock key on, or NUM, when Num Lock is on. The word "Ready" on the left means that Excel is prepared to accept your commands. Most menu and toolbar commands only work when you are in Ready mode. As you work with Excel, you'll see other modes displayed in the status bar, such as Enter when you are entering information into a cell, or Edit when you are changing information in the cell.

- To the left of the horizontal scroll bar are three *worksheet tabs,* and the *tab scrolling buttons.* An Excel workbook can contain literally thousands of worksheets, each on a separate page. You use the worksheet tabs and tab scrolling buttons to move through the workbook, as you'll learn in Lesson 6.

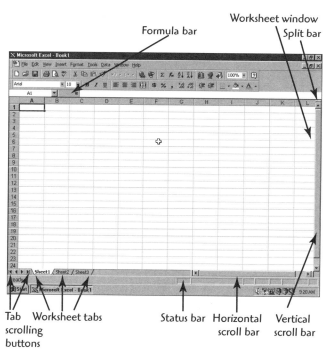

Formula bar · Worksheet window · Split bar

Tab scrolling buttons · Worksheet tabs · Status bar · Horizontal scroll bar · Vertical scroll bar

■ Understanding the Worksheet

Because you'll be spending a lot of quality time in the worksheet, you should be well acquainted with its layout.

Each worksheet is a series of numbered rows and lettered columns. The boxes that contain the column letters are called *column headings.* The boxes that contain row numbers are *row headings.*

Moving Around the Worksheet

The intersection of a row and a column is called a *cell,* and you refer to a cell by its column letter and row number — called it *address* or its *reference.* So the address of the cell in the upper-left corner of the worksheet is A1 because it is in column A and row 1. Note that the column letter always comes first in the address. The cell below A1 is cell A2, and the cell to the right of A1 is B1. Worksheets have 65,536 rows and 256 columns. The columns are numbered A through Z, then AA through AZ, BA through BZ, and so on up to column IV. So each worksheet has a total of 16,777,216 cells! That's a lot of cells.

The cell selected at the current time, which is ready to be filled or formatted, is called the *active* cell. You can always tell the active cell because:

- The cell's address appears in the name box on the left end of the formula bar

- The cell is surrounded by a dark rectangle

- The cell's row letter and column number appear in boldface

As you'll learn in Lesson 2, you can select more than one cell at a time, such as when you want to delete or format several cells in one step. But even when you select more than one cell, only one cell is active.

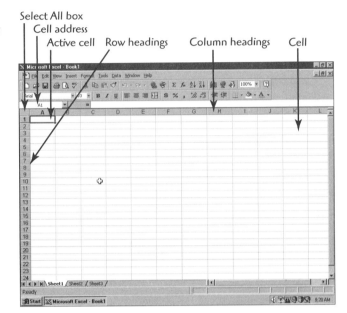

ENTERING INFORMATION INTO WORKSHEETS

To enter information into a cell, click the cell or move to it using the keyboard, and then type. As you type you can use the Backspace or Delete keys to edit the contents, as you would using a word processing program.

Moving Around the Worksheet

To enter or edit information in a worksheet, you need to move from cell to cell. With the mouse, just click the cell that you want to enter information into, edit, or format, scrolling the worksheet as necessary. To use the keyboard, move around the worksheet using the keystrokes shown in Table 1-1.

Moving Around the Worksheet

SCROLLING AROUND

The scroll bars work just about the same as they do in any Windows application. Use the vertical scroll bar to move up and down through rows; use the horizontal scroll bar to move left or right through columns. As you drag the scroll box within the bar, Microsoft Excel displays a *scroll tip*, a box listing the row that will be at the top of the screen or the column that will be at the left edge of the screen when you release the mouse button. If all of your data appears on screen, you can drag the box only enough to move one row or column. To scroll more, just click the scroll arrows at the edges of the scroll bars.

To scroll the worksheet with Microsoft's IntelliMouse pointing device, just rotate the wheel forward or backward. You can also "pan" the worksheet, scrolling it in any direction, by holding down the wheel and dragging in the direction you want to pan. If you don't want to tire your finger by holding down the wheel, just click the wheel as if it were a button and then move the mouse. Click any mouse button to stop panning.

TABLE 1-1 MOVING AROUND EXCEL WITH THE KEYBOARD

To Move	Press
Down to the next row	Enter
One cell in any direction	Arrow key
One cell to the right	Tab
One cell to the left	Shift+Tab
Beginning of the row	Home
Cell A1	Ctrl+Home
Last cell containing data	Ctrl+End
Down one screen	Page Down
Up one screen	Page Up
Right one screen	Alt+Page Down
Left one screen	Alt+Page Up

Reading about it is one thing, but doing it is something else, so try moving about the worksheet now. Cell A1 should be active; if not, click it. Then follow these steps to get some practice moving around the worksheet:

Moving Around the Worksheet

1 Press the Enter key. Cell A2 becomes the active cell, and A2 appears in the name box. The row heading for row number 2 and the column heading for column A are bold.

2 Click cell C5; that's the fifth cell down in the third column. Now C5 appears in the name box and row number 5 and column C are bold.

3 Press Tab to move to the right one cell, into D5. (You could also have pressed the Right Arrow key.)

4 Press Ctrl+Home to move back to cell A1.

As you move down and across the worksheet, Excel scrolls additional rows or columns into view. To move to a specific cell, choose Go To from the Edit menu. Do it now:

5 Select Edit ➤ Go To. Excel displays the Go To dialog box.

6 Type this: **b60000**. The address is for row 60,000 in column B. That's a long way down. Excel is not case-sensitive for addresses, so you can use either uppercase or lowercase when typing in column letters.

7 Click OK. Excel scrolls the worksheet and activates cell B60000.

8 Press Ctrl+Home to move back to cell A1. Excel instantly zips back up 60,000 rows.

When you start typing, the insertion point appears in the cell, whatever you type also appears in the formula bar, and you'll see two additional buttons in the formula bar, as shown here:

- The button containing the X is the Cancel button. Click this button, or press the Esc key, if you change your mind and want to leave the cell unchanged.

- The button containing the check mark is called the Enter button. Click this button, or press Enter or any other cursor movement key, to accept what you've typed and enter it into the cell.

Many of the toolbar buttons and menu commands are dimmed (unavailable) when you are entering information into a cell. To use the dimmed features of the menu or toolbar, you must accept or cancel the entry to return to Ready mode.

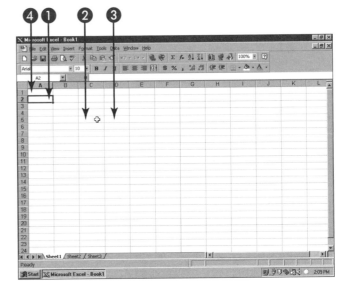

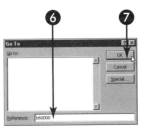

Entering Text

Now you're ready to start a worksheet. You'll begin by entering text. To Excel, text is any information that starts with a letter, and that you don't want to use for a math operation. Excel aligns text on the left side of the cell, although you can change its position, as you'll learn in Lesson 5:

1 Click cell A1 if it's not already active.

2 Type this: **Sales Price Calculation Worksheet**. What you type appears in the cell and in the formula bar. The word *Enter* appears in the status bar, indicating that you are entering data into a cell.

3 Press the Enter key. Excel accepts the entry and moves down to cell A2.

4 Press Enter again. Excel leaves a blank row, and moves to cell A3.

If you type more characters than will fit in the cell, Excel runs the entry into adjacent blank cells. If an adjacent cell has an entry of its own, however, Excel displays only as many characters as fit in the cell. All of the information is still stored in the worksheet, and it appears in the formula bar when the cell is active.

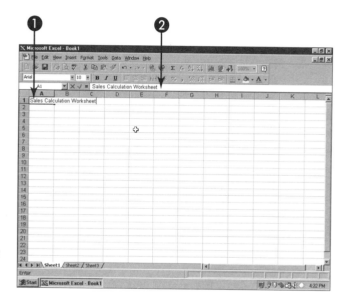

Entering Numbers

To enter a number into a cell, start the entry with a number, an equal sign, a plus sign, or a minus sign. You can enter numbers using commas to separate thousands, and even a dollar sign for currency figures, but it's often better to have Excel add these for you, as you'll learn in Lesson 5:

1 Type **1** and then press Enter. Excel right-aligns the entry within the cell.

2 Type **2** and then press Enter.

3 Type **3** and press Enter.

4 Type **4** and press Enter.

Entering Numbers

⑤ Type **Subtotal** and press Enter.

⑥ Type **Profit** and press Enter.

⑦ Type **Total Sale** but don't press Enter. (You don't have to press Enter if you are going to click another cell.)

⑧ Click cell B3.

⑨ Type **256.00** and then click the Enter button in the formula bar to remain in the cell. Excel removes *trailing zeros* — zeros that come at the end of a number following the decimal point.

⑩ Click the Currency Style button in the Formatting toolbar. Excel adds two decimal places and the dollar sign to the number in the cell. Currency Style is just one of the formats you'll learn about in Lesson 5.

⑪ Click cell B4.

⑫ Type **46.8** and then click the Enter button. Because Excel would remove the trailing zero, don't bother typing 46.80.

⑬ Click the Currency Style button.

⑭ Click cell B5.

⑮ Type **165.25** and then click the Enter button.

⑯ Click Currency Style.

The worksheet on your screen should look like the one shown at right. If it does not, click the cell that is different and type the information shown in the figure.

Entering Dates and Times

You can also enter dates and times into a cell. To enter a date, just type it, using either a slash or a hyphen between its parts, as in 11/16/98. The way it appears in the cell depends on how you type it, but dates always appear in *mm/dd/yyyy* format in the formula bar. If you do not enter a year, Excel adds the current year. So assuming it were 1998, dates would appear as shown in Table 1-2.

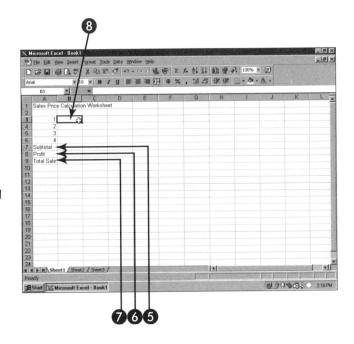

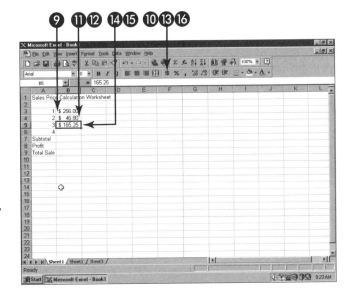

HOW EXCEL HANDLES NUMBERS

Excel does not run long numbers into adjacent cells, as it does with long text entries. If you type a whole number up to 11 digits, Excel automatically widens the column to fit. If the large number includes decimal places, Excel may round off the decimals, displaying the rounded result in the cell but the full value in the formula bar. Excel displays really huge numbers of more than 11 digits in scientific notation, such as 9.78E+08. In scientific notation, Excel indicates the number of decimal places either to the left of the decimal point (with a positive number) or to the right (with a negative number) rather than actually displaying them on screen. In a few cases, you'll just see a series of # signs filling the cell. This means that the number is too large to display and you'll have to widen the column. The # signs usually appear if you format a cell, or change a column width, so the number no longer fits within the cell.

TABLE 1-2 EXCEL'S DATE FORMATS

Typed As	Appears in the Cell As	Appears in the Formula Bar As
Nov 16, 98	16–Nov–98	11/16/1998
11/16/98	11/16/98	11/16/1998
11/16	16–Nov	11/16/1998

To enter today's date in the active cell, press Ctrl+; (semicolon). To enter the current time, press Ctrl+Shift+: (colon). For any other date or time, type the entry into the cell yourself.

Now you can enter the date into your worksheet:

1 Click cell F1.

2 Type **11/16** and then click the Enter button on the formula bar. Excel displays 16–Nov in the cell, aligning the date on the right, just like a number.

You can also type a time by itself, or with a date:

- Enter the hour and the minutes separated by a colon, as in 4:15.

- Optionally add another colon and enter the seconds, as in 4:15:45.

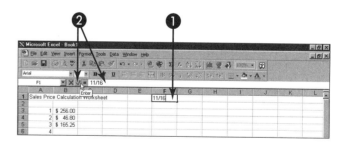

Entering Dates and Times

Don't worry about the Year 2000 problem. If you only enter two digits for the year, Excel adds the remaining two. To account for the turn of the century, however, it adds 20 if you type 00 through 29, changing 11/16/15 to 11/16/2015, for instance. If you type 30 through 99 for the year it adds 19, so 11/16/87 becomes 11/16/1987.

- You can enter the time in either a 12- or 24-hour format, although times are shown in 12-hour format in the formula bar. If you use 12-hour format without indicating AM or PM (or typing A or P), Excel assumes AM.

TIP *You must leave a space between the time and the A (or AM) or P (or PM). If you don't, Excel won't recognize the entry as a time and will treat it as text.*

- To enter both the date and time, separate them with a space, as in 11/16/98 4:15:45.

It's easy to enter dates and times, but there's more to them than meets the eye. Once you enter a date, the cell takes on the date format. Excel then assumes that anything you enter in the cell is a date, and that you want it to appear in the same format. You'll learn how to change the format in Lesson 5, but let's take a look at the consequences here. Cell F1 should be active — if not, click it now:

❸ Type **11/16/98** in cell F1 and then click the Enter button. Excel still displays the date in the cell as 16-Nov, the format of your original entry.

❹ Now try something different. Type **25** and click the Enter button. Excel displays 25-Jan rather than the number 25. That's because Excel has formatted the cell as a date, and converts the number 25 to the date 1/25/1900.

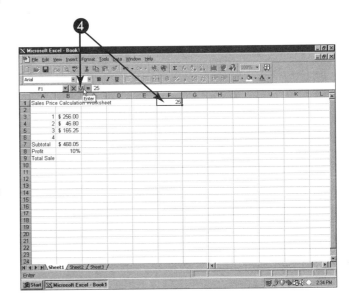

5 Press Ctrl+; (semicolon). Excel enters the current date, displaying it in *mm/dd/yy* format.

6 Press Enter. Excel displays the date in *dd–Month* format, as in your original entry.

Why does Excel convert the number to a date? Excel actually stores dates and times as serial values, so it can perform math on dates, such as calculating the number of days that a bill has been outstanding, or how long a certain task has taken if you record the starting and ending time. Days are numbered starting with 1 for January 1, 1900. So when you entered 25 in a cell formatted as a date, Excel converted it to the date January 25, 1900. The serial number for a time is a decimal number starting with 0.000 for the midnight to 0.99999 for one second before midnight the next day. The serial number for high noon (12 PM) is 0.50.

Entering Formulas

Formulas really take advantage of the power of Excel by letting it recalculate values as you change the contents of cells. Don't let the word *formula* scare you, however; a formula is a just a mathematical operation that uses any combination of numbers and cell addresses.

You must start every formula with an equal sign to let Excel know you want it to calculate and display results. (You can use a plus sign instead, but the equal sign is standard.) To add a series of number together, for example, use a formula such as =34+87+83.

The real power of formulas, however, is in using cell addresses. For example, the formula to multiply whatever is in cell A6 by whatever is in cell B9 is =A6*B9. When you accept the formula, Excel displays the results in the cell but the formula itself appears in the formula bar when the cell is active. If you later change the value in either cell A6 or B9, Excel recalculates the value and displays the new result. You should use cell references wherever you are performing math using the contents of other cells.

Entering Formulas

When you type numbers into most calculators, the math is performed in the order in which you enter it. When you type a formula into a worksheet, however, the math is performed in a certain way. Excel scans the entire formula from left to right, giving precedence to certain operators over others. All multiplications and divisions are done first, and then all additions and subtractions. You can remember this by using the saying "My Dear Aunt Sally" for Multiplication-Division-Addition-Subtraction: something handy I learned in computer school.

Here's an example:

You sell two items worth $100 each, and you want to charge a 10% markup. With a calculator, you'd type 100 +100 * 1.1 to get the result of 220. But if you entered

=100+100*1.1 into the cell, you'd get 210 when you accepted the entry. Excel first multiplies the second 100 by 1.1, yielding 110. It then adds the result to the first 100, getting 210. You'd be cheating yourself. To perform the calculation correctly in Excel, use parentheses to force a different order of calculation, as in =(100+100)*1.1. Operations within parentheses are performed first, and depending on your formula, you may have several levels of parentheses, some inside of others. To ensure that you complete each level, Excel uses Parentheses Matching, color-coding each set to ensure that you have the same number of opening and closing parentheses. The color coding also helps you visualize what values and operators are enclosed within each set.

Now try entering several formulas into your worksheet. Don't forget to type the equal sign to start the formula; leaving it out is the most common mistake beginners make.

NOTE *You'll find a copy of this worksheet, without the formulas, in the Exercise folder of the CD under the name Sales Prices.*

❶ Click cell B7.

❷ Type this: **=b3+b4+b5+b6**. (Remember, Excel doesn't care if you type column letters in lowercase or uppercase — lowercase letters are just easier.) You should include cell B6 in the formula even though it contains no value at the moment, just in case you enter something into it later.

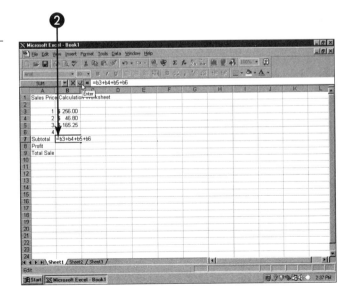

Pointing to Referenced Cells

You can also start a formula by clicking the equal sign in the formula bar, rather than typing the equal sign yourself. When you do this, Excel displays the formula palette shown here:

Now as you enter the formula, Excel calculates and displays the results each step of the way. Don't worry too much if the results look incorrect until you've completed the formula. Keeping an eye on the result, however, may help you locate a problem with your formula.

3 Click the Enter button in the formula bar. Excel calculates the total of the values in those cells and displays the result in cell B7. The formula itself appears in the formula bar because B7 is the active cell. Note that Excel converted the lowercase *b*s to uppercase *B*s.

4 Press the Down Arrow to reach cell B8.

5 Type **10%**, and then press Enter. You can use the percent sign rather than entering a decimal number. Excel performs the calculation using the decimal equivalent anyway. Typing the percent sign applies the Percent format.

Pointing to Referenced Cells

Because you can make a mistake by entering the wrong address in a formula, Excel lets you *point* to a cell to add its address to the formula. To point to a cell, start the formula and then click the cell to add its address to the formula bar.

You should be in cell B9 in the sample worksheet, so now you can see how pointing works. You want to enter the formula =B7+(B7*B8) in the cell to calculate the total sales amount. This formula takes the subtotal, and then adds ten percent of the subtotal to it:

1 Type = (the equal sign). Remember, all formulas start with the equal sign.

2 Click cell B7. The address B7 appears in cell B9 and in the formula bar, and cell B7 is enclosed in the moving border.

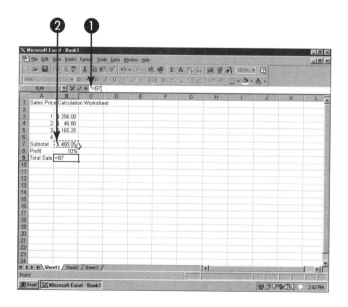

Pointing to Referenced Cells

3 Type **+(** (the plus sign followed by an open parenthesis). You're using parentheses to control the order in which Excel does the math.

4 Click cell B7 again. The formula now appears as =B7+(B7.

5 Type * (the symbol for multiplication).

6 Click cell B8 to enter its reference into the formula.

7 Finally, you need to enter the closing parentheses, but check what happens when you make an obvious mistake in a formula. Press Enter to try to accept the formula without the closing parentheses. You'll see this message box, which reports that Excel has found an error in the formula and it suggests making the correction by entering the closing parenthesis.

8 Click Yes to accept the correction. Excel adds the closing parenthesis and displays the correct result in the cell.

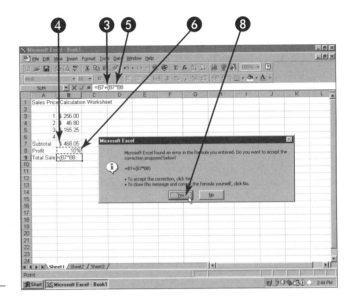

TIP

In some cases, when you're entering simple formulas, Excel just fills in the closing parenthesis for you if you accidentally leave it off.

USING DATES IN FORMULAS

You can use simple formulas to perform math on dates. For example, if cells A1 and A2 contain dates, calculate the number of days between them using the formula =A1-A2.

Excel displays the differences in the format *mm/dd/yy* format — the number of months, days, and years between the dates.

Recalculating Formulas

You should use cell addresses in formulas whenever possible so Excel recalculates the results if you have to change a value in one of the cells. The sample worksheet, for example, used cell addresses, so now see what happens if you change the values of your sale items and profit margin:

① Click cell B6.

② Type **87.65** and press Enter.

The subtotal in cell B7 and the total in cell B9 automatically recalculate to reflect the new information.

③ Click cell B6 and then click the Currency Style button.

④ Click cell B8.

⑤ Type **20**, and then press Enter. (Remember, just click a cell and start typing to replace the value in that cell.) Because the cell is already formatted as a percentage, 20% appears and the total in cell B9 is recalculated for the larger profit. Changing a value in any of the referenced cells causes Excel to recalculate the worksheet automatically.

With the formulas, your worksheet should look like the one in the accompanying illustration — except the current date will appear in cell F1. If a number is incorrect, click the cell, and compare what you see in the formula bar to what you should have entered. Do not simply type the numbers you see in the figure into the cells containing formulas. Go back to the instructions and retype the formula.

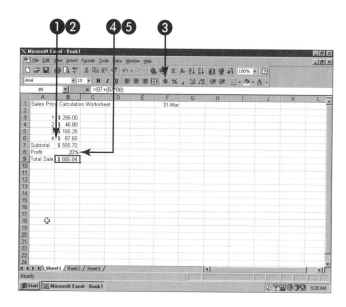

PRESERVING YOUR WORK

Once you've made the effort to complete your worksheet, you certainly don't want to lose it. You should save your workbook, even if you just intend to print it once. You never know when you'll need to make changes to it, or print additional copies.

You should also consider printing your worksheets, even when you're not ready to distribute them. A printed copy makes a good

Saving Your Workbook

backup in the event that you mistakenly delete the workbook file, or save changes to it that you did not intend to keep.

Saving Your Workbook

There's always the question of how often you should save your work onto disk. It pays to save your workbook at regular intervals, or immediately after you create a complex formula or format that you wouldn't want to reconstruct if some computer glitch sent you into the unknown.

NOTE *Before saving your workbook, however, decide where to save your workbook files. You can't save them on the CD, so either save them to a directory on your hard disk or to a floppy disk. When you first start Excel, it assumes that you want to save files in the default folder, a predefined location established by Excel. The default folder where Excel saves file depends on your system. It may be in the Windows\Personal folder, the My Documents folder, or something else. This is also the location where Excel assumes you're storing the workbooks you want to open.*

Once you open or save a file in another location, however, Excel uses that location rather than the default folder for the remainder of the current session — until you save or open a file elsewhere. So it's a good idea to keep track of exactly where your workbooks are located by keeping an eye on the settings in the Save As dialog box. (The folder listed in the Save In list box tells you what folder Excel will currently save your files to.)

To save your workbook, follow these steps:

❶ Click the Save button. If this is the first time you've saved the workbook, you'll see the Save As dialog box shown in the figure at right.

❷ Type **Lesson 1 workbook** in the File Name box. Remember, with Windows 95 a file name can be up to 255 characters long, so take advantage of the feature and enter a name that really describes the work.

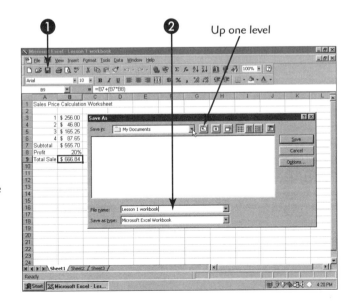

3 Look at the Save In list box. This shows the location on your disk where the document will be saved. To save the file in another location, pull down the Save In list and choose a folder, or double-click the folder icons until you find the correct location.

TIP

You can click the Up One Level button in the Save As dialog box to move up to the folder one level above the folder currently selected in the Save In box.

4 Click the Save command button in the dialog box.

Excel saves documents with the .xls extension. To save your worksheet in some other format — for example, if you want to share it with a Lotus 1-2-3 user — pull down the Save As Type list box in the Save As dialog box and choose the format.

If you make any changes to your workbook after you save it, and you want to keep the changes, you have to save the workbook again. When you click the Save toolbar button this time, however, Excel saves the workbook immediately under the same name without displaying the Save As dialog box. If you want to save a copy of the edited workbook with a different name, choose Save As from the File menu. The Save As dialog box appears so you can enter a new name, or store the new version in a different location on the disk.

USING THE FAVORITES FOLDER

It can be time-consuming to navigate through folders each time you want to open a frequently used workbook that is not saved in the default folder. To save yourself the trouble, take advantage of a special folder called Favorites — a subfolder under your Windows 95 directory that you can open with a single click of the mouse. You can store three types of objects in the Favorite folder — a document such as an Excel workbook, a shortcut to a document, and a shortcut to another folder. A shortcut allows you to access a document or folder from Favorites without having to actually store it in the Favorites folder.

To save a workbook in the Favorites folder, click the Look In Favorites button in the Save As dialog box. Excel opens the Favorites folder so you can save the workbook there. When you later want to open the workbook, click the Look In Favorites button in the Open dialog box, and then double-click the workbook name. (In Lesson 2, you'll learn how to add shortcuts to existing files and folders to the Favorites folder using the Open dialog box.)

Saving Your Workbook

You use the other buttons in the Save As toolbar to determine how your files are listed, and to create new folders in which to store files:

Create New Folder
List
Details
Properties

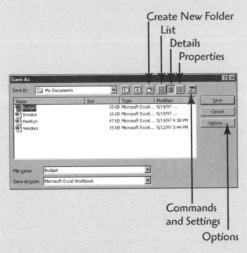

Commands
and Settings
Options

- The Create New Folder button lets you create a new folder in which to store workbook files.

- The List button shows the names of files only, with an icon representing the file type.

- The Details button lists the file names, sizes, types, and dates, as shown here. To sort by either name, size, file type, or the date modified, click the Name, Size, Type, or Modified column headings. Clicking a heading after it has already been selected switches the sort between ascending and descending.

- The Properties button lists specific details about the selected file, including the author, the size of the file, and its creation and revision dates.

- The Commands and Settings button lets you display detailed properties of the selected file; sort the listing by name, type, size, or date; map a network drive; and add or change settings for FTP sites for downloading information from the Internet.

- The Options command button lets you create automatic backup copies of saved files and set passwords for sharing files on a network.

NOTE *There's a completed copy of this worksheet, named Sales Prices Worksheet, in the Solution folder of the CD-ROM in this book.*

Printing Your Worksheet

Printing Your Worksheet

Excel offers a wide variety of printing options. The quickest way to print a copy of your work is to click the Print button on the Standard toolbar. Excel prints a single copy of your worksheet, dividing it into multiple pages if necessary. When the worksheet reappears, you'll see lines indicating the page breaks. To print just a selected range of cells, follow these steps:

1 Select the range.

2 Select File ➢ Print to see the Print dialog box shown at right.

3 Click the Selection option in the Print What section of the dialog box.

4 Click OK.

> You'll learn more about printing worksheets in Lesson 10.

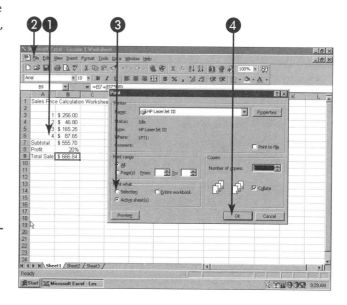

MANAGING WORKBOOKS

When you are done working on your workbook, you can close it, create a new workbook, or open a workbook that's already on your disk. You can actually have more than one workbook open at a time, and can share information between them. (You'll learn how to use multiple workbooks in Lesson 6.)

Keep in mind that you don't have to complete a workbook to save it. You may just run out of time, or decide to continue with the workbook later. You can always open the workbook to complete or print it.

Closing a Workbook

To close the workbook without exiting Excel, click the workbook's Close button (the one at the right end of the menu bar) or choose Close from the File menu. You can also close your workbook and exit Excel at the same time. Click the Close button at the right end of the Excel title bar, or choose Exit from the File menu.

Starting a New Workbook

If you have not saved the workbook since you last changed it, a dialog box will appear, giving you the chance to do so. Click Yes to save the workbook, No to skip saving the changes, or Cancel to keep the workbook open.

- Close your workbook now by clicking the Close button on the menu bar. The worksheet disappears and Excel does not automatically open another one.

Starting a New Workbook

Each time you start Excel, it starts a blank workbook for you. You can create a new workbook at any time, however, even when one is already open on the screen.

- To start a new workbook, click the New button on the Standard toolbar. Do that now. Excel starts a new blank notebook.

You can also choose File ➢ New to start a new blank workbook or to open a workbook already designed for a specific purpose, such as an invoice, expense statement, or purchase order.

Close

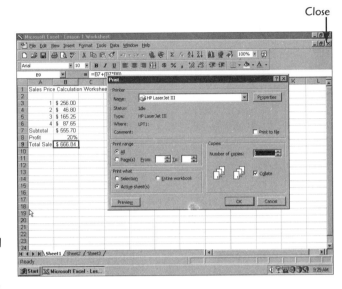

SKILLS CHALLENGE: ENTERING FORMULAS AND RECALCULATING THEIR RESULTS

Now it's your turn to try your own hand at Excel. Excel's automatic recalculation feature helps you solve "what-if" problems by letting you see the effects of changing values on formulas. In this skills challenge, you'll create a worksheet that uses two variables to perform a calculation, and then see what happens when the values change.

There's a copy of this exercise, without the formulas, under the name Workout 1 in the Exercise directory. You can find a copy of the completed exercise under the name Solution 1 in the Solution directory.

❶ If you do not have a new blank worksheet on the screen, click the New button on the Standard toolbar.

What is another way to start a new workbook?

TRY OUT THE
INTERACTIVE TUTORIALS
ON YOUR CD!

② Enter the worksheet shown in the illustration at right.

③ In cell C5, type **20** and apply the Currency style.

> *If you typed 20.00 in the cell, what would have appeared before you applied the Currency style?*

④ In cell H5, type a formula that multiplies the hourly rate in cell C5 by the number of hours in cell G5. Apply the Currency style to the cell.

> *Why should you use cell references in the formula rather than the values within the cells?*

⑤ Enter the corresponding formulas in cells H6 to H10, and apply the Currency style to each. (Hint: Each formula multiples cell C5 by the cell to its left.)

⑥ In cell H12, enter the formula to total the values in cells H5 through H10. Apply the Currency style to the cell.

⑦ In cell H14, type **5600** and apply the Currency style.

⑧ In cell H16, type the formula that calculates the sum of cells H12 and H14.

⑨ Save the workbook with the name **Estimate 1**.

Now let's see how the formulas recalculate. What happens if the labor costs increase $2 per hour?

⑩ Click cell C5 and type **22**. The individual costs, the total labor, and the total recalculate. The total is now $240 higher.

> *When you type 22 in the cell, why does it appear in Currency format?*

⑪ Click cell H14 and type **6000**. The total cost increases by $400. The labor costs are unchanged because cell H14 is not referenced in their formulas.

⑫ Save the workbook with the name **Estimate 2**. (Hint: You can't just click the Save toolbar button to do this.) The worksheet should look like the illustration shown at right.

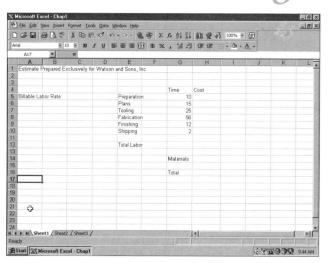

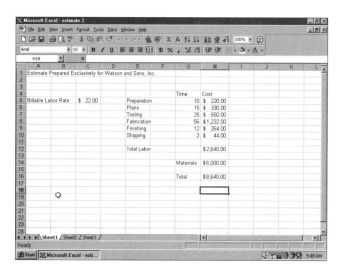

Troubleshooting

 How long can a file name be in Windows 95?

 Close the workbook.

 Does closing the workbook delete it from your disk?

TROUBLESHOOTING

Feeling frenzied? Don't worry, you're doing fine! But if you do have some minor problems, you might gain some insights from this table.

Problem	Solution
Excel won't let me save my work.	You may be trying to save the worksheet to the CD. Select File ➤ Save As, pull down the Save In list, and choose either the floppy disk or the hard disk.
My screen doesn't look the way it does in the figures.	As you'll learn in Lesson 12, you can customize the way Excel looks. Someone who used Excel before you may have turned off the toolbars, or changed something else.
I can't click the Currency Style button.	The button will be dimmed when you are entering information into a cell. Click the Enter button in the formula bar, and then click the Currency Style button.
When I type the formula, the formula itself appears in the cell, rather than the actual results of the calculation.	Make sure you start the formula with the equal sign. Otherwise, Excel assumes that entries starting with letters are text.

WRAP UP

You learned a lot in this lesson, but wasn't it easy? You learned

- How to start Excel

- How to identify the parts of the Excel and worksheet window

- How to enter text, numbers, dates and times, and formulas

- How to print and save workbooks

- How to close workbooks and start new workbooks

If you want more practice, try creating a worksheet that contains your weekly budget, or one that lists the names and birth dates of your friends. Don't be afraid to experiment and practice — you can't break anything!

In the next lesson, you'll learn a whole new batch of essential Excel skills, including how to edit your work and how to get help from Excel.

Working with Worksheets

GOALS

In this lesson, you will learn some essentials for creating worksheets, including:

- Opening workbooks
- Selecting cells
- Changing column width
- Editing your work
- Getting help

60 MINUTES

Opening Workbooks the Easy Way

GET READY

You now know the basics of creating, saving, and printing workbooks. By using text, values, and formulas, you can design worksheets that display information, perform math, and help you make decisions. In this lesson, you'll learn how to open and edit worksheets that you've already created.

If you feel comfortable with what you learned in Lesson 1, you're ready to begin. This lesson refers to the following workbooks:

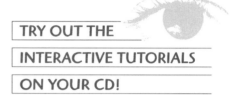

TRY OUT THE
INTERACTIVE TUTORIALS
ON YOUR CD!

File Name	Location
Price Calculation	Exercise directory
Price Calculation Solution	Solution directory
Workout 2	Exercise directory
Solution 2	Solution directory

When you complete this lesson, your edited spreadsheet will look like the one shown at right.

OPENING A WORKBOOK

To view, print, or edit a workbook that you already created, saved, and closed, you have to open it from the disk. Opening a workbook is easy, but you do need to know where the workbook is located on your disk.

With your own workbooks, make sure you know where you saved them. It's best if you use the default folder provided by Excel, but you don't have to. In this lesson, you'll learn several ways to open workbooks.

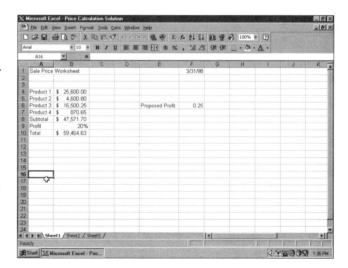

Opening Workbooks the Easy Way

To quickly open one of the last four workbooks you worked with, pull down the File menu, and click the workbook's name at the bottom of the menu. Excel will open the workbook, regardless of its location on your disk.

Opening Workbooks the Easy Way

To open a workbook that is not listed on the File menu, use the Open command in the File menu, or click the Open button on the Standard toolbar. Both options display the Open dialog box. As long as you haven't save or opened a worksheet in some other location during your current Excel session, the dialog box lists the files in the default folder. When the Open dialog appears, just double-click the workbook name to open it. If the workbook is not in the default directory, or that directory is not shown in the Open dialog box, you have to navigate your disk to find the workbook.

As an example, let's open the workbook called Price Calculation in the Exercise directory of the CD that came with this book. This is a copy of the worksheet you created and saved in Lesson 1, along with some other entries that you'll need for this lesson. Insert the CD in your drive, and then follow these steps:

❶ Click the Open button on the Standard toolbar. Excel displays the Open dialog box, listing workbooks in the default directory.

❷ Pull down the Look In drop-down list. Excel displays a list of the drives in your system, as shown to the right.

❸ Click the icon for your CD drive. Your CD may be drive D, depending on your system. Excel displays the directories on the CD.

❹ Double-click the Exercise directory. Excel displays the files in that directory.

❺ Scroll the list of files until you see Price Calculation. Workbook names are preceded by the Excel document icon.

❻ Double-click Price Calculation. Excel opens the file and displays it on your screen.

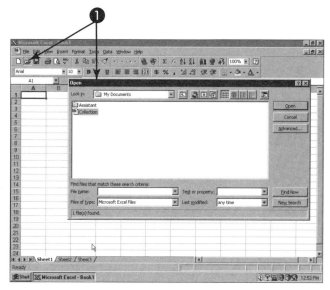

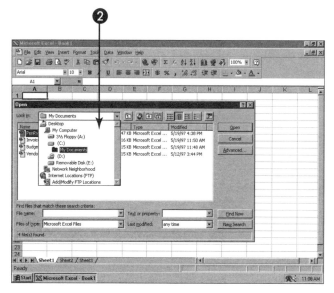

Opening Workbooks the Easy Way

If you ever save a workbook in the Favorites folder, click the Look in Favorites button; then double-click the workbook name to open it. As you know, Favorites can also include shortcuts to documents and folders. So if you already saved a workbook in some other location, you can add a shortcut to it to Favorites. Then rather than navigate to the actual location on your disk, you can access the workbook in Favorites. If you add a shortcut to a folder to Favorites, you can open the folder in two steps: Click Look in Favorites, and then double-click the shortcut to the folder. A shortcut icon looks much like the a regular workbook or folder icon, but with a tiny arrow.

To add a document or folder to Favorites, use these steps:

- Bring up the Open dialog box, and locate the document or folder so its icon appears on screen.

- Click the icon, and then click the Add to Favorites button.

- Click Add Selected Item to Favorites.

If you've already opened the folder, click the Add to Favorites button and click Add "*folder name*" to Favorites.

■ Virus Protection

Some unscrupulous people attach computer viruses to macros. (A macro is a stored set of actions — you can repeat the actions just by running the macro.) The odds are against finding a virus in a macro, but just to be safe, Excel displays the dialog box shown in the accompanying illustration if you open a workbook that contains macros. If you are confident that the macros do not contain any virus, click on the Enable Macros button. For example, you can be confident that the sample workbooks provided by Excel are virus-free. If you are unsure, click on the Disable Macros button, or choose Do Not Open.

In some cases, the workbook will contain macros that cannot be disabled. In this case, you'll see a dialog box asking if you still want to open the workbook, with its macros, or not.

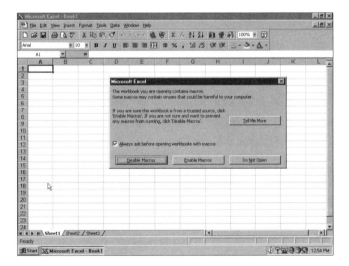

SELECTING CELLS

There are times when you want to perform some function on more than just a single cell. For example, you may want to change the numeric format of an entire column, or you may want to clear the contents of several cells at one time.

To take an action on more than one cell, you have to *select* the cells. When you select cells, all but the active cell become highlighted — the background turns black and any characters appear white — and the entire selected area is surrounded by a thick border.

TIP

Be cautious when you select cells, because all of the cells will be cleared if you press the Del key by accident.

Selecting Cells by Dragging

It is easy to select cells by dragging over them with the mouse. Just make sure that the mouse pointer appears like a white plus sign when you start to drag. As an example, you'll select cells A1 through C10, which is 30 cells in ten rows and three columns:

❶ Point to cell A1. The mouse pointer should look like a white plus sign.

❷ Drag down and over to cell C10. As you drag the cells become highlighted, and the number of rows and columns being selected appears in the formula bar. For example, if you select cells A1 to C10, the formula bar will contain the formula shown in the accompanying illustration.

NOTE

You can also continue dragging past the visible portion of the worksheet — Excel will scroll cells into view as you drag.

❸ Release the mouse button. The cells remain selected. As shown here, the first cell stays white, letting you know that it is the active cell.

❹ Click any cell to deselect the group. You can also deselect the cells by pressing any cursor movement key. But pressing Esc does not deselect the cells.

Selecting Rows, Columns

TIP

You can drag down, up, right, or left, depending on the cells that you want to select and where you start. So if you want to select cells from A1 to C10, you can start in any corner of the block. For example, you can start in cell A1 and drag down and over to C10, or you can start in C10 and drag up and over to A1. Likewise, you can start in A10 and move to C1, or from C1 to A10.

If you don't like dragging, use the Shift key. Click the first cell in the range, and then hold down the Shift key and click the last cell. If the last cell isn't displayed. Just scroll it into view, and then hold down the Shift key and click it. Selecting a large area of the worksheet is easier using Shift+click then dragging. Sometimes is it difficult to stop at a specific cell when dragging into the nonvisible portion of the sheet.

Selecting Rows, Columns, and Entire Worksheets

To select an entire row, column, or worksheet, you don't have to bother dragging at all. Here's how:

1 Point to the column heading F so the pointer appears as the large white plus sign, and click. The entire column is selected. You can also drag over column headings to select adjacent columns.

2 Point to the heading for row 6 and click. To select an entire row, just click on its row heading. You can also drag over row headings to select adjacent rows.

3 Point to the Select All box — it's just above the first row header. Click it to select the entire worksheet.

4 Click any cell to deselect the worksheet.

When you want to select cells, rows, or columns that are not adjacent to one another, use the Ctrl key like this:

- Click on the first cell, row, or column as usual.

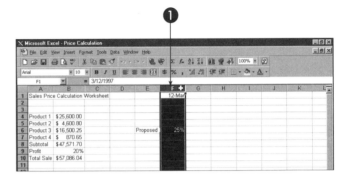

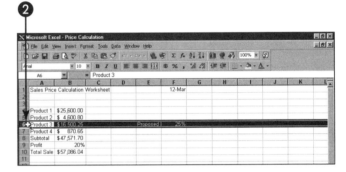

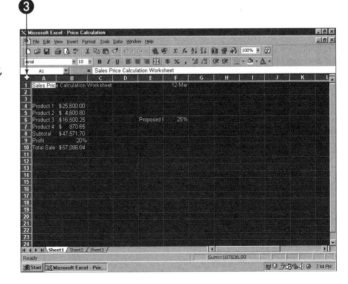

- Hold down the Ctrl key and click on or drag across the other cells, rows, or columns you want to select.

This is standard Windows: when you hold down the Ctrl key and click, Microsoft Excel does not deselect cells already highlighted.

■ Selecting with the Keyboard

You can also select cells entirely with the keyboard. This approach is useful if you're using a laptop computer with a difficult to control (or no) pointing device, or you just don't want to take your hands away from the keyboard.

Table 2-1 shows how to select cells using the keyboard instead of the mouse. Generally, holding down the Shift key while pressing any cursor movement key selects cells in the direction of cursor movement. For example, holding down the Shift key and pressing an arrow key selects the cells in that direction.

TABLE 2-1 SELECTING CELLS WITH THE KEYBOARD

Press	To Do This
Shift+arrow key	Select in the direction of the arrow.
Shift+Home	Select to the start of the row.
Ctrl+Shift+Home	Select to the start of the workbook.
Ctrl+Shift+End	Select to the cell that is the intersection of the last row containing data and the last column containing data.
Ctrl+spacebar	Select the column.
Shift+spacebar	Select the row.
Ctrl+A	Select the entire worksheet.
Shift+backspace	Deselect the cells, returning to the original active cell.
Shift+Page Down	Select to the end of the next screen.
Shift+Page Up	Select to the start of the previous screen.

2

Working with Worksheets

Selecting Cells by Type

You can also use the Ctrl+Shift+arrow key combination to move through groups of information. A *group* of information is a set of cells that contain data. A group ends at the first blank cell, and starts at the first cell containing information. It works this way:

- If the active cell contains information, pressing Ctrl+Shift+arrow selects all of the cells up to the last cell that contains information in the direction of the arrow — to the last cell in the group.

- If the active cell is blank, pressing Ctrl+Shift+arrow selects all cells up the first that contains data — to the start of the next group. If there are no cells with information, Excel selects everything to the end of the row or columns.

- Each time you press Ctrl+Shift+arrow, Excel continues to select cells to the next end or start of another group.

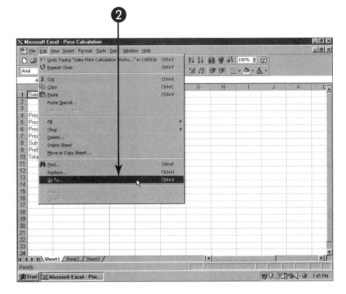

Selecting Cells by Type

Sometimes you may want to select cells based on their contents, such as just cells that contain formulas. In these instances, use the Special option in the Go To dialog box. You'll try that out now by selecting all of the cells that contain formulas:

1 Click cell A1.

2 Select Edit ➤ Go To. Excel opens the Go To dialog box. If you want to select cells in a specific area of the worksheet, you need to highlight them before using the Go To command.

3 Click the Special button.

4 Click the Formulas option button. You can only choose one type of cell using the option buttons. If you choose to select formulas, however, you can click one or more types of formulas.

5 Click OK. Excel selects all of the cells that contain formulas — the type of data you selected.

6 Click the worksheet to deselect the cells.

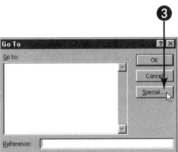

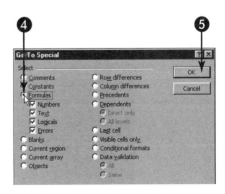

Selecting Cells by Type

■ About Cell and Range References

You may want to refer to a range of cells in a formula, or in a dialog boxes that can act on a range of cells:

- If the range is contiguous — that is, all of the cells are in one group next to each other — enter the address of the cell in the upper-left corner of the range, a colon (:), and then the address of the cell in the lower-right corner. For example, the range A1:C10 (or C10:A1) includes all of the cells that you selected previously.

- If the range is not contiguous, separate the cells with a comma. For example, the range A1,C2,D4 represents a group of three cells.

- You can combine contiguous and noncontiguous references. For instance, A1:C10,D4 means the cells in range A1:C10 as well as cell D4.

    Here are some shortcuts you can take if the cells are all in the same row or column:

All of row 1	1:1
Rows 1 through 5	1:5
All of column B	B:B
Columns A through C	A:C

CHANGING COLUMN WIDTH

As you build your worksheets, you may find that the standard width of the columns is not be sufficient. You may want to display a long text entry even when the cell to its right is not blank, or you may see a series of # symbols when Excel calculates or tries to display a large number. In other instances, why waste space when you have a column that contains short entries, such as a whole column of two letter state abbreviations? By adjusting the width of columns, you control the way that very long and very short entries appear on screen, and how much room they take up on screen and when printed.

2

Working with Worksheets

Adjusting Column Widths

Adjusting Column Widths Automatically

The quickest way to adjust column widths is by using the AutoFit feature. AutoFit makes a column as wide or narrow as needed for its current contents. Try it out:

1 Point to the right boundary of column heading E so the mouse pointer appears as a two-directional arrow, as shown in the top figure at right. The boundary is the line between a column and the one to its right.

2 Double-click. Excel makes the column as wide as the widest entry in the column, in this case the text in cell E6.

Dragging to Set Column Width

To change the column width to any size, drag the right column boundary instead of double-clicking on it. Drag the boundary to the right to widen the column, and to the left to narrow it.
Try it now:

1 Point to the right boundary of column B so the mouse pointer appears as a two-directional arrow.

2 Slowly drag to the right. As you drag, the width of the column in characters will appear in a ScreenTip next to the pointer.

3 When the ScreenTip says 12.00, release the mouse button. If you drag past 12.00, just drag back. You might have to drag back and forth several times to get to the exact column width.

To adjust the width of more than one column at a time, select the columns by dragging over their column headings. Then double-click on any of the column heading boundary lines in the selection to make each column the width of its widest entry, or drag any boundary to make all of the columns the same size.

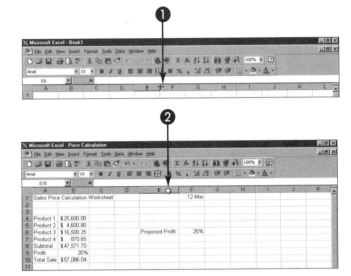

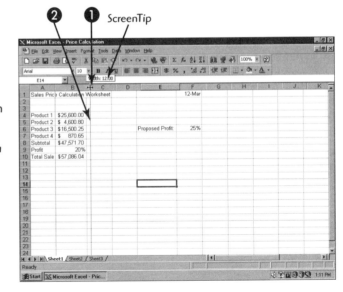

Dragging to Set Column Widths

CHANGING ROW HEIGHT

You can also adjust the height of rows by dragging. Point to the line under the row letter so the mouse appears like a two-directional arrow and then drag down to increase the row height or up to decrease it. Resize several rows by selecting them first. (Remember, you do this by dragging across their row numbers.) To set an exact height, choose Format ➤ Row ➤ Height and enter the height in points. Format ➤ Row ➤ AutoFit makes the row as high as its highest entry.

■ Setting an Exact Column Width

You may want to set a precise column width but might have trouble doing so with the mouse. If so, you can follow these easy steps to set the column width exactly:

- Click any cell in the column.

- Select Format ➤ Column ➤ Width.

- In the dialog box that appears, enter the width in number of characters and then click OK.

NOTE *The AutoFit Selection option in the Format ➤ Column menu, by the way, has the same effect as double-clicking the column heading boundary. You'll learn about the Hide option in Lesson 4.*

EDITING YOUR WORK

To change the contents of a cell you have two choices: type new information into the cell or edit its exiting contents. Retyping is fine when you want to enter an entirely new number or text entry. Just move to the cell and start typing. If you change your mind about the change before you accept the entry by pressing Enter or one of the cursor movement keys, just press Esc or click Cancel to retain the cell's original contents.

Sometimes, however, it is just not practical to retype an entire entry. You may have a typo in just one word of a title, or you want to

Working with Worksheets

2

Editing Text and Numbers

make a minor change in a complex formula. Rather than retype the
entry from scratch, you can switch to Edit mode and make the
change.

Editing Text and Numbers

You can edit an entry either in the cell itself or in the formula bar.
You'll look at both methods here. You'll change the title of the
worksheet in cell A1 to **Sale Price Worksheet**, and the text in cell
A10 to **Total**. You'll start by using the formula bar, and then learn
how to edit within the cell itself:

1 Click cell A1. You must click cell A1 even though the text looks
as through it's also in cells B1 and C1. The information is actually
just in cell A1. You can tell which cell contains the information
by looking at the formula bar. If you click B1 or C1, the formula
bar will be empty. Click cell A1 to see the information in the
formula bar.

2 Click in the formula bar following the word *Calculation*. Excel
displays the insertion point in the formula bar where you click,
and displays the word *Edit* in the status bar. If the insertion
point is not immediately after the word, use the arrow keys to
move it there.

3 Press Backspace until you delete the word *Calculation*. The
word is also deleted from the text in the active cell. Be sure to
delete the extra space so there is only one space between
words.

4 Press the arrow key to move the insertion point after the word
Sales. Place it before the space between the words, immediately
after the letter *s*.

5 Press Backspace to delete the letter *s*. The text should now read
"Sale Price Worksheet."

6 Double-click cell A10. Excel displays the insertion point where
the mouse was pointing. You can also press the F2 key to edit in
the active cell.

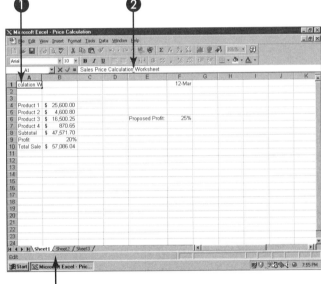

Status bar

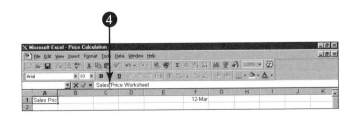

7 Edit the text by deleting the word *Sale*. You can save time when editing in a cell by clicking where you want the insertion point to appear.

8 Press Enter. The word *Ready* appears in the status bar, indicating that you are no longer in Edit mode.

While you are Edit mode, you can switch between editing in the formula bar and editing within the cell by clicking where you want to work. In Edit mode, by the way, the Up Arrow and Down Arrow keys do not work, and the Left Arrow and Right Arrow keys move the insertion point within the text, not from cell to cell.

If you change your mind about editing the entry, just press Esc or click the Cancel button to retain the cell's original contents.

Editing Formulas

You edit formulas just as you do labels and numbers, but with one added advantage — Range Finder.

When you edit a cell that contains a formula, Excel surrounds the referenced cells in color frames, and displays their addresses in the formula in matching colors. For example, suppose a formula references cells A1 and A2, as in =A1+A2. When you activate that cell and get into Edit mode, cell A1 will be surrounded by a blue frame and the address A1 will appear in blue in the formula. Cell A2 will be surrounded by a green frame and the address A2 will appear in green in the formula. This color matching is Excel's way of helping you visualize the construction of the formula and its referenced cells.

You can change a cell reference by typing the new one in place of the old, or by pointing:

1 Click cell B10. This cell contains a formula.

2 Press the F2 key. Excel enters Edit mode, displaying colored frames around cells B8 and B9, with matching colors on the addresses in the formula.

3 Drag over B9 in the formula. When you release the mouse button, the colored frames and matching colors are removed.

4 Click cell F6. Excel replaces the reference to cell B9 with F6.

Undoing Changes

⑤ Click on the Enter box. Excel recalculates the formula using the value in cell F6 as the percentage.

The worksheet on your screen should appear as shown here. If it does not, click on the cell that is different and type the information shown.

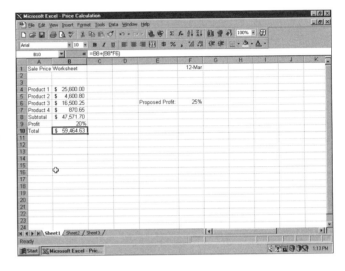

Undoing Changes

If you change your mind about a change you've made to a cell, you may be able to undo it. While you still are in Edit mode and have not yet accepted the entry, just press Esc or click the Cancel button to retain the cell's original contents.

Once you've already accepted the entry, use Excel's Undo feature if you change your mind. Undo lets you cancel almost any action, except saving and printing a worksheet and some other operations. If you made changes to a cell, or deleted its contents or formats, and then changed your mind, use Undo to change everything back again. Let's see how this works:

① Click cell H1.

② Type **1** and then press the Down Arrow key.

③ Type **2** and then press the Down Arrow key.

④ Continue numbering the cells 3, 4, and 5.

⑤ Click the Undo button on the Standard toolbar. The number 5 is cleared from the cell, undoing your most recent action.

⑥ Click the Undo button again to clear the number 4. Excel remembers the last 16 actions that you performed, so if you click on the Undo button a second time, your next-to-the-last action will be undone. Once you've undone all of the actions that Excel has saved, the Undo button will become dimmed.

The Undo button will not undo itself, so if you click Undo and then change your mind, you cannot click Undo again to cancel it. You can, however, click the Redo button. You see, Excel also remembers the last 16 actions that you undid. Click Redo to cancel the previous Undo commands.

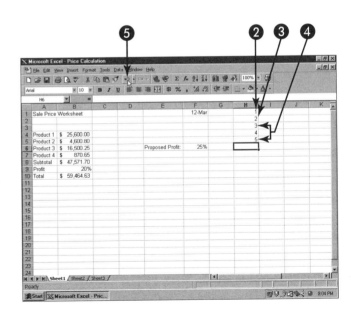

Erasing Information from Cells

Before clicking Undo and Redo, however, you may want to make sure that you are really undoing or redoing what you had in mind. To check out the last action, pull down the Edit menu. The first item in the menu is the Undo command, and its full name indicates the action that you will undo, such as Undo Typing "1" in H7, or Undo Clear. The second item in the Edit menu is the Redo command, and its full name shows the item being redone.

To undo more than a single action at one time, pull down the Undo list by clicking on the down arrow next to the Undo button on the Standard toolbar. Excel displays a list of the actions it can undo, with the most recent on top, as in the accompanying illustration. Click on the top item to undo the last action; the one below it moves up to take its place. You cannot select an individual item from within the list. Clicking the fourth item on the list, for example, undoes it and the three above it at one time. There is a similar Redo list next to the Redo button on the Standard toolbar. Pull down the list to choose one or more items to redo.

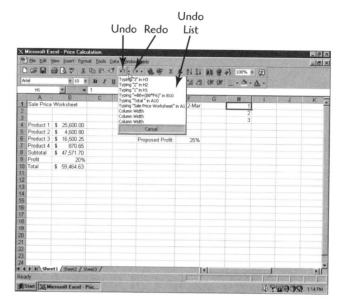

Erasing Information from Cells

If you want to erase all of the information from a cell and leave it blank, you *clear* its contents. In Excel, clearing is a much different operation than deleting:

- When you clear a cell, row, or column, you erase whatever is in it. If you clear column B, for example, the column becomes empty without affecting any other columns.

- When you delete a cell, row, or column, you actually remove it from the worksheet, moving any remaining cells up or over to take the place of the deleted cells. If you delete column B, column C moves over to take its place, and it becomes the new column B, column D becomes C, and so on. You'll learn about deleting cells in Lesson 4.

The easiest way to clear a cell is to activate it by clicking it with the mouse or moving to it with the keyboard, and then press the Delete key. Use the same technique to clear a range of cells, or one or more rows or columns:

❶ Select cells H1 to H3.

Erasing Information from Cells

② Press the Delete key.

Clearing with the Delete key removes the contents of the cell, but not any formats that have been applied to it. Remember when you entered 25 in a cell that had contained the date in Lesson 1? Because you first entered a date into the cell, Excel applied the date format to it. Replacing the date with the number 25 displayed 25-Jan because changing the contents did not change the format. Likewise, clearing the contents of a cell does not change its format. To clear a cell of its formats, you have to use the Clear command from the Edit menu.

③ Click cell F1. This cell contains a date, using the date format.

④ Select Edit ➤ Clear ➤ Formats. Excel removes the date format from the cell, displaying the date's equivalent serial number.

⑤ Press Ctrl+; (semicolon). Excel reinserts the date in the default *mm/dd/yy* format.

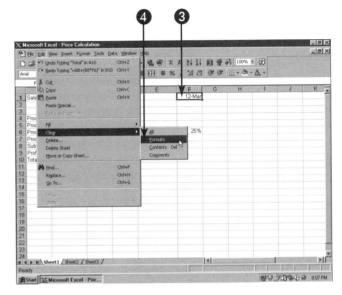

⑥ Click cell F6, the cell that contains the percentage profit.

⑦ Select Edit ➤ Clear ➤ Formats. Excel removes the percentage format but converts the value to its decimal equivalent (0.25) so the results in cell B10 do not change.

Here are the other options in the Clear submenu:

- **All** clears the contents and formats of the cell.

- **Contents** clears the cell but leaves the formats intact (this is the same as pressing the Delete key).

- **Comments** deletes comments that you may have added. Comments are discussed in Lesson 3.

GETTING HELP

Excel always provided a great on-line help system, but Excel 97 really takes help to its limits. There is direct support on the Internet, and a cute little interactive Assistant makes getting help so much fun you'll look forward to needing it.

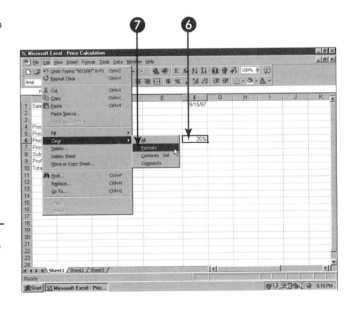

Using the Contents Tab

First you'll take a look at the more traditional help features, and then you'll get to the unique help features of Microsoft Office applications such as Excel. When you need an answer from the Help system, select Help ➤ Contents and Index. Excel displays a dialog box with the three tabs shown at right. Each of the tabs lets you get help in a different way, so learn how to pick the tab for the type of information you're looking for.

Using the Contents Tab

The Contents tab lists general categories of information, with a book icon in front of each. Let's try it out:

❶ Select Help ➤ Contents and Index. If the Contents tab is not displayed, click it now.

❷ Double-click Printing. The book icon next to Printing opens, and Excel displays an additional list of subjects within that category. Some of the items are preceded by a question mark icon. Double-clicking these icons displays a window of information on that topic. Other items are marked with a book icon, just like the major categories. These topics are divided into further subtopics, so continue double-clicking until you see the question mark icon for the subject you need help with.

❸ Double-click the topic What To Do Before You Print.

Excel displays a graphic of a sample worksheet, with individual help topics about the subject shown in rectangles.

❹ Point to the topic Add Headers and Footers. The mouse pointer appears as a small hand. Click the topic to reach a definition or description of the topic, or to open its help window.

❺ Click the Close box in the Help window title bar. The window closes.

Using the Index Tab

The Index tab shows an alphabetical listing of every subject for which Excel offers help. It is often faster to use the index than to navigate

Contents   Index   Find   Help Topics
tab   tab   tab   dialog box

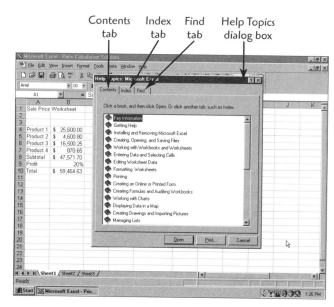

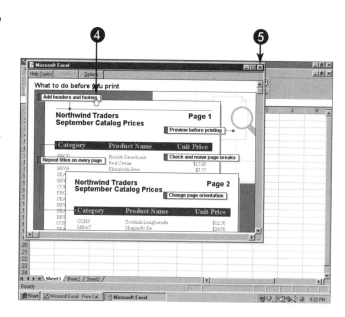

2

Working with Worksheets

Using the Index Tab

though the Contents page. As an example, you'll use the Index tab to get information on printing:

① Select Help ➢ Contents and Index. The Contents tab is displayed because you used it last.

② Click the Index tab. In the text box at the top of the dialog box, enter a word or phrase that describes the subject you are looking for.

③ Type **p**. As you type, Excel scrolls to the part of the help index that begins with that letter.

④ Continue typing **printing**. Excel scrolls to the printing section of the index. When you see topics you're interested in, you double-click them to open their help window.

⑤ Scroll the list of topics until you see the subtopic workbooks.

⑥ Double-click workbooks. Excel displays the help window for this topic.

This is the most common type of help window. It shows you how to perform the function, or lists additional topics that you can select. In this case, the window explains generally how to print a worksheet. The small box with a chevron (>) at the bottom of the window indicates additional information or a subtopic that is available. The box is called a *jump button*. Click the button to jump to that additional information.

The button labeled Show Me will actually open a dialog box for you or perform the function.

Read the information in the box, and if needed, move to related subjects by clicking on the jump buttons. By the way, words and phrases in the help window that have dotted underlines are called defined terms. Click the term to read its definition and then click elsewhere in the help window when you're done. When you are finished with the help system, click its Close box to return to the workbook.

Help windows have three commands:

- **Help Topics** redisplays the Help Topics dialog box.

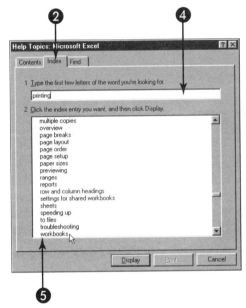

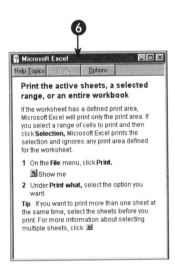

- **Back** returns to the previously displayed help window, but not to the Help Topics dialog box.

- **Options** lets you print the help information, copy it to the Clipboard to paste into another window, change the way that help windows appear, and set bookmarks to quickly return to a specific help window.

Using the Find Tab

The Find tab lets you search the entire help system for a word or phrase. Sometimes what you need help with is not listed as a separate topic in the contents page or index. Searching the system displays a list of all help windows that contain the word or phrase that you enter:

1 Select Help ➢ Contents and Index. You can also click the Help Topics button in any help window. Excel closes the current help window and returns to the Help Topics dialog box.

2 Click the Find tab.

If this is the very first time Find tab is used on your system, Excel asks you to select the type of database of words you want to use. You have three options, as shown here:

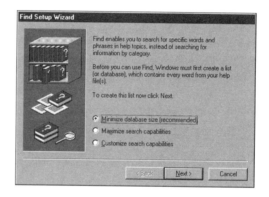

- Select **Minimize Database Size** for simple searches of words or phrases as they appear in the help windows.

- Select **Maximize Search Capabilities** to find subjects with related or similar concepts as the word or phrase you enter.

- Select **Customize Search Capabilities** to specify the help files to search.

Choose the Minimize Database Size option to save time and disk space. Once you make a choice, Excel builds a database of words. The search may take a few minutes or more based on the size of the database, so be patient. Once the database is complete, however, Excel displays a dialog box like the one shown at right.

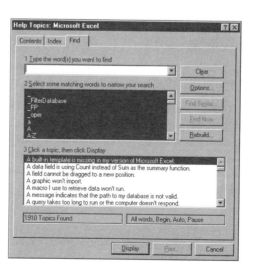

2

Working with Worksheets

Using the Find Tab

You can later choose one of the other database options by clicking the Rebuild button in the Find tab of the Help Topics dialog box. Use the Options button in the dialog box to customize the way Excel matches words in the help windows.

Now let's continue using the Find tab. In the text box numbered 1, type a word or phrase that you are looking for in the help system.

❸ Type **printing**. Excel scrolls the list box numbered 2 to display words in the database that match your entry. Click an item from that list to display the help topics containing that phrase in the bottom list.

❹ Click printing. Excel displays the help topics that contain that word.

❺ Double-click one of the topics in box 3. Excel displays the help topic.

❻ Click the Close button in the help window.

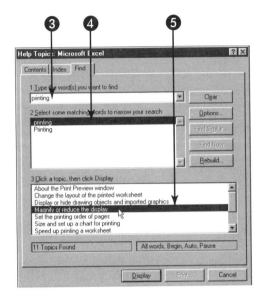

If you need help on a menu, toolbar, dialog box, or other feature that appears on the screen, you can save yourself the trouble of navigating through the help system. Use What's This? help instead. Select Help ➣ What's This? *The mouse pointer will be accompanied by a question mark. Now click the item that you need help with, selecting it from a menu or a toolbar, if necessary. Excel displays a brief description of the feature. Read the information and click elsewhere to remove it from view.*

The Help menu offers several other ways to get information. Choose Microsoft on the Web to select from popular Internet sites and automatically start your Web browser. The Lotus 1-2-3 Help option shows Excel equivalents to Lotus commands. About Microsoft Excel displays license and copyright information, information about your computer system, and explains how to get technical support.

■ Using the Office Assistant

The What's This? help feature is useful but it only displays a brief description of features that are displayed on the screen. The Microsoft Assistant can quickly give you detailed information on almost any Excel feature, and in a way that may amuse and entertain you.

You have probably seen the Assistant in action already, in the form of that small window with the animated paper clip or some other figure. The animation adds a little visual, if not comic, relief to your work, and if your system is equipped for sound you'll hear small sound effects warning you of problems or letting you know that some operation is taking place. If the Assistant is not already on your screen, press the F1 key or select Help ➢ Microsoft Excel Help. If the Assistant is on screen, just click it. Excel displays a balloon asking what you want help with, as shown to the right. Type a word, phrase, or question that describes what you want to do and then press Enter or click the Search button. The Assistant will either display information about a feature or list a number of topics that relate to your question. Click the topic to display its help window.

The Assistant balloon also contains these choices:

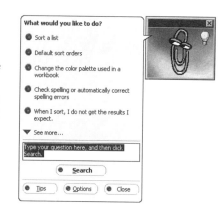

- **Tips** displays a useful hint or shortcut about an Excel feature.

- **Options** lets you customize the way the Assistant works.

- **Close** clears the balloon without removing the Assistant from the screen.

A light bulb icon in the Assistant window means that it has a tip for the feature you are performing. Click the icon to display the tip.

Skills Challenge

To choose from other animated Assistants, and to select other options, right-click the Assistant window, and then choose from these options.

See Tips displays the useful tip of the day

Options lets you customize the way Assistant works

Animate! shows another Assistant animation each time you select it

Hide Assistant closes the window

Choose Assistant lets you select other animated assistants

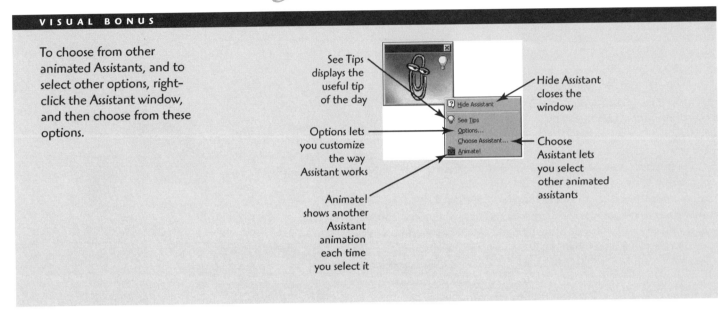

SKILLS CHALLENGE: EDITING A WORKSHEET

You learned a lot in this lesson, so now you should take some time to practice.

Even if everything you do is perfect, you'll still need to make changes to a worksheet now and then. Fortunately, you can open, edit, and save a worksheet as many times as you need. Don't worry if you do not complete the worksheet, or find that you've made some mistakes. Anything can be corrected.

In this exercise, you will adjust the column width and edit text in an existing worksheet, shown in the illustration at right. You can find a copy of this exercise under the name Workout 2 in the Exercise directory. There's a copy of the completed exercise under the name Solution 2 in the Solution directory.

1 Open the file named Workout 2 in the Exercise directory of the CD. Notice that column B is much wider than it needs to be, and columns E and F are too narrow.

2 Select cells D5 to D24, and apply the Currency style. You can apply styles to a selected range just as you can to an individual cell.

1 *How do you select more than one cell?*

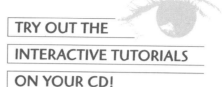

TRY OUT THE
INTERACTIVE TUTORIALS
ON YOUR CD!

3 Adjust the width of columns B, E, and F to fit the widest entry. Double-click the column boundary of a column to make it fit its text.

 2 *What other ways are there to change the column width?*

4 Adjust column G so it is exactly 20 characters wide. Either drag the column and check the width with the ScreenTip, or use the Column Width dialog box.

5 Clear the text in column J.

 3 *What is the difference between deleting and clearing cells, rows, and columns?*

6 Edit cell G15 to read **30 units in need of repair**. Edit the text in the cell, do not retype it.

 4 *How do you choose to edit in the cell or in the formula bar?*

7 Edit cell G16 to read **Keep on low shelf or floor**.

8 Adjust column G to fit its widest entry.

9 Using the File ➢ Save As command, save the worksheet with the name **Stock List**.

The worksheet on your screen should appear as shown in the illustration at right. If it does not, open the worksheet and try again.

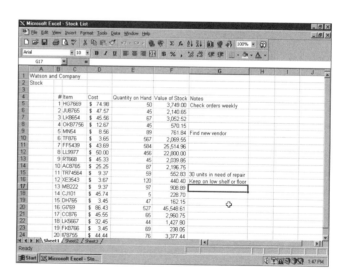

Troubleshooting

TROUBLESHOOTING

You're on a roll now! The more you use Excel, the easier it becomes, even though you're using more sophisticated and powerful techniques. But if you do have a little glitch, check out these tips.

Problem	Solution
I can't find the file I want to open.	By default, Excel lists files with the .xls extension in a default directory (such as My Documents). To list all files in the Open dialog box, pull down the Files of Type list box and select All Files. If the file isn't listed, try other directories.
When I try to select a cell, I move it instead.	Make sure the mouse pointer appears like a large white plus sign before you drag it.
I erased cells that I didn't want to. Do I have to retype everything?	If you clear cells by mistake, click on the Undo button.

WRAP UP

Stand up and stretch; you earned it. In this lesson, you learned a number of essential techniques for creating and working with workbooks. In addition to learning how to open workbooks, you learned these Excel features:

- How to use the Favorites folder

- How to select and edit cells

- How to change the column width and row height

- How to get help

If you want to practice a little more, create one or two worksheets on your own. Use Excel to record your collection of video tapes, stamps, or other object of your affection. Keep track of projects that you're working on, or chores you have to do around the house. In this next lesson, you'll learn timesaving techniques for automating your work.

PART II

Essential Excel Techniques

In this part, you'll learn how to automate your work with Excel, rearrange and format your work, and take advantage of Excel's capabilities to use multiple worksheets and windows. It includes the following lessons:

- Lesson 3: Automating Your Work
- Lesson 4: Rearranging and Previewing Worksheets
- Lesson 5: Formatting Worksheets
- Lesson 6: Using Worksheets and Windows

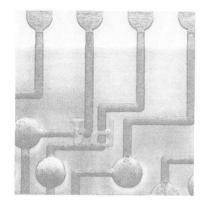

Automating Your Work

GOALS

In this lesson, you will learn timesaving techniques to make your work easier, including:

- Completing series with AutoFill
- Creating custom AutoFill lists
- Pointing to cells from dialog boxes
- Using AutoSum
- Displaying results with AutoCalculate
- Entering labels with AutoComplete
- Selecting labels from a list
- Inserting comments to refresh your memory

Completing a Series with AutoFill

GET READY

Excel has many other ways to automate your work and save time, in addition to automatic recalculation. You don't have to use the techniques that you'll learn about here, but they will save you time. For example, in Lesson 1 you used a rather long formula to total a range of cells: = b3+b4+b5+b6. As you'll learn here, using AutoSum you can perform the same calculation with just a single click of the mouse. The Jump Start briefly introduced AutoSum and AutoFill. In this lesson, you'll learn more about these features, and other ways to save time with Excel.

This lesson refers to the following worksheets:

File Name	Location
Annual Budget	Exercise directory
Final Budget	Solution directory
Workout 3	Exercise directory
Solution 3	Solution directory

When you complete this lesson, you'll have edited a spreadsheet, as shown to the left.

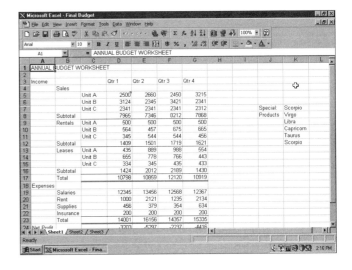

AUTOMATING YOUR WORK WITH AUTOFILL

It is very common to have a series of row and column labels that are sequential entries, such as the days of the week, months of the year, or incrementing numbers. Excel helps you complete these types of entries with a feature called AutoFill. In most cases, you just enter the first of the series, show Excel the range you want to complete, and Excel does the rest for you.

Completing a Series with AutoFill

Some series, such as incrementing numbers or the days of the week, seem obvious. But Excel can recognize and complete other types of series as well. For example, in the steps that follow, you'll use AutoFill to complete the quarters of the year, starting with one entry: Qtr 1.

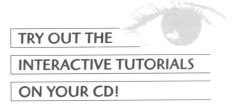

TRY OUT THE

INTERACTIVE TUTORIALS

ON YOUR CD!

Completing a Series with AutoFill

① Open the worksheet Annual Budget in the Exercise folder.

② Click cell D3.

③ Type **Qtr 1** and press the Enter button on the formula bar.

④ Point to the Fill handle — the small black box in the lower-right corner of the selected cell. The mouse pointer should appear like a black plus sign, as shown to the right.

⑤ Slowly drag across the row to the right. As you drag, a ScreenTip appears under the pointer showing the text that will be inserted into the cells that are being selected. Excel recognizes Qtr 1 as the start of the series of months, so the text in the ScreenTip changes to Qtr 2, Qtr 3, and Qtr 4 as you drag.

⑥ Drag until you reach cell G3 and the ScreenTip says Qtr 4, and then release the mouse button. Excel fills in the cells with the quarters.

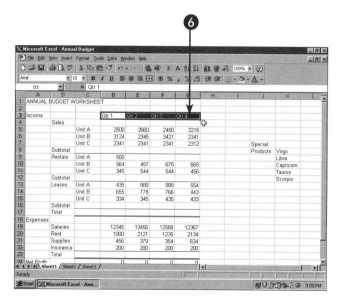

TIP

If you drag down or to the right, Excel increases the values in a series or cycles upward through a fixed set of values. For example, of you drag beyond cell G3 in the steps above, Excel would repeat the same series Qtr 1 to Qtr 4, inserting Qtr 1 in cell H3, Qtr 2 in cell I3 and so on. If you drag up or to the left, Excel decreases the values of cycles downward, such as from Qtr 4 to Qtr 3.

The following table shows some of the other series that Excel will create. In addition to dates, AutoFill completes numeric series that also contain text, such as Plan 1 and Week 1.

TABLE 3-1 STARTING VALUES FOR AUTOFILL

First Value	Series
Jan	Feb, Mar . . .
January	February, March . . .
Mon	Tue, Wed, Thu . . .
Monday	Tuesday, Wednesday . . .

continued

Entering Repeating Values

Suppose you want to skip values in a series, such as using AutoFill to enter all even numbers — 2, 4, 6, and so on. To complete a series such as this, enter and select the first two values of the entries. For example, to insert a series of even numbers, enter 2 in the first cell and 4 in the second cell. Select both cells so Excel can determine the interval between values, and drag the fill handle of the second cell. By looking at the ScreenTip under the pointer as you drag, you can confirm that Excel is completing the series as you intended. If it is not, drag back to the starting cell and release the mouse; then try again using new starting values.

TABLE 3-1 (continued)

First Value	Series
Day 1	Day 2, Day 3 . . .
Week 1	Week 2, Week 3 . . .
Plan 1	Plan 2, Plan 3 . . .
Jan 97	Feb 97, Mar 97, Apr 97 . . .
1st	2nd, 3rd, 4th, 5th . . .
Qtr 1	Qtr 2, Qtr 3, Qtr 4, Qtr 1 . . .
1st Quarter	2nd Quarter, 3rd Quarter . . .
100 Days	101 Days, 102 Days, 103 Days . . .
2,4,6	8,10,12 . . .
11/16/97	11/17/97, 11/18/97 . . .

Entering Repeating Values with AutoFill

If Excel does not know how to complete the series, it will simply copy the contents of the selected cell into the other cells. You can take advantage of this feature to quickly copy the same entry from one cell to the next. Follow these steps:

1 Click cell D9. You want to repeat the value 500 in the other quarters.

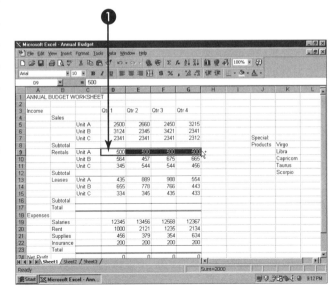

2 Drag the fill handle of D9 to cell G9. The ScreenTip shows that the value 500 is being repeated.

3 Release the mouse button. The same value appears in all of the selected cells.

Creating a Complex Series

Sometimes you don't know the number of cells you need in the series, and you don't want to drag the mouse watching the little ScreenTip. For example, suppose you want to give your class an assignment. You want a paper due every third day during the semester from January 2 to April 30. If the due day falls on a weekend, however, the paper is due the next weekday, and you only want to count weekdays in the three–day work period. Seems complicated? Not at all. The solution is to use the Series dialog box.

Try creating this series of dates now:

1 Click cell I1.

2 Type **1/2** and then click the Enter box in the formula bar. Excel inserts "2-Jan" into the cell.

3 Select Edit ➢ Fill. The submenu that appears includes options for filling a series of cells with the same value in any direction.

4 Click Series. Excel displays the dialog box shown in the accompanying illustration.

5 Under Series In, select Columns. This tells Excel to complete the series down the column, rather that across the row.

6 Leave Date selected under Type. Excel usually chooses the correct type for the data you've selected.

7 Under Date Unit, click Weekday. This skips weekends in the series.

8 In the Step Value text box, type **3** for every third day.

9 In the Stop Value text box, type **4/30**.

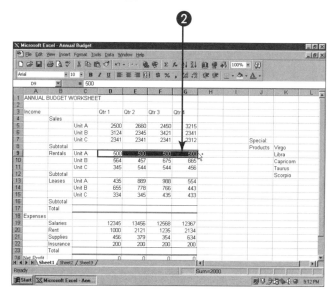

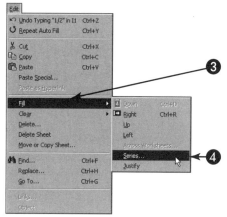

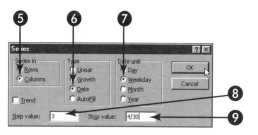

Creating Custom AutoFill Lists

⑩ Click OK. Excel completes the series as you intended, copying the date format from the starting cell as well, as shown to the right.

⑪ Click Undo twice to delete the series.

As another alternative to filling a series:

⑫ Enter the first or more values.

⑬ Drag the fill handle with the *right* mouse button.

⑭ Release the mouse button. A shortcut menu appears.

Choose how to fill the cells. In addition to choosing the type of fill (the Date options are dimmed when you haven't selected date information), you can choose to display the Series dialog box, or select from these options:

- **Copy Cells**: Copies the contents of the selected cells across the range

- **Fill Series**: Completes the series just as if you have dragged with the left mouse button

- **Fill Formats**: Copies the formats from the selected cells into the series but doesn't copy the data

- **Fill Values**: Completes the series but without copying the cell formats

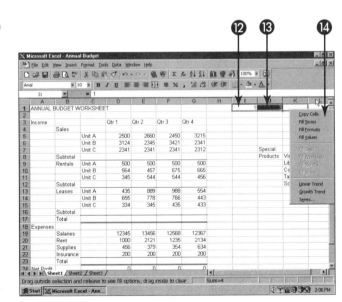

Creating Custom AutoFill Lists

If none of the series options suit your needs, you can create and save your own custom AutoFill series. A series is merely a list of values that AutoFill can complete for you. For example, suppose your company identifies inventory with codes using two letters and three numbers. You can create a custom list so Excel will recognize the first inventory code and complete the series for you.

The Annual Budget worksheet includes a list of similar inventory codes. You can use the entries in the worksheet to create a custom list.

❶ Select cells C26 to H26.

2 Select Tools ➢ Options.

3 Click the Custom Lists tab. Excel displays the dialog box shown in the following illustration. The range of selected entries appears in the Import List from Cells box. The dollar signs in the range represent absolute addresses, meaning that the references will not change when they're moved or copied. You'll learn more about absolute address in Lesson 7.

4 Click Import. Excel inserts the values from the selected cells into the list.

5 Click OK.

6 Click to deselect the cells.

Now whenever you need to enter this series, type the first entry and drag the fill handle.

7 Click cell C25, type **HY765**, and click the Enter button on the formula bar. HY765 is the first item in the series.

8 Drag the fill handle of cell C25 to H25. Excel completes the series from the custom list.

9 Click Undo twice to delete the series.

You can also create the list without typing it in the worksheet first. In the Custom Lists tab of the Options dialog box, click NEW LIST in the Custom Lists box, and then type the series in the List Entries box. Make sure you start with the item that you want to begin the series, and press Enter after each entry. Click Add when you're done.

ENTERING RANGE REFERENCES IN DIALOG BOXES

When you opened the Custom Lists tab of the Options dialog box a moment ago, the range of cells for the list appeared because you had selected the cells ahead of time. If the range was incorrect, or you forgot to select the cells first, you could just type the range reference in the text box. But you can also point to range references under these circumstances. In dialog boxes that can act on a range of cells, look for a Collapse Dialog button next to a text box.

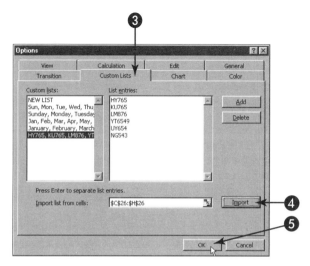

Collapse Dialog button

3

Automating Your Work

Pointing to Cells

This button lets you collapse the dialog box to select the range of cells you want it to act upon. Use the button in either of these ways:

- Click the button to collapse the dialog box (you do not have to click the text box first). The range you select will be inserted into the text box associated with the button.

- Click the text box associated with the button, and then click the first cell of the range in the background of the dialog box.

The difference between the methods is how you expand the dialog box after selecting the cells.

 NOTE *Both methods for collapsing dialog boxes let you point to a cell or range of cells by dragging. Clicking the Collapse Dialog button requires a few more steps than clicking in the worksheet directly, but is the preferred method if the cell or range of cells you want to select is not visible in the background of the dialog box.*

Pointing to Cells via the Collapse Dialog Button

In this exercise, you'll try using the Collapse Dialog button:

1 Select Tools ➢ Options. The Custom List tab of the Options dialog box should be in front. If not, click it now.

2 Delete any reference that may be in the Import List From Cells text box. If you do not delete the address, any range that you select will be added to the address already in the box.

3 Click the Collapse Dialog button. The dialog box collapses and its title bar changes to read Options - Import List from Cells. This tells you which dialog box you are using, and which text box your reference will be recorded in. On the right end of the box is the Expand Dialog button, as shown to the right.

4 Click cell C26, and drag to cell H26. As you drag, a ScreenTip appears with the number of rows and columns next to the

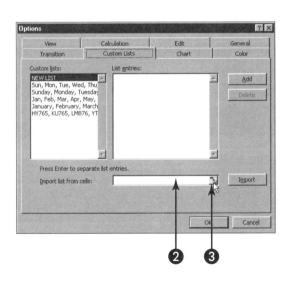

mouse pointer, just as it did in the formula bar when you selected a range.

5 Release the mouse button. The cells are surrounded by a moving border, and the address of the range is in the text box — don't worry for now about how the range address appears.

6 Click the Expand Dialog button. The Options dialog box expands to its full size, and the range you dragged across appears in the Import List From Cells text box.

7 Click Cancel to close the dialog box.

Pointing to Cells by Clicking in the Worksheet

Now you'll try the same thing, but without using the Collapse Dialog or Expand Dialog buttons. You can only use this method if the cell you first want to click is visible. If the cell is obscured by the dialog box, move the dialog box out of the way by dragging its title bar. Don't worry if the last cell you want to select in the range is obscured by the dialog box. Excel automatically collapses the box when you drag within the worksheet.

1 Make sure cell C26 is displayed on screen.

2 Select Tools ➤ Options. If the dialog box obscures cell C26, drag it out of the way by its title bar.

3 Click the Import List From Cells text box and delete any reference there.

TIP

The insertion point must be in a text box that includes a Collapse Dialog button for this technique to work.

4 Click cell C26, and drag to cell H26. As you're dragging, the dialog box should collapse; when you release the mouse button, the dialog box expands automatically.

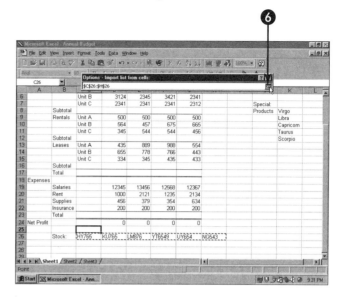

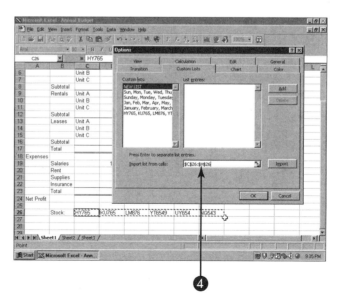

Calculating Totals with AutoSum

USING AUTOSUM

When you want to total the values in a column or row, let AutoSum do it for you instead of typing a formula. It's as easy as clicking the cell where you want the total to appear, and then clicking the AutoSum button in the Standard toolbar. That's the button with the Greek sigma character, as shown to the right.

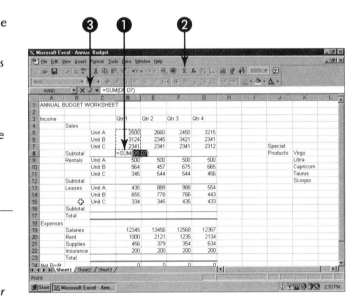

Calculating Totals with AutoSum

In the Jump Start section, you learned how to use the AutoSum button to quickly total a series of numbers. Here you'll review the procedure now that you have more worksheet experience:

❶ Click cell D8 in the worksheet. This cell represents the sum of the values above it, a subtotal of sales.

❷ Click the AutoSum button. Excel encloses the cells above D8 within a moving border and displays a suggested formula =SUM(D5:D7), as shown in the accompanying illustration. As you learned in the Jump Start, SUM is a function that totals the values in a range of cells.

❸ Click the Enter button on the formula bar. AutoSum calculates the total of the cells in the designated range and displays the total in cell D8.

You can also use AutoSum to calculate the totals of cells in a row, but with one small caution: If there are values in the cell above the active cell, Excel will assume you want to calculate those cells instead. In this case, first select the cells in the row along with the blank cell to their right, and then click the AutoSum button.

TIP

You can select either a column or a row of cells containing data, plus a cell below or to the right to contain the total, before clicking the AutoSum button. When you use this method, Excel calculates and inserts the sum in one step, without displaying the moving border for you to confirm the range.

Calculating Subtotals and Totals

Calculating Subtotals and Totals

When you use AutoSum to total the values in a column, Excel adds up the values above it up to the first blank or nonnumeric cell, or to a cell that already contains a SUM function. Likewise, when you use AutoSum to total the values in a row, Excel adds up the values to its left up to the first blank or nonnumeric cell, or SUM function.

You can take advantage of this feature to calculate subtotals and grand totals. For example, if the cell above the active cell contains a SUM formula, Excel assumes you want to add the values of the SUM formulas above (or to the left). This gives you a grand total of the subtotals calculated by SUM functions. Follow these steps to see how this works:

❶ Click cell D12. This cell represents the subtotal of rentals.

❷ Click the AutoSum button. Excel selects cells D9 to D11, stopping at the previous SUM formula, and suggests the formula =SUM(D9:D11).

❸ Click the Enter button on the formula bar.

❹ Click cell D16. This cell represents the subtotal of leases.

❺ Click AutoSum and then press Enter. Excel inserts the formula =SUM(D13:D15), again selecting cells up to the previous total. Cell D17 is active so you can calculate the grand total.

❻ Click AutoSum. Because the cell immediately above D17 contains a SUM function, Excel selects just the subtotals in the column above (the SUM formulas) and suggests the formula =SUM(D16,D12, D8) to total the values in those three cells.

❼ Press Enter to accept and display the grand total.

❽ Click cell D23. This cell is the total of all income categories.

❾ Click AutoSum and then press Enter. Excel inserts the formula =SUM(D19:D22), stopping at the first blank cell in the column.

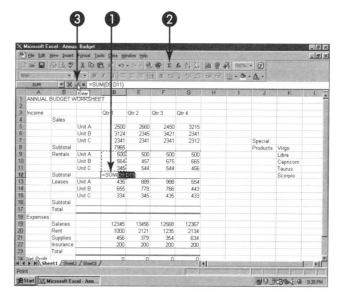

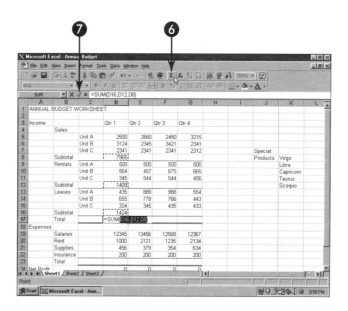

Performing Multiple AutoSums

Always check the range reference suggested by the AutoSum function to confirm that Excel has included the correct cells. When AutoSum suggests a range, the cell reference will appear highlighted. If the range that AutoSum selects is incorrect and you haven't yet accepted or rejected the entry, just drag over the correct cells. The range that you select will be inserted into the function.

Once you accept the entry, you can still change the range by pointing. Click the cell and then click the formula bar. Drag over the range reference to select it (make sure to select just the reference, not any other part of the formula), and then drag over the range you want to insert in its place. Click the Enter button when you're done.

Performing Multiple AutoSums

If you have a series of columns that will each need a total, you can insert SUM functions into them all at one time. For example, your worksheet still needs the remaining subtotals and totals in the other columns. Rather than insert each one individually, you can do them all at once.

❶ Select cells E8 to G8.

❷ Hold down the Ctrl key, and select cells E12 to G12. Holding down the Ctrl key selects this range of cells without deselecting the previously selected range.

❸ Hold down the Ctrl key and select cells E16 to G16.

❹ Hold down the Ctrl key and select cells E17 to G17.

❺ Hold down the Ctrl key and select cells E23 to G23.

❻ Click AutoSum. All of the subtotals and totals are calculated automatically.

The worksheet on your screen should appear as shown here. If it does not, open the worksheet and try again.

At times you can also select an entire range of cells and add totals to rows and columns at the same time. For example, look at the cells in the illustration to the right. Cells C6 to G9 are selected, so if you click AutoSum, Excel will insert the totals for each column and each row.

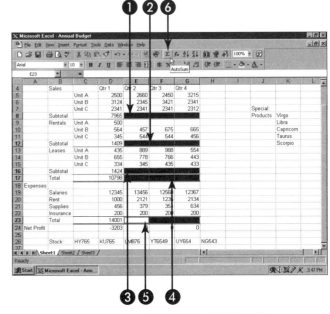

Totals added

Displaying Calculations

Unfortunately, you cannot use this technique to calculate subtotals and grand totals in one step. If you selected cells D5 to G17 in the Annual Budget worksheet, for example, Excel would only calculate the total over the columns, inserting a SUM function in the cells in row 17. It would not calculate subtotals in rows 8, 12, and 16.

USING EXCEL'S OTHER AUTOMATING TECHNIQUES

AutoFill and AutoSum are perhaps Excel's most popular techniques for automating your work, but they are not the only ones. There are other methods for displaying totals, completing entries in cells, and even selecting an entry from a list. You'll be amazed how easy Excel makes it to create a worksheet.

Displaying Calculations with AutoCalculate

Sometimes you might want to see the total, average, or some other calculation on a range of cells without actually entering a SUM formula in a particular cell in the worksheet. That's when you should take advantage of AutoCalculate. When you select a range of cells, Excel automatically adds their values and displays the total in the status bar. You can also change what appears in the status bar to some other operation — such as an average. Try this now:

① Select the range D19 to D22. The status bar will display their total, as shown in the first figure at right.

② Leave the cells selected and right-click anywhere on the status bar. Excel displays a shortcut menu of operations that AutoCalculate can complete.

③ Click Average in the shortcut menu. Excel now displays the average of the selected range instead of the total on the status bar. If you leave the status bar as it is now, Excel will display the average of the next range you select.

④ To again show the total, choose Sum from the shortcut menu.

Entering Text with AutoComplete

Here are the other options in the shortcut menu:

- **Count**: Displays the number of nonblank cells in the range
- **Count Nums**: Displays the number of cells in the range containing numeric values
- **Max**: Displays the highest value in the range
- **Min**: Displays the smallest value in the range

Entering Text with AutoComplete

Because not all cells contain numbers, Excel gives you several ways to automate the entry of text as well. With AutoComplete, as you start typing a text entry, Excel automatically displays an entry from elsewhere in the column that matches those characters. This feature is very useful when you need to add identical or similar text to more than one cell in the column. (It also only works if the list contains no blank cells.) Try it out:

1 Click cell K13.

2 Type **v**. Excel inserts the text *virgo*, matching the only entry in the column that already starts with the letter *v*. If more than one entry starts with that letter, Excel will not suggest an entry until you enter enough matching characters for it to distinguish between the entries that have the same first letters.

3 Press Enter to accept the suggested entry. Excel displays Virgo, matching the case of the existing entry. If you do not want to accept the entry, just continue typing or press the Backspace key.

4 Click Undo.

Picking Entries from a List

If you know there is an entry that you want to copy, you can also insert it by picking from a list. This saves you the trouble of even typing the first letter or so. Here's how:

1 Right-click cell K7.

2 Choose Pick From List from the shortcut menu. A list box appears under the active cell, listing the text entries already in the column in alphabetical order, as shown to the right.

3 Click Scorpio to insert it into the cell.

If you don't want to use the mouse, activate the cell and then press Alt+Down Arrow to display the list. Press the Down Arrow (without the Alt key held down) to choose the entry, and then press Enter.

ADDING COMMENTS TO CELLS

Excel's automation techniques are useful, but your memory may not be automatic when you return to a worksheet sometime later. As you develop your worksheets, you'll create formulas and enter information that is perfectly meaningful as you're doing it. That doesn't mean that you'll remember why you entered the information, or the idea behind the formula, when you open the worksheet some days, weeks, or months from now. Wouldn't it be useful if you could stick one of those little stick-on notes to the worksheet to automatically refresh your memory in the future? Well, you can.

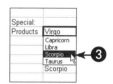

Inserting a Comment

You can add a comment, a small box of text that appears next to the cursor when you point to a cell. You can print comments, if you like, and you can have them displayed all of the time. Comments are great when you want to leave instructions or reminders to others who may be using your worksheet. Follow these steps to add a comment or two now:

1 Click cell D5.

2 Select Insert ➤ Comment. You can also right-click the cell and choose Insert Comment from the shortcut menu. Excel displays a box with the name of the registered user at the top. A small arrow points from the box to the cell.

Inserting a Comment

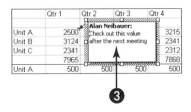

③

TIP *Chapter 12 explains how to change the name that appears with comments.*

③ Type this: **Check out this value after the next meeting.**

④ Click outside of the box. Excel accepts the comment, removing it from the screen. Excel displays a small red triangle in the upper-right corner of the cell, as shown to the right. The triangle lets you know that a comment has been added to the cell.

To display the comment, just point to or click on the cell. Excel displays the *cell tip*, the comment that you inserted, as shown in the third figure at right. You do not have to select the cell. When you move or copy the cell, the comment goes along with it.

Comment triangle

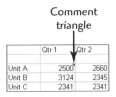

■ Working with Comments

After you add a comment, you can edit and delete it, or display comments so they appear on screen. Here's a summary of ways to work with comments:

Cell tip

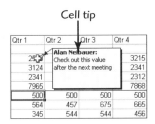

- To edit the comment, select the cell and then choose Insert ➢ Edit Comment. Excel displays the comment so you can edit it. You can also right-click the cell and choose Edit Comment from the shortcut menu.

- To remove a comment, select the cell and then choose Edit ➢ Clear ➢ Comments. Clearing the cell's contents or formats will not remove the comment. You can also right-click the cell and choose Delete Comment from the shortcut menu. Use Edit ➢ Clear ➢ All if you want to clear everything from the cell — contents, formats, and comments.

- To delete all of the comments from a worksheet, press Ctrl+A or click the Select All button, and then choose Edit ➢ Clear ➢ Comments.

- To display a comment so it stays on the screen, right-click the cell and choose Show Comment from the shortcut menu.

Skills Challenge

- To display all of the comments on the worksheet until you want to hide them, select View ➤ Comments. Excel displays all of the comments along with the Reviewing toolbar shown in the illustration at right.

- Hide all displayed comments by reselecting View ➤ Comments, or hide a specific comment by choosing Hide Comment from the shortcut menu.

You can print the comments that are attached to cells but it takes a little planning. If you want to print a comment where it appears on the worksheet, you have to display it first. To print all of the comments, display them all.

You don't have to display comments, however, if you want them printed as a group at the end of the worksheet. Select File ➤ Page Setup. Click the sheet tab and then choose either At End of Sheet or As Displayed on Sheet from the Comments drop-down box.

SKILLS CHALLENGE: TAKING ADVANTAGE OF AUTOMATION

Using Excel's automation features, you can quickly enter text and perform calculations. In this exercise, you will use AutoSum, AutoCalculate, Pick From List, and AutoFill. You can find a copy of this exercise under the name Workout 3 in the Exercise directory. There's a copy of the completed exercise under the name Solution 3 in the Solution directory.

1 Open the file named Workout 3 in the Exercise directory. The worksheet is shown in the illustration at right.

2 Complete the series of column labels from Qtr 1 to Qtr 4.

> **1** *How do you complete a series, other than entering all of the values yourself?*

3 Use AutoSum to insert the totals in row 7 and column G.

> **2** *There are several ways to do this. Which is the fastest?*

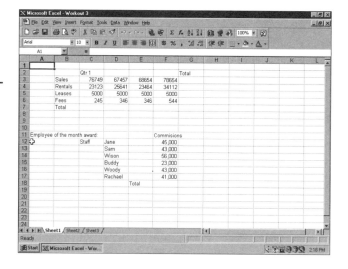

3

Automating Your Work

Skills Challenge

4 Insert the total of the commissions in cell F18.

5 Display the average of the commissions in the status bar. (Hint: Select the cells and right-click the status bar.)

3 *What is the average?*

6 Display the largest commission in the status bar.

4 *Who has earned the largest commission and what is the amount?*

7 Display the smallest commission in the status bar.

5 *Who has the smallest commission and what is the amount?*

8 Return to the default setting so the status bar once again Autocalculates the sum of the selected numbers.

9 Use Pick From List to insert the name of the salesperson with the highest commission in cell D11.

10 Format all of the numbers in the worksheet using the Currency style.

The worksheet on your screen should appear as shown in the accompanying illustration. If it does not, open the worksheet and try again.

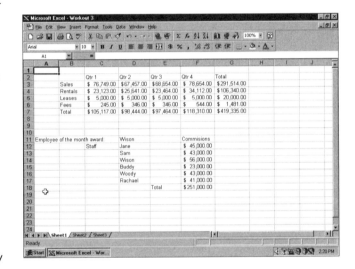

TROUBLESHOOTING

If you have an trouble applying the techniques that you learned in this lesson to your own work, check out these tips:

TRY OUT THE

INTERACTIVE TUTORIALS

ON YOUR CD!

Problem	Solution
AutoFill doesn't work; the cells are blank.	Make sure you are pointing to the AutoFill handle so the mouse pointer appears as a black plus sign. (If it looks like a white plus sign you'll just select the cells you drag across.)
I'm trying to point to cells from a dialog box, but I get too many references.	Remember to delete any reference that may already be there. If you don't, the cells you point to will be added to the reference.
I'm trying to use AutoSum, but Excel wants to include in the range the year that I'm using as a column label.	When you enter a year such as 1998, Excel treats it as a number and may include it in the AutoSum range. To enter a year as text, precede it with an apostrophe, as in '1998.
AutoSum is giving me the wrong result.	Before accepting the AutoSum range, check it carefully. Make sure the SUM function includes the cells you want to total. If you have problems, select the cells first, including the cell where you want the sum to appear, and then click the AutoSum button.
I don't see the sum of the selected range in the status bar; instead I see some other statistic.	You or someone else probably selected the other statistic. Right-click the status bar and select Sum from the shortcut menu.

3

Automating Your Work

Wrap Up

WRAP UP

The automation features you learned in this lesson can really save you time. Take advantage of them when possible, because they can save you even more time when you need to change and recalculate a worksheet. As a quick recap, this lesson described how to:

- Use AutoFill to complete a series of entries
- Create custom AutoFill ranges
- Add subtotals and totals with the AutoSum button
- Perform multiple AutoSum functions by selecting cells
- Display the total, average, count, minimum, and maximum values of a range in the status bar
- Use AutoComplete to enter text
- Select values from a list
- Add comments to cells

Excellent work. Now it's time to relax. If you still want a little more practice, create a worksheet for your own budget. Use AutoSum to total the income and expense categories, and add a formula to compute your leftovers. In Lesson 4, you will learn how to make some major changes to a worksheet.

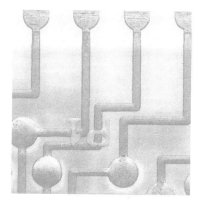

Rearranging and Previewing Worksheets

GOALS

In this lesson, you will learn more advanced techniques for completing and editing your worksheet, including:

- Moving and copying information
- Performing math when moving and copying cells
- Transposing rows to columns
- Inserting and deleting rows, columns, and cells
- Hiding columns and rows
- Previewing your worksheets before printing

60 MINUTES

Get Ready

GET READY

Now it's time to delve a little deeper into Excel, learning techniques to create more sophisticated worksheets even more easily than before. Sometimes you create a worksheet, only to find that you left out rows or columns, or entered information into the wrong cells. Have no fear. In this lesson, you'll learn how to move and copy information, and even how to perform math while you're doing so. You'll also learn how to insert and delete cells, rows, and columns.

This lesson refers to the following workbooks:

File Name	Location
Product Sales	Exercise directory
Product Sales Solution	Solution directory
Workout 4	Exercise directory
Solution 4	Solution directory

By the end of this lesson you'll have created the worksheet shown in the accompanying illustration.

MOVING AND COPYING INFORMATION

Sometimes you insert information in the wrong location, or you want to add the same entry to selected cells in the worksheet. Excel lets you move and copy information — text, numbers, and formulas — anywhere in the workbook. When you move information, you delete it from one location and place it in another. When you copy information, you create a duplicate of it in another location. In both cases, placing the information in a cell automatically deletes anything that was already there.

Now you'll learn a variety of ways to copy and move information.

■ Moving and Copying via the Clipboard

If you've worked with other Windows programs, you probably know how to move or copy information using the Clipboard. The

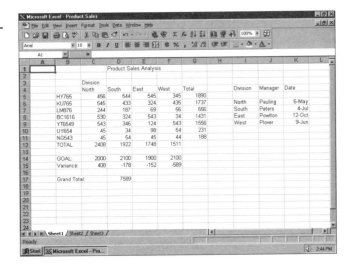

TRY OUT THE
INTERACTIVE TUTORIALS
ON YOUR CD!

Clipboard is an area in memory where you can temporarily store information. Here's the general procedure:

- Select the cells containing the information you want to move or copy.

- Cut (to move) or copy the information to the Clipboard.

- Move to the location where you want to place the information.

- Paste in the data from the Clipboard.

TIP *The shortcut keys Ctrl+D and Ctrl+R are two of the quickest ways to copy an entry from one cell to others. To copy the contents of a cell to cells below it, select the cell and the ones that you want to fill, and then press Ctrl+D. To copy the contents of a cell to the cells on the right, select the cells and press Ctrl+R.*

To cut or copy the selected cells, so you can move or copy them to the new location, use any of these techniques:

- Click the Cut or Copy button in the Standard toolbar.

- Choose Edit ➢ Cut, or Edit ➢ Copy.

- Right–click the cell and choose Cut or Copy from the shortcut menu.

- Press Ctrl+X (Cut) or Ctrl+C (Copy).

The cut or copied cells will be surrounded by the *moving border*, a blinking frame, and inserted into the Clipboard. To paste the cells, click the cell that you want to be the upper-left corner of the range into which you'll paste the cells, and then use any of these techniques:

- Press the Enter key.

- Click the Paste button in the Standard toolbar.

- Choose Edit ➢ Paste.

- Right–click and choose Paste from the shortcut menu.

- Press Ctrl+V.

Using Drag and Drop

If you use any technique other than pressing Enter to paste the cells, the moving border remains on screen. As long as the moving border is visible, you can paste the same information repeatedly — a real time-saver if you want to copy information to several locations. Just press Esc to remove the border when you are done copying the cells.

Before actually pasting a range of cells that's on the Clipboard, you only need to click the cell that will be the upper-left corner of the new location. You do not have to select an entire range. However, make sure that there are enough empty cells in the range that's receiving the data, so you do not overwrite existing data when you perform the paste operation.

Using Drag and Drop

One of the easiest ways to move and copy information is through a procedure called *drag and drop*. This means that you drag the information using the mouse, and then drop it in another location by releasing the mouse button. You can drag and drop a single cell, or a range of contiguous cells. The techniques for moving and copying information with drag and drop are almost identical. The only difference is that to copy the information, you must hold down the Ctrl key when you release the mouse button:

❶ Open the workbook Product Sales in the Exercise folder.

❷ Select the cell or cells that you want to move. In this case, click cell A1.

❸ Point to the border around cell A1 so the mouse pointer appears like an arrow. (If the mouse pointer looks like a white plus sign instead, you're pointing inside the cell.)

❹ Drag to cell D1. As you drag, an outline of the selected cell or cells moves with the mouse, and a ScreenTip reports the location where the cells will be dropped if you release the mouse button, as you can see here.

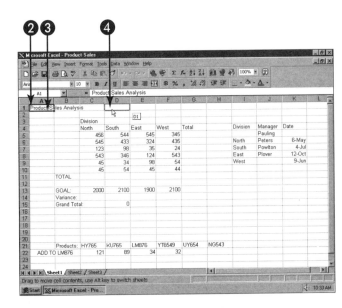

⑤ Release the mouse button to deposit the text from A1 into cell D1.

To copy the information using drag and drop, hold down the Ctrl key when you release the mouse button. A small plus sign next to the mouse pointer indicates that you are copying rather than moving the information. You don't have to hold down Ctrl while you are dragging, just when you release the mouse. This makes it easy to change your mind between moving and copying any time before you actually release the mouse button.

Using Drag and Drop with Rows and Columns

In addition to using drag and drop on selected cells, you can drag and drop entire rows and columns.

To move or copy an entire row, follow these steps:

① Click the row header to select it. To move or copy multiple rows at one time, drag over their row headers to select them.

② Point to the top, bottom, or left border around the selected row or rows so the mouse pointer appears as an arrow. (You can't point to the row header itself or to the lines between row borders.)

③ Drag the row(s) up or down. As you drag, the destination row appears in a ScreenTip with the pointer.

④ Release the mouse button to move the row of data. To copy the data, release the mouse button while holding down the Ctrl key.

You can move or copy an entire column using the same technique — just click the column header or drag across the column headers.

Using the Drag and Drop Shortcut Menu

One of the problems with drag and drop is that you need to hold down the Ctrl key to copy a cell. To copy a cell without holding down the Ctrl key, and to choose from other drag-and-drop options, drag with the right mouse button instead of the left. When you release the mouse button, Excel displays the shortcut menu shown at right.

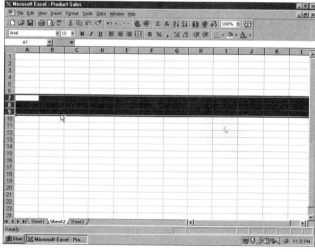

Transposing Cells

To make a copy of the cell that you dragged, choose Copy Here from the shortcut menu. You can also move cells, copy just the formats applied to cells but not the contents, and copy the value of a formula rather than the formula itself. If you copy just the value, the cell will not be updated if you change any of the cells addressed in the original formula.

The Link Here command inserts the address of the selected cells, rather than the contents of the cell. You'll learn more about this command in Lesson 7. You'll learn about the Create Hyperlink Here option in Lesson 9, and about the Shift options later in this lesson.

USING PASTE SPECIAL

For even more control over what gets inserted into a cell, use the Paste Special command. This command only works when you are copying cells, not moving them, but it lets you choose what parts of a cell you want to paste — such as the formulas, values, formats, or everything. Choosing values, for example, will paste the values from the cells, but not any formulas that calculated the values. This means that the values will remain constant and will not be updated if you change any of the cells addressed in the original formula.

When you normally paste cells, a blank cell that you copy (or cut) will be pasted as a blank cell, clearing the original contents of the cell. The Paste Special command allows you to choose Skip Blanks, so Excel will not paste blank cells, retaining the original contents in the pasted area.

You'll look at two special uses of the Paste Special command now.

Transposing Cells

The Transpose option lets you paste cells from a row into a column, and vice versa. You would use this command, for example, if you typed a series of entries as row titles and then decided to use them for column labels. Try this out now:

❶ Select cells C21 to H21. These titles were typed in a row, and you want to enter them into a column.

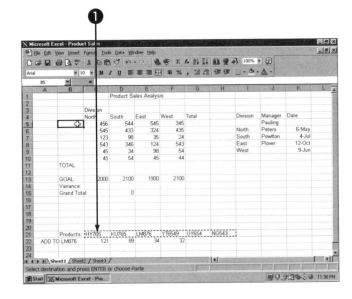

Performing Math with Pasted Cells

2 Click the Copy button in the Standard toolbar.

3 Click cell B5. You want to copy the six selected titles down column B, starting in B5.

4 Select Edit ➤ Paste Special. Excel displays the Paste Special dialog box shown in the illustration at right.

5 Click Transpose and then click OK. The column titles now appear as row labels in column B.

6 Press Esc to remove the moving border from cells C21 to H21.

7 Clear the original cells. Select cells B21 to H21, and then press the Delete key.

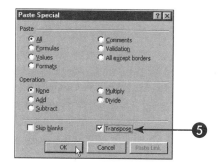

NOTE
Do not try to transpose cells that contain formulas. Because Excel will copy the cells using a relative reference, they will not contain the same results as in their original location.

The worksheet on your screen should appear as seen here. If it does not, open the worksheet and try again.

Performing Math with Pasted Cells

In most cases, you want the pasted cells to replace the current contents of the destination cells. But sometimes, you may want to combine the current contents and the information in the Clipboard using a mathematical operation.

In the practice worksheet, for example, there is a row containing some additional supply expenses. These need to be added to their corresponding values already in the supply row. In this case, you want to add the values rather than replace them. Do that now:

1 Select cells C22 through F22. These cells contain the values you want to add to the supplies.

2 Click the Copy button on the Standard toolbar. The contents of all four cells are copied to the Clipboard.

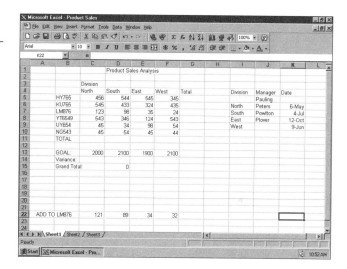

4

Rearranging and Previewing Worksheets

Moving and Copying Formulas

3 Click cell C7; this will be the upper-left corner of the range that receives the copied data.

4 Select Edit ➢ Paste Special. The options in the Operation section of the Paste Special dialog box let you add, subtract, multiply, or divide the contents of the cut cells and the values in the selected cells.

5 Click the Add option in the Operations section. For other occasions, you can also choose an option from the Paste section.

6 Click OK. The values of the copied cells are added to the original contents of the destination cells.

7 Press Esc. The moving border is cleared from the cells.

8 Finally, erase the contents of the original cells. Select cells A22 to F22, and press the Delete key.

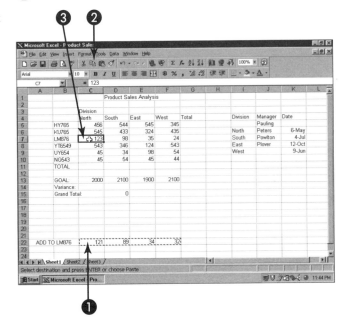

Moving and Copying Formulas

Moving and copying works the same for formulas as it does for other entries, with a major special benefit. If you move a cell that contains a formula, the exact same formula is inserted into the new location. It still references the same cells it did in its original position. When you copy a cell with a formula, however, Excel inserts it using a *relative reference*. This means that the cell references in the formula are adjusted to refer to the corresponding cells in the new location.

As an example, you'll add a formula to your practice worksheet, and then copy it across the row. You want the same formulas in the first three worksheets:

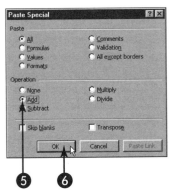

COPYING WITH THE FILL COMMAND

When you want to copy the contents of one cell to another, you can also use the Edit ➢ Fill command, or the fill handle. Remember, if the entry in a cell is not recognized as a series, Excel copies the contents when you drag the fill handle. If it is the start of a series, such as Jan or Monday, drag the fill handle with the right mouse button and choose Copy Cells from the shortcut menu that appears.

Moving and Copying Formulas

1 Click cell C11. You could insert the totals for all of the columns by selecting cells C11 to F11 and clicking AutoSum. However, you'll fill in these other cells using AutoFill so you can see the effect of copying formulas.

2 Click the AutoSum button in the Standard toolbar.

3 Click the Enter button on the formula bar. Excel inserts a formula that adds the values in the cells above. Look at the cell references in the formula — SUM(C5:C10).

4 Now, instead of repeating these steps to add similar formulas to total the remaining columns, just copy the formula. Point to the fill handle of cell C11. (You can use any method, although you'll use the fill handle for now.)

5 Drag the fill handle across to cell F11. When you release the mouse button, the sum of each column appears.

6 Click cell D11. Notice that Excel copied the formula by changing the reference to be relative to the cells above. The formulas in the other cells have been adjusted as well.

As you saw here, Excel does not see a relative reference as something absolute. The formula inserted in cell C11, for instance, means "add the values in the six cells immediately above here." So when Excel copied the formula, it changed the references to have the same meaning — the six cells just above the cell containing the formula.

The relative reference works on any formula, except those containing absolute references, which you'll learn about in Lesson 7. Now try adding and then copying another formula:

7 Click cell G5.

8 Click AutoSum and press Enter. Excel inserts the sum of the cells to the left.

9 Click cell G5.

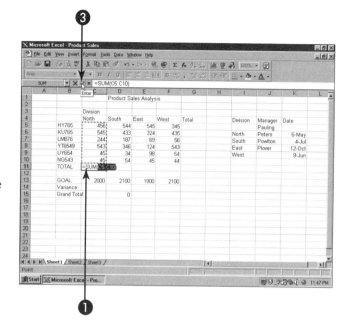

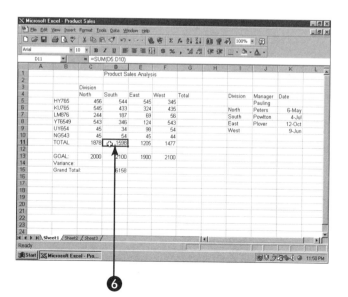

Inserting Rows and Columns

10 Drag the fill handle of cell G5 down to cell G10. The formula is copied when you release the mouse button.

Finally, create the formulas for the variance:

11 Click cell C14.

12 Type **=C11–C13** and click the Enter button. The formula subtracts the actual sales from the target.

13 Drag the fill handle of cell C14 across to cell F14.

The worksheet on your screen should look like the bottom figure on this page. If it does not, open the worksheet and try again.

INSERTING AND DELETING CELLS, ROWS, AND COLUMNS

Planning your worksheet is important, but you won't always be able to think of everything. Fortunately, Excel lets you insert and delete cells, rows, and columns. Depending on where you insert or delete, Excel may automatically adjust formulas that include cells that have been affected.

As usual, there are several ways to insert and delete in a worksheet. Whichever method you choose, check your work carefully when you're done. Although it is easy to insert and delete, it is just as easy to cause unexpected errors, especially when you insert or delete in ranges referenced in formulas.

TIP
If you do run into trouble when inserting or deleting information, click the Undo button in the Standard toolbar or select Edit ➤ Undo.

Inserting Rows and Columns

When you insert into a worksheet, existing rows, columns, or cells shift down or to the right to make room. You can insert blank rows, columns, and cells, and then add information into them. You can also insert cells that already contain information.

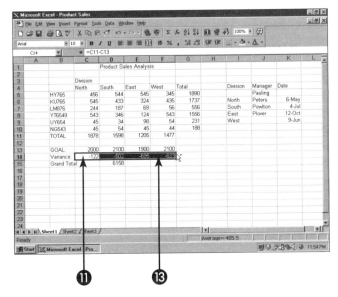

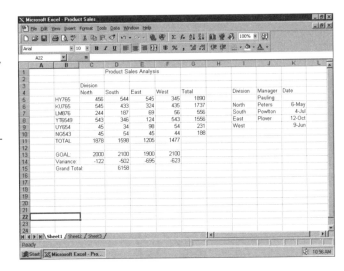

Inserting new blank rows and columns is easy. Just right-click the row or column header and choose Insert from the shortcut menu, or click anywhere in the row and choose Insert ➤ Rows. The new row or column will be inserted, and the entire worksheet below that row or to the left of that column will be renumbered. New rows are inserted above the current row, and new columns to the left of the current column. If you insert a new row 3, for example, what was row 3 becomes row 4, and the remaining rows are renumbered appropriately.

When you insert a row or column into a range that's included in a function, such as SUM, Excel adjusts the range to include the new row or column.

As an example, try inserting an additional row of expenses. You would use the same approach to insert columns:

① Right-click the row header for row 15. You want to insert a new row 15 above this row.

② Choose Insert from the shortcut menu. Rows starting with number 15 shift down, and Excel inserts a new row 15.

③ Right-click the row header for row 8.

④ Choose Insert from the shortcut menu.

⑤ Enter the information shown in the illustration at right into the new row.

When you enter values in the row, the total and variance values recalculate. For Excel to adjust the range in the function, the inserted row must replace a row within the range. For example, the SUM function in cell C12 of your worksheet now references the range C5 to C11. If you now inserted a new row 12, the range would not be adjusted because row 12 was not included in the SUM function range.

Notice that inserting the row added extra cells between the information in columns I, J, and K. You'll take care of that later.

⑥ Click cell G7.

⑦ Drag the fill handle of cell G7 to cell G8. This copies the formula to the new row, using a relative reference so the values in the row are totaled.

4

Rearranging and Previewing Worksheets

Deleting Cells, Rows, and Columns

TIP

To insert several rows or columns at one time, select the number of rows or columns you want to insert before right-clicking and choosing Insert. To insert three rows, for instance, drag to select three entire rows.

Deleting Cells, Rows, and Columns

When you delete a row, column, or cells from a worksheet, existing cells move up or to the left to take their place. As with insertion, Excel may automatically adjust ranges in formulas that have been affected, so check your work carefully.

To delete a row or column, right-click its header (or drag across several headers to delete several rows or columns) and choose Delete from the shortcut menu or choose Edit ➤ Delete.

Sometimes, however, you don't want to delete an entire row or column, but instead want to delete selected cells. In the worksheet, for example, you now have extra blank cells separating the division information in columns I, J, and K. Rather than use drag and drop to move up the information, you'll delete the extra cells:

❶ Select cells I8 to K8.

❷ Right-click the selected cells and choose Delete from the shortcut menu to see these options. The two Shift Cells options delete just the selected cells, moving existing cells up or to the left.

❸ Select Shift Cells Up, if it is not already selected.

❹ Click OK.

Excel doesn't shift up the entire row below the inserted cells, it just shifts the number of cells that you are deleting.

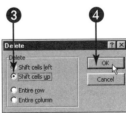

Inserting Cells

When you don't want to insert an entire row or column, you can insert just a cell or group of cells. When you go this route, however, Excel doesn't shift down the entire row below the inserted cells, or shift to the right the entire column. Instead, it shifts just the number of cells that you are inserting. For example, look the Product Sales workbook on your screen. Notice that the names of the managers in column J do not match up with the divisions in column I.

NOTE *If you're not careful, inserting cells could shift some values away from the labels that describe them. Before inserting cells, check the rows or columns that follow to make sure your action will not wind up misaligning information.*

As an example, you'll correct the problem with the managers in the worksheet:

1 Click cell J5.

2 Right-click the cell and choose Insert from the shortcut menu. Excel displays this dialog box.

3 Click Shift Cells Down if it is not already selected. This choice will move down the cells in just the column below the selected cell, not affecting other columns in the worksheet.

4 Click OK.

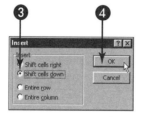

The Shift Cells Right option in the Insert dialog box will shift to the right just the cells in the selected rows, not affecting other rows in the worksheet. This means that values will no longer be aligned with their original column labels.

The Entire Row and Entire Column options insert the same number of rows or columns as there are in the selected range.

■ Inserting Moved or Copied Cells

In addition to inserting new blank cells, you can insert cells, rows, or columns that you cut or copy from elsewhere in the worksheet.

To use the Clipboard to insert cells, follow this procedure:

1 Cut or copy the cells.

2 Select the destination location.

Rearranging and Previewing Worksheets **4**

Hiding Rows and Columns

3 Right-click and choose Insert Copied Cells (or Insert Cut Cells) from the shortcut menu, or select Insert ➤ Copied Cells (or Insert ➤ Cut Cells).

4 Choose Shift Cells Right or Shift Cells Down from the dialog box that appears, and click OK.

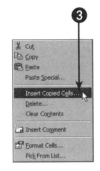

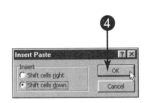

To insert by drag and drop, hold down the Shift key when you release the mouse button to insert the moved cells. Hold down the Ctrl and the Shift keys to copy the inserted cells. You can also drag and drop with the right mouse button to select from these options when you release the mouse button:

- Shift Down and Copy
- Shift Right and Copy
- Shift Down and Move
- Shift Right and Move

HIDING AND REVEALING ROWS AND COLUMNS

At times, you might not need to see a row or column that you've entered into your worksheet, but may not want to actually delete it. Rather than remove the row or column entirely, you can hide it from view. This conceals the row or column but leaves it in the worksheet so its cells can be referenced in formulas. It's also easy to bring hidden rows and columns back into view.

Hiding Rows and Columns

Unlike deleting, hiding does not change existing row numbers or column letters. If you hide column C, for example, your columns will appear to be lettered A, B, D, E, and so on.

As an example, try hiding rows 14 through 17, which contain information supplemental to the actual sales figures:

1 Drag over the row headers for rows 14 to 17. Make sure the pointer appears as a large white plus sign before you begin dragging. The rows should be selected.

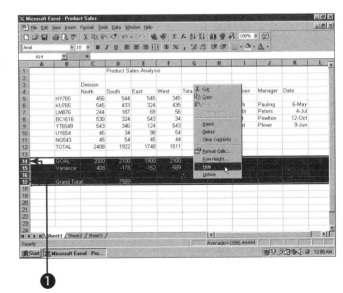

Unhiding Rows and Columns

2 Right-click the selected rows and choose Hide from the shortcut menu, or select Format ➤ Row ➤ Hide. The rows, and their row numbers, no longer appear.

Even though the rows no longer appear, their cells are still referenced in formulas, and any formulas within the rows will continue to be recalculated.

To hide columns, select them and choose Hide from the shortcut menu, or choose Format ➤ Column ➤ Hide.

Unhiding Rows and Columns

To unhide a row, select a range of cells in the rows that come before and after it, and then choose Format ➤ Row ➤ Unhide. If you select the entire rows before and after the hidden rows, you can also right-click the selected rows and choose Unhide from the shortcut menu.

Try that now:

1 Drag to select rows 13 and 18. You could also select any range of cells in those rows.

2 Choose Format ➤ Row ➤ Unhide.

Use a similar strategy to unhide columns. In other words, select a range of cells in the columns that come before and after the hidden column or columns, and choose Format ➤ Column ➤ Unhide; or select the entire columns before and after the hidden columns, right-click the selected columns, and choose Unhide from the shortcut menu.

If you hid column A or row 1, you cannot select rows or columns on both sides. In this case, use either of these techniques:

- To unhide every row and column in the worksheet, click the Select All button to select the entire worksheet and then choose Format ➤ Row ➤ Unhide or Format ➤ Column ➤ Unhide.

- To unhide only row 1 or column A, not others elsewhere in the worksheet, select Edit ➤ Go To. Type A1 in the Reference box, and click OK. This selects cell A1, although you won't see it on the screen. Then, select Format ➤ Row ➤ Unhide or Format ➤ Column ➤ Unhide.

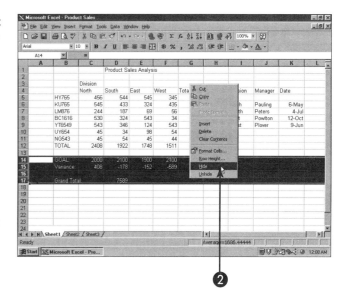

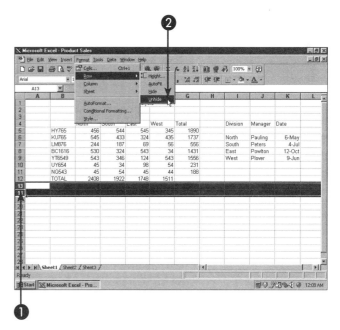

4

Rearranging and Previewing Worksheets

Skills Challenge

PRINT PREVIEW

Now that your worksheets are getting more sophisticated, you may want to preview them before you print. This way you can see how your formats will appear on paper. Preview shows the worksheet exactly as it will print, so you can make sure there aren't any formatting or other problems before you waste paper.

Click the Print Preview button in the Standard Toolbar or select File ➤ Print Preview. Excel displays the worksheet in Preview mode and displays the toolbar shown in the illustration at right.

The Zoom function is on by default. When you point to the page, the pointer is shaped like a magnifying glass. To enlarge a section of the page, click it. Click again to return to the full-page display. You can also zoom in and out by clicking the Zoom button.

When you're done looking at the preview, click Close. Excel displays the page break lines, just as if you printed it. You'll learn about the other options in the Preview window in Lesson 10.

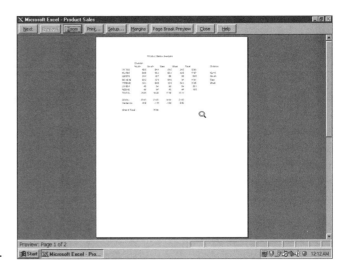

SKILLS CHALLENGE: REARRANGING A WORKSHEET

The skills that you learned in this lesson can give you quite an edge. By moving and copying cells, and taking advantage of the Paste Special dialog box, you can turn even the simplest worksheet into an Excel wonder. This exercise let you practice these important skills. In fact, you'll complete a worksheet starting with these few entries.

There is a copy of this exercise under the name Workout 4 in the Exercise directory. You can find a copy of this completed exercise under the name Solution 4 in the Solution directory.

1 Open the file named Workout 4 in the Exercise directory. It should look like the illustration at right.

2 In column A, complete the series of days from Monday to Friday.

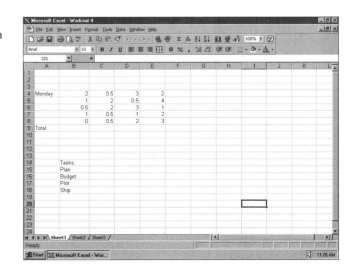

3 Copy the label Total from cell A9 to cell F3.

 What other ways are there to copy information?

4 Enter the totals for the tasks in row 9, and for the days in column F.

5 Widen column A so you can see the complete day names.

6 Copy and transpose the task labels from cells B15:B18 to cells B3:E3.

 Can you also transpose cells from a column into rows?

7 Insert a new row 9 to leave a space between the values and the totals.

 When you insert a row, where is it inserted and what happens to the current row?

8 Enter the title **Billable Time** in cell D1.

9 Enter the text **Week of March 5** in cell A1.

10 Delete rows 15 to 19.

 Do you have to delete the rows one at a time?

The worksheet on your screen should appear as shown to the right. If it does not, open the worksheet and try again.

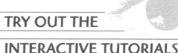

TRY OUT THE
INTERACTIVE TUTORIALS
ON YOUR CD!

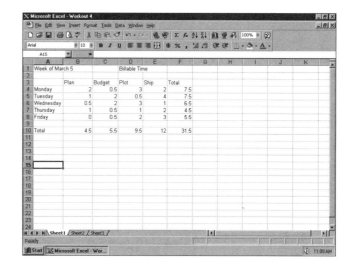

Rearranging and Previewing Worksheets

Troubleshooting

TROUBLESHOOTING

Once you start moving and copying, and using all of the features of Paste Special and drag and drop, things can go slightly haywire, so check your results carefully. Remember that you can always use the Undo command to corrects mistakes if you catch them quickly enough. However, if you have any problems using the techniques you learned in this lesson — and Undo doesn't help — check with the table here.

Problem	Solution
Excel won't let me drag and drop. What's the story?	There is a setting that lets you turn off the drag and drop feature. See Lesson 12 to learn how to turn it back on.
I tried to use Paste Special to add copied value. It seemed to work, but the original numbers returned when I press Enter to move to the next row.	After closing the Paste Special dialog box, do not press Enter. When the moving border is still around the selected cells, pressing Enter pastes their values. Press Esc to remove the moving border before pressing Enter.
Wow! I transposed a series of numbers and they're all wrong.	The numbers were probably formula results. You cannot transpose them if they use relative references. Copy and link each individually.
The Paste Special option is dimmed on the Edit menu — I can't select it.	You probably cut cells instead of copying them, or didn't copy anything first. You can only select Paste Special when cells have been copied to the Clipboard.
I can't unhide a row or column.	To unhide every row and column, click on the Select All button before choosing the Unhide command.

WRAP UP

Sit back, relax, and think for a moment. There was a lot of powerful information in this lesson, so let's recap. You learned how to:

- Move and copy information using the Clipboard or drag and drop

- Drag with the right mouse button to choose the type of drop operation — such as moving, copying, or inserting

- Use the Paste Special command to select what gets pasted, to perform math on copied values, or to transpose cells

- Insert and delete rows, columns, and cells

- Hide and unhide rows and columns

- Preview the worksheet before you print it

If you feel like you need a little more practice, open the Annual Budget workbook that you used earlier and try inserting and deleting rows and columns. Try making a copy of the entire worksheet transposed — with the quarters in rows, and the income and expenses in columns. Check your work to make sure the totals and profit value are correct. Do it, and you deserve a good rest. In the next lesson, you'll learn how to format your worksheet to make it look its best.

4

Rearranging and Previewing Worksheets

Formatting Worksheets

90 MINUTES

GOALS

In this lesson, you will learn how to format the appearance of your worksheet, including:

- Changing the font, size, color, and style of characters in a cell

- Adjusting the position of characters in a cell

- Merging and splitting cells

- Formatting numbers

- Setting the pattern and background of cells

- Changing the borders around cells

- Applying a ready-made format to the entire worksheet

Get Ready

GET READY

Whether you plan to print your worksheet or display it on screen, it should be easy and pleasant to read. Formats such as fonts, fill patterns, colors, borders, and rotated text can enhance your work, making it easier to see trends and the points you want to get across.

This chapter refers to the following workbooks:

File Name	Location
Units Sold	Exercise directory
Units Sold Solution	Solution directory
Workout 5	Exercise directory
Solution 5	Solution directory

When you complete this lesson, you'll have the skills needed to create eye-catching, formatted worksheets. By the end of this lesson you'll have created the worksheet shown in the illustration at right.

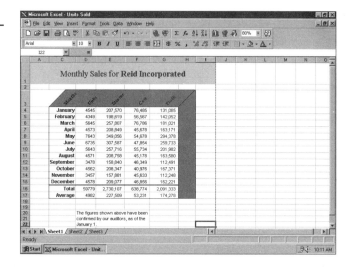

FORMATTING METHODS

In this lesson, you'll learn three general ways that you apply formats to your worksheet:

- Many formats are available on the Formatting toolbar shown labeled here. Some of the buttons are toggles. They appear pressed down when the format is applied; you can click them again to turn off the format. Other buttons apply a style that you turn off by choosing another style. This chapter explains how to use each of the buttons and pull-down lists on the Formatting toolbar.

- You can also format your worksheet using the Format ➤ Cells command. This command displays a dialog box that offers all of the formats available in the Formatting toolbar, and more.

- Finally, you can use a feature called AutoFormat to format an entire worksheet, or any section of it, by choosing from a list of predefined formats.

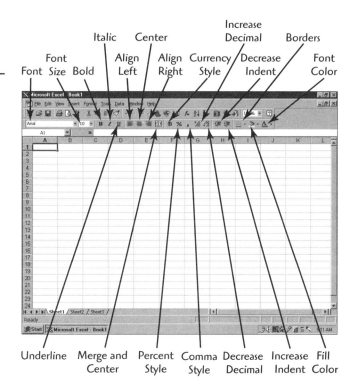

Applying Formats with the Toolbar

Whichever method you choose, you must be in Ready mode to apply all except character formats. You cannot apply most formats while you are entering or editing information in a cell. To format a range of cells, or entire rows or columns, just select the area you want to format and then choose the formats. There are no special formats that apply to rows or columns, other than the column width and row height.

Now that you have the background, you're ready to go.

TRY OUT THE

INTERACTIVE TUTORIALS

ON YOUR CD!

FORMATTING CELL CONTENTS

You can change the font, size, style, and color of the contents of a cell, whether the contents consist of text, a number, or a date. You can format individual characters in a text entry; however, the entire number or date must have the same format.

To apply the same format to the entire cell, apply it in Ready mode. You can also apply formats to the cell, or selected characters in the cell, as you enter or edit cells. If you are entering a number, the entire number will be formatted as its first character when you accept it. The formats only appear in the cell, not in the formula bar.

Applying Formats with the Toolbar

The toolbar is the easiest way to format characters because it is just a click away:

1 Open the workbook Units Sold in the Exercise directory.

2 Click cell A1.

3 Pull down the Font list in the Formatting toolbar. Excel lists the fonts installed on your system.

4 Scroll down through the list and choose Times New Roman. Excel will use the selected font for text you enter in this cell. It will not affect text in other cells.

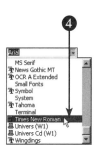

5

Formatting Worksheets

Applying Formats with the Toolbar

Instead of scrolling the Font list, type the first letter of the font you want to select. Enter T, for example, to automatically scroll the list to the fonts whose names begin with T.

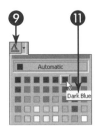

5 Pull down the Font Size list. Excel displays the sizes available in the current font. The sizes are in points. There are 72 point in a vertical inch, so an 18-point font is a quarter-inch high.

6 Choose 20. Excel increases the row height to accommodate the larger font.

7 Type **Monthly Sales Analysis for Reid Incorporated**.

8 Click the Enter button on the formula bar.

9 Point to the Font Color button. The ScreenTip and color on the button indicate what color will be applied if you click.

10 Pull down the Font Color list. A palette of colors appears, as shown here. Excel displays a ScreenTip with the color's name when you point to it.

11 Click Dark Blue. Excel applies the color to the cell and makes it the new color on the button face. So unless you choose another color, dark blue will be applied the next time you click the Font Color button. Your color selection will not affect new text that you type in other cells, but only in this cell.

12 Drag over cells C3 to G3. You can also apply formats to a range of selected cells.

13 Select Times New Roman from the Font list, and choose 12 from the Font Size list. Excel increases the row height to accommodate the larger font.

14 Select cells G3 to G17.

15 Click the Font Color button on the toolbar. The text turns dark blue, the last color you select from the color palette. You have to click away from the cells to deselect them and to see the color.

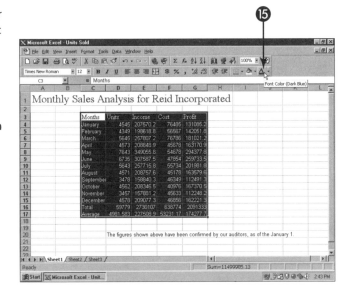

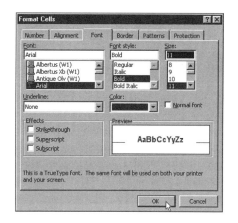

Applying Formats

Applying Formats with the Format Cells Box

The Format Cells dialog box lets you apply even more formats than the Formatting toolbar. And it has an additional benefit. As you choose options from the dialog box, you can preview how the text will appear, so you can cancel your selections if you do not like the results. As when using the toolbar, you can apply formats to text as you type or edit it, or to the all of the text by selecting the cell first.

Display the Format Cells dialog box by right-clicking a cell and choosing Format Cells from the shortcut menu, or by selecting Format ➢ Cells. The dialog box has a number of tabs for applying a variety of formats.

Use the dialog box now to format text:

1. Select cells C3 to G3.

2. Select Format ➢ Cells.

3. Click the Font tab if it's not already in front. Excel displays the Format Cells dialog box shown here. As you select options, the sample text in the Preview section shows you the effects of your choices.

4. Click Bold in the Font Style list.

5. Click 11 in the Size list.

6. Click OK.

7. Select cells C4 to C17.

8. Select Format ➢ Cells, click Bold in the Font Style list, choose 11 in the Size list, and click OK.

9. Notice that Excel does not automatically widen columns to adjust to the larger font. Widen column C now to see the full text within the column.

In addition to the font and size, the Format Cells dialog box lets you choose a style (regular, italic, bold, bold italic), font color, underline, and various special effects. Checking the Normal Font check box returns all of the settings to their defaults. The underline methods include Single and Double underlining, and Single Accounting and Double Accounting. The accounting underline

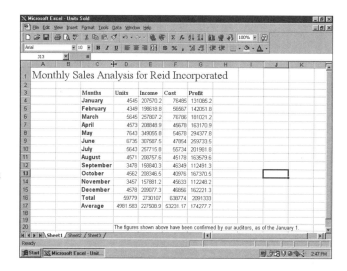

5

Formatting Worksheets

Formatting Parts of a Cell

methods draw the line almost the full width of the cell even if it contains no characters.

NOTE *When you underline, the line appears just below the text in the cell, but above the bottom cell gridline. If you apply a border to the bottom of the cell, as you'll learn how to do later in this lesson, the line appears on the gridline, and extends for the full width of the cell. The accounting underline styles run almost the full width, stopping just short of the left and right cell borders.*

Formatting Parts of a Cell

You do not have to apply the same format to all of the text in a cell. As you are typing in a cell, just select the formats that you want to apply to the next characters you type. If you already entered the characters, double-click the cell to place the insertion point within it, drag over the characters you want to format, and then select options from the Formatting toolbar or Format Cells dialog box.

Try this now:

1. Double-click cell A1.

2. Drag over the words *Reid Incorporated.*

3. Click the Bold button in the Formatting toolbar.

4. Click the Enter button on the formula bar.

The worksheet on your screen should look like the one shown at right. If it does not, go back and apply the formats again.

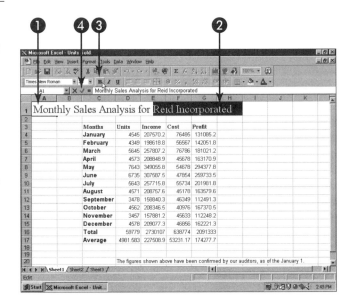

CHANGING THE ALIGNMENT OF TEXT

Alignment formats determine where the characters appear in the cell. There are several formats available in the Formatting toolbar, and even more options in the Format Cells dialog box. The alignment of text can also be affected by the size of the cells. In addition to changing column width, you can combines several cells into one, and you can control the way in which long entries are divided between lines within a cell.

Aligning Horizontally

Horizontal alignment determines the position of the data relative to the left and right sides of the cell. You can use the alignment buttons on the Formatting toolbar and the Alignment tab in the Format Cells dialog box to set horizontal alignment. You'll use both methods now to change the alignment of text in your worksheet:

1 Select cells C3 to G3. Remember, you can format individual cells or a selected range of cells using the same techniques.

2 Click the Center button in the Formatting toolbar. The labels become centered. If you wanted to return the cells to their default alignment, you could just select them and click the Align Left button.

3 Select cells C4 to C17. You want to align these cells on the right.

4 Click the Align Right button. The labels become even with the right side of the column.

5 Select cells A1 to I1. You want to center the title over the worksheet.

6 Click the Merge and Center button. Excel combines all of the selected cells into one large cell, and centers the text within it.

TIP

You should usually wait until you have finished adjusting the width of columns before centering text across cells. If you center it first and then change column width, the text may no longer appear centered.

You can also adjust the horizontal alignment using the Alignment tab of the Format Cells dialog box, shown in the following illustration. The Horizontal alignment options in the dialog box control the position of the text between the left and right sides of the cell. The options are General (the default setting), Left, Center,

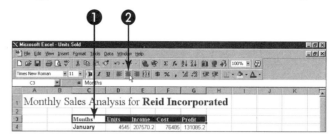

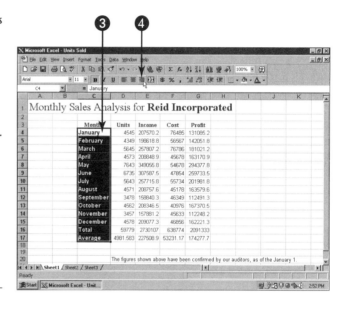

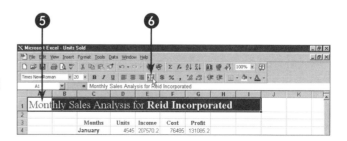

5

Formatting Worksheets

Aligning Vertically

Right, Fill, Justify, and Center Across Selection. The Left, Center, and Right options are the same as their corresponding buttons on the Formatting toolbar, while the Center Across Selection option works the same as the Merge and Center toolbar button.

The Fill option repeats the characters in the leftmost cell in the selected empty cells to the right, and the Justify option divides long text entries into multiple lines, adding spaces between words to fill the cell to its left and right edges.

The Indent option in the Format Cells dialog box, and the Increase Indent and Decrease Indent buttons on the Formatting toolbar, control the spacing between the left cell boundary and the start of the text. You'll learn about the other features in this dialog box later in the lesson.

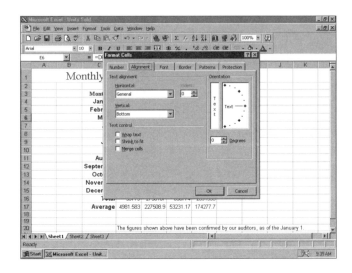

Aligning Vertically

The vertical alignment determines the position of the data relative to the top and bottom of the cell. You won't notice much difference in vertical alignment with the default cell height, because text seems to be centered within the row. However, the default vertical alignment is actually set at the cell bottom. To see how vertical alignment affects text, start by making a row higher:

❶ Right-click the row 1 header.

❷ Choose Row Height from the shortcut menu. You'll see a dialog box in which you enter the row height, as shown to the right. You want to make the row higher so you can center the title within it.

❸ Type **50** in the Row Height box.

❹ Click OK. Excel makes the row 50 points high. (Remember, there are 72 points in an inch.) The text appears along the bottom of the row.

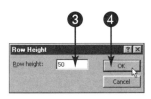

❺ Select Format ➢ Cells, and then click the Alignment tab.

❻ Pull down the Vertical list and choose Center. Other vertical alignment options are Top, Bottom, and Justify.

7 Click OK, and then click to deselect the cell. The text is centered vertically within the row. You'll learn about the Justify option in the Vertical list a little later in this lesson.

▶ Rotating Text in Cells

Another way to align text in a cell is to rotate it. Text can appear vertically down a cell, or rotated anywhere between 90-degrees clockwise and 90-degrees counterclockwise:

1 Select cells C3 to G3. You are going to rotate these labels so they appear on an angle.

2 Right-click the selected cells and choose Formats Cells. The Alignment tab is displayed because it is the last tab you used. You want to rotate the text at a 45-degree angle. You can type the angle into the Degrees box or click the degree point in the Orientation section.

3 Click the degree point at the two-o'clock position, as shown here. The number 45 appears in the Degrees box. To print the text vertically, you would click the vertical word *Text*.

4 Click OK, and then click to deselect the text. The text is formatted as shown in the figure at right.

The worksheet on your screen should look like the one shown here. If it does not, go back and apply the formats again.

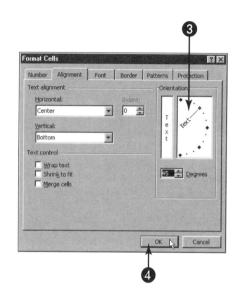

▶ Formatting Long Text Entries

When you type a long text entry, characters run over into blank cells on the right. But if the cells to the right are not blank, not all of the text will appear on screen and when you print the worksheet. You can widen the column, but that's not practical if the text is very long.

The solution to long text is to have Excel format it for you. Excel can either divide the text into more than one line within the cell, or it can shrink the text so it just fits in the cells:

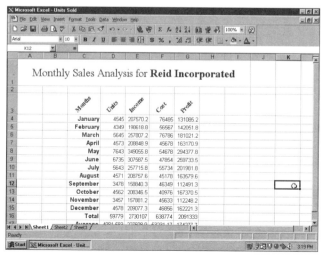

Splitting a Merged Cell

❶ Right-click cell D20 and choose Format Cells. The Alignment tab should appear; if not click it now.

❷ Click Wrap Text.

❸ Click OK. Excel divides the text into multiple lines so it fits in the current column width. The Justify horizontal and Justify vertical alignments would yield similar results, but Justify horizontal would also add space between words so they fill the width of the cell.

The Shrink to Fit option will reduce the font size of the text so it fits into the cell without dividing it into lines. If the text is much wider than the cell, however, it will become too small to read.

Splitting a Merged Cell into Separate Cells

Wrapping the text in cell D20 did not increase the column width. It fit in the text by making the row rather high, and only one or two words fit on a line. You could widen the column, but then it would be wider than the others.

Rather than widen the column to place more words on each line, you can merge a group of cells to create one larger cell. Merging is similar to using the Merge and Center button, but the text within the cell is not centered unless you center it yourself. As an example, try clicking cell F1. You can't because there is no cell F1 anymore — cell A1 has replaced it.

Merge the long text into one cell now:

❶ Select cells D20 to F22. The text will fit nicely into these cells.

❷ Select Format ➤ Cells. The Alignment tab should appear.

❸ Click Merge Cells.

❹ Click OK. The cells are combined into one, and the text is now divided into just three lines.

NOTE *Even if you merge cells, you need to wrap the text for long entries to be divided into multiple lines. In this example, the text appears in multiple lines in the merged cell because you previously used the wrap format.*

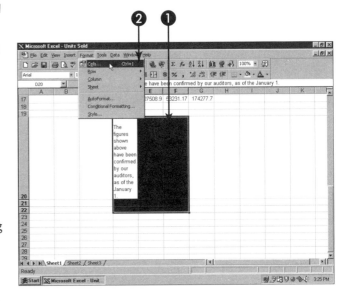

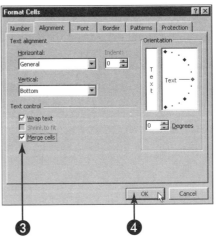

Applying Number Formats

To unmerge cells, click the merged cell, display the Format Cells dialog box, and deselect the Merge Cells check box.

The accompanying illustration shows how your worksheet should appear. The illustration uses 75% magnification to show the entire worksheet. (You'll learn how to change the magnification of the screen yourself in Lesson 12.)

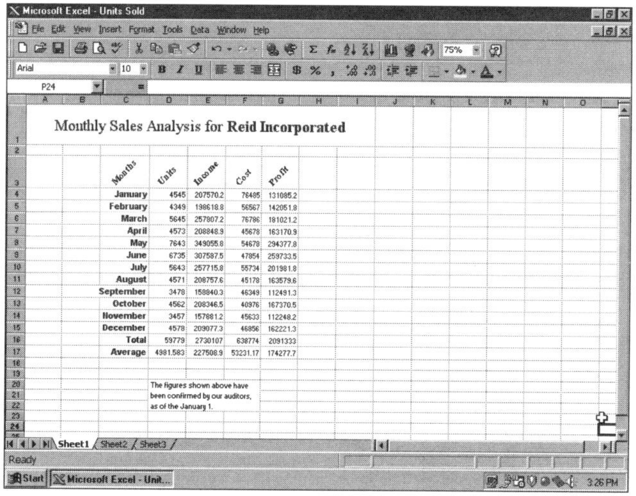

NUMBER FORMATS

Back in Lesson 1, you applied the Currency format to several cells by clicking the Currency Style button. The style displays numbers with dollar signs, commas separating thousands, and two decimal places.

There are other number formats in the Formatting toolbar, and even more in the Format Cells dialog box. The Comma style, for example, is just like Currency but without the currency symbol. The Increase Decimal and Decrease Decimal buttons insert or delete another decimal position with each click.

Applying Number Formats with the Toolbar

The worksheet contains three columns of numbers that represent currency amounts, but they are not formatted as currency. In addition, some of the values in columns E and G contain significant decimal digits that do not fit in the cells.

PERCENT FORMAT

The Percent format displays numbers with a percent sign. If a cell contains the value 0.05, the Percent format displays it as 5%. If the cell contains the value 5, it is displayed as 500%. Once you apply the Percent format, however, you can enter percentages as nondecimal numbers. Typing 6 in a cell that has the Percent format, for example, will display 6%. If you type a value into a cell using the percent sign — for instance, if you type 12% — the Percent format is automatically applied to that cell.

Applying Number Formats

Because you're not really concerned about the decimal amounts in these cells, and it is obvious that they refer to currency, you can display the values in Comma format but without any decimal places:

① Select cells E4 to G17. You don't need to select column D because it contains whole numbers that do not represent currency amounts.

② Click the Comma Style button on the Formatting toolbar. All of the cells now display two decimal digits, with thousands separators.

③ Click the Decease Decimal button twice. Excel removes the decimals, rounding off the whole dollar amounts.

④ Click cell D17. For this exercise, there's no need to have the decimal digits in this cell.

⑤ Click the Decease Decimal button three times. The value changes from 4981.583, to 4981.58, to 4981.6, and then to 4982.

ROUNDING PROBLEMS

When you decrease decimals, Excel removes decimals from display, but still stores the decimal values within the cell. In fact, the decimals appear in the formula bar when the cell is active. This way, the decimals are still used when the cell is referenced in a formula.

In the worksheet, decreasing decimals will appear to round off values — if the removed digit is a 5 or higher, the next remaining digit is rounded up in the display. If you use a calculator to check the math using the displayed values, it may seem as though Excel made an error. For example, suppose you have the values 100.43 and 100.20 totaling 200.63, as shown here.

```
100.43
100.2
200.63
```

If you decrease the decimals in all three cells to none, it appears as if Excel added 100 and 100, and arrived at 201:

```
100
100
201
```

Although both of the first two cells rounded down to 100, the sum rounds up to 201. When you have a large worksheet, this rounding problem may not be noticeable, but it can be obvious with just a few numbers.

Selecting Number Formats

▶ *Selecting with the Format Cells Dialog Box*

The number formats available in the Formatting toolbar are just a few of those that Excel offers. There are many more formats that you can apply to numbers, and additional formats for dates, times, text, and other types of entries. There are even fraction formats that display decimal values as fractions.

Take a look at some of the options now:

① Click a blank cell on the worksheet. By default, this cell has the General format applied.

② Select Format ➢ Cells.

③ Click the Number tab. Excel displays the options shown here. When you select an option from the Category list, additional options for your choice appear to the right of the list.

④ Click Number in the Category list. Options appear that let you select the number of decimal places, whether to use the comma to separate thousands, and choose how negative numbers appear.

⑤ Click Accounting in the Category list. You can now choose the number of decimal places, as well as the symbol or abbreviation used to represent currency.

Choose the format that best fits the values in the cells, and can be understood by those reading your worksheet. The Scientific format, for example, is excellent for displaying very large or small numbers, but would not be appropriate for accounting information. To apply a format, select options.

⑥ Click OK.

⑦ Click Cancel to close the dialog box.

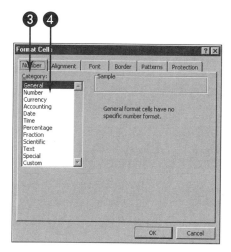

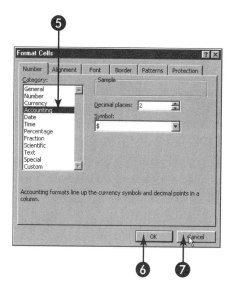

5

Formatting Worksheets

Using the Toolbar to Add Borders . . .

ADDING BORDERS, FILL COLORS, AND FILL PATTERNS

The grid lines that appear around cells on the screen do not print by default — their purpose is to make it easy to identify rows and columns. Grid lines on the printed worksheet can help you keep track of rows and columns, so you may want to add such lines — called borders — to make your worksheets easier to read. By adding borders, and by adding colors and patterns to cells, you can add some pizzazz to a worksheet, whether you're going to print it or view it on the screen.

Using the Toolbar to Add Borders and Fill Colors

It is easy to add borders around a cell using the Borders button on the Formatting toolbar. The picture on the button shows the borders that will be inserted when you click the button. You can apply one or two individual lines around a cell, or insert a complete border around it with one click. If you select a range of cells, you can also insert borders between them.

You can also use the Formatting toolbar to add a fill color. Select fill and text colors carefully, because some combinations may be difficult to read, especially when you're printing with a monochrome printer. When you print colors on a monochrome printer, Excel converts the colors to shades of gray. To display characters in reverse, select a dark fill and light text color.

Now follow these steps to add borders and fill colors to your worksheet:

① Select cells C3 to G17. You want to place a border around this entire section of the worksheet.

② Pull down the Borders list. A palette of options appears, as shown to the right. Take a moment to look at each one. Excel displays the same ScreenTip — the word Border — when you point to any one of them.

③ Click the complete border option with the thinner line — the second option from the right in the bottom row. (The last

option in that row inserts a thick border. The second option from the left in that row adds lines to every grid line in the selected range.) Excels adds the lines, with 45 degree lines following contour of cells in row 3.

4 Select cells C3 to G3. You want to add a fill color and a line below these cells.

5 Hold down Ctrl and select cells H3 to H17. Adding the same fill color here will give the worksheet a three-dimensional look.

6 Pull down the Borders list and click the bottom border button — the second option from the left in the top row. Leave the cells selected when you're done.

7 Pull down the Fill Color list. A palette of colors appears along with the option No Fill. When you point to a button, Excel displays a ScreenTip listing the fill color.

8 Click Light Blue — the third from the right in the third row. You need to pick a light color so the dark blue label *Profit* still shows up.

9 Click to deselect the cells.

10 To complete the shadow effect, add a line to the side of the cells in column H. First select cells H3 to H17.

11 Pull down the Borders palette and click the right border button. There is already a line below these cells from a previous step.

12 Click to deselect the cells. If you look closely at cell H3, you'll notice that the diagonal line next to the label *Profit* does not seem to extend to the corner.

13 Drag the right boundary line of column H to the left until it meets the end of the diagonal line.

NOTE *Removing the default gridlines from the screen is discussed in Lesson 12.*

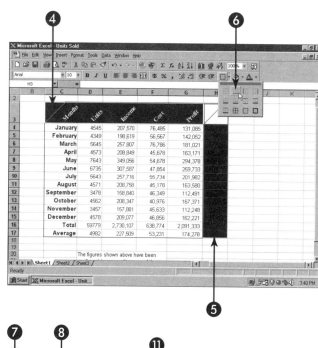

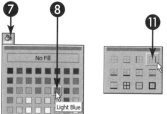

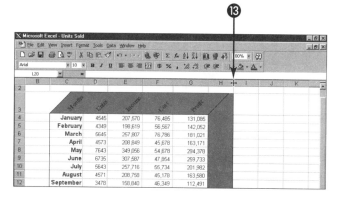

Using the Format Cells Dialog Box

Your worksheet will resemble the illustration shown at right, with a light blue background behind the labels. If your worksheet looks different, go back and try again.

Using the Format Cells Dialog Box

The Format Cells dialog box lets you add borders and background fills as well. In addition, it enables you to choose the line style and add a pattern to the background fill. Line styles include dashed, dotted, and diagonal borders in your choice of 56 colors:

1 Select C15 to G15. You want to add a line separating the monthly details from the summary values.

2 Select Format ➤ Cells and click the Border tab. Excel displays the dialog box shown here. The sample shows the current borders applied to the selection, so there are lines on the left and right.

3 First select the type of line you want to add. In this case, click the double line in the Style section.

4 Next you need to choose a line position. In addition to using the three preset layouts — None, Outside, and Inside — you can add or remove a border by clicking its button or its position in the sample area of the Border section. Click the Bottom Line border. A double line appears at the bottom of the sample, as shown to the right.

5 Click OK, and then click to deselect the cells. The double line appears along the bottom of the row.

TIP

When you're selecting options in the Border page of the Format Cells dialog box, the buttons for lines that have been applied appear pressed down. Your Line Style choice applies to the next line position you choose. Clicking on a position button applies the current selected line style to that position.

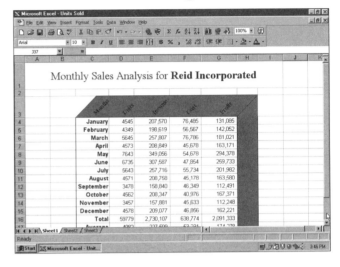

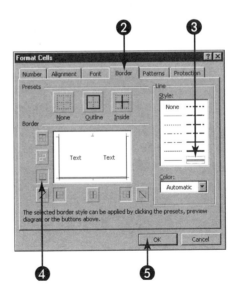

Adding a Pattern

Patterns include dotted and crosshatch patterns. You can choose the color of the pattern as well as the fill color behind it. For example, you can select yellow vertical lines over a red background fill. Try it now:

1 Right-click cell A1 and choose Format Cells from the shortcut menu. You can actually right-click anywhere in the title because it is one large cell.

2 Click the Patterns tab. Excel displays the dialog box shown here. You choose a background color from the displayed palette, and a pattern and pattern color from the Pattern pull-down list.

3 Pull down the Pattern list to see these choices:

The choices on the top of the palette are shades of gray and patterns. The colors will be used in place of black for the pattern. A ScreenTip will appear with the name of the pattern or color you point to.

4 Click the Thin Vertical Stripe pattern — the second from the left in the third row. The palette closes when you select an option.

5 Pull down the Pattern list again and click Yellow. The vertical lines turn yellow, as shown in the Sample box.

6 Finally, choose a background color to appear behind the pattern. Click Neon Green — the fourth from the left in the fourth row down. (Note that no ScreenTip appears when you point to a fill color.)

7 Click OK.

TIP

Choose text colors wisely and coordinate them with the shading color and pattern. Some color combinations may be difficult to read.

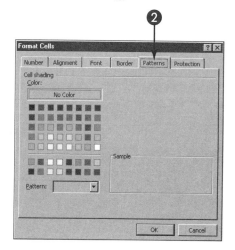

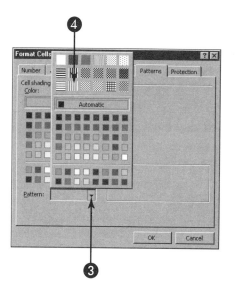

5

Formatting Worksheets

Adjusting the Worksheet Position

Excel's Color Palette

The color palette in the Patterns tab of the Format Cells dialog box contains 56 color choices. The palette is divided into three sections, although you can use choose any of these colors for anything, including the contents of cells, charts, and drawing objects. You'll learn more about adding colors to charts in Lesson 13, and about drawing objects in Lesson 15.

Click no color to restore the default black color.

Standard colors recommended for any use.

Colors suggested for chart fills.

Colors suggested for chart lines.

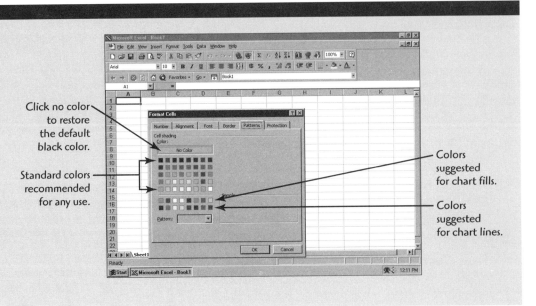

Adjusting the Worksheet Position

You've made quite a few changes to this worksheet, and some may have affected its position on the page. Now you'll check the position of the worksheet in Print Preview and then take care of any formatting problems:

1 Click the Print Preview button. Because you changed the number format, several columns became wider so the worksheet and title no longer appear centered on the page.

2 Click Close in the Print Preview toolbar.

3 Now remove column B to shift the worksheet over to the right. Point to the right boundary of column B. The mouse pointer should look like a two-directional arrow.

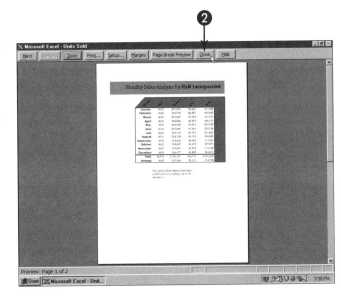

Applying an AutoFormat

4 Drag the boundary to the left, all the way to column A so the ScreenTip shows Width: 0.00. You cannot use the Hide command because the cells in row 1 are merged. If you hide the column, columns A through I will be hidden.

5 Save your workbook under a name of your choice.

The worksheet on your screen should resemble the second figure on this page, again displayed at 75% magnification. If it does not, go back and apply the formats as shown.

AUTOFORMAT

Applying individual formats can exercise your creativity but is also time-consuming. Instead of applying your own formats one at a time, you can format an entire worksheet with a few clicks. The AutoFormat command lets you completely format an entire range of cells, or even the entire worksheet, by choosing from a list of ready-made designs.

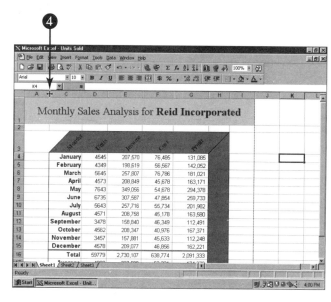

Applying an AutoFormat

To use AutoFormat, start by selecting any cell within a block of cells that you want to format. If you want to format just part of the block, or cells in several blocks at one time, select the range first. Here's how:

1 Reopen the unaltered version of the Units Sold workbook in the Exercise directory. It should be listed at the bottom of the File menu.

2 Select any cell in the range C3 to G17. Because C3 to G17 is a range surrounded by blank cells, Excel automatically chooses the entire range for the AutoFormat command.

3 Select Format ➢ AutoFormat. Excel selects the block C3 to G17, and displays the AutoFormat dialog box. The Table Format list contains the names of all the built-in designs. When you click a design in the list, a sample worksheet using that style appears in the Sample box.

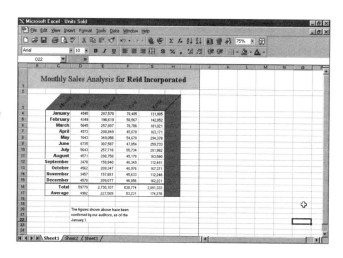

5

Formatting Worksheets

Modifying AutoFormats

④ Click Classic 3 in the Table Format list.

⑤ Click OK. Excel applies all of the styles from the format to the selected cells, as shown to the right.

Excel displays an error message if you select AutoFormat when you have not selected a range of cells, or if the active cell is not within a range that contains entries. If this occurs, click OK to remove the message, select the range, and then try again.

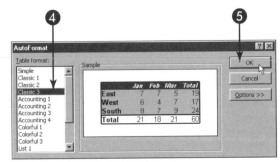

Modifying AutoFormats

AutoFormat styles can affect most of the formats applied to cells. If you want to use some of the formats that you've already applied yourself, you can choose aspects of the AutoFormat style that you do not want to apply. As an example, try choosing an AutoFormat style without using its border styles:

❶ Select any cell in the range C3 to G17 and then select Format ➤ AutoFormat.

❷ Click Options. Excel expands the AutoFormat dialog box to display additional options, as shown in the bottom figure on this page. You use the Formats To Apply section to determine what elements of the selected format to apply.

❸ Select Colorful 2. This style includes several fill colors, fonts, and borders.

❹ Deselect the Border check box in the Formats to Apply section. The style's borders are removed from the Sample panel and will not be applied to the selected block of cells.

❺ Click OK. Excel applies the formats to the selected cells.

❻ Close the workbook.

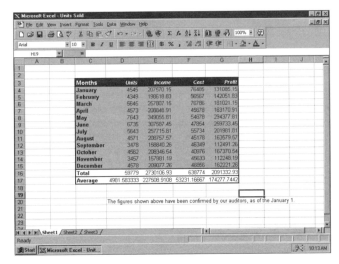

SKILLS CHALLENGE: CREATING A BUSINESS FORM

Most formats are easy to apply, but some combinations can present a challenge. In this exercise, you'll create an invoice form. You'll apply a number of formats, so take your time and follow the steps carefully.

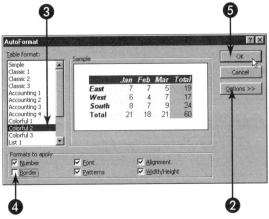

Skills Challenge

The completed worksheet is shown in Print Preview mode in the illustration at right. Periodically as you work, go into Print Preview and compare your worksheet with the illustration. Don't worry too much if it doesn't look exactly the same or it extends into a second page — it will be correct when you're all done.

One of the more interesting formats in this exercise is text that appears to have lines centered on both sides, as shown in the bottom figure on this page.

You create this effect by merging cells in two rows that contain the text, and then adding a border to the cells in one row before and after it:

1 Open Workout 5 in the Exercise directory.

2 Change cell A1 to 16-point bold.

3 Change cells A2 to A4 to bold.

4 Change cell H2 to 8-point bold.

5 Merge cells H6 to I7. (Hint: Select them and choose Merge Cells from the Alignment tab of the Format Cells dialog box.)

 What effect does merging have on cell grid lines?

6 Format cell H6 to 20-point bold and italic.

7 Set the horizontal and vertical alignment of cell H6 to Center.

 What are the two ways to change the horizontal alignment?

8 Add a double bottom line under cells A6 to G6.

3 *What are the two ways to add double-bottom lines?*

9 Set the width of columns E and F to 2.71.

4 *Can you set the two adjacent columns to the same width by dragging?*

10 Place a light outside border around cells A8 to G13.

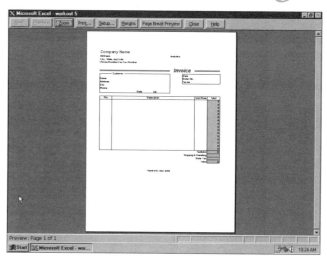

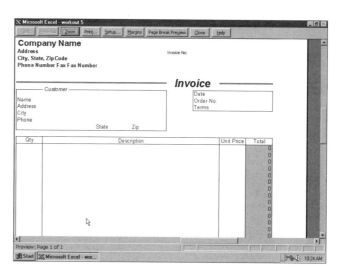

Skills Challenge

⑪ Merge cells B7 and B8.

⑫ Format cell B7 to bold italic.

⑬ Set the horizontal and vertical alignment of cell B7 to Center.

⑭ Place an outside border around cells I8 to K10.

⑮ Place a double-bottom line under cells J6 and K6.

⑯ Place an outside border around cells A15 to K31.

⑰ Place a bottom border under A15 to K15.

⑱ Center the contents of cells A15, J15, and K15 horizontally.

⑲ Select B15 to I15 and click the Merge and Center button.

⑳ Place a right border on cells A15 to A31.

㉑ Place left and right borders on cells J15 to J31.

㉒ Place outside and inside borders around the range K32 to K35.

㉓ Right-align cells J32, J34, and J35.

㉔ Merge cells I33 and J33.

㉕ Right-align I33.

㉖ Add a light fill color to cells K16 to K35. Select a light color or shade of gray so the text is not obscured.

㉗ Merge and center cells A38 to K38.

㉘ In cell K16, add the formula =A16*J16.

㉙ Use AutoFill to copy the formula from K16 down through K31.

㉚ In cell K32, use AutoSum to insert a formula totaling the values from the range K16 through K31.

㉛ In cell K35, add the formula =K32+K33+K34.

You'll find a copy of the completed workbook under the name Solution 5 in the Solution directory.

TRY OUT THE

INTERACTIVE TUTORIALS

ON YOUR CD!

TROUBLESHOOTING

Formatting enables you to create professional-looking worksheets for onscreen display and printed distribution. However, formats can affect each other, and can cause some unwanted results. If you have trouble with some formats, check out these tips.

Problem	Solution
I just can't get the lines where I want them.	When you have this problem, remove all of the lines from the cells and start over. Also remember that the lines in adjacent cells will affect the current cell. For example, selecting the no border option for cell B2 will remove a bottom border that you previously added to cell B1.
I cleared a column, but information in merged cells next to it was deleted as well.	When you merge cells, the large cell will take on the name of the cell in the upper-left corner of the original range. However, the cell will be affected by actions on any of the other merged cell columns. For example, if you merge cells D11 and E11, the cell will be called D11. Even though the text appears to be in cell D11, it will be affected by formats and actions you take on column E as well. Formatting column E in bold, for example, will boldface the text in the merged cell D11.
I really can't tell what formats have been applied to a cell.	Select the cell and display the Format Cells dialog box. The applied formats will be indicated in the various tabs of the dialog box. For example, to see what borders have been applied, click the Border tab and examine the sample area that represents the cell, and the Line Style and Color settings.

continued

Wrap Up

Problem	Solution
I'm typing in a cell but nothing appears.	Check the font color and fill color. If they are the same, nothing will appear. Make sure the font color is not set to white with an unfilled cell. To find out if there really is anything in a cell, even when you can't see anything, click the cell and look at the Formula bar. If you see anything in the Formula bar then there are contents in the cells but you are using a color scheme that makes them invisible.

WRAP UP

There's a lot to formatting cells, but you did a good job. Refresh yourself by reviewing some of skills you learned in this lesson:

- How to format cells using the Formatting toolbar and the Format Cells dialog box

- How to change the font, size, number format, color, and position of text

- How to add borders and fill colors to cells

- How to format entire worksheets using AutoFormat

There's only one way to get really good at formatting, and that's practice, practice, practice. Experiment as much as possible, keeping a record of formats that you prefer, and ones that give you problems. If you feel like investigating styles some more, open the Units Sold workbook and try out other AutoFormat styles. Pick a style and try to re-create it by applying individual formats.

In the next lesson, you're going to work with more than one worksheet at a time, learn how to refer to three-dimensional ranges (cells on more than one worksheet), and even work with multiple workbooks.

Using Worksheets and Windows

2 HOURS

GOALS

In this lesson, you will learn how to work with multiple worksheets, windows, and workbooks. After you complete this lesson, you will be able to:

- Insert, delete, and rename worksheets

- Enter information into multiple worksheets

- Refer to 3D ranges — that is, ranges that span several worksheets

- Divide the worksheet window into several panes

- Freeze rows and columns so they stay in view when you scroll

- Display multiple workbook windows

Get Ready

GET READY

You learned in Lesson 1 that an Excel workbook is made up of one or more worksheets. Although each workbook typically starts with three sheets, you can have as many as your computer allows. We created one workbook with over 5000 pages, although it is highly unlikely you'd ever need that many.

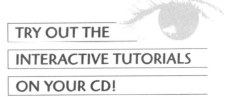

TRY OUT THE

INTERACTIVE TUTORIALS

ON YOUR CD!

This chapter refers to the following workbooks and files:

File Name	Location
Multiple Sheets	Exercise directory
Sales Analysis	Exercise directory
Sales Analysis Solution	Solution directory
Annual Product Sales	Exercise directory
Workout 6	Exercise directory
Solution 6	Solution directory

The workbook named Sales Analysis Solution is a copy of the Sale Analysis workbook as it will appear when you've completed the lesson. Refer to this workbook if you experience any difficulty. When you complete this lesson, you'll be able to work with multiple worksheets and workbooks. You will know how to move and copy information between them, and how to refer to 3D ranges of cells. When you are done, you will have created a workbook consisting of four worksheets, as shown to the right. (Note the named worksheet tabs in the illustration.)

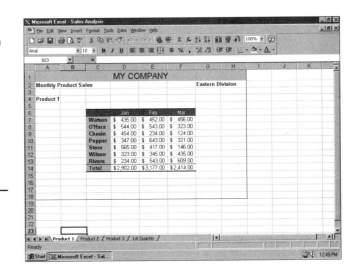

USING MULTIPLE WORKSHEETS

Because worksheets are so large — remember, each has over 16 million cells — what's the sense in having so many of them?

In the past, files in spreadsheet programs contained only one page. So if you had related sets of data you could either place them in separate files or you could place more than one set of data or chart on the same page. This approach had several drawbacks,

Switching Between Worksheets

however. You had to scroll through the worksheet to find specific information, and it was too easy to make a mistake by referencing the wrong cells or accidentally erasing or overwriting information. In addition, it was difficult, if not impossible, to use the information in one file to perform calculations in another.

When you have multiple pages, you can store a series of related worksheets on separate pages in one workbook file. For example, suppose your business plan includes a number of worksheets and charts. Rather than store each one as a separate file, create each on its own sheet in the same workbook. When you save the workbook, Excel saves all of the worksheets and charts together. Open the file to access the entire business plan. If you need to use the worksheets on another computer, you just need to copy the one file that contains everything.

In addition, the sheets in a workbook can share information. A formula in one worksheet can refer to cell addresses in another worksheet. For instance, you can use the first 12 sheets of the workbook to store each monthly budget. The thirteenth page, or the fourteenth if you are superstitious, can contain a summary and yearly totals, drawing on the subtotals in the previous sheets. Changing a referenced cell on one sheet will automatically affect the results on the summary page.

Switching Between Worksheets

To change to a different worksheet in a workbook, you click the sheet tabs — the index tabs just above the status bar. Click the tab marked Sheet2, for example, to display that worksheet. (Displaying a new worksheet is also called *activating* that sheet.) You can also press Ctrl+PgUp and Ctrl+PgDn to move from worksheet to worksheet.

Take a look at a workbook with 12 worksheets now:

1 Open the workbook Multiple Sheets on the Exercise directory. The workbook contains 12 sheets. Cell A1 is the active cell in Sheet1.

2 Click the Sheet2 tab. That sheet of the workbook is displayed.

3 Click cell A10. The active cell of Sheet2 is now A10.

4 Click the Sheet3 tab.

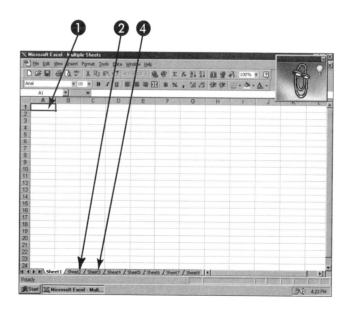

Switching Between Worksheets

5 Click cell B8 to make it the active cell.

6 Click the Sheet1 tab. A1 is still the active cell on this sheet. You didn't change the active cell here by selecting different cells in another worksheet.

7 Click the Sheet2 tab. Notice that cell A10 is still active. The three sheets have different active cells.

When your workbook contains many sheets, you can use the tab scrolling buttons to the left of the sheet tabs to scroll the sheet tabs into view. The buttons are shown in the figure at right.

Clicking a tab scrolling button does not change which worksheet is visible, it just scrolls the tabs into view. Once you see the tab for the sheet you want to access, click the tab to activate the sheet. To scroll the tabs and choose a specific page at the same time, right-click any of the tab scrolling buttons and choose a worksheet name from the menu that appears.

8 Click the Scroll to End button. The tabs scroll to display the Sheet 12 tab, but Sheet2 is still active.

9 Click the Scroll Left One Tab button twice. The tabs scroll, without changing the active sheet.

10 Hold down the Shift key and click the Scroll Left One Tab button. Excel scrolls an entire set of tabs in the direction of the arrow. You can also hold down the Shift key and click the Scroll Right One Tab button.

11 Right-click any of the tab scrolling buttons. Excel displays a shortcut menu listing up to 15 sheets in the workbook.

12 Click Sheet 3. The tabs are scrolled and the sheet is activated.

13 Select File ➢ Close to close the workbook.

If there are more than 15 sheets in the workbook, the shortcut menu will include the option More Sheets. Click More Sheets to display a list box of all worksheets in the workbook. Double-click the sheet you want to open, scrolling the list if necessary.

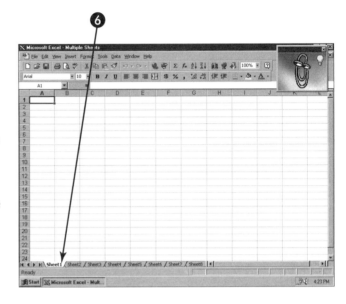

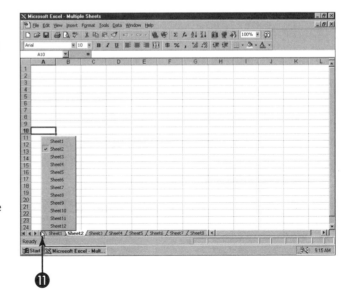

Renaming Worksheets

Renaming Worksheets

The workbook's file name identifies the purpose of the entire book. Likewise, the sheet name shown in the sheet tab should identify the material in the worksheet. By default, Excel gives worksheets the rather boring and uninformative names Sheet1, Sheet2, and so on. To change the worksheet name, double-click the sheet tab and type. Try it now:

1 Open the workbook Sales Analysis in the Exercise folder. The worksheet contains the default three sheets, with information already entered into them.

2 Double-click the Sheet1 tab. The name Sheet1 becomes selected.

3 Type **Product 1**. Typing the new name deletes the selected entry.

4 Double-click the Sheet2 tab.

5 Type **Product 2**.

6 Double-click the Sheet3 tab.

7 Type **Product 3** and press Enter.

You can also rename a sheet by right-clicking on the tab and choosing Rename from the shortcut menu that appears.

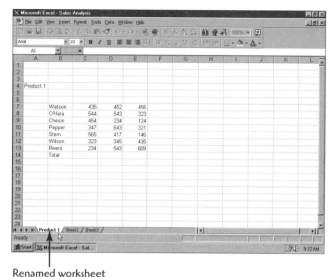

Renamed worksheet

Inserting Worksheets

If the default three sheets aren't enough for your workbook, insert additional sheets. An inserted sheet appears before the current one in the workbook. If Sheet2 is active, for instance, the inserted sheet is placed between Sheet1 and Sheet2. You can move sheets within a workbook, and even between workbooks, so don't worry if you want the new sheet at some other location. Try inserting a new worksheet now:

1 Click the Product 3 tab.

2 Select Insert ➢ Worksheet. Excel inserts a new worksheet to the left of the previously active worksheet.

Deleting Worksheets

To insert more than one sheet at a time, select several existing sheet tabs before selecting Insert ➤ Worksheet. For example, to insert three sheets, select three sheet tabs. To do this, click the first tab, hold down the Shift key, and click the last tab. To select all of the sheets, right-click any tab and choose Select All Sheets from the shortcut menu. Selecting multiple sheets is called grouping, and you'll learn more about that soon.

TIP

If you regularly have to add worksheets to your workbook, the default of three worksheets is clearly not enough. You can increase this default by using the Tools ➤ Options command, as you'll learn in Lesson 12.

▶ Deleting Worksheets

To delete an entire sheet:

1 Click its sheet tab if it's not already active.

2 Select Edit ➤ Delete Sheet. Excel displays a warning that the sheet will be permanently deleted from the workbook , meaning that any information on the sheet will be lost.

3 Click OK to delete the sheet, or click Cancel to retain it.

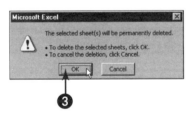

You cannot delete all sheets in a workbook — you must leave at least one. If you want to delete everything, close the workbook and start over. You can always delete the workbook using standard Windows 95 techniques.

Keep in mind that deleting a sheet is different than clearing the sheet's contents. To erase what's on the sheet but leave the sheet itself in the workbook, click the Select All button and then press Del. To remove the formats as well as contents, use Edit ➤ Clear ➤ All, as you learned in Lesson 2.

Inserting or deleting worksheets affects formulas that reference cells in those sheets, so review your formulas carefully.

Moving and Copying Worksheets

Moving and Copying Worksheets

You can rearrange the order of worksheets if you insert a sheet in the wrong location, or simply want to change a worksheet's position in the workbook. You can also make copies of existing worksheets. There are two ways to move or copy a worksheet — by using drag and drop, or by using a dialog box.

You can use drag and drop to move almost anything in Excel, including cells and graphics, so it is a good technique to master. You'll try it now by moving the newly inserted sheet to the end of the workbook:

① Click the inserted sheet's tab and hold down the mouse button. A sheet icon will appear with the pointer and a small down arrow at the left side of the sheet tab, as shown here:

② Drag the sheet icon to the right of the Product 3 tab and then release the mouse button. The sheet now appears at the end of the workbook.

③ Double-click the sheet tab of the inserted sheet.

④ Type **1st Quarter** to rename the sheet.

⑤ Press Enter.

To copy rather than moving a sheet, hold down the Ctrl key while dragging the sheet tab. A small plus sign appears on the sheet icon. This reminds you that you are copying the sheet instead of moving it. The new sheet has the same name as the original but with the number 2 in parentheses. If you make additional copies, they will be numbered consecutively.

Use the shortcut menu for even more control over moving and copying sheets. Here's how:

⑥ Right-click the tab for the sheet you want to move or copy, and then choose Move or Copy from the shortcut menu. Excel displays the dialog box shown in the illustration at right.

⑦ In the To Book list, choose the workbook in which you want to place the sheet. The default selection will be the current workbook, but you can also select (new book) from the list to place the sheet in a new workbook, or you can select the name of any other open workbook.

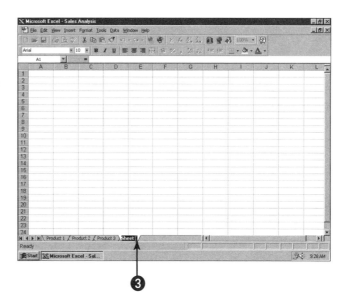

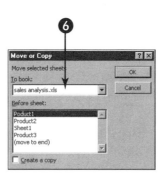

Hiding and Displaying Worksheets

If you are only using a few worksheets, you can extend the horizontal scroll bar more to the left to make it larger and easier to use. Point to the small rectangle on the left of the scroll bar — the one at the end of the sheet tab area. When you point to the rectangle, the mouse pointer turns into a two-directional arrow. Drag to the left to widen the scroll bar. You can actually drag the line as far as you want, so it is covering the sheet tabs and the tab scrolling buttons. If you drag the bar too far, just drag it back to the right.

8 In the Before Sheet list, choose the sheet that you want to follow the one you are moving or copying. To place the sheet at the end of the workbook, select (move to end).

9 To make a copy of the sheet at the new location, select the Create a Copy check box.

10 Click OK.

Your worksheet tabs should be named and in the order shown at right.

If your tabs are in a different order, select and drag the tabs as needed. The names of the original three sheets should be the same as the value in cell A4 of the sheets. The 1st Quarter sheet should be empty, and should be the last sheet in the workbook.

Hiding and Displaying Worksheets

Sometimes there is information in a worksheet that you do not want some users to change or see. Excel provides a number of features for protecting cells, objects, and entire workbooks. When you do not want someone to see or change an entire worksheet, you can hide the sheet from display. The sheet tab will not appear on screen, but the sheet and all of its information are still there. Any cells in the sheet that are referenced will still be used in formulas, and any formulas in the sheet will continue to be updated.

To hide a sheet, use these steps:

1 Make the sheet active by clicking on its tab.

2 Select Format ➤ Sheet ➤ Hide.

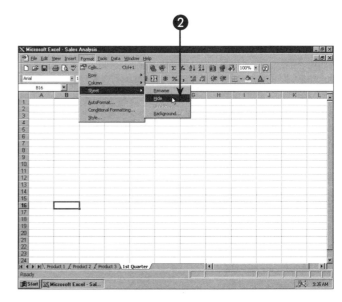

Addressing Cells in Worksheets

❸ To redisplay the sheet, select Format ➢ Sheet ➢ Unhide to see a list of hidden sheets, then click the sheet you want to display and click OK.

Addressing Cells in Worksheets

Formulas can reference cells in any sheet of the workbook. The general syntax when referencing a cell on another worksheet is *Sheetname!Address.* Sheet1!A1, for example, represents cell A1 on Sheet1 of the workbook. Jan!B2 represents cell B2 in the sheet named Jan.

You can reference a cell in a formula by typing its address or by pointing, just as you do for cells in the active worksheet:

❶ Click the cell where you want to enter the formula or reference.

❷ Type = and begin the formula.

❸ When you reach the position where you want the cell reference, click the sheet the tab for the worksheet to be referenced.

❹ Select the cell or range of cells to be referenced.

❺ Enter the next mathematical operator and complete the formula, or click the Enter button if you are done.

Using Groups to Affect Multiple Worksheets

When you select multiple worksheets, Excel considers them to be a group. (Remember, select multiple sheets by holding down the Shift or Ctrl keys while you click the worksheet tabs.) This means that any action you take on one of the sheets — such as data entry, formatting, clearing and deleting, and using AutoSum — will be repeated on the others. For example, suppose you want to create a series of monthly budgets, and you want the same title on a series of worksheets. Rather than retype the title on each sheet, you can create a group of the sheets and enter the title only once. Excel will duplicate the title on the other sheets of the group.

All of the sheets in the group must be consecutive, and you must start by selecting either the first or the last sheet of the group. You cannot start by selecting a sheet in the center of the group:

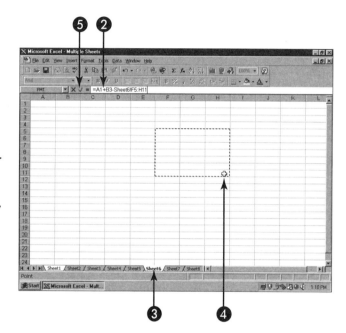

Using Groups

❶ Click the Product 1 sheet tab.

❷ Hold down the Shift key and click the Product 2 tab. Excel inserts the notation (Group) to the right of the workbook name in the title bar, as shown to the right.

❸ Hold down the Shift key again and click the Product 3 tab.

❹ Click cell A2.

❺ Type **Monthly Product Sales**. The text will be repeated on every sheet of the group.

❻ Click cell G2.

❼ Type **Eastern Division**.

❽ Click the Product 2 sheet tab. The entries you made in the Product 1 sheet also appear here. If the sheet is scrolled to some other location, press Ctrl+Home to scroll the sheet so you can see the entries.

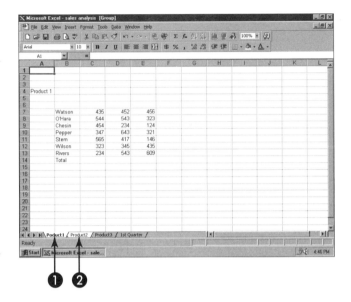

❾ Click the Product 3 tab and confirm that the entries were repeated here as well.

❿ Click the 1st Quarter tab.

Excel deselects the sheets and removes the Group indicator from the title bar. The entries do not appear on this sheet because it was not part of the group.

 NOTE

To ungroup the sheets yourself, click a tab of a worksheet outside of the group, or right-click a tab and choose Ungroup Sheets from the shortcut menu. If all sheets are selected, ungroup them by clicking on any single tab.

If you need to edit an entry that you made to the entire group, you have to regroup the worksheets.

⓫ Right-click the Product 3 tab. Excel activates that worksheet and displays the shortcut menu.

⓬ Choose Select All Sheets from the shortcut menu. Excel groups all of the worksheets in the workbook.

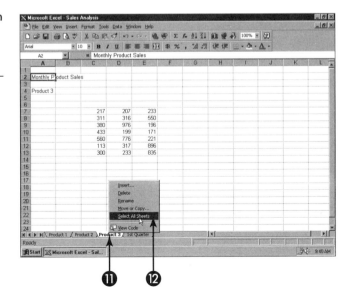

⑬ Click cell A1.

⑭ Type **MY COMPANY** and click the Enter button in the formula bar. Excel repeats the entry in all four of the selected sheets.

⑮ Change the font size to 16 point. The format is repeated on all of the grouped sheets.

⑯ Drag over the range A1 to H1, and click the Merge and Center toolbar button. The title is centered in the cells.

⑰ Click cell C6.

⑱ Type **Jan** and click the Enter button.

⑲ Drag the AutoFill handle of cell C6 to cell E6. The series Jan to Mar is completed in all of the selected sheets.

⑳ Click the Product 1 tab. Excel deselects the sheets. Your entries have been repeated on all of the sheets, as shown to the right.

㉑ Right-click the Product 1 tab.

㉒ Choose Select All Sheets from the shortcut menu.

㉓ Select cells B7 to B14. You will be copying the selected entries to the other selected sheets.

㉔ Select Edit ➢ Fill ➢ Across Worksheets. Excel displays a dialog box asking if you want to fill All, Contents, or Formats, as shown here.

㉕ Select All and then click OK. The contents and formats of the selected cells are copied to the same cells on the other selected worksheets.

㉖ Select cells C14 to E14, the cells to store the totals.

㉗ Click the AutoSum button. The totals are inserted in each of the cells.

㉘ Click the Product 2 tab. The totals are repeated here and in the same cells of the other selected sheets.

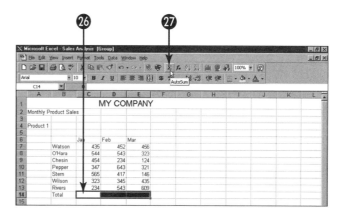

Selecting 3D Ranges

Selecting 3D Ranges

A *3D range* is a group of cells in more than one worksheet. Select a 3D range when you want to clear or format the same cells in a number of consecutive sheets, or when you want to reference the cells in a formula. To enter a 3D range, use the format Sheet1:SheetN!Cell1:CellN, where N represents the last sheet or last cell in the range. For example, the range Jan!:March!A1:C10 represents the group of the same 30 cells (A1 through C10) in the first three sheets of the budget workbook. You'll use 3D ranges later to complete your first quarter budget:

1 Click the 1st Quarter worksheet tab.

2 Click cell C7. The formula in this cell will reference cells in other sheets.

3 Type = to start the formula. To use the technique described here you cannot click the equal sign in the formula bar; you must type the equal sign yourself.

4 Double-click the AutoSum button. Excel inserts the SUM() function with the insertion point within the parentheses.

5 Click the Product 1 sheet tab. Excel adds the sheet name to the function in the formula bar.

6 Hold down the Shift key and click the Product 2 and Product 3 sheet tabs. The range in the input line appears as =SUM('PRODUCT 1:PRODUCT 3'!).

7 Click cell C7 in the Product 1 sheet. The range in the input line appears as =SUM('PRODUCT 1:PRODUCT 3'!C7).

8 Click the Enter button. The formula totals the values of cell C7 in the first three worksheets. The 1st Quarter sheet appears with the formula inserted and calculated.

9 Drag the fill handle of cell C7 across to cell E7. Excel copies the formula across the cells.

10 Release the mouse button, but leave the cells selected.

11 Drag the fill handle in cell E7 down to cell E13. The formula is repeated in all of the cells (C8:E13), inserting the total from the previous three worksheets.

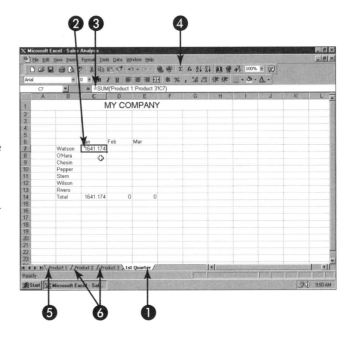

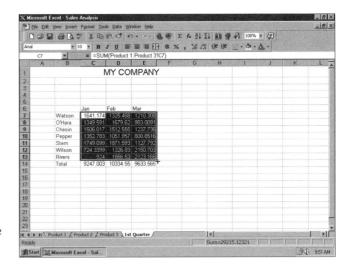

⑫ Click cell A2.

⑬ Type **1st Quarter Totals** and press Enter.

Formatting 3D Ranges

You can also use group mode to apply the same formats to cells on more than one sheet, and to move or copy cells. As an example, you can complete the worksheet by moving a group of cells over one column, and then formatting the worksheet to give it an attractive appearance:

❶ Right-click the Product 1 tab. Excel activates that worksheet and displays the shortcut menu.

❷ Choose Select All Sheets from the shortcut menu. Excel groups all of the worksheets in the workbook.

❸ Select the range B6 to E14.

❹ Point to the border of the selected cells. The mouse pointer should be shaped like an arrow.

❺ Drag the selection one column to the right so the ScreenTip is C6:F14, and then release the mouse button. The same range of cells is also moved on the other sheets in the group.

❻ Select Format ➢ AutoFormat.

❼ Click Classic 2 in the Table Format list, and then click OK.

❽ Select cells D7 to F14.

❾ Click the Currency Style button. In Currency style some values are too wide for the column width.

❿ Select Format ➢ Column ➢ AutoFit Selection. The columns widen to display the numbers they contain.

⓫ Select cells A1 to H18.

⓬ Pull down the Border list in the Formatting toolbar and click the thin outside border — the second button from the right on the bottom row.

⓭ Click cell A1.

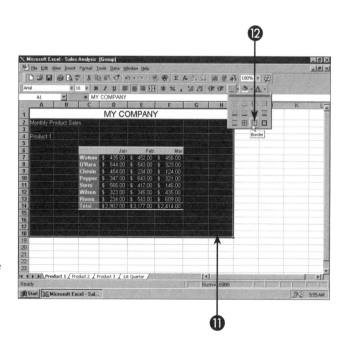

Splitting Worksheets into Panes

⑭ Pull down the Fill Color list on the Formatting toolbar, and select a light fill color.

⑮ Select cells A2 to H4.

⑯ Click the Bold button on the Formatting toolbar.

Click the 1st Quarter tab to see the worksheet you added to this workbook. It should appear as in the illustration to the right. If your worksheet does not contain the same values, check your formulas.

Now save and close the workbook before continuing with this lesson.

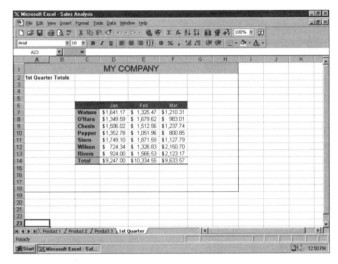

USING PANES

As your worksheets get larger, you'll spend more time scrolling just to find the information you're looking for. For example, suppose you were entering information in row 1000 and needed to refer to a cell in row 1. You'd have to scroll back to row 1, look at the cell, and then scroll back again to row 1000. You could use the Go To command rather than scrolling, but that would still take a few steps.

Instead of scrolling in cases like these, you can divide the window into several *panes*. Panes are areas of the screen that display different portions of the same worksheet. So, for example, you could divide your screen into two horizontal panes — one displaying row 1, the other row 1000. You could then see both areas of the worksheet at the same time, and even switch back and forth between the two to input information or to reference addresses.

Splitting Worksheets into Panes

You create panes by using the split box or the Split command on the Window menu. The split box is the small rectangle at the top of the vertical scroll bar (just above the upward-pointing arrow) and the small rectangle to the right of the horizontal scroll bar (just to the right of the rightward-pointing arrow).

To split the worksheet window into two horizontal panes, so you can see two different sets of rows, follow these steps:

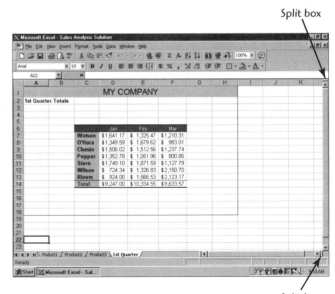

Split box

Split box

Splitting Worksheets into Panes

1 Open the worksheet Annual Product Sales in the Exercise directory. The worksheet extends to cell N51 so you cannot see the entire worksheet on the screen.

2 Point to the split box above the vertical scroll bar so the mouse pointer appears as a two-directional arrow.

3 Drag down. As you drag, a gray split line appears across the screen showing where the window will be split.

4 When the line is on row 10, release the mouse button. If you drag down too far, just drag back up. You can make the panes any size you want.

TIP *You can double-click the split box to quickly divide the window into two equal-sized panes, or to divide the window just above or to the left of the active cell.*

To change the size of the panes, drag the split box or the split line across the window. The split only affects the current worksheet, so each sheet can have a different pane configuration, or no panes at all.

As shown in the illustration at right, each pane has its own scroll bars and the two panes are *synchronized* in the direction of the split. This means that if you split the screen horizontally, you can scroll each pane up and down independently to display different rows in each page. When you scroll left or right, however, the columns in the panes move together.

Now see how the panes affect scrolling:

5 Press the Right Arrow key to scroll to column N. Scrolling one pane in the direction of the split (horizontally, in this case) will scroll the other as well.

6 Press Ctrl+Home. Cell A1 is selected in the active pane.

7 Click the bottom pane. To move from one pane to another, click the pane with the mouse or press the F6 key.

8 Scroll the bottom pane until you see row 51. Scrolling in this direction is not synchronized; you can scroll up and down to see different rows in horizontal panes.

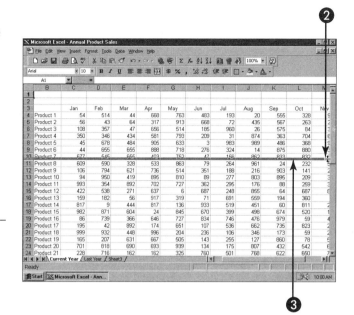

Independent scroll bars

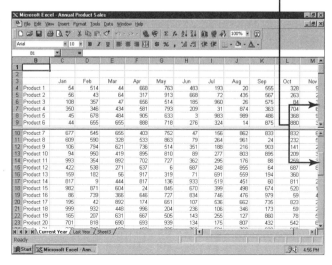

Removing the Split

▶ Removing the Split

When you no longer need to work with a split window, remove the split so your worksheet appears as a single pane:

1 Point to the split box or split bar.

2 Drag up all the way off the window. The pane is removed, displaying the worksheet as a single pane again.

TIP *There are two other ways to remove the split. You can double-click the split box or split bar, or Select Window ➤ Remove Split.*

▶ Creating Vertical Panes

In addition to horizontal panes, you can create vertical panes, and divide the screen into four panes:

1 Point to the split box to the right of the horizontal bar so the mouse pointer appears as a two-directional arrow.

2 Drag to the left. As you drag, a gray split line appears across the screen showing where the window will be split.

3 When the split line is on column F, release the mouse button. You can now scroll the panes to display different columns in each. Scrolling rows will be synchronized.

4 Select Window ➤ Remove Split. The window is no longer split.

5 Press Ctrl+Home.

6 Select Window ➤ Split. Excel creates four panes, as shown in the figure at right. If cell A1 is active, the panes equally divide the screen, as shown in the following illustration. If any other cell is active, the window splits horizontally and vertically at the active cell. You can also create four panes by dragging the split bars individually. Each set of side-by-side panes can show different columns of the same rows. Each set of stacked panes can show different rows of the same columns.

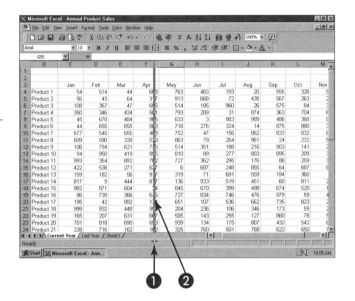

7 Select Window ➤ Remove Split.

NOTE *Keep in mind that regardless of the number of panes, you are still working with only one worksheet. So changes you make in one pane are automatically reflected in the same cells in the other pane.*

Freezing Titles in Panes

When you scroll a long spreadsheet, the column and row labels may scroll off the edge of the screen. This makes it difficult to identify the row or column you want to enter information into.

By "freezing" titles, you prevent an area of the spreadsheet from scrolling off the screen. You can freeze columns, rows, or both. When you use the Freeze command, whatever is above and to the left of the active cell becomes fixed. For example, if cell C7 is active, columns A and B and rows one through seven will be fixed and will not scroll out of view:

1 Click cell C4. Select the cell to mark the frozen rows and columns.

2 Select Window ➤ Freeze Panes. Excel displays solid black lines indicating the rows and columns that will not scroll off of the screen.

3 Press the Right Arrow to scroll to column N. Columns A and B do not scroll so you can reference the product numbers.

4 Press the Down Arrow to scroll to row 51. Rows 1 through 3 do not scroll so you can reference the months.

5 Select Window ➤ Unfreeze Panes to "unfreeze" the frozen columns and rows so they can scroll out of view once again.

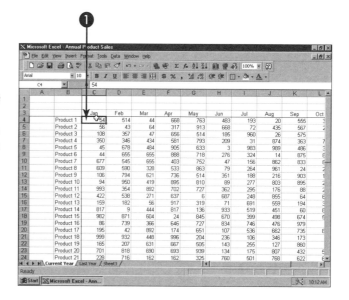

USING MULTIPLE WINDOWS

To take advantage of Excel's resources, you can even display more than one worksheet or workbook on the screen at the same time.

Dividing a Worksheet into Windows

Most of the techniques for working with several windows are standard Windows 95. So if you've worked with multiple windows before — in Microsoft Word or some other application, for example — you already know the basics. If you're new to Windows 95, you'll learn about using multiple windows in this lesson.

Dividing a Worksheet into Windows

Panes only affect the active worksheet. If you want to see more than one sheet of your workbook on the screen at a time, you need to divide the screen into more than one window. You do so in three basic steps:

❶ Create a new window for the same workbook.

❷ Arrange the multiple windows on the screen.

❸ Change sheets in one of the windows.

As an example, you'll look at both the Current Year and Last Year sheets of your workbook at the same time:

❶ Click the Last Year sheet tab.

❷ Select Window ➢ New Window. Excel creates another window displaying the same workbook and worksheet. The notation :2 appears after the file name in the title bar, indicating that it is the second window for the workbook.

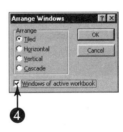

❸ Select Window ➢ Arrange. Excel displays the dialog box shown here.

❹ Select the Windows of Active Workbook option. This prevents Excel from displaying other open workbooks at the same time.

Next you choose how you want the windows arranged.

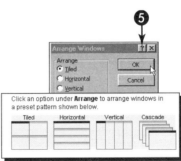

❺ Click the help button and then click inside the Arrange area. The following What's This? help message shows the various options. Accept the default Tiled; when you choose this option, each window retains its own title bar, sheet tabs, and sheet scrolling buttons. The active window will also have scroll bars. Click OK.

6 Click the Current Year sheet tab in the active window. The two windows are unsynchronized, so scrolling one will not affect the other.

7 Click the Close box of the active window. This closes the window but not the workbook, so Excel won't bother asking if you want to save a modified file.

8 Click the Maximize button of the window.

Displaying Multiple Workbooks

You can have multiple workbooks open at one time and then switch back and forth by selecting one from the Window menu. When one workbook is open, just open another or start a new one. To change windows, either press Ctrl+F6, or pull down the Window menu and click the name of the workbook you want to display.

   You can use the Arrange command to arrange windows from multiple workbooks. (In this case, you do not need to create a new window, since that's only useful for multiple windows from a single workbook.) Once multiple windows are on screen, you can use standard Windows techniques to adjust their size and position by dragging. As an example, you'll start a new workbook and arrange two workbook windows on the screen:

1 Click the New button in the Standard toolbar. Excel starts a new blank workbook, moving the existing one into the background.

2 Select Window ➢ Arrange. The Arrange Windows dialog box appears. Make certain that the Windows of Active Workbook option is not selected. If it is, the Arrange command only affects the current workbook, not others that are open but in the background.

3 Click Cascade.

4 Click OK. Excel overlaps the worksheet windows. When windows are cascaded, you can see the title bars of each window, but only the window in the foreground is active. To switch between windows, just click the title bar of the window you want to go to.

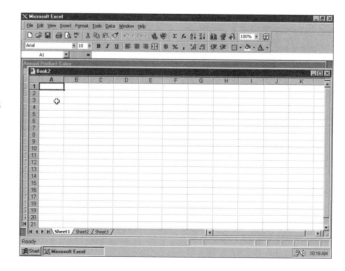

Saving Multiple Workbooks

5 Select Window ➢ Arrange.

6 Click Vertical and then click OK. The two workbook windows are now side by side. To choose a window when more than one is displayed, click anywhere in the window, or select Window from the menu bar and then click the window name.

While more than one window appears on screen, only one is active, or ready for you to use. Inactive windows have a dimmed title bar and no scroll bars.

To arrange the windows so they do not appear at the same time, maximize one of the windows by clicking on its Maximize button in the title bar.

7 Click the window displaying the blank new workbook.

8 Click its Maximize button. Any other windows move into the background, maximized as well.

9 Close both workbooks.

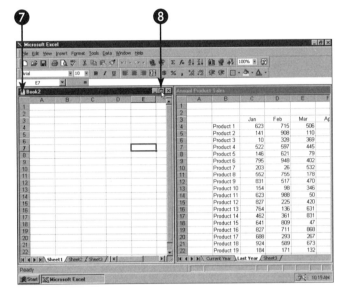

Saving Multiple Workbooks

When you have multiple workbooks open, saving or closing one has no effect on the other. If you exit Excel with more than one unsaved workbook open, you'll be asked if you want to save the active workbook. The message box also contains the option Yes To All. Choose Yes to All to save all of the open workbooks without being asked if you want to save each individually, Choose Yes to be prompted for each workbook.

If you want to later open all of the currently open workbooks in the same configuration of windows as they appear, choose File ➢ Save Workspace. In the dialog box that appears, type a workspace name and then click Save. If you have not saved any of the workbooks since saving them last, you'll be asked if you want to save each one — there will be no Yes To All option.

Workspaces are saved in a special file with the .xlw extension. The files will be listed in the Open dialog box but with an icon that differs from the icon for regular documents. To reopen all of the files, in the configuration in which they were saved, just open the workspace file.

MOVING INFORMATION BETWEEN WORKSHEETS, PANES, AND WINDOWS

One important benefit of using multiple worksheets and workbooks is that you can easily share information between them. In fact, you can share information just as you learned to move or copy data within a sheet.

To use the Clipboard, display the worksheet containing the information you want to move or copy, select the information, and then click the Cut or Copy button on the Standard toolbar. Next, display the worksheet or workbook where you want to place the information, click where you want to paste in the data, and then click the Paste button.

You can also drag and drop information. To drag between displayed panes or windows, just select and drag the information right across the pane or window boundaries.

Excel makes it especially easy to copy information between sheets of a workbook even without using panes. Just hold down the Alt key as you drag and point to the sheet tab of the worksheet where you want to insert the data. As soon as you point to the tab, Excel displays the worksheet, so you can then release the Alt key (but keep the mouse button held down). Drag to the location where you want to insert the information and release the mouse button.

SKILLS CHALLENGE: WORKING WITH MULTIPLE WORKSHEETS

The ability to work with multiple worksheets, panes, and windows is an important one. Not only can you view multiple worksheet projects at one time, you can share information between them, moving and copying information between sheets and building formulas that refer to cells in other sheets. In the following exercise, you'll reinforce some of these important Excel skills.

In this exercise, you will organize the sheets of a workbook, and share information between them. You'll insert, rename, and move worksheets, as well as fill and copy information across them:

TRY OUT THE

INTERACTIVE TUTORIALS

ON YOUR CD!

Skills Challenge

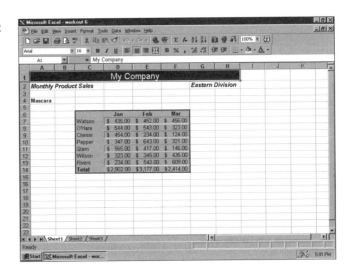

1 Open Workout 6 in the Exercises folder of the CD. The first sheet of the workbook is shown in the accompanying illustration.

2 Rename the sheets using the labels in cell A4. For example, change the name of Sheet1 to Mascara.

 What are the two ways to rename a worksheet?

3 Change the order of the sheet so the tabs are in alphabetical order.

4 Insert a new sheet at thee end of the workbook. (Hint: You'll have to insert the sheet and then move it.)

 What are the two ways to move a worksheet?

5 Copy the contents and formats of cells A1 through H14 to the new worksheet. (Hint: Select the last two sheets and use the Edit ➤ Fill ➤ Across Worksheets command.)

6 Clear the contents of cells D7 to F13 in the new worksheet.

 Does clearing cells on one worksheet affect the contents of the other worksheets in the workbook?

7 Change the text in cell A4 and the worksheet tab to Eye Shadow.

8 Move the Eye Shadow sheet so the sheet tabs are in alphabetical order.

9 Display the Lipstick and Eye Shadow sheets at the same time. (Hint: Create a new window for the workbook, arrange them tiled on the screen, and then select the appropriate worksheets.)

 Can you use panes to display two worksheets from one workbook at the same time?

10 Use drag and drop to move the contents of cell A18 in the Lipstick sheet to cell A3 in the Eye Shadow sheet.

Troubleshooting

 5 *Can you drag and drop between worksheets when they are not displayed at the same time? If so, how do you do this?*

11 Close the window containing the Lipstick page. (You have to select it to display the Close box.)

 6 *Does closing the window also close the workbook?*

12 Maximize the remaining window.

13 Check your progress, and then save and close the workbook.

The Eye Shadow sheet of the workbook is shown in the accompanying illustration. If your worksheet is different, try to determine which formats are incorrect, and then correct them. If need be, reopen the worksheet and start over, working slowly through the steps.

A completed copy of this workbook is under the name Solution 6 in the Solution directory.

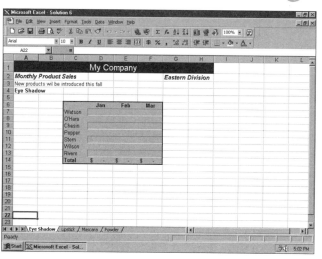

TROUBLESHOOTING

As you can see, it is easy to work with worksheets and workbooks. Not much can go wrong, but if it does, check out these tips.

Problem	Solution
I try using the Arrange command to see more than one worksheet, but all I see is one window.	To see more than one window of the same workbook, you have to first use the Window ➤ New Window command. In the Arrange Windows box, be sure to select the Windows of Active Workbook check box.

continued

Using Worksheets and Windows

6

Troubleshooting

Problem	Solution
I used the Window menu but my workbook just disappeared!	You may have clicked on the Hide option in the Window menu by mistake. This command hides the current workbook. To redisplay the workbook, select Window ➢ Unhide and select the workbook in the dialog box that appears.
I'm freezing the panes but they are still scrolling.	Freezing only prevents the panes from scrolling in one direction. Freezing rows prevents them from scrolling up or down but not left or right; freezing columns prevents them from scrolling left or right but not up or down. The idea is to keep row or column labels from scrolling out of view. If you want the column headings to remain on screen, freeze the rows in which they are placed. Then when you scroll the window up or down, the column headings remain displayed. To keep row headings displayed, freeze the columns in which they are located.
I'm having trouble using drag and drop between windows.	Because of the small window size, it is sometimes it is difficult not to drag too far, scrolling the window when you don't want to. If you can't get the cells in the correct location, drop them in any blank area. Then, maximize the window and try dragging the cells again, or use the Clipboard to cut and paste them.

very long page title

WRAP UP

Just imagine what you can do by working with more than one worksheet or workbook at a time. But for now, relax and stretch a little, keeping in mind all that you learned:

- How to give sheet tabs more meaningful and useful names

- How to change the order of worksheets by dragging their tabs

- How to insert and delete sheets as needed

- How to select multiple sheets by using the Shift key, or by choosing Select All Sheets from the shortcut menu

- How to divide a worksheet window into panes to see two or four different areas at one time

- How to freeze panes to keep row and column labels on the screen while you scroll through your data

- How to create a new window to see more than one worksheet at a time

- How to open and arrange multiple workbooks

Still feel up to a challenge? See how many windows you can open, and the interesting ways that you can arrange them. Use standard Windows techniques to change the window sizes.

In Lesson 7, you will learn special techniques for preventing mistakes, including protecting your worksheets from unauthorized users and controlling the information that can be entered into cells.

PART III

Key Excel Features

This part shows you how to prevent and correct errors using special Excel techniques, how to use functions to perform calculations, and how to connect to the World Wide Web and link information between projects. It includes the following lessons:

- Lesson 7: Preventing and Correcting Worksheet Errors
- Lesson 8: Working with Formulas and Functions
- Lesson 9: Excel on the World Wide Web

Preventing and Correcting Worksheet Errors

2 HOURS

GOALS

In this lesson, you learn how to prevent and correct many common errors that occur in worksheets. After completing this lesson, you will be able to:

- Correct mistakes and expand abbreviations with AutoCorrect

- Check spelling

- Use absolute cell references in formulas and functions

- Lock cells so they cannot be changed

- Hide cells so they cannot be seen

- Protect your worksheets and workbooks with passwords

- Validate cell entries

Get Ready

GET READY

No matter how careful you are, it's all too easy to make small mistakes in your worksheets. Unfortunately, even small mistakes can create big problems, especially where numbers are concerned. You can help avoid mistakes by planning your worksheet before creating it, and by taking advantage of all that Excel has to offer. In this lesson, you learn some useful Excel features for preventing and correcting some common worksheet errors.

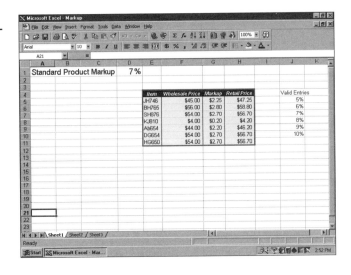

This lesson refers to the following workbooks:

File Name	Location
Markup	Exercise directory
Markup Solution	Solution directory
Workout 7	Exercise directory
Solution 7	Solution directory

When you are done with this lesson, you will have created the workbook shown at right, which uses absolute references.

PREVENTING MISTAKES WITH AUTOCORRECT

In many cases you won't have an data validation rules for text and numbers, but you can still take some steps to avoid and correct errors. Excel's AutoCorrect feature helps you avoid typographical errors by checking your typing on the fly. For example, if you mistakenly type two capital letters at the start of a word, Excel automatically changes the second uppercase character to lowercase. If you accidentally turn on Caps Lock and type an initial lowercase letter, Excel turns Caps Lock off for you and reverses the case of what you typed.

In addition, Excel automatically corrects common typographical errors — such as replacing "teh" with "the" and "you;re" with "you're." In fact, you can add your own common typos to the list, and even use this feature to insert text when you type an abbreviation for it.

TRY OUT THE

INTERACTIVE TUTORIALS

ON YOUR CD!

Creating Custom AutoCorrect Entries

To see how AutoCorrect works, Select Tools ➢ AutoCorrect to display the dialog box shown at right.

The check boxes at the top of the dialog box indicate which AutoCorrect features are turned on:

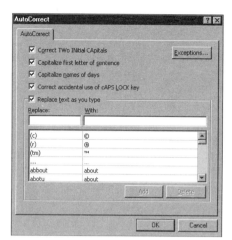

- **Correct TWo INitial CApitals**: Sometimes you hold down the Shift key just a little too long when typing an initial capital letter. If you type two initial capitals, Excel changes the second one to lowercase.

- **Capitalize first letter of sentence**: When you type in cells and comment boxes, Excel capitalizes the first letter after an end-of-sentence punctuation mark, such as a period, question mark, and exclamation point.

- **Capitalize names of days**: Excel capitalizes the first letter of day names. This only affects the names when they are spelled out, not when they are abbreviated.

- **Correct accidental use of cAPS LOCK key**: If you press the Caps Lock key by mistake and then type a sentence, the first letter will be lowercase, the remaining uppercase. When this happens, Excel turns off Caps Lock and reverses the case of the characters.

- **Replace text as you type**: Excel changes anything that you type that's listed in the Replace column with the corresponding entry in the With column. The columns contain a long list of common typographical errors. Make sure to keep this check box selected or most of Excel's AutoCorrect features won't work.

Clearing a check box turns off the feature. To remove a specific item from the Replace Text as You Type list, click it and then click the Delete button.

Creating Custom AutoCorrect Entries

If you misspell a certain word often, you can add your misspelling and the correct spelling to the AutoCorrect list. Then when you type the word the same incorrect way again, Excel corrects it for you. Take advantage of this feature to enter long phrases or complex words by typing an abbreviation. For example, suppose the name of your company is Reid's Educational Service Bureau. Rather than type the

7

Preventing and Correcting Worksheet Errors

Creating Custom AutoCorrect Entries

full name whenever you needed it, wouldn't it be easier just to type "resb" and let Excel enter the full name for you? Do that now:

❶ Start a new workbook, and then select Tools ➢ AutoCorrect.

❷ In the Replace box, type **resb**.

❸ Press Tab to reach the With box.

❹ Type this: **Reid's Educational Service Bureau**.

❺ Click Add.

❻ Click OK.

Now whenever you type the abbreviation "resb," Excel expands it for you:

❼ Click cell A1.

❽ Type **resb**.

❾ Press Enter. The full name appears: Reid's Educational Service Bureau. Clear the contents of the cell.

When creating AutoCorrect entries, avoid using abbreviations that are complete words themselves. For example, if your business is called California Association of Teachers, you wouldn't want to create the AutoCorrect entry using the abbreviation cat. If you did, each time you actually wanted to use the word "cat" it would expand to California Association of Teachers.

TIP

AutoCorrect entries that you create in one Office 97 application will be available to all of the Office 97 applications. For example, AutoCorrect entries you create in Excel 97 will be available in Word 97, and vice versa.

■ AutoCorrect Exceptions

The exceptions command button in the AutoCorrect dialog box lets you indicate instances when you do not want to capitalize the first letter of a sentence or change two initial capital letters. Shown at right is the dialog box that appears when you click Exceptions.

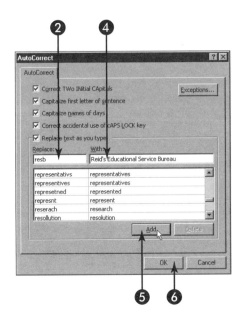

The options in the Don't Capitalize After list are common abbreviations that end with a period. Without this feature, suppose you typed **Make an appt. for Monday**. Excel would think that you ended the sentence with the word "appt." and would capitalize the first letter of the word "for." When "appt." is listed as an exception, Excel does not treat the period after it as the end of the sentence. If you use other abbreviations that end with a period, add them to the exceptions list if they're not already there.

In the Initial Caps tab of the AutoCorrect Exceptions dialog box, you can enter words that you do not want AutoCorrect to change. Excel doesn't provide any default examples, but it is becoming more common for product and trade names to have odd capitalization. For example, suppose you sell a software product that you've named DBasement. If you just entered the product name into a cell, AutoCorrect would change the letter *B* to lowercase. To prevent this, click the Initial Caps tab and add your product name to the exceptions list.

CHECKING YOUR SPELLING

Even the best spellers can make mistakes, and only fairly common misspellings are corrected by AutoCorrect. Excel's spell checker compares each word in your worksheet against those in its dictionary. When it finds a word that is not in the dictionary, it reports the word as a possible error, and may even list some suggested spellings.

NOTE *The spell checker feature in Excel is similar to the one in Microsoft Word. In fact, all Office 97 applications share the same dictionary. You can add a word to the dictionary, such as your name, so it will not be reported as an error in any Office 97 program.*

Correcting Spelling Errors

To begin the spell check, use any of these methods:

- Click the Spelling button on the Standard toolbar.

Correcting Spelling Errors

- Select Tools ➤ Spelling.
- Press F7.

When Excel finds a word that appears misspelled, it may show you a list of other spellings. You can choose one of the words from the list, type the word again yourself, or tell Excel to ignore the word because it is indeed spelled correctly. You can also add the word to the dictionary so Excel does not stop on it again, and you can create an AutoCorrect entry from the word so Excel corrects it automatically as you type.

To see how spell check works, you'll first create a worksheet with some obvious errors:

1 Enter the worksheet shown in the illustration at right, exactly as it appears. Make sure to enter the typos and duplicated words.

2 Click cell A1. You can start the spelling check from any cell. If you do not start in cell A1, however, Excel starts in the active cell and checks to the end of the worksheet, then checking whether it should return to the start of the sheet to continue checking.

3 Click the Spelling button on the Standard toolbar. Excel finds the first word that is not in its dictionary, activates the cell, and displays the Spelling dialog box shown here. The Not in Dictionary prompt lists the word the way it is spelled in your worksheet, with some suggested spellings in the list box. The Change To box shows the selected word in the Suggestions list, which in this case happens to be the correct spelling.

4 Click Change to correct the misspelling. If the correct spelling is elsewhere in the list, double-click it. If the word is not in the list, you can type the correct spelling in the Change To box and then click Change.

NOTE *When you choose Change, Excel makes the replacement and continues searching, but stops at the next occurrence of the misspelling. If you select Change All, Excel automatically replaces other*

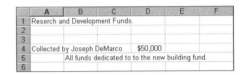

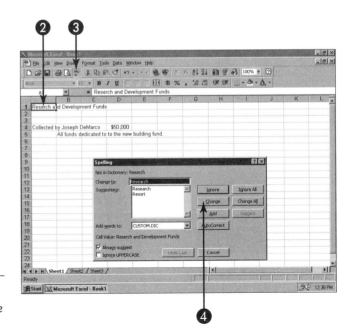

occurrences of the same misspelling. Use Change All with care. You might get some unanticipated results.

5 Excel now stops on the name DeMarco, which is spelled correctly. Click Ignore.

NOTE When you click Ignore, Excel skips just this occurrence of the word, but stops on other occurrences later in the worksheet. If you click Ignore All, instead, Excel leaves the word unchanged and continues the spell check, without stopping on the same word again.

6 Excel now stops on the double *to to*. The Not in Dictionary box is labeled Repeated Word, and the Change To box is empty. Click Delete to erase the duplicate. That was the last error, so Excel displays a message reporting that the entire sheet has been checked.

7 Click OK. The errors in the worksheet are now corrected.

8 Close the workbook without saving it. You'll be opening a new workbook in the next exercise.

TIP When Excel finds a possible misspelling, it activates the cell but does not highlight or select the misspelled word. With long cell entries, the error may not be obvious if you're looking at the cell, so always check the Not in Dictionary prompt to see which word Excel has located.

NOTE To delete occurrences of a misspelled word from the worksheet, wait until the word appears in the Not in Dictionary prompt and then press Del to erase the suggested spelling in the Change To box. The Change and Change All buttons change to Delete and Delete All. Click Delete All to delete all occurrences of the word, or click Delete to delete the current occurrence.

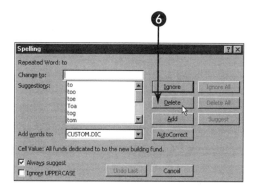

6

Other Spelling Options

The other options in the Spelling dialog box give you some additional choices. Review this summary of the options before spell checking important documents.

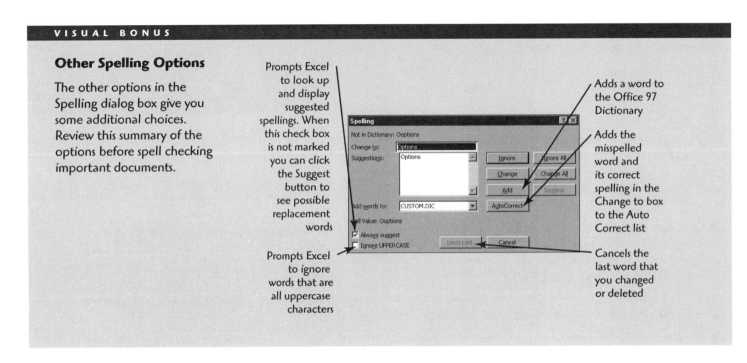

Prompts Excel to look up and display suggested spellings. When this check box is not marked you can click the Suggest button to see possible replacement words

Prompts Excel to ignore words that are all uppercase characters

Adds a word to the Office 97 Dictionary

Adds the misspelled word and its correct spelling in the Change to box to the Auto Correct list

Cancels the last word that you changed or deleted

ABSOLUTE REFERENCES

Excel's ability to copy a formula using a relative reference is a great time-saver, but sometimes an unwanted one. Remember, when a cell address in a formula is a relative reference, Excel will change the addresses when you copy the formula to another cell. There may be times when you don't want the reference to change. When you create and copy such a formula, Excel changes the references anyway, and if you don't look closely you won't notice that the results are incorrect.

The worksheet in the accompanying illustration is an example. It calculates a product's retail cost by multiplying the wholesale cost by a standard markup percentage, which is in cell D1. To calculate the markup on the wholesale cost in cell F5, you'd could enter the formula =F5*D1 in cell G5. But what if you then copied that formula down in column G to calculate the retail costs of the other products? It wouldn't work because Excel would adjust the reference so cell D1 would not be used by the markup in each formula.

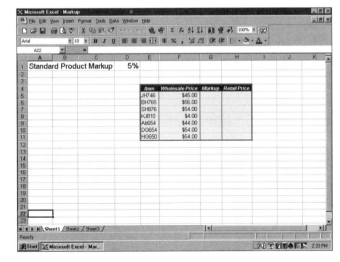

The Problem of Relative Addresses

When you want a cell address in a formula to stay the same, regardless where the formula is copied, you use an *absolute reference*. To create an absolute reference, type a dollar sign ($) in front of each part of the address that you want to remain constant.

The Problem of Relative Addresses

You are now ready to enter the formulas to calculate the markup and the retail prices. The markup formula must reference the percentage in cell D1. To see how relative addressing can create problems, first enter the formula without the absolute address, so you can see what happens:

1 Open the Markup workbook in the Exercise directory.

2 Click cell G5.

3 Type this: **=F5*D1**. The formula multiplies the price by the markup percentage.

4 Click cell H5.

5 Type this: **=F5+G5**. The formula adds the markup to the wholesale price to yield the retail price.

6 Click cell G5.

7 Drag the fill handle to cell G11.The formula is copied using a relative reference, and the values are calculated as zero, which is incorrect. You'll learn why shortly.

8 Click cell H5.

9 Drag the fill handle to cell H11. Because of the relative references in column G, the error is compounded by adding no markup to the wholesale costs in column H, as shown in the illustration at right.

Adding Absolute Addresses

The formula =F5*D1 certainly worked well in cell G5, but copying it down the column resulted in incorrect value. Here's why. When Excel copied the formula to cell G6, it changed to =F6*D2, which multiplies the wholesale cost by the blank cell D2. Excel modified the references to both cells F5 and D1, when you really want to always refer to cell D1.

Using a relative reference, the formula =F5*D1, when in cell G5, means "multiply the value one cell to the left by the value in the cell four rows up and three columns to the left." This works fine in cell G5 because the markup amount is indeed four rows up and three to the left. In cell G6, however, the wholesale price for the item is still one cell on the left, but the markup is no longer four rows up and three to the left.

Adding Absolute Addresses

To make this worksheet work, you have to refer to cell D1 in each of the formulas in the markup column. You could type each formula yourself, using cell D1 as the reference, but Excel supplies a better way. Enter the address of D1 with an absolute reference so it will not change when copied down the column. If you use the absolute reference $D$1, neither the row nor the column reference changes when copied.

You can take care of the problem now by changing the reference to cell D1 to an absolute reference:

❶ Double-click cell G5. Excel surrounds cells F5 and D1 in frames, and displays their addresses in matching colors within the formula.

❷ Edit the formula to be **=F5*$D$1**, and then press Enter. You do not want to change the reference to cell F5 because you want Excel to adjust it relatively.

❸ Click cell G5.

❹ Drag the fill handle to cell G11. The correct markup and retail figures are now displayed, as shown in the illustration at right.

❺ Click cell G6.

Item	Wholesale Price	Markup	Retail Price
JH746	$45.00	$2.25	$47.25
BH765	$56.00	$2.80	$58.80
SH876	$54.00	$2.70	$56.70
KJ810	$4.00	$0.20	$4.20
Ab654	$44.00	$2.20	$46.20
DG654	$54.00	$2.70	$56.70
HG650	$54.00	$2.70	$56.70

Adding Absolute Addresses

MIXING RELATIVE AND ABSOLUTE REFERENCES

In the preceding exercise, you added the dollar sign to both the column letter and row number in the cell address, but you don't always need to do so. For example, the reference to $C5 tells Excel to always refer to column C when you copy the formula, but to change the reference to row 5. Similarly, the reference C$5 tells Excel to maintain the row number 5 as you copy the formula, but to change the reference to column C. These are called *mixed references*.

The formula in cell G6 is =F6*$D$1. When you copied the formula down the column, only the reference to cell F5 changed. This way, the formula always multiplies the wholesale cost in the cell to its left by the markup in cell D1. The absolute reference, indicated by the dollar signs, tells Excel not to change the reference to column D and row 1. In addition, if you want a larger profit, you can quickly change all of the markup amounts and retail prices by changing just the percentage in cell D1.

NOTE *Excel makes it easy to enter absolute references using the F4 key. When you type a cell address in the formula bar, press F4 to toggle between a relative address and the possible combinations of absolute addresses. If you enter the address G8, for example, press the F4 key to cycle through the references $G$8, G$8, $G8, and then back to G8.*

PROTECTING WORKSHEETS AND WORKBOOKS

Even once you create the perfect worksheet, things can still go wrong. One of the most common problems occurs when a user mistakenly changes something they shouldn't — such as typing a value in a cell that contains a formula, or deleting the contents of a referenced cell.

In this section, you'll learn four ways to protect your work. You can protect the contents of cell from being changed, and you can hide a formula so a user will not see how a value is calculated. You can also prevent a user from inserting and deleting worksheets or making other changes to the structure of the workbook, and you can

Protecting Cells from Changes

password protect your workbook to prevent it from being opened or changed by unauthorized users.

Protecting Cells from Changes

The most basic protection you can give a worksheet is to lock cells. Locking a cell prevents anyone from changing its contents. By default, every cell in the worksheet is locked, but the mechanism that implements locking, called worksheet protection, is turned off. Turning on worksheet protection locks all cells in the worksheet. If you want to lock just specific cells, leaving most unlocked, you have to unlock those cells before turning on worksheet protection.

NOTE *Formulas in locked cells still recalculate when referenced cells change.*

To try your hand at this, you'll lock and hide some cells on the Markup workbook. You'll lock cells so users cannot change the markup amount, and so they cannot change or even see the formulas. In fact, the only cells you'll allow the user to change are the wholesale prices. Because the locking feature is turned on for all cells by default, you have to turn off locking for the cells you want the user to be able to change:

1 Select cells F5 to F11. These are the cells that you'll allow users to change.

2 Select Format ≻ Cells. You can also right-click the selected cells and choose Format Cells from the shortcut menu.

3 Click the Protection tab. Excel displays the options shown here.

4 Deselect the Locked check box, if it is checked. This turns off locking for the selected cells.

5 Click OK.

Before the other cells in the worksheet are actually locked, however, you must turn on worksheet protection, as you'll soon learn.

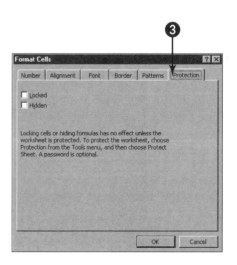

Hiding Formulas from Display

Hiding Formulas from Display

When you hide a formula, it will not appear in the formula bar when the cell is active. This is a handy feature when you do not want users to see how you've performed a calculation. Formulas are not hidden by default. You must first tell Excel which formulas to hide, and then turn on worksheet protection to actually hide them.

Now, you want to hide the cells with formulas so they do not appear when the cell is selected. Follow these steps:

1 Select cells G5 to H11 — the cells that contain formulas you want to hide.

2 Select Format ➢ Cells. The Protection tab should already be selected. If not, click it now.

3 Click the Hidden check box to select it, and hide the formulas in the selected cells.

4 Leave the Locked check box selected so the cell will also be locked.

5 Click OK.

6 Click to deselect the cells.

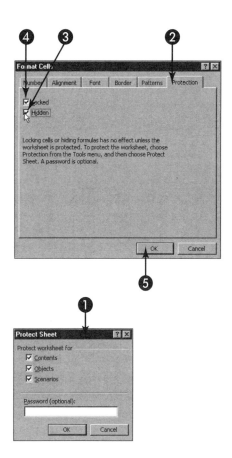

Turning on Worksheet Protection

Now that you set the desired attributes, you have to turn on worksheet protection to implement them:

1 Select Tools ➢ Protection ➢ Protect Sheet. Excel displays the dialog box shown at right. You want to protect all parts of the worksheet, so don't deselect any check boxes.

2 Click OK. The worksheet is now protected. The cells that still contain the locked attribute are locked and the designated formulas are hidden.

3 Try changing the value in cell D1. As soon as you start typing in a locked cell, Excel displays a message indicating that the cell is protected.

4 Click OK to remove the message.

7

Preventing and Correcting Worksheet Errors

Turning on Worksheet Protection

5 Click cell G5. The cell contains a formula, but the formula does not appear on the formula bar because it is hidden.

6 Click cell F5, type **35**, and click the Enter button in the formula bar. Even though the formula in cell H1 is locked and hidden, its value is still recalculated.

7 Click Undo to restore the original values.

8 Now remove the protection by selecting Tools ➤ Protection ➤ Unprotect Sheet. The worksheet is no longer protected, so all of the cells can be changed and the formulas will be displayed.

 NOTE

When the worksheet is protected, you can press the Tab key to move among the unlocked cells. Pressing Tab or Shift+Tab will not move to locked cells.

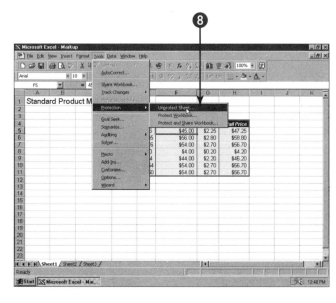

■ Protecting the Structure of Workbooks

In addition to protecting the cells in worksheets from change, you can protect the structure of your workbook. Start by selecting Tools ➤ Protection ➤ Protect Workbook. In the dialog box that appears, you can select one or both of two types of protection — the structure and the windows:

- Choose Structure to prevent users from deleting, moving, hiding, unhiding, renaming, or inserting sheets.

PROTECTING SHEETS WITH A PASSWORD

When you protect the sheet you can also designate a password. You'll need to then use the password to unprotect the sheet. If you do enter a password, it will appear as a series of asterisks as you're typing to keep it secure from prying eyes. Passwords are case sensitive, so type it exactly as you want it, including uppercase and lowercase letters. When you click OK, another box appears asking you to renter the password. This helps to ensure that you did not enter the incorrect password.

As you'll soon learn, you can also password protect the entire workbook. With a workbook password, you can "lock" every cell without setting options for individual sheets.

Password Protecting Workbooks

- Choose Windows to prevent users from changing the size and position of worksheet windows.

  You can also enter a password that will be required to unprotect the workbook.

Password Protecting Workbooks

Turning on worksheet protection only affects the active worksheet, not the entire workbook. When you want to protect the entire workbook without setting options for individual sheets, you can set a password that users must know to open or modify the workbook. You designate the password when saving the workbook, so if you already saved it, you need to use the File ➢ Save As command.

When you want to add a password, follow these steps:

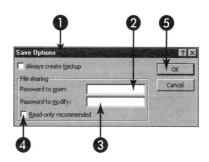

1 Select File ➢ Save As and click the Options button. Excel displays the dialog box shown to the right.

2 In the Password to Open text box, type the password users must enter to open the workbook.

3 In the Password to Modify box, type the password users must enter to edit the worksheet.

4 To simply recommend that users open the workbook so it cannot be changed, select the Read-Only Recommended check box.

5 Click OK.

6 Confirmation boxes will appear for each of the passwords you entered. Retype the appropriate password in each, and then click OK.

7 Click save to save the worksheet.

If you specified a password, a message will appear when the workbook is opened. The user must type the correct password to either open or modify the workbook. If you select the Read-Only Recommended option, a message will appear *suggesting* that the user open the workbook in read-only mode so it cannot be changed. The user can elect to open it in read-only mode, open it normally, or not open it at all.

Password Protecting Workbooks

VALIDATING DATA

Worksheet and workbook protection and passwords cannot prevent an authorized user from making a mistake. For example, suppose you design a great looking worksheet that multiplies the total of an invoice amount by a discount percentage. By mistake, however, some user enters 100% as the discount rather than 10%. All of a sudden you're giving your product away. Invalid input is one of the primary causes of inaccurate results, and it can be disastrous.

The solution to the problem is *data validation* — making sure that invalid information cannot be entered. In the markup problem, for example, you could limit the entry to some number between 5% and 10%, or any other range of values that you felt was appropriate. You can even display a message when the cell is selected, telling the user what entries are valid, and you can have a special message appear when incorrect information is entered. You can also create a message that appears even when you're not limiting data entry, just as a little friendly reminder.

You validate entries in these steps:

1. Specify the type of criteria, such as a numeric value, the length of text, or matching an entry in a list.

2. Indicate an operator, such as less than or not equal to.

3. Specify the allowed values or ranges.

4. Choose whether you want the user to be able to leave the cell blank.

5. Create an optional input message box, with a title and message.

6. Create an optional error message, with a graphic, title, and message.

Adding Data Validation

Adding Data Validation to a Worksheet

As an example, you'll add data validation to the Markup workbook:

1 Click cell D1. You can specify data validation rules on a cell-by-cell basis.

2 Select Data➤Validation. Excel displays the dialog box shown to the right. If the Validation option is dimmed on the Data menu, make sure you are in Ready mode and that the worksheet is not protected.

3 Click the Settings tab if it is not already selected. The options in the Data list, and the availability of other options in the dialog box, depend on your selection in the Allow list.

4 Pull down the Allow list and look at the available choices. The options determine the type of entry that can be made into the cell.

5 Choose Decimal. Text boxes labeled Minimum and Maximum appear.

6 Pull down the Data list and check out the options.

7 Leave the setting set at the default, Between. This lets you designate a range of proper values.

8 Click the Minimum text box, and type **.05**. You can also click the Collapse Dialog button and select a cell containing the minimum value.

9 Click the Maximum text box, and type **.1**.

10 Deselect the Ignore Blank check box. When this box is checked, the user can delete the contents of the cell. A blank cell will be calculated as no markup. Deselect this box to ensure that a valid entry will be in the cell.

11 Click OK.

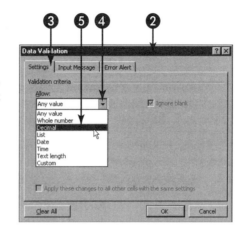

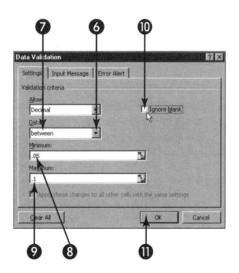

Displaying Messages

⓬ Now try to enter an invalid entry into the cell. Type **100** and then press Enter. Excel displays a generic error message reporting that you've entered invalid information.

⓭ Click Retry. If you select Cancel, Excel restores the existing value to the cell.

⓮ Type **5%** and press Enter. Excel now accepts this valid entry.

Some other possible combinations of validation are shown in Table 7-1. The default Any Value option in the Allow list provides no validation. The Custom option lets you enter a validation formula. The check box labeled Apply These Changes to All Other Cells with the Same Settings will apply any changes you made to the validation rule to any other cells that were already formatted with the same rules.

TABLE 7-1 DATA VALIDATION

Allow	Data	Options
Whole number	not between	minimum 25, maximum 50
Decimal	greater than or equal to	0.5
List		B1:B9
Date	greater than	1/1/76
Time	between	minimum 5 P.M., maximum 7 P.M.
Text length	less than or equal to	10

Displaying Messages

If you don't know the rules, you can't play the game. Data validation can be confusing to a user who doesn't know what entries are expected, and the generic message that appears doesn't help very much. You can forget what entries are valid even when you create the validation rules yourself.

To help yourself and others enter valid information, you can display two types of messages. The input message appears on screen when you select a cell. The error alert message appears when you make an improper entry. Now try adding the messages to cell D1:

1. Click cell D1.

2. Select Data ➤ Validation.

3. Click the Input Message tab. Excel displays the dialog box shown in the bottom illustration at right. Make sure the check box is selected. If it is deselected, your message will not appear.

4. Click the Title text box.

5. Type this: **Wholesale Price Markup**.

6. Click the Input Message text box.

7. Type this: **You must enter a decimal number between .05 and .1, or a percentage between 5% and 10%.**

| NOTE | *The Clear All button in the dialog box removes all validation rules and messages that you have applied.* |

Now you'll enter an error alert message. Like the input message, it has a title and message, but you can also select how strictly the rule should be applied. These are the following options:

- **Stop**: Excel does not allow you to enter an invalid entry.

- **Warning**: Excel reports that your entry is invalid, but gives you the option to reenter or accept it.

- **Information**: Excel displays the message you designate but accepts your entry anyway and continues.

Each type of message is accompanied by a different graphic.

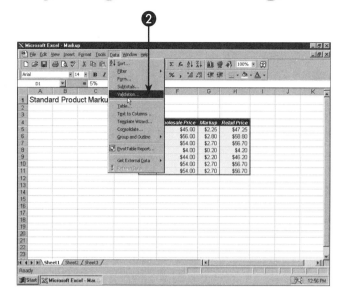

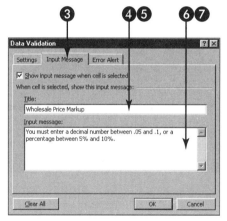

Preventing and Correcting Worksheet Errors

7

Limiting Values to a List

8 Click the Error Alert tab. Excel displays the dialog box shown at right. Make sure that the check box is selected. If it is deselected, your message will not appear.

9 Pull down the Style list.

10 Select Warning.

11 Click the Title text box.

12 Type this: **Wholesale Price Markup**.

13 Click the Error Message text box.

14 Type this: **You did not enter a value in the proper range. Type a decimal number between .05 and .1, or a percentage between 5% and 10%. Select Retry to enter another value. Select Cancel to keep the current value.**

15 Click OK. The input messages appears on screen because cell D1 is already selected, as shown to the right. If you are using the Office Assistant, the message appears with it. Otherwise, the message appears near the cell.

16 Type **100** and press Enter. The Error Alert message appears.

17 Click Retry.

18 Type **.05** and press Enter.

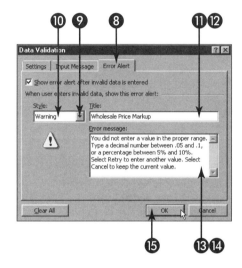

Limiting Values to a List

In some cases, you have a specific list of valid entries. For example, when filling in an invoice, you may want to limit the shipping company to FedEx, UPS, or DHL. Rather than requiring that users remember which shippers are allowed, you create display drop-down list that lets them select the appropriate choice.

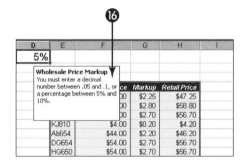

Limiting Values to a List

To create a list, enter the valid entries elsewhere in the worksheet, and then indicate the range of cells containing those entries in the Data Validation dialog box. For example, if you allow the markup to be any decimal between .05 and .1, users could enter something such as 6.5787%. To limit the entry to a whole numbers, create a list of those that are allowed. Try that now:

1 Enter **Valid Entries** in cell J4.

2 Type **5%** in cell J5.

3 Type **6%** in cell J6.

4 Select cells J5 and J6.

5 Drag the fill handle of cell J6 to J10 to generate the numbers 7%, 8%, 9% and 10%.

Now that you've created the list of valid entries, you have to specify its location in the Data Validation dialog box. This tells Excel where to check for the list of valid entries:

6 Click cell D1.

7 Select Data ➢ Validation to display the Data Validation dialog box shown to the right.

8 Click the Settings tab.

9 Move the dialog box out of the way (drag its title bar) so you can see column J.

10 Pull down the Allow list.

11 Select List. Excel dims the Data box and displays a text box labeled Source and a check box labeled In-Cell Dropdown.

12 Drag over the contents of the Source text box to select it.

13 Drag over cells J5 to J10. The dialog box collapses, and as you drag, the range of cells appears in the Source text box. The box expands when you release the mouse button.

14 Click OK. The drop-down list arrow appears to the right of the cell.

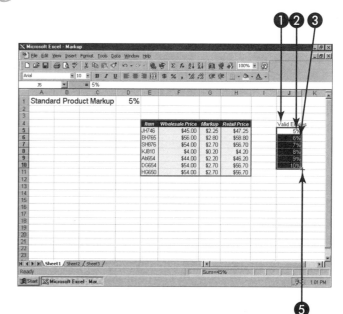

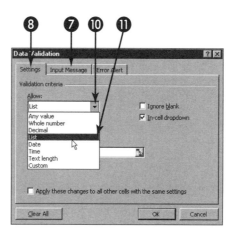

Skills Challenge

⑮ Pull down the drop-down list. Excel displays the values in the list range that you just selected.

⑯ Select 7% from the list.

⑰ Save and close the workbook.

Use a list and drop-down box to ensure that entries match specific values. You can also type a value directly into the cell, rather than use the drop-down list, but that value it must be in the list.

SKILLS CHALLENGE: CREATING A FAILSAFE WORKSHEET

Now take some time to practice your new skills. In this exercise, you'll create a payroll worksheet that calculates state, local, and social security taxes using absolute references. You'll also format the sheet with borders and shading. Then, as a finishing touch, you'll protect the worksheet so users must enter information in a valid range, and so they cannot change any of the tax percentages or formulas:

❶ Open Workout 7 in the Exercise folder.

❷ In cell E7, enter the formula =**B7*C7**.

 What does the formula =B7*C7 calculate?

❸ In cell F7, enter the formula =**(D7*1.5)*B7**.

 Why can you use relative addresses in columns E, F, and G?

❹ In cell G7, enter the formula =**E7+F7**.

❺ In cell H7, enter the formula =**G7*$C$2**. (Hint: Type =G7*C2, and then press F4.)

 Why do you need an absolute address in the formula =G7*$C$2?

❻ In cell I7, enter the formula to calculate the local income tax. (Hint: The formula multiples cell C7 by the absolute reference to C3, =C7*$C$3.)

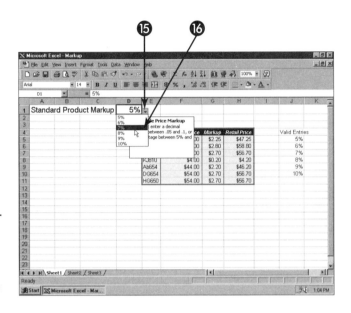

TRY OUT THE
INTERACTIVE TUTORIALS
ON YOUR CD!

7 In cell J7, enter the formula to calculate the social security tax. (Hint: You must use an absolute reference to the social security percentage.)

8 In cell K7, enter the formula to calculate the net pay. (Hint: Subtract from cell G7 the values in cells H7, I7, and J7.)

9 Use AutoFill to copy the formulas to row 20.

10 Insert the totals in cells C21 through K21. (Tip: Select the cells and click the AutoSum button.)

11 Apply the Currency format to cells E7 through K22.

12 Format row 6 so the text in the cells can wrap to the next line, and is centered vertically and horizontally. (Hint: Use the Alignment page of the Format Cells dialog box.)

13 Change the height of row 6 to 25.

14 Apply the borders and fill pattern shown in the accompanying illustration.

15 Set the data validation for cells B7 to B20 to accept decimal values between 0 and 15. Enter an input and error alert message of your choice.

4 *Why should you set a data validation rule for these cells?*

16 Set the data validation for cells C7 to C20 to accept decimal values between 0 and 40, with input and error alert messages of your choice.

17 Set the data validation for cells D7 to D20 to accept decimal values between 0 and 10, with input and error alert messages of your choice.

18 Turn off cell locking for cells B7 to D20. (Hint: Select the cells and use the Protection tab of the Format Cell dialog box.)

19 Turn on sheet protection.

5 *What other ways are there for you to protect this workbook?*

7

Preventing and Correcting Worksheet Errors

Troubleshooting

⑳ Try changing the state tax rate in cell C2.

 6 *What happens when you change the state tax rate?*

TROUBLESHOOTING

You covered a lot in this chapter — and learned some very useful and powerful Excel features. Check out these handy tips if you have problems applying these techniques to your own work.

Problem	Solution
I used the dollar signs to indicate an absolute reference but the calculation is still incorrect.	First make sure you are referencing the proper cell. Second, make sure you typed the dollar sign ($) rather than another character, and check that the symbol is in front of just the parts of the reference you want to remain absolute. In most cases, it should be in front of both the column letter and row number, but there are exceptions.
I made sure that the cells were locked in the Format Cells dialog box but I can still change their values.	You must turn on worksheet protection to activate the locking mechanism. Select Tools ➢ Protection ➢ Protect Sheet, and then click OK.
I specified that a worksheet should be "read-only" but people are still changing it.	The Read-Only Recommended option only suggests that users open it in read-only mode but doesn't require that they do so. If you want to protect cells from certain users, turn on worksheet protection for the locked cells and designate a password in the Protect Sheet dialog box, so a password is needed to turn off protection.

Wrap Up

WRAP UP

Absolute references, worksheet protection, and data validation certainly give you a variety of ways to fine-tune your worksheet. As you develop your own projects, keep these keys items in mind:

- Create AutoCorrect entries to streamline your input.

- Check your spelling before printing a worksheet.

- Use absolute references when you don't want a cell address in a formula or function to change when copied.

- All of the cells in a worksheet are set to be locked. To protect some but not all of the cells, you need to unlock the cells that you want users to be able to change.

- You must turn on worksheet protection for cell locking to go into effect.

- The Hide option in the Format Cells dialog box prevents a formula from appearing on the formula bar when the cell is selected.

- Assign a password to the entire workbook using the Save As dialog box.

- Data validation lets you control the information that can be typed into a cell.

- If you use data validation, enter input and error alert messages to keep your users informed of the validation rules.

- Use the List validation option to limit acceptable entries to those that you designate in a list.

Now that you've successfully completed this lesson, try adding data validation rules to important worksheets, and make sure you don't really need absolute addresses.

You're ready to move on to Lesson 8. There you'll learn how to use the power of Excel's functions to perform sophisticated math operations with ease. You'll also learn how to refer to cells by a label or name, rather than a row and column address.

7

Preventing and Correcting Worksheet Errors

Working with Formulas and Functions

2 HOURS

GOALS

In this lesson, you will learn how to use formulas and functions to perform calculations. After you've completed this lesson, you will be able to:

- Use row and column labels as cell names in formulas
- Define cell names and range names
- Use a wide range of Excel functions for performing simple to complex calculations

Get Ready

GET READY

Excel's ability to automatically recalculate formula results when the referenced data changes makes it a powerful problem solver. You use cell references in formulas so they are recalculated automatically when the addressed cells change. To make formulas even easier to create and use, you can assign names to cells and cell ranges, or use the row and column labels that are part of the worksheet to refer to the cells.

You can also use Excel's functions to easily perform complex mathematical operations using a keyword, such as Average or Sum. A function is a special predefined formula that takes supplied values, performs an operation, and returns another value. These are just some of the powerful techniques you will learn in this lesson.

This lesson refers to the following workbooks:

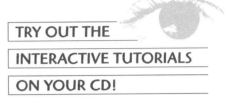

TRY OUT THE
INTERACTIVE TUTORIALS
ON YOUR CD!

File Name	Location
Sales and Commissions	Exercise directory
Index	Exercise directory
Sales and Commissions Solution	Solution directory
Index Solution	Solution directory
Workout 8	Exercise directory
Solution 8	Solution directory

Refer to the workbooks Sales and Commissions Solution and Index Solution when you have completed the exercises to check your work. The Solution 8 workbook contains the completed worksheet that you'll create in the Skills Challenge. When you are done with this lesson, you will have used formulas and functions to create the workbook shown at right.

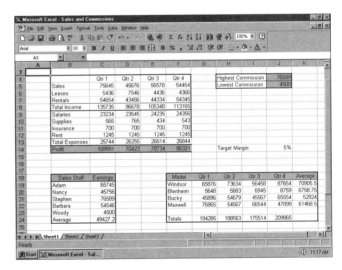

USING LABELS FOR CELL REFERENCES

Cell references in formulas give Excel its power, but cell addresses aren't always easy to use. If you forget what cell contains the information you want to use, you have to scroll to locate the address.

Using Labels as Cell References

Although Range Finder helps you correct formula problems by color coding cells, you still have to determine what the references represent. For example, a year after creating a worksheet, will you understand the purpose of =B5–C5 without having to study the worksheet?

When you use cell names instead of addresses, formulas become even easier to enter and understand. The formula =Income–Expenses will have some meaning long after you forget the cell addresses of the references. You can name cells or ranges of cells yourself, or have Excel name them for you. When you create the names yourself, you can use any names that you find informative and meaningful. When Excel creates the names, it use the labels that you've already entered. In fact, you may be able to refer to a cell by using the labels as well, as you will soon learn.

Using Column and Row Labels as Cell References

Many worksheets use labels above columns and to the left of rows. You can use these labels instead of cell addresses to reference cells, without giving the cell a formal name.

Look at the worksheet in the accompanying illustration. You can use the combination of the row and column labels, in either order, as the address of a cell. For example, you can refer to cell C5 as either Sales Qtr1 or as Qtr1 Sales. Cell E9 would be Salaries Qtr 3 or Qtr 3 Salaries. You can use the labels for the cell any place you would use the address, as in the formula =Sales Qtr 1 + Leases Qtr 1 + Rentals Qtr 1 to add two expense items.

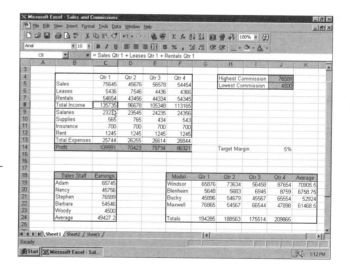

NOTE

Using labels to identify cell addresses makes formulas easy to read, but can involve a lot of typing. You'll learn later how to name cells and cell ranges yourself to create informative and shorter cell names.

Now you'll use labels to enter formulas:

1 Open the workbook named Sales and Commissions in the Exercise directory.

Omitting Row or Column Labels

② Click cell C14. This cell needs a formula to compute the net profit, subtracting expenses from income.

③ Type **=Total Income Qtr 1-Total Expenses Qtr 1**. The formula subtracts the value in cell C13 from the value in C8. Cell C8 is referenced as **Total Income Qtr 1**, because it is in the Total Income row and the Qtr 1 column. Cell C13 is called **Total Expenses Qtr 1** because it is in the Total Expenses row and the Qtr 1 column. You have to spell the label name just as it is in the worksheet, although case is not important.

④ Press Enter. The value is calculated and displayed.

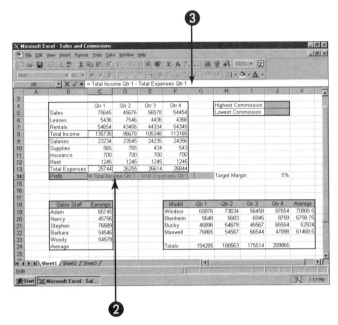

Omitting Row or Column Labels

If you are using the reference in the same column as the cell, you do not have to refer to the column name. Likewise, if you are using the reference in the same row as the cell, you do not have to refer to the row label. For example, the formula in cell C14 could also be simply =Total Income – Total Expenses because the formula is in the Qtr 1 column.

See how this works now:

① Click cell C16.

② Type = **Profit** and press Enter. Excel accepts the entry as a reference to cell C14, the cell in the Profit row of the current column.

③ Click cell G5.

④ Type = **Qtr 1** and press Enter. Excel accepts the entry as a reference to cell C5 because it is in the Qtr 1 column of the current row.

⑤ Click cell A16.

⑥ Type =**Profit** and press Enter. Excel displays the value 0, not referencing any cell. That's because there is no Profit value in column A or in row 16.

⑦ Click Undo three times to reverse your last three actions.

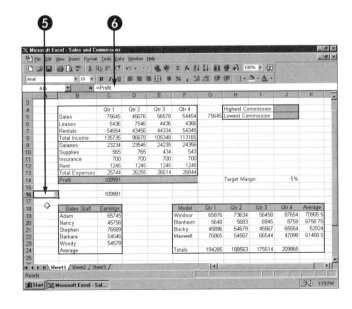

Defining Label Ranges

LABEL NAMES ARE RELATIVE

When you use a label name in a formula or function, Excel treats it as a relative reference. You can then copy the formula to other cells, or use AutoFill to copy it, changing its reference as appropriate.

Defining Label Ranges

Even if you can omit a row or column label, typing long labels, such as Total Expenses, can take longer than finding and entering the cell address. Instead of typing labels yourself, you can point to cells to add their labels to a formula. However, before you can point to a cell to use its label, you have to define a *label range.* A label range is the group of row and column labels that you want to use in formulas. Defining the label range assigns the row and column labels to the cells. Then when you click a cell at the intersection of the labels, Excel places the labels rather than the cell address into the formula. Try it now:

1 Select cells C4 to F4. This range contains the column labels you want to use to refer to cells in this section of the worksheet.

2 Select Insert ➣ Name ➣ Label. Excel displays the Label Ranges dialog box. The range appears in the Add Label Range text box and the Column Labels option button is selected.

3 Click Add. Excel inserts the range into the Existing Label Ranges list.

4 Click OK.

5 Select cells B5 to B14. These are the row labels you want to use.

6 Select Insert ➣ Name ➣ Label. The range B5:B14 appears in the Add Label Range text box and now the Row Labels option button is selected.

7 Click Add. Excel inserts the selected range into the Existing Label Ranges list.

8 Click OK.

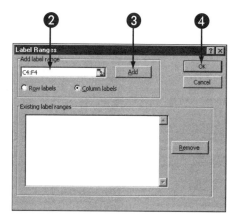

Defining Label Ranges

⑨ Click cell D14. Even though you could just use AutoFill to enter the remaining formulas in this row, you'll enter it yourself to see how Excel uses the label ranges.

⑩ Type = to start the formula, and then click cell D8. Excel inserts the reference to **Qtr 2 Total Income** rather than to cell D8.

NOTE *You have to name both the row and column labels for Excel to automatically use the label names in formulas.*

⑪ Press - (minus sign) and then click cell D13. Excel inserts the reference to **Qtr 2 Total Expenses**.

⑫ Click the Enter button on the formula bar. Excel inserts the results of the formula.

⑬ Drag the AutoFill handle of cell D14 to cell F14. Excel copies the formula into the other cells, adjusting the labels using relative references.

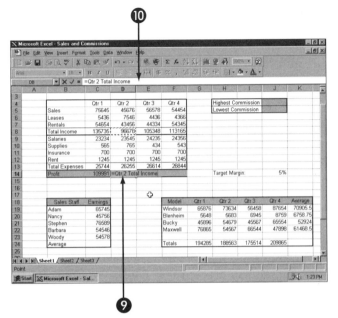

CHANGING LABELS

If you change the name of a referenced label, Excel automatically makes the same change to every formula in which the name is used. You do not have to make the changes yourself. Changing cell B13 to Total Costs, for example, changes the labels in the formulas in the Profit row as well.

However, if you delete a referenced label, Excel won't know how to refer to it and displays #NAME? in the cell. This error message means that the cell contains a reference to a label that does not exist. If you delete a label by mistake, click Undo. Retyping the label will not correct the problem.

If you misspell one of the label names, Excel may display an error message. The message will report a suggested correction, using the correct spelling from the corresponding label. If the suggestion is correct, click Yes. Otherwise, click No and make the correction yourself. Excel makes the suggestion when you make a minor spelling error to one of the labels. If you really mess up, the #NAME? error message appears.

NAMING CELLS AND RANGES

Labels are convenient for use in formulas, but they have limitations:

- You cannot refer to the labels on another worksheet, even if you use the sheet reference.

- You cannot use the label to refer to a range of cells.

- You cannot use the label name to move to the cell.

- You cannot use labels if the worksheet doesn't have them!

Instead of using labels in these instances, you have to use cell or range names. For example, in the Budget workbook, you could name the range C5 to C7 as Q1Income, and then refer to the name in a formula such as =SUM(Q1Income).

TIP

Unlike label names, cell and range names can only be one word — no spaces are allowed.

There are several ways to name cells and cell ranges. You can define a cell or range name yourself, or you can have Excel create the names for you.

CELL AND RANGE NAMES ARE ABSOLUTE ADDRESSES

Unlike label names, which are relative, cell and range names are absolute. When you use a cell name in a formula or function, Excel automatically treats it as an absolute address. If you want to be able to copy a formula using relative addressing — so the reference changes as it is copied — do not use cell names. However, when you need to use absolute addressing, referring to cell names saves you the trouble of adding the dollar signs. You'll see how this works in the Skills Challenge at the end of the lesson.

Defining Cell Names

Defining Cell Names

If a cell or range of cells is not associated with any label, you name it yourself. Because cell names must be unique, use names that clearly identify the cell, and that will be easy to remember. You'll be able to pick the name from a list, and even print a table showing your names, but it is easier if you can remember the ones you'll need often.

You must be in Ready mode to name cells:

❶ Click cell J14.

❷ Click the name box at the left end of the formula bar. The cell address will become selected.

❸ Type **Margin**. You're entering a name that represents the purpose of the value in the cell.

❹ Press Enter. Excel accepts the name, but it keeps the cell active. Notice that the cell name, not its address, now appears in the name box.

Not only can you now type the name of the cell instead of its address, you can quickly move to the cell. When you pull down the name list, Excel displays all of the named cells. Click the name of the cell or range that you want to make active.

❺ Click cell A3.

❻ Pull down the name list. You'll see the name you just gave cell J14.

❼ Click Margin in the list. Excel selects cell J14. If you choose a range name, the entire range will be selected.

You can also name a cell or range by selecting Insert ➢ Name ➢ Define to display the Define Name dialog box, typing the name for the cell, and then clicking OK.

Letting Excel Name Cells

If the cell or range of cells that you want to name has labels, you can have Excel automatically name the cells for you. For example, look at cells C19 to C23 in the sample worksheet. Each of the cells in

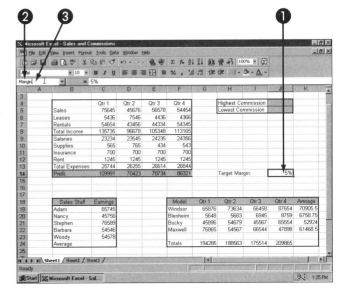

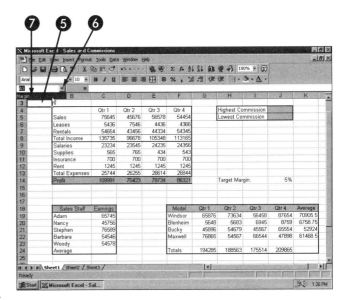

Letting Excel Name Cells

column C is identified by a label in column B. You can't use the labels by themselves to identify the cells, but you can have Excel name them for you:

1 Select cells B19 to C23 — these are the cells containing the labels and the cells you want to name.

2 Select Insert ➢ Name ➢ Create to see the Create Names dialog box. These options let you designate the position of the labels in relation to the cells. Excel automatically determines that the values in column C have labels to their left (note that the Left Column check box is selected), so you do not have to change any options.

3 Click OK.

4 Click to deselect the cells. Each of the cells is now named using the label to its left. (C19 is named Adam, and so on.)

5 Click cell C20. Its name, Nancy, appears in the name box instead of its cell address.

In the preceding steps, you named each of the individual cells in the range. You can also give a single name to the entire range, such as a row or column of cells. To do so, just select the range of cells as well as the labels. Excel will use the row label as the names of the selected ranges in the row, and the column labels as the names of the cells in the column.

6 Select cells F18 to K22.

7 Select Insert ➢ Name ➢ Create. Excel selects the Left Column and Top Row check boxes.

8 Click OK. Excel uses each row label as the name for the range of cells to its right, and each column label as the name for the cells below it in the column.

9 Click to deselect the cells.

10 Drag over cells G19 to G22. Their range name — Qtr_1 — appears in the name box. (Because names cannot include spaces, Excel replaces them with underscore characters.)

11 Click to deselect the cells.

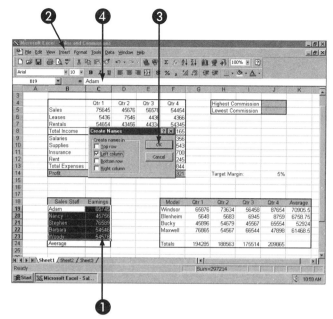

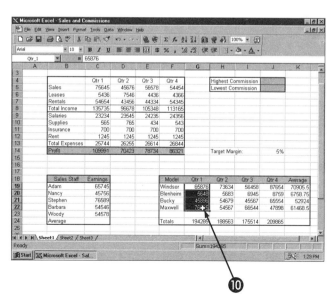

8

Working with Formulas and Functions

Using Cell and Range Names

⑫ Pull down the name list to see all of the defined names.

⑬ Click Bucky. The range of cells associated with that name is selected.

Using Cell and Range Names

You can use a cell or range name anywhere that you would use an absolute cell reference. Either type the name in place of the address, or select it from a list of names. Try it now.

① Click cell J4. This cell is designed to show the highest amount of commissions from the group of cells B18 to C24.

② Type =**Stephen**, and press Enter. The value assigned to the name Stephen appears in the cell. Cell J5 is now active, representing the lowest earnings.

③ Select Insert ➤ Name ➤ Paste to see a box listing the named cells and ranges, as shown to the right.

④ Click Nancy and then click OK. The value assigned to the name Nancy appears in cell J5.

The Paste Name dialog box also contains the option Paste List. Click this button to insert a list of names and their references into the current worksheet location.

TIP

Remember, cells names are absolute. For example, you could calculate the sum of cells G19 to G22 using the formula =SUM(Qtr_1) in cell G24. But, you cannot drag the fill handle to copy the formula across to cell J24. Excel would not adjust the reference, so you'd get the same value in all four cells.

Converting Addresses to Names

Your worksheet already contains SUM functions in row 24, but it is not too late to use the cell names to make the functions easier to read. You can *apply* cell names to addresses you've already entered. Follow these steps:

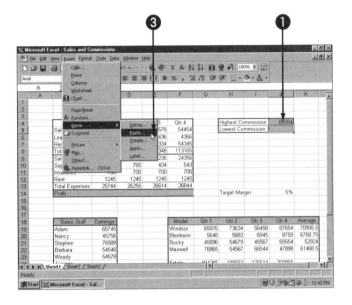

Converting Addresses to Names

1 Select cells G24 to J24.

2 Select Insert ➤ Name ➤ Apply to see the Apply Names dialog box shown in the bottom illustration at right. Here you select the names that you want to replace. By default, all of the names are selected, but you can click to deselect or select those you want. You can leave the name selected.

3 Click OK.

4 Click cell J24. The formula now refers to the cell name rather than its address.

The other choices in the Apply dialog box let you customize the way this feature works:

- **Ignore Relative/Absolute**: Excel replaces the reference with the name whether the address is absolute or relative. Unchecking this option causes Excel to only replace absolute references.

- **Use Row and Column Names**: By default, if a cell dos not have its own name but is part of a named range, Excel uses the range row and column headings to refer to it. Deselect this option if you do not want range names used.

- **Options**: Expands the Apply Names dialog box, providing choices to omit row or column range names if the cell is in the same row or column, and to use range names in either row-column or column-row order.

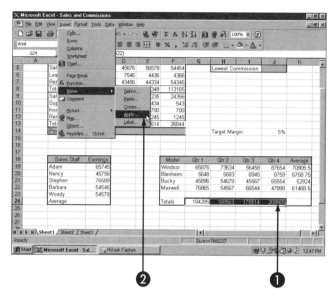

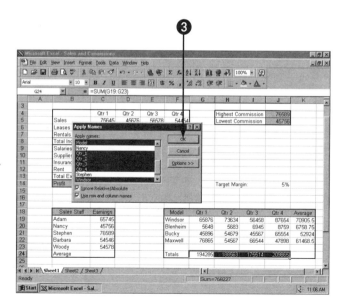

FUNCTIONS

A function is a special predefined formula that takes supplied values, performs an operation, and returns another value. You already used the SUM function to calculate the total of a series of numbers. It certainly is easier to enter =SUM(A1:A40), than it would be to type =A1+A2+A3 and so on. Because functions can act on a range of values, they offer other advantages as well.

Consider the AVERAGE function. This function computes the mathematical mean (the average) of a range of values. The average is the total of the values divided by the number of values, and the

Using Functions

syntax of the function is =AVERAGE(*range*). Excel automatically calculates the total and the count, and then computes the average.

Now how would you perform the same operation without using a function? You'd need a formula that looked something like =(B1+B2+B3...and so on)/X, where X is the number of cells. If you wanted to add another value into the average, you'd have to make two changes to the formula: insert the additional cell into the parentheses, and increase by one the count that you were using for the division.

When you use the function, however, you only need to change the range. In fact, if you insert a new row into the range to store the value, Excel changes the range for you.

In addition to the SUM and AVERAGE functions, two other commonly used functions are MIN and MAX. They result in, respectively, the minimum value in the specified range of cells and the maximum value of the range.

Using Functions

Functions use the syntax =*NAME*(*arguments*). *NAME* is simply the name of the function. The arguments, in parentheses, are the cell references, values, or other instructions that the function needs to do its work. There are some functions that don't have any arguments, and there are others for which some arguments are optional. For example, the function =TODAY() inserts the current date in the cell, without any argument. The SUM function that you've already used can have one argument — the range of cell to total — or up to 30 separate arguments for each cell or value, as in =SUM(A1,C5,H7,H2000).

NOTE *You can type a function name in either uppercase or lowercase; Excel changes the name to uppercase when you finalize the entry by pressing Enter or one of the cursor movement keys.*

If you know the name of the function you want to enter, and its arguments, just activate the cell that you want to contain the function results, and then type = followed by the function name and arguments. You can point to cells or cell ranges to add their addresses

Using Functions

to the argument. For example, if you type **=AVERAGE(** to initiate the AVERAGE function, you can then drag over the range of cells that you want to average to insert their addresses into the function.

If you do not know the function name or arguments, get help from Excel using the Formula Palette. This is an onscreen guide that shows you the syntax and arguments of the function you choose. You display the palette by using the Paste Function dialog box that appears when you choose the Paste Function toolbar button, or by selecting a function from the name list.

1 Click cell B24. Type **Minimum**. Click cell C24. The easiest way to add a simple function to a cell is to type it directly into the cell.

2 Typle **=MIN(C19:C23)** and press Enter. The lowest value (45756) in the specified range is now displayed.

3 Click cell B24 again. Type **Maximum**. Click cell C24.

4 Type **=MAX(C19:C23)** and press Enter. The highest value (76589) in the range is now displayed.

5 Click cell B24. Type **Average**. Click cell C24. In the next step, you will use the Paste Function button to create an average value for the range.

6 Click the Paste Function button in the Standard toolbar. (It's just to the right of the AutoSum button and has *fx* on its face.) Excel inserts the = sign into the cell and formula bar, and displays the Paste Function dialog box. The Function Category list shows the categories of functions; the Function Name list shows the functions within the selected category. The Office Assistant also appears asking if you want help on the function.

7 Click No for now.

8 Choose All in the Function Category list. Excel displays all the functions, in alphabetical order. You can also use the Recently Used category to see the functions that you've recently entered.

9 Scroll the Function Name list and double-click AVERAGE. Excel displays the Formula Palette, shown at right. The palette contains a text box and Collapse Dialog button for each argument. It includes a general description of the function, and of the

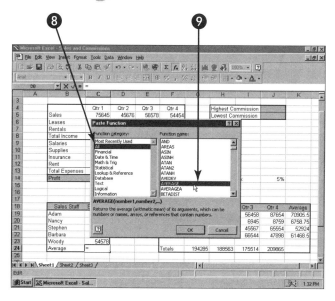

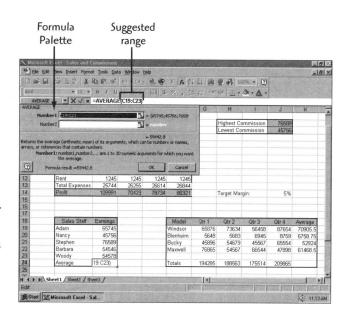

Formula Palette   Suggested range

Working with Formulas and Functions

8

Using Functions

argument for the selected text box. Excel has already suggested the range, using the cells containing data above the active cell. Notice that the range appears to the right of the argument text box, and the calculated result of the function appears at the bottom of the dialog box.

⑩ Click OK. Excel inserts the function into the cell.

Using Functions with Multiple Arguments

The AVERAGE function is relatively easy to use, especially when Excel suggests the correct argument, as in the previous example. The AVERAGE function you just used only took a single argument. To see a function with several arguments, you'll compute the payment amount for a 20–year, 5% mortgage for $50,000. The function is called PMT, for payment, and it includes three required and two optional arguments.

The required arguments refer to the mortgage rate, the number of payments to be made, and the amount of the loan. The optional arguments indicate whether there is any cash value at the end of the payments and whether payments are made at the beginning or end of each period.

❶ Click cell E31. The cell is next to the label "Mortgage Payments on New Building."

❷ Click the Paste Function button on the Standard toolbar. Excel displays the Paste Function dialog box. You can also select Insert ➢ Function.

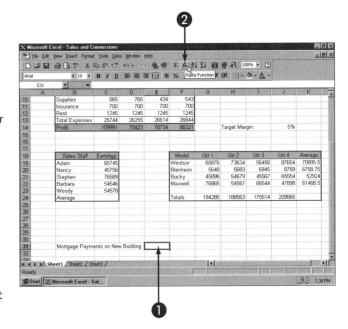

CHOOSING FUNCTIONS FROM THE NAME LIST

Another way to choose a recently used function is to use the name list. When you enter the equal sign to start a formula, the name list changes from a list of cell names to a list of functions. Pull down the name list to display the most recently used functions. Click the function you want

to use to insert it into the formula bar and to display the Function Palette. If the function you want to use is not shown, click More Functions to display the Paste Function dialog box.

---

③ Click Financial in the Function Category list. If you do not know which category the function is in, choose All.

④ Double-click PMT in the Function Name list. Excel opens the Formula Palette with the arguments for the PMT function. The insertion point is in the Rate argument.

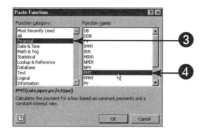

⑤ Type **5%/12**. This calculates the monthly interest on a 5% annual loan. The result is shown to the right of the text box. Nothing appears as the Formula Result because there are three required arguments.

⑥ Press Tab. The insertion point moves to the Nper (number of periods) argument.

⑦ Type **20*12**. This calculates the number of monthly payments — the result appears as 240.

⑧ Press Tab. The insertion point moves to the Pv (present value) argument.

⑨ Type **-50000**. Enter the value of the mortgage as a negative number. As you type in this argument, values appear to the right of Formula Result at the bottom of the Formula Palette.

⑩ Click OK. The results of the function appear in the cell.

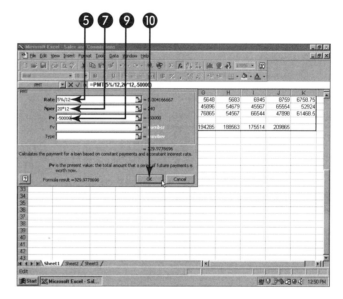

If you click Paste Function when the active cell already contains a function, Excel displays the Formula Palette.

NESTING FUNCTIONS

You can use a function as the argument of another function; this is called *nesting*. For example, the ROUNDUP function rounds a number up to a specified number of decimal places. If you want to round up the mortgage payments calculated by the PMT function to the next highest dollar amount, you'd enter the formula:

```
=ROUNDUP(PMT(5%/12,20*12,-50000),0)
```

Notice that the entire PMT function is one of the arguments of ROUNDUP. The other argument is the desired number of decimal places. There is also a function called ROUNDDOWN that rounds down a value, and a function called ROUND that rounds up or down depending on the value.

Using Functions

A FUNCTION REFERENCE

Excel includes hundreds of functions, ranging from the simple to the sublime. Functions such as AVERAGE and SUM are rather straightforward. Other functions require specialized financial or statistical knowledge. For example, although the PMT function was easy to use, you might need a more in-depth knowledge of finance to use the two optional arguments. There are also functions such as ATANH, which returns the inverse hyperbolic tangent of a number, and MINVERSE, which returns the inverse matrix for a matrix stored in an array. Needless to say, functions such as these require some specialized knowledge!

Excel's functions are divided into nine categories:

- Financial
- Date and Time
- Math and Trigonometry
- Statistical
- Lookup and Reference
- Database
- Text
- Logical
- Information

Let's take a look at the categories now, along with some functions that you might find useful.

■ Financial Functions

Financial functions perform financial calculations and operations, such as calculating accrued interest, the present value of an investment, and the yield to maturity of an investment.

Getting Help with Functions

Use the Excel Help system if you need detailed information about a function. Click the Help icon (the question mark button) in the Formula Palette to select help options from Office Assistant, or cruise the Help system using its contents and index features. Here's is a typical help window.

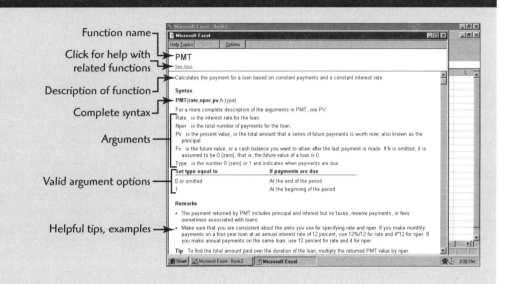

Function name

Click for help with related functions

Description of function

Complete syntax

Arguments

Valid argument options

Helpful tips, examples

Some of the arguments that you find include the number of payment periods, the amount of payments, rate of interest, and interval type. For example, the PMT function has two optional arguments — future value and type of payment. The type of payment argument indicates whether payments are made at the end or beginning of each period.

■ Date and Time Functions

Date and time functions perform calculations using dates, times, and days. For example, the formula =TODAY()-I23 calculates the number of days since the date in cell I23. The function TODAY() does not require any arguments, but you must still use the parentheses.

Statistical Functions

The function DATEVALUE converts a date string to its serial number, as in DATEVALUE("2/4/97"). Common arguments include a date string, a date, or time serial number. As explained in Lesson 1, Excel actually stores dates and times as serial values, so it can perform math on dates.

■ Math and Trigonometry Functions

Math and trigonometry functions perform simple and complex mathematical calculations, such as calculating the square root or rounding a value. In fact, you've already used a function in this category when you clicked the AutoSum button to insert the SUM function. This category also includes the RAND and RANDBETWEEN functions for generating random numbers. Use =RANDBETWEEN (1,100) to get a random number between 1 and 100. The RAND() function returns a random decimal number between 0 and 1.

Statistical Functions

Statistical functions perform statistical operations, such calculating the average and median of a range, the minimum or maximum value, or the standard deviation and variance.

Although the average is the statistical mean, the median return the number in the middle of a set of numbers. This means that half of the set has higher values and half has lower values. If the set has an even number of values, the function calculates the average of the two numbers in the middle. The numbers in the range do not have to be in order.

As an example of statistical functions, you'll make a major improvement to the Sales and Commissions workbook. The references in cells J4 and J5 refer to the highest and lowest commission figures. You entered information into these cells by looking at cells C19 to C23 to determine the highest and lowest values. If the values in these cells change, however, the items in J4 and J5 may no longer be valid. Rather than manually entering the new information into J4 and J5, you can use functions that will update the cells for you, automatically inserting the highest and lowest values:

Lookup and Reference Functions

1 Click cell J4.

2 Type **=MAX(C19:C23)**. This function displays the highest value in the range of cells.

3 Press Enter to reach cell J5.

4 Type **=MIN(C19:C23)**. This function displays the lowest value in the range of cells.

5 Click cell C23.

6 Type **4500**. The MIN function in cell J5 automatically updated the value for the new lowest amount in the range.

7 Close the workbook without saving it — a completed version is in the Solution folder under the name Sales and Commissions Solution.

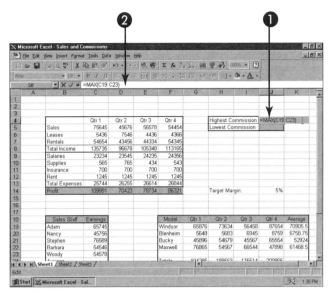

Lookup and Reference Functions

Lookup and reference functions let you find values in a range of cells. They are rather specialized, but the INDEX function, which locates a value based on the row and column, can be extremely useful in business applications.

To see its versatility in action, you'll use the function now to create a *lookup table*:

1 Open the Index workbook in the Exercise folder.

When preparing an invoice, the user must determine the correct shipping and handling charges — the intersection of the shipper being used (cells E8 to H8) and the zone where the package is being shipped to (cell D9 to D13). Rather than manually look for the intersection, you're going to use a function to find it for you by typing the shipper number in cell B3 and the zone in cell B4.

2 Click cell B3.

3 Type **3**. This represents the shipper number you want to locate in the table.

4 Click cell B4.

5 Type **2**. This represents the zone you want to locate in the table.

Lookup and Reference Functions

⑥ Select cells E9 to H13.

⑦ Click the name box.

⑧ Type **Charges** and press Enter. You've named the range so you can refer to it easily in the function.

⑨ Click cell B5.

⑩ Type **=INDEX(Charges,B4,B3)**. The arguments tell Excel to look at the range of cells defined by the name Charges, and to return the value for the zone in cell B4 and the shipper in cell B3. In this case, the charge is the value in cell G10.

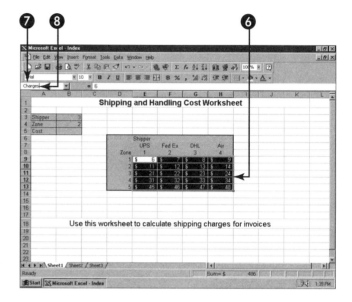

■ Database Functions

Database functions help analyze information in a range. All of the functions use the same three arguments: *database, field,* and *criteria.* The *database* argument is the range of cells that contains the values, *field* is where the data that you want to analyze is located, and *criteria* are cells that indicate conditions values have to meet to be included in the process.

■ Text Functions

The text functions perform operations on text rather than numbers. For example, the LEFT function returns a specified number of characters from the left side of a label. If cell A10 contains the phone number 609–345–0987, the function =LEFT(A10,3) returns the area code, and the function =RIGHT(A10, 8) returns the rest of the number (seven digits and one dash).

The CONCATENATE function combines two labels. If cell F4 contains Quarter 1 and cell F5 contains Profits, the function = CONCATENATE(F4,F5) returns the text Quarter 1 Profits.

■ Logical Functions

Logical functions return whether a condition is true or false. The functions are AND, FALSE, IF, NOT, OR, and TRUE . For instance, the function =AND(A1<50, B3=3) returns true if both the conditions are met — the value in cell A1 is less than 50 and the value in cell B3 is 3).

Lookup and Reference Functions

The most powerful of the logical functions is =IF. This function returns one value if a condition is true, another if the condition is false. The syntax is =IF(*condition, value-when-true, value-when-false*).

As an example, suppose you use a worksheet to prepare an invoice. If the order is over $500, you do not charge shipping. Otherwise, the shipping charge is 5% of the order amount. If the order amount were in cell G20, you would use this function to calculate the amount: =IF(G20>500,0,G20*5%)

■ Information Functions

Information functions let you determine the type of information in a cell. They can return the value in a cell, they can return a code indicating the type of value, and they can indicate whether the cell is blank or contains an error.

For example, the TYPE function lets you know what kind of entry is in a cell, returning a number using the codes shown in Table 8-1.

TABLE 8-1 CODES RETURNED BY TYPE FUNCTION

Entry	Returns
Number	1
Text	2
Logical value	4
Formula	8
Error	16
Array	64

For example, consider the nested function =IF(TYPE(C1)= 1,C1/2,"NA"). If the entry in cell C1 is a number, the function divides the number by 2. Otherwise, it inserts the characters "NA".

Skills Challenge

SKILLS CHALLENGE: CALCULATING DEPRECIATION USING FUNCTIONS

By using Excel's functions, you can create quite sophisticated worksheets. In this exercise, you'll create a depreciation table — just in time for tax season! — using the fixed-declining balance method. Don't know exactly what that is? It doesn't matter, but briefly, the fixed-declining method depreciates the bulk of the cost in earlier years, taking smaller depreciations on the remaining amounts in subsequent years. Excel makes it easy by providing a function. You'll also design the worksheet so it uses cell names so you won't have to enter absolute addresses.

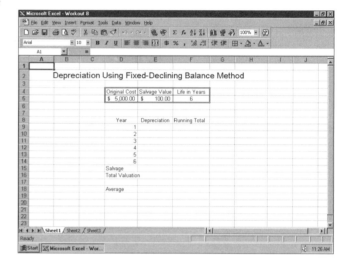

1 Open the Workout 8 workbook, shown in the illustration at right. Cell D5 contains the value of the item you are depreciating; cell E5 contains the salvage value; and cell F5 contains the number of years you are depreciating the item. The names for the other columns and row labels of the worksheet have already been created.

2 Use the Insert ➢ Name ➢ Create command to assign cell names to cells D5, E5, and F5.

 What cells do you have to select to assign these cell names?

3 Click cell E9 and use the Paste Function button to select the DB function from the Financial category. The Formula Palette for the function is shown at right. You want to enter the function once, and then copy it down the remaining cells in column E.

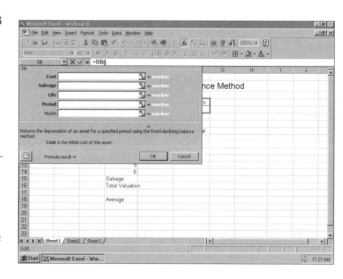

 How many required and optional arguments does the DB function have?

TIP

Because you always want to reference the same cells, enter the references to the Original Cost, Salvage Value, and Life in Years using their cell names. Remember, the cell name is the same as the column label above it but with underscore characters in place of spaces — as in Original_Cost.

4 Enter the reference to the cell containing the Original Cost using the cell's name.

TRY OUT THE

INTERACTIVE TUTORIALS

ON YOUR CD!

3 *How does Excel treat the spaces between words when it creates a cell name?*

5 Enter the reference to the cell containing the Salvage Value using the cell's name.

6 Enter the reference to the cell containing the Life in Years of the item using the cell's name.

7 In the Period text box, enter the reference to the cell containing the year. (Hint: The period is the label of the row in which you're placing the function, in this case cell D9. Use a relative address because you want the reference to change when you copy the function.)

8 Click OK, and then copy the function to the remaining cells.

 9 Enter the formulas in the Running Total column. (Hint: The running total is the depreciation in the current row plus the running total in the previous column. The first year has no previous running total, so simply enter the address of the depreciation in the format =E9. The formula in the next row is =F9+E10, and so on.)

10 Enter the reference to the Salvage Value in cell F15. Apply the Currency format.

4 *Can you use either a name or cell address for the reference?*

11 Enter the sum of the total depreciation and the Salvage Value in cell F16.

12 Enter the average periodic depreciation in cell E18.

The final worksheet is shown at right. You'll find a copy of the completed workbook, called Solution 9, in the Solutions folder of the CD. Check your own work against this workbook if you run into difficulty.

8

Working with Formulas and Functions

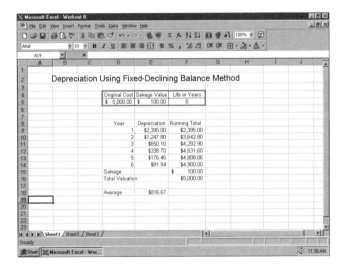

Troubleshooting

TROUBLESHOOTING

As you use labels and names, and add formulas and functions to your worksheets, you have to pay attention to the details. Minor errors can lead to major mistakes, and it can be frustrating to use Excel's more complex functions. Check out these handy tips if you have problems applying these techniques to your own work.

Problem	Solution
I'm using cell names but my formulas are coming out wrong.	Remember that label ranges and cell names are not the same. When you assign label ranges, the resulting labels are treated as relative addresses. When you use cells name, however, they are treated as absolute addresses. Make sure you use the correct one for the task you are performing. For example, if you want to copy cells using the AutoFill handle, do not use cell names in the formula if you want the addresses to change relatively.
I get error messages when I use a function.	Excel requires you to use the proper number and type of arguments in functions. Although some arguments are optional, you must use the required ones in the proper order, and with the correct type of information. Use the Paste Function command and the Formula Palette to enter functions. Both give you cues to the arguments, and the Formula Palette even lets you enter arguments by pointing to cells.

Problem	Solution
The IF function just doesn't seem to work.	The IF function is powerful but it can be complex. First make sure that you are using the correct syntax, and that the IF condition is correct. With conditions such as =IF(C4–A1) make sure that rounding is not causing a problem when you have applied Currency or other styles. For example, two values can look the same on screen but the cells may actually contain slightly different information. A function may calculate the result as 5000.005 and display $5000.00. When compared to a cell that actually contains $5000.00, the condition will be false, even though they appear the same.

WRAP UP

You should use formulas and functions whenever possible in a worksheet so results are automatically recalculated when you change values. Using labels and names for cells and ranges of cells makes formulas easier to create and troubleshoot. Take advantage of Excel's power by using these techniques that you learned in this lesson:

- Use column and row headers to quickly refer to cells in your worksheet.

- Use label ranges when you want to add labels to functions and formulas by pointing to cells.

- Label ranges are treated as relative references.

- Use cell names to apply custom names to cells — name the cells yourself or let Excel create them for you from labels.

- Cell names are treated as absolute addresses.

- Perform math easily using built-in functions.

Wrap Up

■ Use the Paste Function button and the Function Palette to add functions to your worksheet.

When you have time, practice using cell labels, and cell and range names, and functions in your worksheet. Open a workbook that you've already created and apply names. Take a look at the built-in functions, using either the Paste Function button or the Help system, to discover what functions are available.

Interested in exploring the Internet and the World Wide Web? In Lesson 9, you'll learn how to browse the Web from with Excel, create hyperlinks in your worksheet, and even publish your work to the Web.

Excel on the World Wide Web

2 HOURS

GOALS

In this lesson, you will learn how to access the Internet and the World Wide Web from Excel. You will learn how to:

- Browse and search the Web from within Excel
- Create hyperlinks on your worksheet
- Create links to data
- Publish worksheets to the Web

Get Ready

GET READY

You are not alone. There's a big, wide world out there and most of it is connected over the Internet through the World Wide Web. When you want to make the connection, there's no need to stop what you're doing in Excel. You launch your Web browser, go to a home page, and search the Web directly from Excel. You can even create links in your worksheet to access Web pages, and to open or use data from other worksheets. Have a worksheet to share with the world? Use Excel to publish the worksheet to the Web so the world can read it.

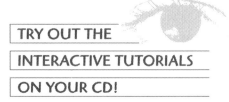
If you're unfamiliar with the Internet and the World Wide Web, pick up a good beginning book at any computer or book store. There are plenty to choose from.

This lesson refers to the following workbooks:

File Name	Location
Proposal	Exercise directory
Personnel	Exercise directory
Schedule	Exercise directory
Proposal Solution	Solution directory
Workout 9	Exercise directory
Solution 9	Solution directory

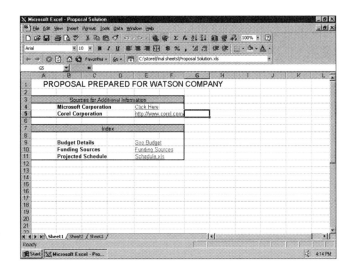

Refer to the workbooks Proposal Solution (shown here) and Solution 9 to check the results of your work. When you are done this lesson, you will have created the workbook shown to the right.

CONNECTING TO THE WORLD WIDE WEB

Easy access to the World Wide Web is built right into Excel, but you'll need to have a account set up with an Internet service provider (ISP) before taking advantage of it. Your account and Internet software must be set up and able to run before you can connect to the Web from within Excel.

There are many ways to connect to the Internet. You can have a *dial-up account* through an ISP such as AT&T WorldNet, Erol's, or a similar service. This means that to access the Internet, your system has to dial the phone and create a connection with the ISP before your Web browser is started. You can also connect to the Internet through your company network or intranet. This lesson discusses making the connection through a dial-up account. If you connect in some other way, consult your system or network administrator.

The Internet features of Excel are optimized to use the Microsoft Internet Explorer Web browser. In addition, the illustrations in this lesson, and the step-by-step exercises, were developed with Internet Explorer. Some of the features work just as well with Netscape Navigator — the other big name browser on the market — but if you're running Navigator you won't be able to use all of the techniques discussed in this lesson.

Web pages you see on your screen may be different than those illustrated on this book. The World Wide Web is constantly changing. Companies refine and change their Web pages, and options that are available one day may be gone the next. But even if your screen looks different that the ones shown in this lesson, the basic principles still apply.

■ The Web Toolbar

Excel and other Office 97 applications let you share information with the world through the Internet. To make it easy, Excel offers a special Web toolbar, shown in the following illustration, that lets you access the Web much as you can from Microsoft's Internet Explorer Web browser. The Web toolbar is similar to the toolbar in Microsoft's Internet Explorer, and provides access to the same resources. A bookmark or home page that you create using one toolbar will automatically be available in the other. Don't worry if some of this terminology is new to you — you'll learn all about bookmarks, home pages, and other Web features in this lesson. When you first display the Web toolbar, some of the buttons may be dimmed. These are features that aren't available until you connect to the Web.

To display the toolbar, use any of these techniques:

- Click the Web Toolbar button in the Standard toolbar.

- Right-click any toolbar and select Web from the shortcut menu.

- Click a hyperlink field.

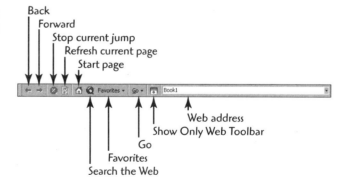

Back
Forward
Stop current jump
Refresh current page
Start page

Web address
Show Only Web Toolbar
Go
Favorites
Search the Web

Connecting to the Start Page

The toolbar buttons are explained in Table 9-1.

TABLE 9-1 WEB TOOLBAR BUTTONS

Toolbar Button	Purpose
Back	Returns to the previously open Web page
Forward	Moves forward to the page you were on before you used the Back command
Stop Current Jump	Stops retrieving the page being loaded into your computer
Refresh Current Page	Reloads the current page, retrieving the most recent version of the information at the site you are connected to
Start Page	Opens the designated home page
Search the Web	Opens a search page for locating information on the Internet
Favorites	Creates bookmarks and jumps to frequently used sites or documents
Go	Opens a specified site, and lets you change the start page and search page
Show Only Web Toolbar	Toggles the display of other toolbars
Address	Lists recently visited sites

Connecting to the Start Page

The start page (called the home page in some Web browsers) is the page that automatically appears when you first connect to the Web. To launch your Web browser and open the start page, click Start Page in the Web toolbar. Your start page depends on your system and on your Internet service provider. The default home page depends on how Internet Explorer was set up on your system. It may be one of Microsoft Corporation's Web sites — such as http//home.microsoft.com or http://www.msn.com/default.asp — or your ISP's main Web page.

Searching the Internet

If you have an ISP and your Internet software is all set up, try the Web toolbar now:

1 Start Excel.

2 Click the Web Toolbar button. The Web toolbar will appear just above the formula bar.

3 Click Start Page. If you have already connected to the Internet before this, your Web browser will appear with the start page displayed. If you have a dialup account, the Connect To dialog box appears, so continue with these steps.

4 Click Connect. Your browser dials the phone, connects to your Internet service provider, and then moves to the start page designated by your system.

5 Close the browser window and disconnect from your service.

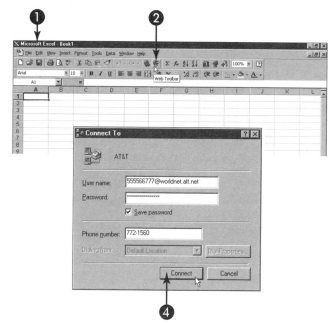

Searching the Internet

The search page is a Web page that lets you enter text and select a service for locating the text on the Internet. From within Excel, click the Search The Web button to open the page, launching your browser if it is not already open. The layout of the search page varies. The page gives you the option of choosing from the most popular search companies, searching the Microsoft Network, or the Microsoft Web site. Your search page may differ. If you're already working in Internet Explorer, click its Search button to access a search page:

1 Click Search the Web. If you are already connected to the Internet, your browser will jump to the search page. If the Connect To dialog box appears, click Connect. The search page appears after the connection is made.

2 In the text box for typing in search terms, type a word or phrase representing what you want to find.

3 Click the button for the search engine you want to use.

4 Click Search. Your request will be sent to the search company, and then a list of sites containing your search phrase appears. Each item in the list is a hyperlink, so click an item to jump to its site.

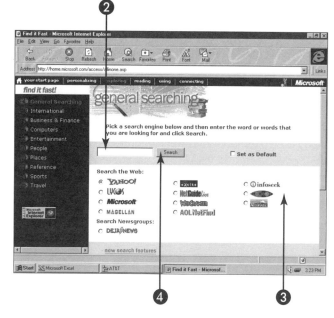

Changing Start and Search Pages

There are millions of Web pages on the Net, so don't be surprised if your search results in hundreds or even thousands of possible references. In many cases, a large percentage of the references will not be what you're looking for. To save time, refine your searches by entering a specific search phrase, and surround multiple words in quotation marks, such as searching for "Olympic National Park" rather than just the word *Olympic* or *Park*.

Each search company has its own syntax for refining searches, but most will interpret a phrase in quotation marks to mean that you're looking for all of the words in that order. You can also usually use a plus sign to indicate that a word must be in the site, such as +Olympic +Park to retrieve sites that contain both words, rather than one word or the other.

If your search results are not what you intended, look for links labeled Options or Help for more information about the search company you are using.

TIP

In your start page, the button to begin the search may be labeled Get it Now, Seek, or something else, but it's usually next to the text box where you enter your search phrase.

Changing Start and Search Pages

You can change the start and search pages to other Web sites. You can also designate an Excel workbook on your computer, the network, or the company intranet as the start page. Before changing your start or search pages, however, record the default pages that are being used. Although Internet Explorer will let you quickly restore the default start and search pages, not every Web browser is that accommodating.

From within Excel, you can change the start and search pages to the current document that you have open. This is useful if you want to quickly open a particular workbook, even if it is not on the Net. Here's how:

1 Open the workbook that you want to use for the start page or search page.

2 Display the Web toolbar.

3 Pull down the Go list.

4 Click Set Start Page or Set Search Page. A dialog box asks if you want to change your start or search page to the current page.

5 Click Yes.

To set the start or search page to a Web site, use Internet Explorer. This is the technique:

6 Launch Internet Explorer.

7 Select View ➢ Options.

8 Click the Navigation tab.

9 Pull down the Page list and select Start Page or Search Page.

10 If the page you want to use is open, click the Use Current button; otherwise, enter the site in the Address text box. Click Use Default to reinstate the default start or search pages for Internet Explorer and Excel.

11 Click OK.

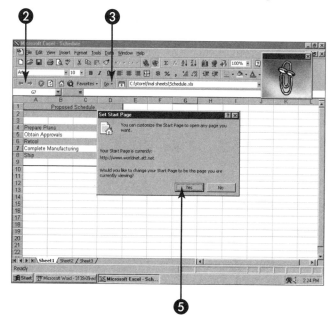

NOTE

If you have Netscape Navigator, you can also change your start page, but the process is different. From with the browser, pull down the Options menu and click General Preferences. Click the Appearance tab of the dialog box that appears, as shown in the illustration at right. In the Startup section, click the Home Page Location option button, and then enter the path of the start page in the text box.

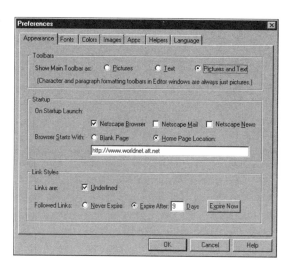

USING FAVORITES

When you find a site that you may want to return to, designate it as a favorite. (These are called bookmarks in some programs.) Excel saves a shortcut to the site in the Windows/Favorites folder on your hard drive. You can then jump directly to the site without having to type

Adding Favorite Web Sites

its Web address or surf through a series of other sites. You can also add a workbook to the Favorites list to make it easily accessible.

Excel and Internet Explorer share the same Favorites folder, so your sites and workbooks are just a click away in both programs.

Adding Favorite Web Sites

If you want to add a Web site to the Favorites folder so you can quickly reach it from Excel, you have do so within Internet Explorer. Use these steps:

1 Start Internet Explorer, connect to your ISP, and navigate to the site.

2 Pull down the Favorites list on the Internet Explorer toolbar.

3 Click Add to Favorites. You can also select Favorites ➤ Add to Favorites. The address of the current site will appear in the Add to Favorites dialog box. Your dialog box may have additional options, depending on the version of Internet Explorer you are using.

4 Click OK.

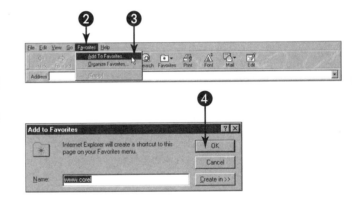

Your favorites may be organized into related folders. To store a site in a folder, click the Create In button in the Add to Favorites dialog box, click the folder in which to store the favorite, and then click OK.

When you want to jump to a favorite site, pull down the Favorites list in either Excel or Internet Explorer. A list of your recently added favorites will appear at the bottom of the menu, so just click the location you want to jump to.

TIP

Launching your Web browser and navigating the Internet from Excel takes a lot of Windows 95 resources. Don't be surprised if the unexpected occurs or you receive an error message. For example, if your workbook closes when you jump to a site on the Internet from within Excel, just reopen the workbook when you disconnect.

Adding Favorite Workbooks

If the favorite site isn't listed, you can choose it from the Favorites folder. To select a site from within Excel, pull down the Favorites list, select Open Favorites, and then double-click the site name. From within Internet Explorer, pull down the Favorites list and click Organize Favorites. Then select the site from the dialog box that appears.

Adding Favorite Workbooks

Do you have a workbook that you use often? You can add a workbook to the Favorites list so it is just a click away. The procedure is similar to adding a favorite site. You'll see the differences now by adding the workbook Proposal to the Favorites list:

1 Open the Proposal workbook from the Exercises folder.

2 If the Web toolbar is not on screen, click the Web Toolbar button.

3 Pull down the Favorites list in Excel.

4 Click Add to Favorites. Excel's Add To Favorites dialog box is similar to the Save As dialog box, except the Save As Type option is set to Internet Shortcuts, and the default folder is Favorites. The name of the open workbook appears in the File Name box, followed by its path using hyphens in place of backslashes, as shown here.

5 Click Add to add the shortcut to the folder.

6 Now close the workbook, so you can see how to use the Favorites list.

7 Pull down the Favorites list and click the workbook name.

Because Excel and Internet Explorer share the same Favorites list, you can also open the workbook while in the browser. Internet Explorer, however, opens the workbook into an "in-place window," as shown to the right. Notice that the window has the Excel menu bar, formula bar, and worksheet window, but the Internet Explorer toolbar. To display the Excel toolbars, click the Tools button, the rightmost button on the Internet Explorer toolbar.

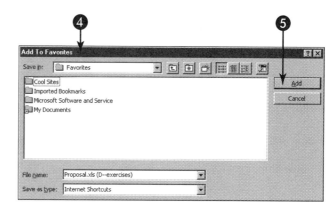

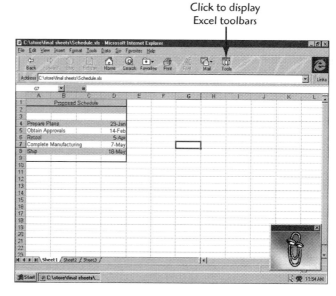

Click to display Excel toolbars

9

Excel on the World Wide Web

Hyperlinks

Using Netscape Navigator

Although Netscape Navigator looks different on screen than Internet Explorer, they have many elements in common. Here's a look at a typical Search page in Netscape Navigator 3.0.

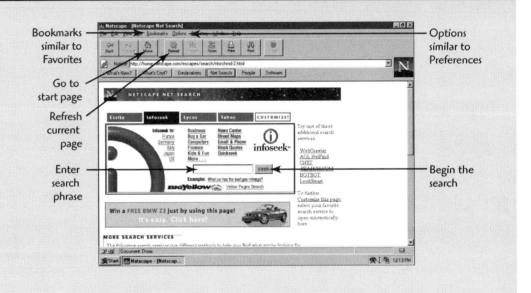

Bookmarks similar to Favorites

Go to start page

Refresh current page

Enter search phrase

Options similar to Preferences

Begin the search

HYPERLINKS

A *hyperlink* is a quick connection between your workbook and a site on the Web, a document or another workbook on your computer, the network, or the intranet. When you click a hyperlink, Excel automatically jumps to the Web page or opens the document.

The following illustration shows a good use for hyperlinks. The worksheet contains information about vendors. Column D contains hyperlinks to each manufacturer's Web site. Hyperlinks appear underlined in blue. If this was your worksheet, and you needed information about a product, you could just click the manufacturer's hyperlink to launch your Web browser (if it were not already running), connect to the Web, and open the site.

Creating Hyperlinks

The link in the worksheet can be any text, not necessarily the site address. In the previous illustration, for example, the links are displayed as "click here" messages. You may want to display the actual address itself, but most are rather long and, depending on the circumstances, might not appear in full. Web address can also be quite complex, and sometimes really do not indicate the actual contents of the site, so it is often useful to give links a more meaningful name.

To create a hyperlinks, just click the Insert Hyperlink button in the Standard toolbar and enter the link's address. Try it now:

❶ Open the Proposal workbook from the Exercise folder, if it is not already open.

❷ Click cell E4.

❸ Type **Click Here**. Remember, the hyperlink doesn't necessarily have to be the site address — any text will do. If you want the address to appear in the cell, however, leave the cell blank.

❹ Click the Enter button.

NOTE *You must be in Ready mode to create the link.*

❺ Click the Insert Hyperlink button in the Standard toolbar or select Insert ➢ Hyperlink. Excel displays the Insert Hyperlink dialog box.

❻ In the Link to File or URL text box, type this: **www.microsoft.com**. You can pull down the Link to File or URL list to see your most recently linked sites.

❼ Click OK. The text in the cells now appears as a link, underlined and in blue.

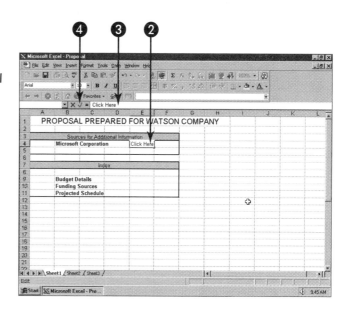

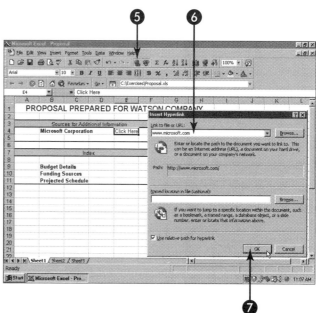

Excel on the World Wide Web — 9

Browsing for the Address

TIP

In case you're wondering, URL is short for uniform resource locator, and means an address for a Web site.

8 Point to cell E4. The mouse pointer looks like a hand and a ScreenTip appears with the address of the link. Notice that Excel adds http:// to the address — this is required to locate the site on the Web.

9 Click the hyperlink. Excel makes the connection, and opens the Web site.

NOTE

Remember, Excel's Internet features are designed and optimized for Microsoft Internet Explorer. If you are using Netscape Navigator or another Web browser, your system may behave differently than described here.

10 Disconnect from your service provider.

Browsing for the Address

Don't worry if you do not know the address of the site you want to add to the link. You can browse for the site on the Net, and Excel will insert the address into the Link to File or URL box for you.

Try it now:

1 Click cell E5. You'll leave the cell blank this time so the site address is used as the link text.

2 Click Insert Hyperlink. Excel displays the Insert Hyperlink dialog box.

3 Click Browse. Excel displays the Link to File dialog box, which you use to create a link to a workbook, to a site in the Favorites folder, or to another site on the Web. To insert the address of one of your favorites as the link, for example, navigate to the Windows/Favorites folder, and then double-click the site shortcut.

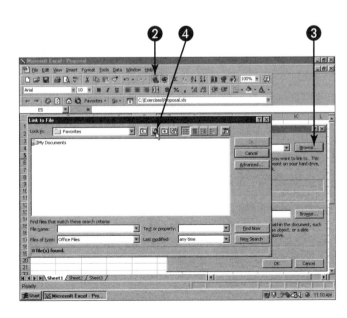

4 Click the Search the Web button. Excel launches your browser and connects to your search page.

5 Type a word or phrase that interests you, and then begin the search by clicking on the Search button (or its equivalent).

6 Surf the Web until you find an interesting Web site. The address of the first site you select is inserted into the Link to File or URL text box.

7 Drag over the text in the Internet Explorer address box.

8 Right-click the selected address and choose Copy from the shortcut menu.

9 Click Microsoft Excel in the Windows 95 taskbar to return to the Insert Hyperlink dialog box. If you're done surfing the Net, you can first disconnect from your Internet service provider.

10 If the address in the Link to File or URL box is not the correct one, drag over it and press Ctrl+V. Excel pastes in the copied address.

11 Click OK.

12 Click cell B5.

13 Enter the name of the company of the site you selected.

■ Changing a Link

Unlike other cell contents, you cannot click a hyperlink to edit it, since clicking jumps to the site of link immediately. To change the URL of a link, or the link text, first move to the cell with the keyboard; then press F2 or click the formula bar.

You can also work with hyperlinks by right-clicking the cell and choosing Hyperlink from the shortcut menu to see these options:

- **Open**: Jumps to the hyperlink, replacing the site currently in the browser if it is already open

- **Open in New Window**: Jumps to the site and opens it in a second window

Hyperlinking to Cells and Files

- **Copy Hyperlink**: Copies the hyperlink address to the Clipboard so you can paste it in another location

- **Add to Favorites**: Adds the hyperlink to the Favorites folder

- **Edit Hyperlink**: Displays the Edit Hyperlink dialog box, which is the same as Insert Hyperlink except for the title

- **Select Hyperlink**: Selects the hyperlink; this is just the same as moving to the link with the keyboard

LINKING TO WORKBOOKS AND WORKSHEETS

So far, you've used Web sites for hyperlinks. A hyperlink can also be to another workbook or a location in the current workbook. This type of link lets you move to a cell, sheet, or workbook with just a click.

You can also create a link to the data within a worksheet. This is not a hyperlink, but a link that establishes a connection between the two cells. Whatever is in the linked cell will appear in the cell containing the link.

Hyperlinking to Cells and Files

You can use the Insert Hyperlink command to create a hyperlink that moves to a location in the current workbook or to a related workbook. Use these type of links to quickly access other worksheets or workbooks. To create a link to a cell, either use the Edit ➤ Paste as Hyperlink command, or drag and drop the cell with the right mouse button. You'll experiment with both methods now:

1. Select cell B28.

2. Point to the border around cell B28 so the mouse pointer appears as an arrow.

3. Hold down the right mouse button and drag up to cell E9 and release the mouse button.

4. Select Create Hyperlink Here. The text in the dragged cell appears as a link.

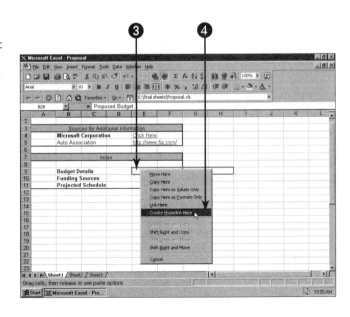

Hyperlinking to Cells and Files

5 Type **See Budget**. What you type replaces the text in the cell.

6 Press Enter.

7 Scroll down and click cell I28.

8 Click Copy.

9 Scroll up and click cell E10.

10 Select Edit ➤ Paste as Hyperlink. Excel creates a hyperlink in cell E10 that will take you to cell I28.

11 Click cell E10. Excel jumps to the linked position.

Remember, to drag and drop to another sheet, hold down the Alt key and point to the sheet tab.

To insert a hyperlink to another workbook, enter its name in the Insert Hyperlink dialog box. Do that now by creating a link to the workbook called Schedule in the Exercise folder:

12 Click cell E11.

13 Click the Insert Hyperlink button. Excel displays the Insert Hyperlink dialog box. The insertion point is in the Link to File or URL box.

14 Click Browse.

15 Pull down the Look In list and click the listing for your drive. The folders in the drive appear in the list box.

16 Double-click Exercise. A list of files in that folder appears.

17 Double-click Schedule. The name of the file appears in the Link to File or URL box. You can use the Named Location in File box to enter a named cell or range that you want to jump to when the workbook is opened.

18 Click OK.

19 Click cell B13. Excel opens the linked workbook.

20 Close the Schedule workbook, but leave the Proposal workbook open.

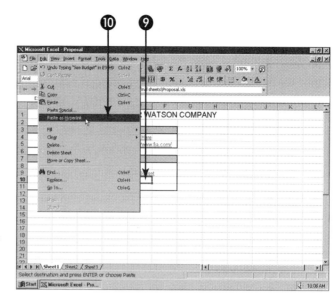

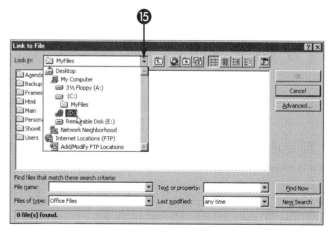

Excel on the World Wide Web — 9

Creating Data Links

NOTE

The Use Relative Path for Hyperlink check box in the Insert Hyperlink dialog box is on by default. If you do not enter the complete path of the file in the Link to File or URL box, Excel assumes the file is in the currently active directory. You can then move the file to another location that you plan to change to in Excel. If you clear this check box, the path is set to the exact location where the file was located when you created the link.

▶ Creating Data Links

Use a data link when you want to display information from one workbook into another. This is similar to paste linking a cell within a workbook, except the data is external, from another file on the disk.

For example, in the Proposal workbook, a key element of the proposal is the employee pay rate. Although the pay rate is shown in cell D32, it is based on the rate given in another workbook. If you later change the pay rate in that workbook, the value in Proposal is no longer accurate unless you change the pay rate there as well. If you link the value in cell D32 to the rate information in the other notebook, the proposal will always be up to date.

To link cells in one workbook to another, you use the Paste Link command. This inserts a link to the cells that are pasted. Here's how it works:

1. Open the Personnel workbook in the Exercise directory. As you learned in Lesson 6, the Proposal workbook moves into the background.

2. Click cell C11.

3. Click Copy.

4. Press Ctrl+F6 to change to the Proposal workbook.

5. Click cell D32.

6. Select Edit ➢ Paste Special.

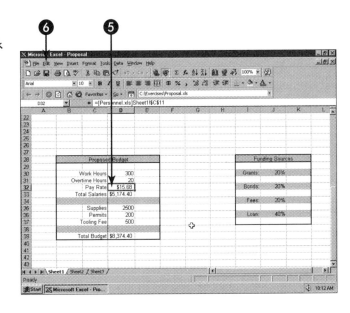

Updating a Data Link

7 Click the Paste Link button in the Paste Special dialog box. The workbook and worksheet name and the cell address appear in the formula bar. The value from cell C11 in the Personnel workbook appears in the cell. In the formula bar, you'll see the address of the cells including the workbook name and absolute reference to the cell — '[Personnel.xls]Sheet1'!$C$11.

8 Press Ctrl+F6 to change to the Personnel workbook.

9 Type **20.50** in cell C11.

10 Press Ctrl+F6 to change to the Proposal workbook. The value has changed in cell D32 in this workbook as well.

11 Press Ctrl+F6 to change to the Personnel workbook.

12 Close the Personnel workbook, leaving Proposal open.

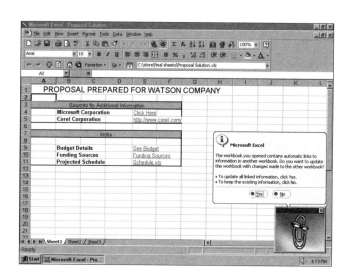

Updating a Data Link

Because both workbooks were open when you changed the linked information, it was updated in both locations at the same time. You do not have to open both workbooks, however, to ensure that the cell containing the link is up to date.

When you open a workbook that contains data links, even when the workbook containing the data is closed, you'll see a message like the one shown here. (If you do not have Office Assistant running, the message appears in a plain dialog box, but the options are the same.) Click Yes to update the link so the worksheet contains the most current information. Click No if you want to leave the worksheet as is, without updating the link.

By default, the links are set to update automatically, every time you open the file. However, if you've had the file open and another user changes the linked information on the network, the information may be out of date.

To update the links yourself, use this procedure:

1 Select Edit ➢ Links to see the dialog box shown in the illustration at right. It lists all of the links in the workbook.

2 Click the links you want to update.

3 Click Update Now.

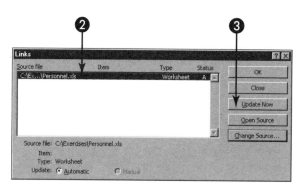

Installing the Internet Assistant

Use the Open Source button to open the workbook associated with the link, and use the Change Source button to link the cell with another location.

PUBLISHING WORKSHEETS ON THE WEB

When you want to share your worksheet with others, there's no better way than to publish it on the Web. Web documents are created using special instructions called HTML (Hypertext Markup Language) tags. These tags tell the Web browser how to format and display the information on screen.

Creating a Web page by writing the HTML tags can be a time-consuming and frustrating process. Fortunately, Excel does all of the work for you with the Internet Assistant.

Installing the Internet Assistant

First, check whether Internet Assistant is already installed on your system. Pull down the File menu and look for the item Save as HTML. If the item is on your menu, you're ready to go. If not, try this:

① Select Tools ➤ Add-Ins. This opens the Add-Ins dialog box.

② If there is a check box for Internet Assistant Wizard, click it.

③ Click OK.

If the Internet Assistant Add-In is not available, you have to add it to your installation:

④ Insert your Excel or Office CD into the drive.

⑤ Close all Office applications.

⑥ Click the Start button in the Windows taskbar.

⑦ Select Settings ➤ Control Panel.

⑧ Double-click Add/Remove Programs.

⑨ Click Excel 97 or Office 97.

⑩ Click Add/Remove. A dialog box appears telling you to insert the CD.

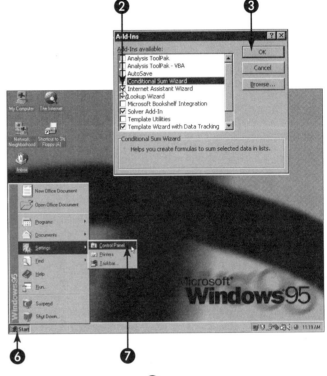

⑪ Click OK. The Setup dialog box appears.

⑫ Click Add/Remove.

⑬ If you installed Excel from the Office Suite CD, click Excel and then Change Option.

⑭ Click Add-In and then Change Option.

⑮ Click the Internet Assistant Wizard check box.

⑯ Click OK.

⑰ Click Continue.

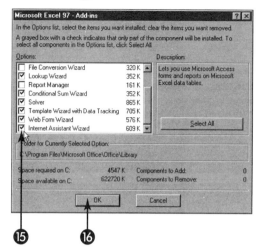

Creating Web Pages

Once the Internet Assistant add-in is installed, you're ready to create a Web page. The Internet Assistant uses a series of dialog boxes to take you step by step through converting your worksheet into an HTML document that you can display on the Web. You'll go through the steps now, assuming that you have Internet Assistant and a Web browser in your system. The Proposal workbook should still be open:

❶ Select cells A1 to H15. You can select cells after you start the Internet Assistant if you want.

❷ Select File ➤ Save as HTML. The first Internet Assistant dialog box appears. The selected range of cells appears in the list box. You can add additional ranges, remove them, and change their positions using the options in the dialog box.

❸ Click Next. The next dialog box offers two options. You can either create a new Web page complete with a header and footers, or you can add the range to an existing Web document. Accept the default and create a new page. To add the range to an existing Web page you have to know a bit about HTML.

❹ Click Next. Excel displays the third Internet Assistant dialog box. Here you enter information that you want to appear on the page. By default, the title of the page is the name of the workbook, and the header is the name of the worksheet. You can change these as desired.

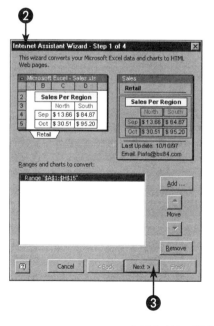

Creating Web Pages

Creating a Web page in HTML format is just the first step in making your worksheet available on the Internet. To allow access to your page, you have to upload the HTML pages to your Web server.

If you manage your own Web site, this means copying the HTML pages to a specific folder on your network or on the hard disk. Check with your system administrator for information on adding the file to your own Web page.

If you connect to the Web through an Internet service provider, find out whether it gives you space on its system for personal Web pages. Most do, including America

Online, CompuServe, Prodigy, and AT&T WorldNet. The specific steps involved in uploading your Web page varies, so consult your ISP for details.

For example, America Online makes available a number of Web publishing tools that help you design a Web page and upload it to the system. You can download the tools from America Online for free. CompuServe offers a similar program, called the Publishing Wizard. Chances are that your ISP has detailed instructions explaining how to publish your HTML pages to your personal Web site.

5 Click the box labeled Description Below Header. The description will appear under the header, as illustrated in the dialog box.

6 Type this: **Watson Company Proposal**.

7 Click the two check boxes to insert horizontal lines above and below the worksheet data. Excel fills in the Last Update On and By text boxes using the information about the worksheet. If you want the browser to send you e-mail, click the Email box and enter your e-mail address.

8 Click Next. The final dialog box offers some options for more advanced users that you don't have to be concerned with here.

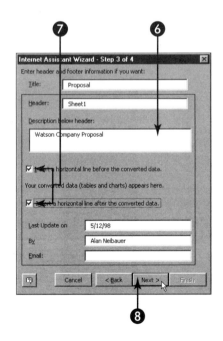

9 Click Finish. The Web page is saved in your current directory with the name MyHTML.htm.

You can now display the HTML page in your browser using the File ➤ Open command. The illustration at right shows a completed HTML file in Internet Explorer.

SKILLS CHALLENGE: CREATING LINKS TO THE WEB

The unlimited resources of the Web make it fertile ground to expand your knowledge and exercise your imagination. In this workout, you'll have the opportunity to surf the Net to locate sources of information and software. You will also create a data link with a cell in another worksheet:

1 Open the Workout 9 workbook, shown in the bottom illustration at right.

2 Display the Web toolbar if it's not already on screen.

3 Use the Web toolbar to connect to the start page.

What start page is used by your system, and will everyone's start page be the same?

4 Click cell H6, and then insert a hyperlink to the site www.microsoft.com.

Do you have to type the http:// designation for a URL when creating a hyperlink?

5 Change the text of the hyperlink in cell H6 to **Connect to Microsoft.**

6 Add a hyperlink to the Hewlett Packard Corporation Web page in cell H9.

How do you find an address if you do not know what it is?

7 Change the text of the hyperlink in cell H9 to **Connect to HP**.

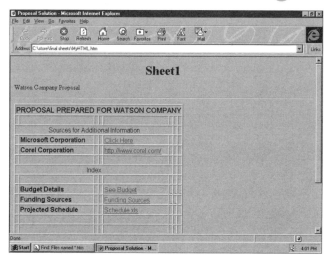

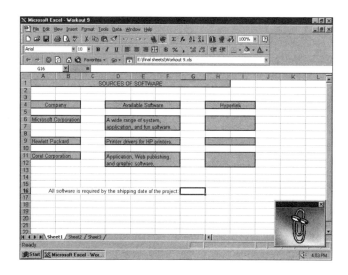

Troubleshooting

 Add a hyperlink to the Corel Corporation Web page in cell H11.

 4 *What is the address of the Corel Corporation's main site?*

TRY OUT THE
INTERACTIVE TUTORIALS
ON YOUR CD!

9 Add the Corel Corporation Web site to your Favorites list.

10 Change the text of the hyperlink in cell H11 to **Connect to Corel**.

11 In cell G16, add a data link to cell D8 in the first sheet of the Schedule workbook that you'll find in the Exercises directory.

4 *What value appears in cell G16 and what address appears in the formula bar?*

12 Test the hyperlinks by moving to the Hewlett Packard Web site.

13 Test the data link by changing the value in cell D8 of the Schedule workbook to June 10.

 5 *Was the change reflected in Workout 9 and, if so, why?*

TROUBLESHOOTING

It is easy to get enamored with the Web, but before you get lost in the Internet check out these troubleshooting tips.

Problem	Solution
I'm using the browse feature but no site, or the wrong Web site, is inserted into the hyperlink.	To make sure the link is correct, select and copy the address in the location text box of your browser. When you return to the Hyperlink dialog box, press Ctrl+V to insert the address into the box. You cannot use the Paste button or the Edit menu to paste the text.

Problem	Solution
I'm getting error messages when I try to open a document that has data links.	Make sure that the workbook containing the linked data is still on your disk, and in the same location it was in when you created the link. If you moved the workbook, you'll have to reestablish the link. You can do this by using the Edit ➤ Links command, clicking the link in the Links dialog box, and then using the Change Source command to choose the workbook in its new location.
I don't have Internet Explorer. Now what?	If you have another Web browser, it may be registered in Windows 95 to handle Internet shortcuts, and it will probably open automatically. Remember, Excel's Internet features are optimized for Internet Explorer. Some of the features illustrated in this lesson may not be available with other browsers, and some of the techniques may not work at all. If you have difficulty launching or working with your browser from within Excel, just switch to the Windows 95 desktop and launch the browser as you would normally.
My start page and search page are nothing like what's described here. What's the story?	If you set up your browser as part of a package from an ISP, such as AT&T WorldNet, your start page and search page are determined by the ISP. Many service providers have their own pages, custom designed just for them. You may even see a custom set of toolbar buttons on the browser window.

9

Excel on the World Wide Web

Wrap Up

WRAP UP

There's a lot to the Web, so don't be frustrated if it at first seems overwhelming, especially if you are using Excel with Netscape Navigator. In this lesson, you learned how to use Excel to access the Web. Among other things, you discovered how to:

- Display the Web toolbar when you want to access the Web from Excel.

- Set your start page and search page to the sites you want. (Excel and Internet Explorer share a common start page and search page.)

- Mark Web pages and Excel workbooks as favorites so you can return to them easily. (Excel and Internet Explorer share a common set of favorites.)

- Add hyperlinks to access Web sites from within workbooks. Hyperlinks can also access other workbooks.

- Use data links to link information between workbooks.

- Use Internet Assistant to publish a workbook to the Web.

Try out Internet Assistant with various workbooks, experimenting with Internet Assistant options. Build a worksheet that serves as an index to the sites you use most often. Have fun with Excel and the Web.

Now that you've created some attractive-looking workbooks on screen, it's time to improve their appearance when printed. In Lesson 10, you learn how to set up pages for printing. Among other things, you find out how to include headers and footers, repeating rows or columns on each page, and more!

PART IV

Organizing and Customizing Excel

This part shows you how to create attractive printouts, find and sort information, and customize Excel to suit the way you like to work. It includes the following lessons:

- Lesson 10: Arranging and Printing Worksheets
- Lesson 11: Finding and Arranging Information
- Lesson 12: Customizing Excel

Arranging and Printing Worksheets

GOALS

In this lesson, you will learn how to format the printed appearance of your worksheet. You will learn how to:

- Determine where pages end by inserting and changing page breaks
- Set and remove print areas
- Create headers and footers
- Repeat rows or columns on every page
- Change the size of your printouts
- Choose what other elements print with the worksheet
- Determine the order of printed sheets

Get Ready

GET READY

So far, you've been dealing with worksheets on the screen. In this lesson, however, you'll concentrate on printing worksheets for maximum impact.

The lesson refers to the following workbooks:

File Name	Location
Sales Statistics	Exercise directory
Sales Statistics Solution	Solution directory
Workout 10	Exercise directory
Solution 10	Solution directory

Refer to the workbooks Sales Statistics Solution and Solution 10 to check your own work, or in case you run into difficulty with the exercises or challenges.

When you are done with this lesson, you will have created the workbook shown to the right. (Because this entire worksheet is shown in Print Preview, you get a good sense of its overall layout but may not be able to see the details. When you're viewing a worksheet this way, remember that you can click the Zoom button in Print Preview to get a more closeup view of your worksheet.)

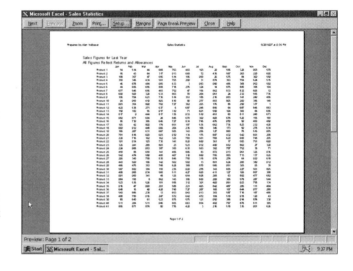

PRINTING WORKSHEETS

When you click the Print button in the Standard toolbar, Excel prints your worksheet automatically, using its default printing settings. It prints everything from cell A1 to the last cell containing information.

You can select what to print, and how to print it, however, using the Print dialog box. The dialog box appears when you choose Print from the File menu. When you do so, the worksheet is not printed immediately; instead the dialog box appears and you can set print options.

TRY OUT THE

INTERACTIVE TUTORIALS

ON YOUR CD!

■ Specifying What to Print

Take a look at the Print dialog box, shown in the illustration at right. In addition to the All option in the Print Range section, you can choose to print a specific range of pages. Enter the number of the first page you want to print in the From text box, and the last page in the To text box. Making an entry in either or both will automatically select the Page(s) option button. To print a single page, enter the number of the page you want to print in both boxes.

Use the options in the Print What section to specify how much is printed. Choose Selection to print just the selected cells. Choose Active Sheet(s) to print only the selected sheets, and select Entire Notebook to print every sheet that contains data.

To print more then one copy of the worksheet, increment the Number of Copies setting. You can also specify whether to collate the pages of the worksheet. When the Collate check box is selected, for example, Excel prints one complete set of pages of the worksheet, and then prints another complete set, and so on. If you deselect the Collate box, the Copies area changes to look like the second illustration at right.

Excel will now print all copies of the first page, then all copies of the second, and so on.

Enter page range here

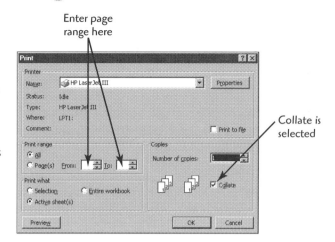

Collate is selected

Collate is not selected

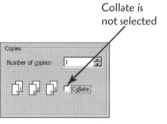

Establishing a Print Area

If you do not want to print the entire worksheet, you can establish a *print area* — a designated range of cells that Excel prints automatically when you print the worksheet. This saves you the trouble of selecting cells first, and then choosing the Selection option in the Print dialog box. Here's how:

❶ Open the Sales Statistics workbook in the Exercise folder.

❷ Select cells A1 to H13.

❸ Select File ➢ Print Area ➢ Set Print Area.

❹ Click to deselect the cells. Excel displays a dashed line around the cells indicating the print area.

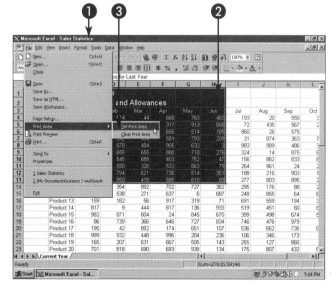

10

Arranging and Printing Worksheets

Establishing a Print Area

5 Click Print Preview. Only the selected cells appear on the preview window, and only that range will print. When you display the Print dialog box, the All option will still be selected in the Print Range section but only the print area will actually print.

TIP *You can designate a different print area for each sheet of the workbook.*

6 Click Close to close the Print Preview screen.

7 Select cells B3 to J17.

8 Select File ➢ Print Area ➢ Set Print Area. You can only designate one print area in a worksheet at a time. This new print area replaces the one you set previously. You can confirm this, if you want, by switching to Print Preview.

9 Select File ➢ Print Area ➢ Clear Print Area. The lines around the print area are removed, and now the entire worksheet will print.

WORKING WITH PAGE BREAKS

When you print a large worksheet, Excel divides it into pages, showing dotted page break lines on screen. You can see where the pages will be divided in Print Preview before you print the worksheet. If you don't like where Excel divides the pages, you can set your own page breaks. In fact, Excel offers two ways — using the Insert menu or Page Break Preview.

There is a difference, however, between the page breaks that Excel inserts automatically and the breaks that you add yourself. Excel's page breaks are *soft breaks*. This means that the information that prints on a page will change as you insert and delete rows or columns. For example, suppose the information in row 52 appears just under a page break that Excel has inserted. If you delete a row above the page break, the rows are renumbered, and the information that was in row 52 now prints above the break.

5 Print area

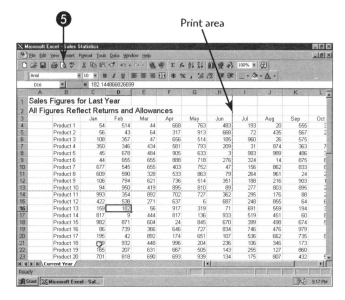

9

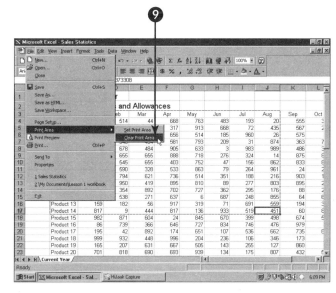

Inserting Page Breaks

Page breaks that you add yourself are *hard breaks*. This means that the break will always occur at that position of the worksheet, regardless of how many rows or columns you delete or insert. Using the previous example, suppose you add a page break just before row 52. The information in that row will now always start at the top of a new page, even if you delete rows above the page break position.

Inserting Page Breaks

Changing page breaks lets you control what rows and columns print on each page of the printout, so you can insert either a vertical or horizontal page break, or both. A vertical page break is one that divides columns across pages, displaying a vertical line down the worksheet. A horizontal page break divides rows across pages, displaying a horizontal line across the worksheet.

For example, suppose you want to print the first 20 rows on one page, and the remaining rows on additional pages. You need to insert a horizontal page break. Here's how to create one:

1 Click cell A21. When inserting a horizontal page break, you should activate the cell in column A that you want to be in the first row on the next page.

2 Select Insert ➤ Page Break. Excel inserts the page break line between rows 20 and 21, so row 21 begins a new page.

3 Select Insert ➤ Remove Page Break. Excel eliminates the page break. To remove a horizontal page break, you must be in the row immediately under the page break line.

Now, suppose you want to print the first four columns on one page. You need to insert a vertical page break:

4 Click cell E1. When inserting a vertical page break, you should activate a cell in row 1 in the column that you want to be the first column on the new page.

5 Select Insert ➤ Page Break. Excel inserts the page break line between columns D and E.

6 Select Insert ➤ Remove Page Break. Excel deletes the page break. To remove a vertical page break, you must be in a cell in the column just to the right of the page break.

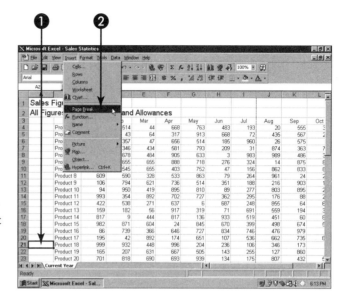

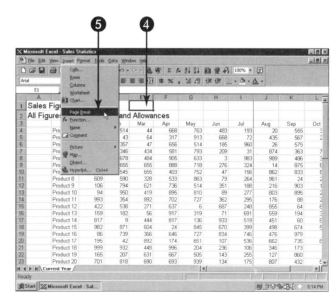

10

Arranging and Printing Worksheets

Using Page Break Preview

To insert both horizontal and vertical page breaks at one time, activate a cell that's not in column A or row 1. Activate the cell that you want to be in the upper-left corner of the new page. For example, to print cells A1 to F14 on one page, click cell G15, and then select Insert ➢ Page Break. You must select the same cell to remove both page breaks at the same time. To remove just the horizontal or vertical breaks, select a cell immediately under or to the right of the break line.

Using Page Break Preview

For even more control over how the worksheet is divided into pages, and to adjust page breaks visually, use the Page Break Preview mode. Unlike Print Preview, Page Break Preview is a "live" view of the worksheet. This means that it lets you edit, type, and format the sheet, as well as adjust the position of page breaks.

Try it now:

1 Select View ➢ Page Break Preview. You can also click Print Preview, and then click the Page Break Preview button. A message reports that you can adjust the position of page breaks by dragging them with the mouse.

2 Click OK to clear the message. In this mode, in addition to showing page break lines, Excel marks the number of each page, as shown in the accompanying illustration.

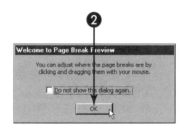

The solid dark lines indicate the end of the printable portion of the worksheet; the dashed lines indicate the automatic page breaks inserted by Excel. The nonprinting areas of the worksheet are shown in gray. The size of the page number indicators — shown in gray on the page — indicate how full the page is.

To change a page break, just drag the break line. Next you'll divide the columns more evenly between page 1 and 3:

3 Move cursor between the headers for columns I and J.

④ Drag the dashed line until it is between columns G and H.

NOTE

After you move a dashed line, it becomes solid, indicating that has been set manually and is now a hard page break. You can also drag the solid lines at the end of the printable areas to adjust their page break position. If you decide you don't like where you set a page break, just drag it back.

⑤ Now divide the rows between pages more evenly. Scroll down until you see the dashed page break line under row 49.

⑥ Drag the line up until it's just under row 32. Notice that the page number indicators are all the same size, indicating that each page now contains approximately the same amount of information.

⑦ To return the worksheets to the default automatic page breaks, right-click the worksheet and select Reset All Page Breaks from the shortcut menu.

You can also insert a page break manually. Instead of using the Insert menu, right-click the cell where you want the break to appear, and then select Insert Page Break from the shortcut menu. Delete a page break by right-clicking the cell below or to the right of the page break line and selecting Remove Page Break from the shortcut menu.

In Page Break Preview, you can also set and clear the print area using the shortcut menu. Select the cells that you want to print, and then right-click the selection and choose Set Print Area from the shortcut menu. All of the cells, except for those selected, will become gray. Clear the print area by right-clicking and choosing Reset Print Area.

To exit Page Break Preview, select View ➢ Normal.

SETTING UP THE PAGE

Now that you know all of the ways to print worksheets, you can concentrate on arranging your worksheets to look good. You can

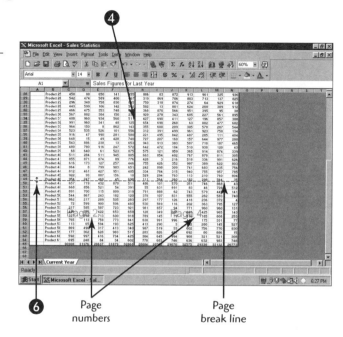

Page numbers

Page break line

Setting Page Options

adjust the margins, size, and orientation of the printed page, change the size of the printout, and create titles, headers, and footers.

For complete control over the layout of your page, use the Page Setup dialog box shown in the illustration at right. Display the dialog box now using any of these techniques:

- Select File ➤ Page Setup.
- Select View ➤ Header and Footer.
- In Print Preview, click the Page Setup button.
- In Page Break Preview, right-click and select Page Setup from the shortcut menu.

The dialog box has four tabs, so you'll look at them one at a time.

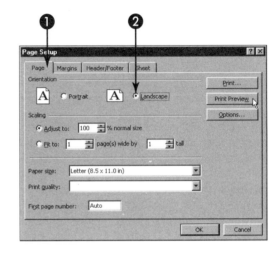

▶ Setting Page Options

The Page tab of the Page Setup dialog box lets you change the size and orientation of the printed page, the print quality, and the print scale.

Use the Paper Size list to select the size of the page, and use the Print Quality list to select the resolution. The options available in these lists are determined by the printer Windows is using.

Select either Landscape or Portrait under Orientation. In portrait (vertical) orientation, the rows of the worksheet print across the narrower side of the page. In landscape (horizontal) orientation, the rows print sideways down the wide part of the page. Portrait is the default orientation, but printing in landscape is a good way to fit more columns on a page, although with fewer rows:

❶ Click the Page tab if it is not already displayed.

❷ Click Landscape.

❸ Click Print Preview. The worksheet is now arranged across the length of the sheet, as shown to the right.

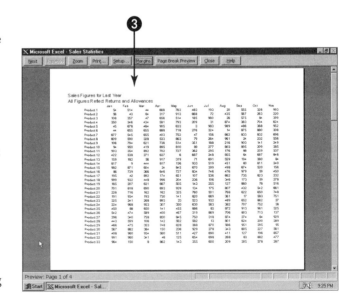

Use the First Page Number box if you want the page numbering to start with something other than 1 for the first page. You'll learn more about page numbering in the sections on headers and footers later in this lesson.

Setting Margins

The Scaling section determines the size of the printout. Use these options if you want to reduce the entire printout to fit into a smaller area, or if you want to expand it to fill more sheets. To squeeze more on the page, reduce the value in the Adjust to box to something less than 100% normal size. If you want a worksheet to fill a specific number of pages, click Fit To, and enter the numbers in the two text boxes next to that option.

For example, in landscape orientation, all but one column fits on the page. Moving the columns over would reduce the worksheet from 4 pages to 2 pages:

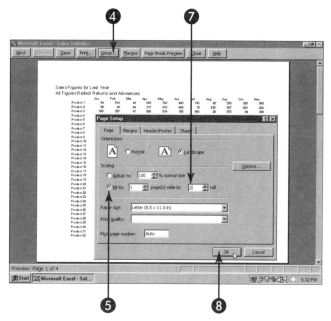

4 Click Setup in the Print Preview toolbar.

5 Click Fit To.

6 Press Tab to select the text box next to the Tall option.

7 Type **2** in the list box.

8 Click OK.

9 If the first page of the worksheet does not appear, click Previous. Now all of the columns fit on the page.

Setting Margins

Use the Margins tab of the Page Setup dialog box to set the page margins and the distance between headers and footers and the edge of the page.

When you click one of the a text boxes, such as Top, the margin being affected is indicated by a darker line with small triangles on either side.

You can also center the worksheet vertically or horizontally on the page, or both. Selecting Vertically, for example, centers the worksheet between the top and bottom margins. Centering only has an effect when the worksheet does not fill the entire page:

Margin affected

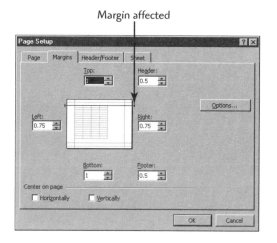

Setting Margins

1. You should still be in Print Preview, so click Setup to display the Page Setup dialog box.

2. Click the Margins tab.

3. Click Horizontally. The sample page adjusts to show the worksheet centered between the left and right margins.

4. Click Vertically. The sample page shows the worksheet centered between the top and bottom margins.

5. Click OK to return to Print Preview.

6. Click Next. The second page of the worksheet is now centered on the page.

7. Click Close to return to the worksheet in Normal view.

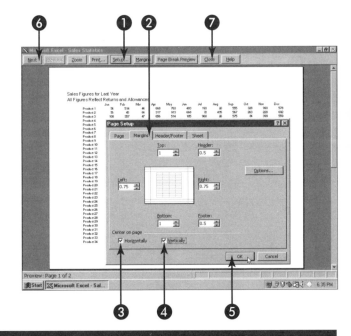

Changing Page Layout in Print Preview

You can also change the margins and column widths in Print Preview. Click the Margin button to display margin and column indicators, as shown here. Drag a dotted line to change the margin size or header or footer area. Drag column boundaries to change the width of columns.

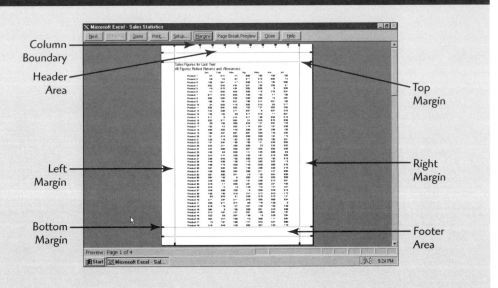

Column Boundary

Header Area

Left Margin

Bottom Margin

Top Margin

Right Margin

Footer Area

Selecting Standard Headers and Footers

Headers and footers help identify the pages of your worksheet, and can be invaluable if multiple pages become separated. By default, headers print a half-inch from the top of the page; footers print a half-inch from the bottom. You can change the starting position of headers and footers in the Margins tab of the Page Setup dialog box, or by dragging their lines in Print Preview. Although Excel sets aside a half-inch for headers and footers, you can create larger headers and footers and Excel will show fewer rows on the page.

Headers and footers do not appear on screen in Normal view or in Page Break Preview. To see headers and footers, display the worksheet in Print Preview:

1 Select View ➤ Header and Footer. This opens the Page Setup dialog box with the Header/Footer tab in front.

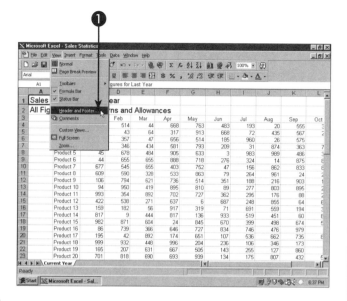

NOTE

To select from some standard headers, pull down the Header list. Standard headers include combinations of page numbers, your name and date, sheet numbers, and workbook name. You can also select from a similar set of standard footers by pulling down the Footer list.

2 Pull down the Header list.

3 Scroll through the list and select the item that contains your full name (or the name of the registered user), the page number, and the date. The sample panel shows how the header appears across the page, as shown to the right.

4 Pull down the Footer list, and select the name of the workbook. The workbook name appears centered.

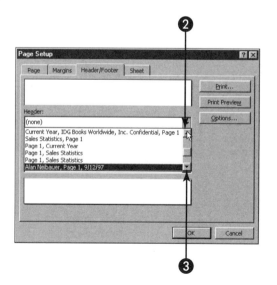

Creating Custom Headers and Footers

If none of the standard headers or footers are appropriate, create a custom header or footer. You can start with one of the standard headers or footers and then modify it, or you can select None in the Header or Footer list to start from scratch:

10

Arranging and Printing Worksheets

Creating Custom Headers and Footers

1 Click Custom Header. Excel displays a dialog box that shows the text from the selected standard header. Use the buttons in the dialog box to change the font, and to add other elements to the text.

You can customize three sections: Left, Center, and Right. Each section represents where the text will be positioned on the page. The text in the Left section is currently selected.

2 Press the Home key to deselect the text and move the insertion point to the left edge of the Left section.

3 Type **Prepared by**, and then press the spacebar.

4 Press Tab to reach the Center section. The notation &[Page] tells Excel to print the page number in the header. You'll change the section to display the workbook name.

5 Delete the text in the Center section.

6 Click the Workbook Name button. Excel inserts the notation &[File], which represents the workbook name.

7 Press Tab to reach the Right section. You want to add the time to this section of the header.

8 Press End to reach the end of the text in the section.

9 Press the spacebar.

10 Type **at** and press the spacebar.

11 Click the Time button.

12 Click OK to return to the Page Setup dialog box.

13 Click Print Preview to see the new header. (You can click the header to magnify it if you want a better view of the text.)

Font Page number Numbers of pages Date Time Workbook name Worksheet tab name

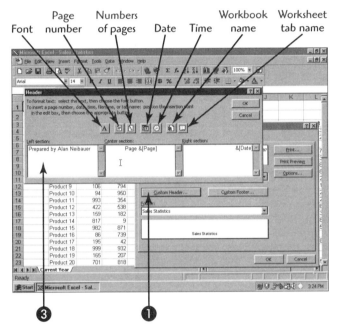

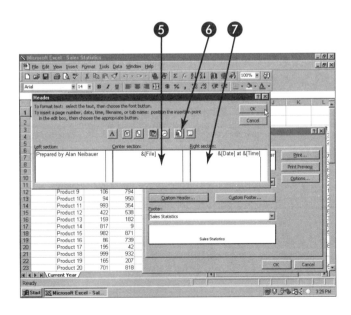

Setting Sheet Options

Finally, you'll change the footer so it just contains the page number and total number of pages:

⑭ Click Setup.

⑮ Pull down the Footer list and select Page 1 of ?.

⑯ Click OK.

⑰ Click Close to return to Normal view.

⑱ Print the worksheet.

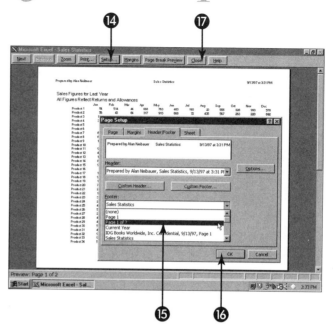

Setting Sheet Options

The Sheet tab of the Page Setup dialog box, shown in the following illustration, lets you control what gets printed on the page, as well as the order in which pages are printed.

Print titles, for example, are rows or columns that print on every page of the worksheet. For instance, the Sales Statistics workbook will now print on two pages, in landscape orientation. However, the worksheet title in rows 1 and 2, and the months in row 3, will only print on the first page. If the second page gets separated from the first, the user will not have the month names to reference each column. (And even if the pages don't get separated, it can be distracting to have to flip back to the first page for the identifying month and product names.) If you tell the user to look at the figures for June, for example, he or she would have to count over to the sixth column of figures. To solve this problem, you can designate the first three rows as print titles.

The options in the Print section of the dialog box determine some features about the overall look of the printout:

- **Gridlines**: Prints the normally nonprinting grid lines that you see on the screen. The grid lines between cells print as dotted lined.

- **Black and White**: Ignores colors that you've selected for text, printing everything in black. Use this option if you do not have a color printer, or if you want to print in black on a color printer to save time (and color ink!).

Setting Sheet Options

- **Draft Quality**: Speeds up printing by not printing the custom borders that you've entered and most graphics.

- **Row and Columns Headings**: Prints the row numbers and column letters along with the worksheet. This option is useful to help you later reference cells on screen.

- **Comments**: Lets you select not to print the comments that may appear on screen or to print them in a group at the end of the worksheet.

You'll look at these options now by setting print titles:

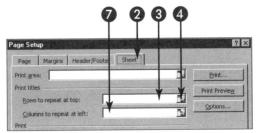

1. Select File ➢ Page Setup.

2. Click the Sheet tab. If you select Setup from Print Preview, some of the options in this dialog box will be dimmed.

3. Click the Rows to Repeat at Top text box.

4. Click the Collapse Dialog button to the right of this text box.

5. Drag over the row headers for rows 1 to 3. The notation $1:$3 appears in the collapsed dialog box, indicating that these rows are print titles.

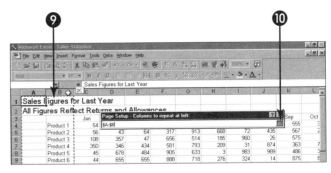

6. Click the Expand Dialog button at the right end of the collapsed dialog box.

7. Click the Columns to Repeat at Left text box.

8. Click its Collapse Dialog button.

9. Drag over the column headers for columns A and B.

10. Click the Expand Dialog button.

11. Click Print Preview to see the first page of the worksheet.

12. Click Next to see the next page. Notice that the rows and columns designated as print titles appear on that page as well.

13. Click Close.

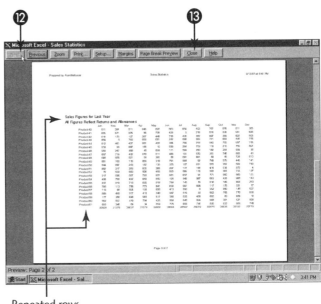

Repeated rows and columns

SETTING THE PAGE ORDER

The Page Order options determine how the pages of the worksheet are numbered. By default, a large worksheet is printed Down, Then Over. The first page (page 1) contains as many rows and column as can fit. The second page (page 2) contains additional rows of the same columns. The remaining pages are printed until all of the rows have been printed. Then, Excel returns to the top of the worksheet and begins printing the columns that would not fit on the first set of pages.

You can also select to print the worksheet Over, Then Down. Now the second page (page 2) contains additional columns of the same rows as the first page. The remaining pages are printed until all of the columns have been printed. Then, Excel returns to the left edge of the worksheet and begins printing the rows that would not fit on the first set of pages.

These illustrations show the order of pages in the two options.

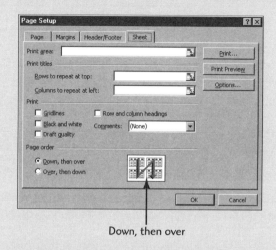

Down, then over

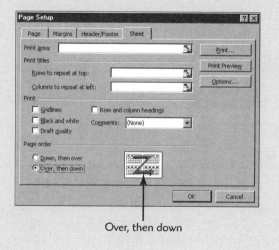

Over, then down

10

Arranging and Printing Worksheets

Skills Challenge

SKILLS CHALLENGE: WORKING WITH LARGE WORKSHEETS

Large worksheets are relatively easy to work with on screen, but may present several challenges when printing. In this exercise, you'll use a worksheet that has 96 rows and over 50 columns, experimenting with a variety of page layout and printing features:

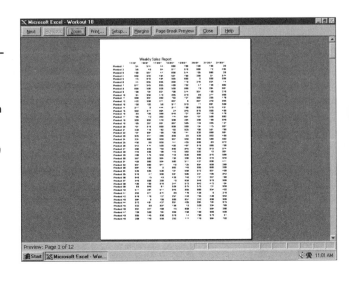

1 Open the Workout 10 workbook, which is shown to the right in Print Preview. This workbook is similar to the Sales Statistics workbook you used in the lesson — only larger!

2 Change to Page Break Preview to determine how many pages this worksheet takes up.

3 Adjust the page breaks to print an equal number of rows on each page. (Hint: This will result in 48 rows on each page.)

 What are two methods that you can use to change page breaks?

4 Reduce the scale to 85%.

 How would you reduce the worksheet to fit on a specific number of pages?

5 Set the first two rows as print titles.

6 Set column A as a print title.

 Does creating print titles affect the number of pages, or the page break positions.

7 Insert a header into the worksheet with your name on the left, the workbook name in the center, and the page number on the right.

 How would you use a standard header as the basis for a custom header?

8 Insert a footer into the worksheet with the date and time in the center.

```
TRY OUT THE
INTERACTIVE TUTORIALS
ON YOUR CD!
```

⑨ Center the pages horizontally and vertically.

⑩ Change the page order to Over, Then Down.

⑪ Change to legal-sized paper.

⑫ Change to landscape orientation.

⑬ Print a copy of the entire worksheet.

The second page of the worksheet is shown in the illustration at right in Print Preview. Notice the layout and orientation of the page, and the print titles that are repeated on the page.

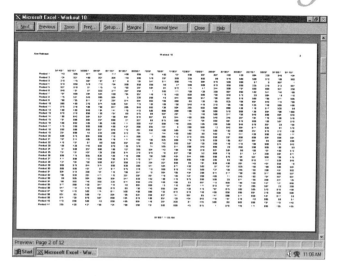

TROUBLESHOOTING

The larger the worksheet, the bigger the headaches? Not necessarily. However, printing and organizing large worksheets does require some attention to detail. If you have problems laying out worksheets for printing, maybe these tips can help.

Problem	Solution
When I print my worksheet only a certain section actually prints. I want to print the whole thing.	You have a print area set. First, select File ➢ Print Area ➢ Clear Print Area. That should remove the print area. If not, select File ➢ Page Setup, and click the Sheet tab. Make sure the Print Area text box is empty.
I get one row (or one column) all alone on a whole page.	This is an easy one. Try making the margins just a little narrower — this might move the straggling row or column onto the other page. If that doesn't work, or you don't want to reduce the margins, reduce the print scale.

continued

10

Arranging and Printing Worksheets

Troubleshooting

Problem	Solution
I tried changing page breaks in Page Break Preview but I messed things up. Now I can't get the original pages breaks back.	In Page Break Preview, right-click the worksheet and choose Reset All Page Breaks from the shortcut menu.
Help! I'm trying to designate the first column or two as print titles but Excel selects the entire page!	You probably used the Merge and Center feature to center text across the page. When you use this feature, you cannot select individual columns as print titles. First, split the cell into columns: Select Format ➢ Cells, click the Alignment tab, clear the Merge Cells check box, and click OK. Next, select the text that you want centered and move it over so it appears centered on the page. If it does not look centered, delete the row, and then add the same text to the center section of the header. Now you can select columns for print titles.
I want to add my Excel printout to another document and I want to start numbering the pages with a number other than 1.	Select File ➢ Page Setup, and click the Page tab. In the First Page Number text box, type the number that you want to print on the first page of the printout. This only sets the number, however; you still must insert the page number code in a header or footer.

WRAP UP

Time for a stretch. The techniques that you learned in this lesson can be applied to every worksheet, not just large ones:

- Before printing a worksheet, look at its layout in Print Preview, and check the page breaks in Page Break Preview.

- Use a print area when you want to print a section of your worksheet without having to select it each time. Just remember to clear the print area when you're ready to print the entire worksheet.

- Use headers and footers to identify your worksheet, and to help keep pages in order.

- Add print titles when your worksheet is more than one page, so readers can identify columns and rows by their headings.

- Select a print order based on how you want readers to look at the pages in your worksheet.

- Center small worksheets horizontally so they appear neatly arranged on the page.

- Print row and column headings on your reference copies of worksheets.

Now go back to some of the worksheets you created earlier and check out their page layout. Add headers and footers to identify the worksheets, and find other ways to enhance their printed appearance.

In the next lesson, you will learn how to find information in your spreadsheet, and how to sort rows and columns. You'll also learn how to use filters that temporarily hide information that you are not interested in so you can hone in on the data you need.

10

Arranging and Printing Worksheets

Finding and Arranging Information

2 HOURS

GOALS

In this lesson, you will learn how to find information in a worksheet, and how to change the arrangement of information. You'll learn how to:

- Use the Find and Replace features
- Sort worksheets
- Filter information
- Outline data

Get Ready

GET READY

Having all of the information you need in a worksheet is only half the battle. Finding specific information when you need it is the other half. In this lesson, you'll learn several ways to locate information, and to arrange your worksheet to make it easier to find information.
You'll use the following workbook files:

File Name	Location
Division Sales	Exercise directory
Outline	Exercise directory
Division Sales Solution	Solution directory
Workout 11	Exercise directory
Solution 11	Solution directory

When you complete this lesson, you'll be able to find and arrange the information in a worksheet. You will extract matching information using a filter, and will create an outline, as shown to the right. Check your own work against the workbooks Division Sales Solution and Solution 11.

Outlined rows   Outlined columns

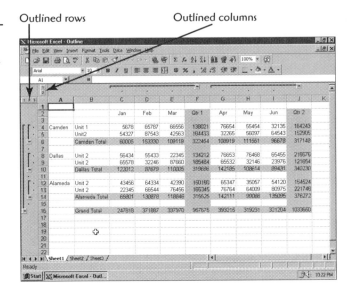

FINDING AND REPLACING INFORMATION

If you're working with a small worksheet, it's easy to find information simply by scanning down the rows and across the columns. To change something, just click the cell and type the new information, or use the editing skills you learned in Lesson 2. Finding and replacing information manually, however, has its problems, especially as your worksheets grow larger. If you're not careful, for example, you may not locate all the instances of the information you're looking for. When you use the Find and Replace commands, you let Excel do the work for you, making it easy to locate information, and to change information no matter how many times it occurs within the worksheet.

Using the Find Command

Using the Find Command

The Find command locates instances of information that you're looking for, whether it's a word, phrase, number, date, or any type of information that you can enter into a cell. Take a look at this feature now:

TRY OUT THE
INTERACTIVE TUTORIALS
ON YOUR CD!

11

Finding and Arranging Information

① Open the Division Sales workbook in the Exercise folder.

② Select Edit ➤ Find. Excel displays the dialog box shown at right.

③ Type **South** in the Find What text box. You use the options in the Search list to choose the direction of the search.

> **NOTE**
> You can also select the direction in which Excel searches the worksheet. Choose By Rows for Excel to search across the first row, and then across the second row, and so on. Choose By Columns to have Excel search down the rows in the current column, then move over and search the next column, and so on.

④ Make sure the Look In list is set to either Formulas or Values. If the Look In List is set to Comments, Excel only searches through comments in the worksheet.

> **NOTE**
> When you select Values, Excel finds matches when the information is contained in a cell. When you select Formulas, Excel also matches entries where the information is contained in a formula, but not necessarily displayed in a cell.

⑤ Click the Match Case check box to select it. Excel will find text that matches the exact combination of uppercase and lowercase letters that you entered in the Find What box. For example, it will not locate the word *south* — with a lowercase *s*.

⑥ Click Find Entire Cells Only. If you leave this box unchecked, Excel will locate any occurrence of the word *South* even if it is part of another word, such as *Southland*, or a longer entry, such

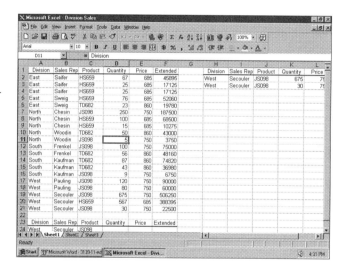

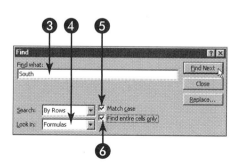

Using the Replace Command

as *South Bend.* If you select this option, Excel only locates cells that just contain the word *South.*

7 Click Find Next. Excel selects the first cell containing the word *South.*

8 Click Find Next four more times. Excel locates the next occurrences of the word *South.*

9 Click Find Next again. Excel returns to the start of the worksheet and continues searching. It does not stop when it reaches the end of the worksheet.

10 Click Close.

If it cannot locate any occurrence of the set of characters you're looking for, Excel displays a message to that effect. Click OK to clear the box. If there is only one occurrence of the word, Excel remains at that cell each time you click Find Next.

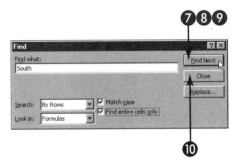

Using the Replace Command

The Replace command not only finds the characters you're looking for but replaces them with something else of your choosing. For example, did you spell a client's name wrong? Do you need to change an address or other piece of information, no matter how many times it appears in the worksheet. That's when you can use Replace. You'll try it now with two replacements. You'll start by changing each occurrence of the product number TD762 to TD682. The Replace command searches the entire worksheet, so it doesn't matter where you start. To make a replacement within a specific range of cells, select the cells first:

1 Select Edit ➤ Replace. Excel displays the dialog box shown to the right. The Find What text box contains the same text you entered in the last Find operation. Similarly, the status of the Match Case and Find Entire Cells Only check boxes have the same settings they had in the most recent Find operation.

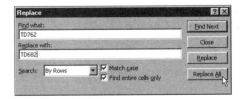

TIP

You can also open the Replace dialog box by clicking the Replace button in the Find dialog box.

Using the Replace Command

2 Type **TD762**.

3 Press Tab to go to the Replace With text box.

4 Type **TD682**.

5 Make sure the Match Case and Find Entire Cells Only check boxes are checked. These options ensure that you do not change other cells by accident.

6 Click Replace All. Every occurrence of TD762 is changed to TD682. If you change your mind about making the replacement, click Undo.

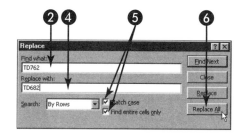

Sometimes you do not want to change every occurrence of a word, phrase, or value. In the Division Sales workbook, for example, the number 675 appears in both the Quantity and Price columns. Suppose you want to change the price of an item from $675 to $685. If you use the Replace All feature, you'll also change the amount in the Quantity column.

In this case, you have two options. You can select the Price column and then use the Replace command; if you do this, Excel only makes the replacement in that column. You can also find and replace the values one at a time. Try using that method now:

7 Click cell A1. (In your own work, you don't need to move to the top of the worksheet because Excel will search the entire worksheet.)

8 Select Edit ➢ Replace. If the Find dialog box is already on screen, click the Replace button to display the Replace dialog box.

9 Type **675** in the Find What text box.

10 Press Tab to reach the Replace With text box.

11 Type **685**.

12 Click Find Next. Excel selects the first cell containing the value 675 — the one in the Price column.

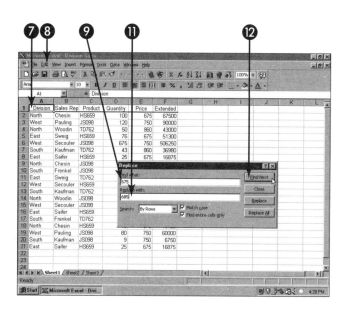

Using the Replace Command

TIP

If necessary, move the Replace dialog box out of the way by dragging its title bar to see the located set of characters.

13 Click Replace. Excel replaces 675 with 685 and then finds the next occurrence of 675 — this one is also in the Price column.

14 Click Replace. Excel makes the replacement and selects the cell containing 675 in the Quantity column. You do not want to change this value.

15 Click Find Next. Excel locates the next occurrence of the characters without making the replacement. If necessary, again move the Replace dialog box out of the way.

16 Click Replace five more times until Excel again selects the cell in the Quantity column.

17 Click Close.

SORTING INFORMATION

In many cases, you'll create your worksheet by adding information in a specific order. If you do need to switch rows or columns you can always drag and drop them to new positions. Other times, you'll enter data based on how you receive it. For example, suppose you're entering information about the members of your club. You'll probably add new members to the end of the worksheet, so those that have belonged the longest will be at the top. But what happens if you're copying the information from a card file that you've been keeping? Your records might then be in name order — the same way they are in your file.

Do you have to keep them in that order? No way. You can sort the rows and columns of your worksheet, easily and quickly.

Performing a Quick Sort

As an example, you'll sort the rows of the Division Sales workbook. You'll start by sorting them by division, the information in the first row. You can quickly sort rows using these buttons in the Standard toolbar:

1 Click any cell in column A that contains information.

2 Click Sort Ascending. Excel rearranges all of the rows, except row 1, so the values in column A are in ascending order.

NOTE *By default, Excel treats the top row as columns headings and doesn't sort it with the rest of the worksheet.*

3 Click Sort Descending. Excel places the values in descending order.

4 Click any cell in column D that contains information.

5 Click Sort Ascending. Excel now rearranges the rows by quantity, placing the smaller orders at the top.

If you select a range of cells first, before sorting, only those selected cells will be sorted. The remaining cells in the rows will stay unsorted. This is usually undesirable. For example, in the Division Sales workbook, the sales person named Woodin is in the North division. When you sort the rows of the worksheet, Woodin remains in that division because all of the cells in his row are moved at the same time.

Now find out what happens if you select cells before sorting:

6 Select columns B and C.

7 Click Sort Ascending. Only the cells in those columns are rearranged, so it now appears as if Woodin is in the West rather than the North division.

8 Click Undo.

Sort ascending   Sort descending

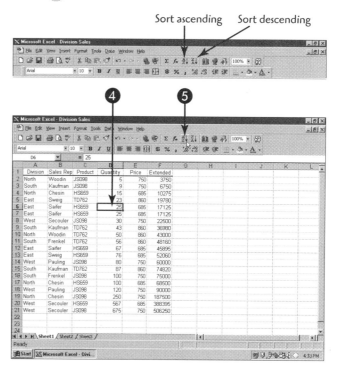

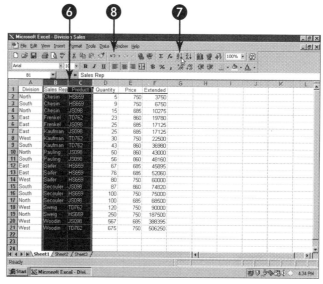

Sorting on Multiple Columns

Sorting on Multiple Columns

The Sort Ascending and Sort Descending buttons only let you sort on one column at a time. Suppose, however, you want to sort the table by Division and then by Sales Rep? This means that all of the divisions will be sorted first, and then the names of the salespersons will be sorted within each division. To sort on more than one column (their official name is *keys*), you use the Data ➤ Sort command.

Now try sorting on three columns:

① Click cell A1 and select Data ➤ Sort. Excel selects all of the cells in the contiguous block of cells, and displays the Sort dialog box. The dialog box lets you sort on up to three columns, choosing an ascending or descending sort for each.

② Make sure that the Header Row option button at the bottom of the dialog box is selected. (If you select the No Header Row button, the first row will be sorted along with the others.)

③ Pull down the Sort By list. You'll see a list of the column labels in the first row.

④ Select Division from the list.

⑤ Pull down the first Then By list.

⑥ Select Sales Rep from the list.

⑦ Pull down the second Then By list.

⑧ Select Extended.

⑨ Select the Descending option button next to Extended. You'll sort the extended prices of the orders in descending order, listing the largest orders for each sales rep first.

⑩ Click OK. The worksheet is now sorted by three columns, as shown to the right. Notice that it is sorted first by division, within division by sales rep name, and within each sales rep row by extended prices.

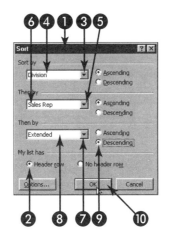

Sorting on Multiple Columns

■ Selecting Sort Options

The Options button in the Sort dialog box displays the dialog box shown to the right, which lets you customize the sorting process.

Information is usually sorted in either alphabetic, numeric, or date order, depending on what's in the column. This is called the *normal* sort order. Although this order is usually what you want, there are exceptions. For example, if your column contains months (Jan, Feb, Mar, and so on), sorting them normally will place them in alphabetical order, not month order. The same situation applies to days of the week. To select a month or day sort, pull down the First Key Sort Order list to see these options.

Select the type of sort you want. The list will also contain any custom lists that you've created.

Here are the other options in the dialog box:

- **Case Sensitive**: Select this option to differentiate between uppercase and lowercase letters. By default, the case of letters is not considered. With a case-sensitive ascending sort, numbers are placed first, then lowercase letters and uppercase letters.

- **Sort Top to Bottom**: This is the default setting. Select it to rearrange the rows of the worksheet.

- **Sort Left to Right**: Select this option to rearrange the columns. When you select this option, the Sort By and Then By lists show the row numbers.

USING FILTERS

Even if you sort the worksheet, you may still need to scroll to the section of the sheet that you are interested in reading. In addition, when you want to look at specific information in a worksheet, data that you are not interested in can be distracting. Wouldn't it be better if you could temporarily hide all of the information that you don't need to see? You can, with a filter. A filter lets you display just the rows that you are interested in viewing — for example, all the rows with data about the South division, or all rows in which the value in the Extended column is over 50,000. The information that you don't want to display isn't deleted from the worksheet, it's just hidden from view. You can easily redisplay the information whenever you want.

Applying an AutoFilter

Filters are designed for information that is organized like a database. This means that it has column headings that explain the type of information in each column. In database terminology, each column heading is called a *field*. Each row under the column headings contains information about another object in the database, and each row is called a *record*. For example, in the Product Sales workbook, each row/record contains the information about a single order. For a set of rows and columns to be considered a database, there must also be no blank rows between the records, but at least one blank row following the last record.

Applying an AutoFilter

The AutoFilter command lets you select the rows you want to see by choosing from a list of values in a column. For example, suppose you just want to see the sales for a specific sales rep, or all orders for a certain product. It's easy:

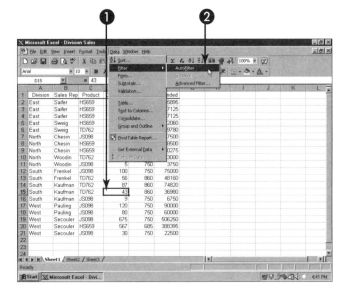

❶ Click any cell in the range A1 to F21. To apply an AutoFilter, you must select a cell in the range of information you want to filter.

❷ Select Data ➤ Filter ➤ AutoFilter. Next to each column label, Excel displays drop-down lists that let you select the information you want to view.

❸ Click the down arrow at column B. You'll see a list of the names in that column, along with other options, as shown to the right.

❹ Click Chesin. Excel conceals all of the rows in the worksheet, except those containing Chesin in the Sales Rep column. The rows numbers of the remaining rows are shown in blue to designate that a filter has been applied. Notice that the row numbers are not sequential, showing that some rows are hidden from view.

❺ Click the down arrow at column B.

❻ Click (All). Excel removes the filter, displaying all of the rows once again.

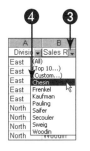

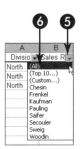

Applying an AutoFilter

You can apply more than one filter to select records on multiple columns. For instance, suppose you want to see all sales for product JS098 in the North division. You'll need to apply filters on two columns:

7 Click the down arrow at column A.

8 Click North. Excel displays only the rows containing North in column A.

9 Click the down arrow at column C.

10 Click JS098. Now you only see the North rows that also have product JS098.

Each filter uses the rows that are shown. So once you applied a filter for North, any other filter uses just those rows. Next see how this works:

11 Click the down arrow at column A.

12 Click (All). Because a filter is still applied at column C, Excel now lists all divisions that have project JS098. Choosing (All) did not list every row because a filter is applied in another column.

13 Click the down arrow at column A.

14 Click West. Now rows from the West division with product JS098 are displayed.

15 Click the down arrow in column C.

16 Select (All). This removes the filter in column C, but leaves the filter applied to column A. The worksheet now shows all sales in the West division, regardless of the product.

17 Click the down arrow at column A.

18 Select (All). All of the filters are removed, displaying every row.

TIP

To quickly display all of the records when you have one or more filters in place, select Data ➤ Filter ➤ Show All.

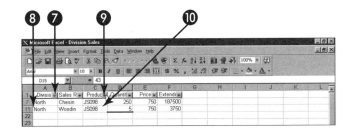

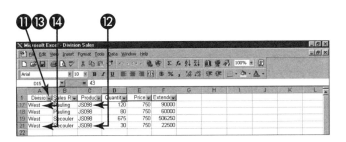

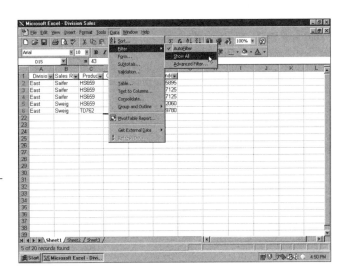

Using the Top 10

Using the Top 10

The Top 10 option in the AutoFilter list lets you select rows that fall in an upper or lower area, not just the top 10. You can only use this option, however, in columns containing numeric values. For example, a teacher might want to list the students with the highest (or lowest) five grade point averages, or students that fall in the top (or bottom) percentiles.

To use this option, you need to set three parameters:

- Top or bottom

- The number of rows or percentile to display

- Whether to display items or those falling in the specified percentile

Start by displaying the records with the top five highest extended prices:

1 Click the down arrow at column F.

2 Click Top 10.

Excel opens the dialog box shown to the right. The first list box is set at Top, so you can leave it that way. The second list box should be selected, with its contents highlighted.

3 Type **5**. You can leave the last list box set at Items, because you want to display five rows rather than a specified percentage.

4 Click OK. The worksheet now displays the five rows with the highest amounts in the Extended column.

5 Click a cell in column F.

6 Click Sort Descending. Excel sorts the rows while leaving the filter in place.

Now try using the Top 10 option to find the bottom ten percent of all orders:

7 Click the down arrow at column F.

8 Click Top 10.

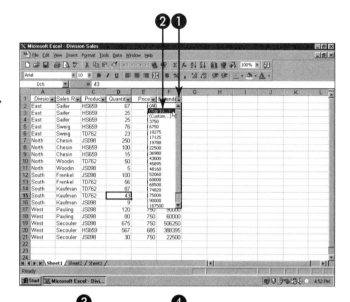

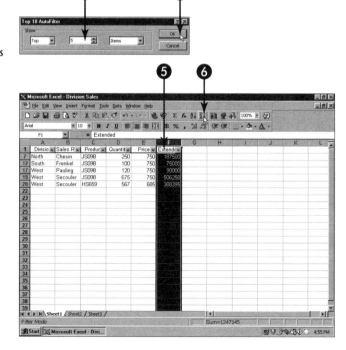

⑨ Pull down the first list box in the Top 10 AutoFilter dialog box and select Bottom.

⑩ Press Tab to move to the second list box.

⑪ Type **10**.

⑫ Pull down the last list box in the dialog box and select Percent.

⑬ Click OK. Excel displays just two rows, representing the bottom 10 percent of the Extended price column.

⑭ Select Data ➢ Filter ➢ Show All. All of the rows are again displayed.

Designing Custom Filters

The AutoFilter pull-down lists only let you choose information that matches a specific value, such as the sales representative Secouler, or a quantity of 100. There will be instances, however, when you're looking for a more general match, such as all orders over $50,000, or the rows for both the North and West divisions. If you're a teacher, for example, you may want to list students with grades over 90, or just between 80 and 89.

To search for this type of information you have to create a custom filter. A custom filter lets you select information based on one or two criteria using these comparison operators:

equals
does not equal
is greater than
is greater than or equal to
is less than
is less than or equal to
begins with
does not begin with
ends with
does not end with
contains
does not contain

To see how this works, you'll start on the next page by displaying rows for orders over $50,000:

Designing Custom Filters

1 Click the down arrow at column F.

2 Select Custom.

Excel displays the dialog box shown in the illustration at right. Notice that the box includes the text *Show rows where*, followed by the column label (*Extended* in this case). You use the top row of boxes to enter the first comparison operator.

3 Pull down the first list box; it lists 12 comparison operations.

4 Select *is greater than or equal to*.

5 Press Tab to reach the second box. Here you can either type the value to use for the comparison, or pull down the list and select one of the items already in the column. In this case, there is no item for $50,000 so you'll have to enter the value yourself.

6 Type **50000**.

7 Click OK. Excel displays rows where the extended price is at least $50,000.

8 Select Data ➢ Filter ➢ Show All to turn off the filter and display all records again.

In the previous example, you used the filter to locate numeric information. You can also use a filter for text. For example, try locating all sales representatives whose names start with the letter *S*:

9 Click the down arrow at column B.

10 Select Custom.

11 Pull down the first list and select *begins with*.

12 Press Tab to reach the second box.

13 Type **s**.

TIP

Filters are not case sensitive, so you can enter either an uppercase or lowercase letter here.

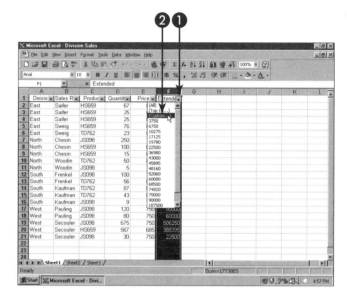

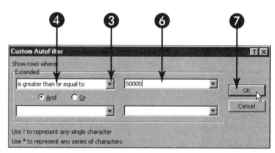

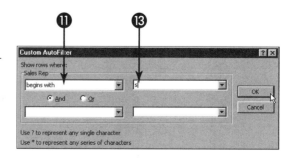

Filtering with Operators

⑭ Click OK. Excel displays the records for three sales representatives, whose names begin with the letter *S*.

⑮ Select Data ➢ Filter ➢ Show All.

Filtering with Two Comparison Operators

Using two comparison operators lets you refine your searches even more than using a single operator. When you use a second comparison operator, however, you have to choose whether to perform an *and* operation or an *or* operation. If you use an *and* operation, both comparisons must be met by the information in the column. If you use an *or* operation, at least one comparison must be met.

For instance, suppose you want to list rows for sales in the North and West divisions. Is this an *and* or an *or* operation? It cannot be an *and* operation because a row would have to have both North and West in the Division column to meet both criteria. It is an *or* operation because the row has to have either North or West in the column. In fact, apply that filter now:

❶ Click the down arrow at column A.

❷ Select Custom to access the Custom AutoFilter dialog box.

❸ Leave the operator set at *equals*. The insertion point should be in the second text box.

❹ Pull down the list and select North.

❺ Click the Or option button.

❻ Pull down the first list in the second row, and select *equals*.

❼ Pull down the second list in the second row and select West.

❽ Click OK. Only rows for the North and West divisions are displayed, as shown to the right.

❾ Select Data ➢ Filter ➢ Show All.

Because a cell can only contain one value, when would you ever use the *and* operation? This is trickier. Generally, you never use the *and* operator and the equals comparison operator. You only use it with comparisons that can both be true. Next, you'll use the *and*

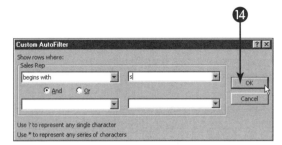

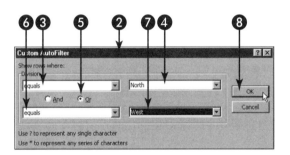

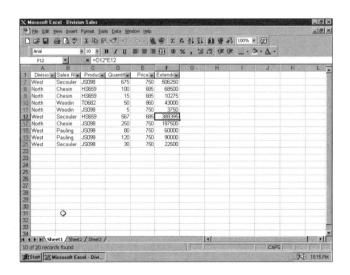

Filtering with Operators

operator in two examples. First, you'll find rows where the extended prices are between $50,000 and $100,000:

10 Click the down arrow at column F.

11 Select Custom to access the Custom AutoFilter dialog box.

12 Pull down the first list and select *is greater than or equal to*.

13 Press Tab to reach the second box.

14 Type **50000**. The And option button is selected by default — leave it that way.

15 Pull down the second list and select *is less than or equal to*.

16 Press Tab to reach the second box.

17 Type **100000**.

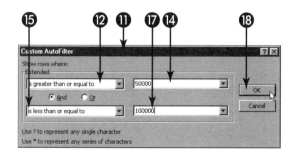

NOTE
Although a cell cannot be equal to both 50000 and 100000 at the same time, it can meet both of these conditions. If a value is both greater than or equal to $50,000, and less than or equal to $100,000, then it falls between those two values.

18 Click OK. Excel lists the six rows that meet both conditions.

19 Select Data ➢ Filter ➢ Show All.

Finally, you'll use an *and* operation to locate text. In this case, you want to find the rows for sales representatives whose last name begins with the letter *S*, but excluding Secouler. The first comparison will be "begins with S." This will display rows for sales representatives whose last names begin with the letter *S*. The second comparison will be "does not equal Secouler."

But is this an *and* or an *or* operation? If you used an *or* operation, Excel would list rows for every salesperson except Secouler, regardless of the first letter. Although the name Chesin, for example, does not start with the letter *S*, it does not equal Secouler, so it would be listed. In this case, you need an *and* operation to exclude rows for salespeople besides Secouler whose names do not begin with *S*.

Creating an Advanced Filter

⑳ Click the down arrow at column B.

㉑ Select Custom to access the Custom AutoFilter dialog box.

㉒ Pull down the first list and select *begins with*.

㉓ Press Tab to reach the second box.

㉔ Type **s**.

㉕ Pull down the first list in the second row, and select *does not equal*.

㉖ Pull down the second list in the second row and select Secouler.

㉗ Click OK. The filter does its job, listing all sales representatives whose last names begin with an *S*, except Secouler.

㉘ Select Data ➢ Filter ➢ Show All.

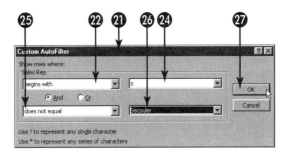

Creating an Advanced Filter

Custom filters are quite flexible, but they are limited to only two conditions, also called criteria. When you need to perform a more complex filter operation, use a criteria range instead. A *criteria range* is an area of the worksheet where you enter the criteria you're looking for, rather than using the AutoFilter dialog box.

In the first row of the criteria range, you enter the column names containing the information you are looking for. In the rows below the column names, you enter the criteria:

❶ Select cells A1 to F1.

> **NOTE**
> *You only need to copy the field names you will be searching on. However, the field names must be exactly the same as those in the columns of information, so it is easier to copy and paste all the field names rather than retyping them.*

❷ Click Copy.

❸ Click cell A23. (Leave at least one blank row between the database and the criteria range.)

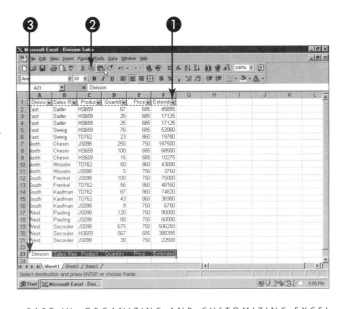

4 Click Paste, and then press Esc to remove the moving border around cells A1 to F1.

5 Click cell A24. Use the rows under the field names to enter criteria.

6 Type **West**. Excel will use this for an exact match.

7 Enter **Secouler** in cell B24.

8 Enter **JS098** in cell C24.

TIP

Criteria in the same row are treated as an and *condition.*

9 Click any cell in the list of data you want to filter.

NOTE

It isn't absolutely necessary to click a cell in the data because you can later point to the range of cells you want to search. But doing this saves you a step later.

10 Select Data ➤ Filter ➤ Advanced Filter. Excel displays the Advanced Filter dialog box, as shown in the illustration at right.

11 Make sure that the Filter the List, In-Place option is selected. This option means that the filtering will be performed on the rows themselves.

12 Click the Criteria Range box.

13 Drag to select cells A23 to F24 on the worksheet. These cells represent the criteria. While you select the range, the Advanced Filter dialog box collapses to show the range selected.

14 Click OK. Excel uses the criteria in the range to filter the rows, with the results shown to the right.

15 Select Data ➤ Filter ➤ Show All.

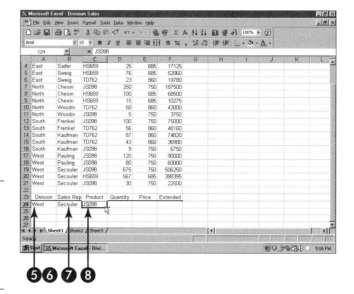

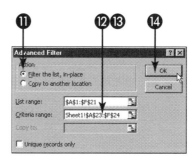

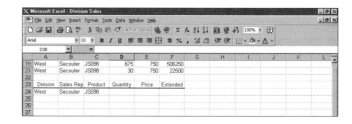

Creating an Advanced Filter

When you enter criteria in more than one row, Excel treats it as an *or* condition. You can use as many rows as you need. Just check your criteria carefully for the correct logic.

The Copy to Another Location option in the Advanced Filter dialog box lets you make a copy of the records that meet the criteria. In addition to setting the List Range and the Criteria Range, you can select a Copy To location. This option is very helpful for creating a separate list of specific records, while leaving all of the records displayed in their original location.

Next use the criteria already in the worksheet to create a separate table:

16 Click any cell in the range A1 to F21.

17 Select Data ➢ Filter ➢ Advanced Filter to access the Advanced Filter dialog box.

18 Click Copy to Another Location. The Copy To text box becomes active.

19 Click the Copy To box; this is where you designate where to place the copied records.

20 Type **H1**. You only need to enter the upper-left corner of the range to be copied.

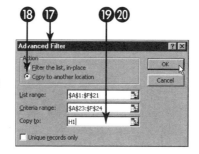

NOTE

If you choose the Unique Records Only option, you'll get a list with only one copy of records that are repeated.

21 Click OK. Excel makes a copy of the rows that meet the criteria, including the column labels, as shown at right.

22 Save and close the workbook.

CREATING OUTLINES

Often finding information would be much easier if you just didn't have so much of it. Although you can delete information from a worksheet, sometimes a better possibility is to temporarily hide some of the details that you're not interested in.

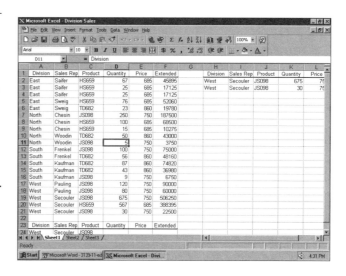

11

Finding and Arranging Information

Automatic Outlining

When you outline a worksheet, you divide it into levels, much like the levels in a document outline. When you want to see just the summary information, without the details, you *collapse* the outline. When you want to look at the details again, you *expand* the outline. With Excel, you can collapse and expand rows as well as columns.

Automatic Outlining

If your worksheet is organized suitably, you can have Excel create the outline for you. Excel will use subtotals and totals, or similar formulas, to determine the outline levels. Try your hand at it now:

1 Open the Outline workbook in the Exercise folder. The worksheet is organized into three sections of rows, each section relating to a different geographical area. The columns are organized into two general sections, Qtr 1 and Qtr 2.

2 Select Data ➤ Group and Outline ➤ Auto Outline.

Excel divides the worksheet into levels, indicated by the outline levels shown in the bottom illustration at right.

Now take some time to understand the way Excel outlines the worksheet. Along the left side of the screen are the level indicators for the rows. The numbers 1, 2, and 3 represent three levels:

- 1 represents the fewest details, just the grand total in row 16.

- 2 represents the next amount of details, the subtotals in rows 6, 10, and 14.

- 3 represents the most amount of details — all of the rows.

The lines, boxes, and other symbols graphically represent the levels. For example, the long line on the far left represents level 1, the three short lines represent level 2, and the dots represent level 3. The minus sign in the boxes at the end of the lines show that the levels are expanded.

Along the top of the worksheet are the level indicators for the columns. The numbers 1 and 2 represent these levels:

- 1 represents the fewest details, Qtr 1 and Qtr 2.

- 2 represents the most details — all of the columns.

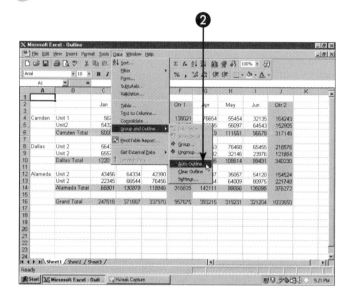

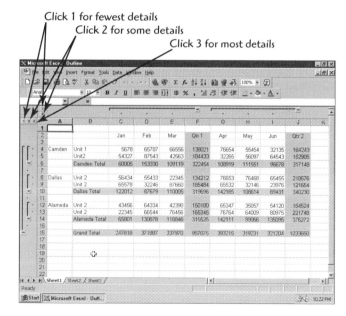

Click 1 for fewest details
Click 2 for some details
Click 3 for most details

Collapsing and Expanding Outlines

There are only two levels because there is no grand total column. The lines, boxes, and dots indicate the levels of the columns.

Collapsing and Expanding Outlines

When you collapse an outline, you show fewer levels, and thus fewer details. For example, you may want to see just the grand totals, or just the quarterly totals. Or, you may want to see the subtotals for the three cities but not the details — the individual values that comprise the subtotals.

When you expand an outline, you show more levels, and more details.

You click the level numbers to expand and collapse all of the rows or columns represented by the levels. You click the boxes at the end of the lines to expand or collapse individual sections of the outline.

Try it now:

1 Click the number 1 in the row levels (the number 1 in the 1, 2, and 3 to the left of the worksheet). Excel collapses the outline, displaying just the grand total, as shown to the right. The plus sign in the box indicates that the level is collapsed.

2 Click the number 1 in the column levels (just above the worksheet). Excel collapses the columns, showing only the quarterly totals.

3 Click the number 2 in the row levels. Excel displays the subtotals.

4 Click the box with the plus sign next to row 6. Rather than expanding all of the levels, Excel expands just the level indicated by the plus sign, showing the details for Camden.

5 Click the box with the plus sign above column J. Excel expands the Qtr 2 details, the values for April, May, and June.

6 Click the number 2 in the column levels. The columns are completely expanded.

7 Click the number 3 in the row levels. The worksheet is now fully expanded.

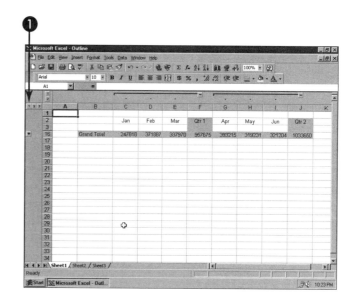

Skills Challenge

⑧ Select Data ➤ Group and Outline ➤ Clear Outline. The outline level indicators are removed.

When automatic outlining is in place, you can also show and hide details using the Data ➤ Group and Outline menu. Select the row or column that you want to expand, and then select Data ➤ Group and Outline ➤ Show Detail. To collapse a level, select it and choose Data ➤ Group and Outline ➤ Hide Detail.

You can also select just one cell in the row or column, not the entire row or column itself, before showing or hiding details. However, if the cell is in a collapsed row and column, Excel expands both the row and the column when you choose Data ➤ Group and Outline ➤ Show Detail. Likewise, if the cell is in an expanded row and column, both the row and the column are collapsed if you choose Data ➤ Group and Outline ➤ Hide Detail.

■ Creating an Outline Manually

If you do not have subtotals and totals, Excel may not be able to create the outline automatically. You can still create the outline, but you have to do it manually.

Start by selecting all of the rows or columns that you want in level 1. If you are manually outlining the Outline workbook, for example, you would select rows 4 to 16. Then select Data ➤ Group and Outline ➤ Group.

Next, select the rows or columns that you want in one of the next level groups, such as rows 4 to 6, or columns C to F. Then select Data ➤ Group and Outline ➤ Group.

Continue selecting and grouping the other sections of the outline.

To ungroup a specific section, select it and choose Data ➤ Group and Outline ➤ Ungroup. Remove all of the levels by selecting Data ➤ Group and Outline ➤ Clear Outline.

SKILLS CHALLENGE: FILTERING AND OUTLINING A WORKSHEET

Now it's time to practice the skills you learned in this chapter. In this exercise, you will sort a worksheet using a custom order, and use an outline to view a worksheet without all of its detail:

TRY OUT THE

INTERACTIVE TUTORIALS

ON YOUR CD!

1 Open the Workout 11 workbook, shown to the right.

2 Apply an AutoFilter.

 What conditions have to be met before you can apply an AutoFilter?

3 Filter the worksheet to display only freshman students.

 What happens to the rows that do not meet the filter conditions?

4 Filter the worksheet to display only freshman students taking Spanish.

5 Filter the worksheet to display the grades in the top 15th percentile.

 Do you have to first remove the previously applied filters? If so, why?

6 Display all of the rows.

7 Sort the worksheet on the two columns — first by Class and then by Name. (Hint: To sort by class, you have to create a custom list. Do so by using the Tools ➢ Options ➢ Custom Lists command, and creating a list with the items Freshman, Sophomore, Junior, and Senior — in that order, making sure you spell everything correctly. To sort by two columns, you need to use the Data ➢ Sort command.)

8 Insert a blank row after each group of student names, such as after Green, O'Hara, and so on.

9 Insert the average of each student's grades. For example, insert a blank row under the last row for Green, and then add the average of cells D2 and D3.

10 Insert a blank row after each group of classes, such as after the last freshman, the last sophomore, and so on.

11 Insert the average for each class.

12 Insert a blank row between classes to improve readability.

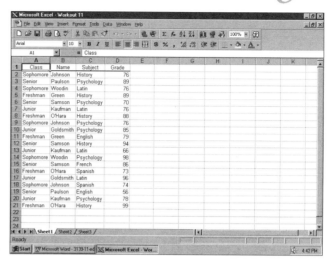

11

Finding and Arranging Information

Troubleshooting

⑬ Add an average for the entire school at the end of the worksheet. If you have difficulty inserting the averages, refer to the file Solution 11 in the Solution folder. The worksheet with averages is shown to the right.

⑭ Apply an Auto Outline.

 4 *How does Excel know where to separate the rows of the worksheet into outline levels?*

⑮ Collapse the outline to display just the class averages. (Hint: This should be level 2. The results should appear as shown in the bottom right figure.)

⑯ Expand the outline to display student and class averages.

 5 *What is the purpose of creating, expanding, and collapsing outlines?*

⑰ Collapse the outline to display just the school average.

⑱ Expand the entire outline.

⑲ Clear the outline.

TROUBLESHOOTING

Sorting, filtering, and outlining are powerful Excel features, but they can lead to some unexpected results. Don't be surprised if information you know you entered no longer seems to exist, or is not where you typed it. If you have problems with the techniques you learned in this lesson, check out these troubleshooting tips:

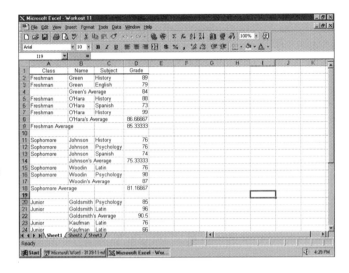

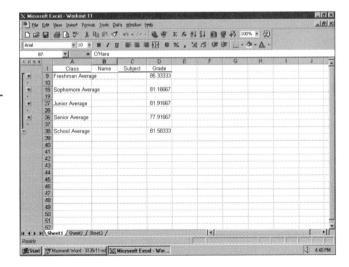

Troubleshooting

Problem	Solution
I'm searching for information that I know is in the worksheet, but Excel can't find it.	Make sure that the Match Case and Find Entire Cells Only check boxes are cleared. If these are set, Excel may be missing text that uses different cases, or is part of a longer cell entry. Also make sure that the Look In list is not set to Comments—unless that's where you want to search.
The Sort Ascending and Sort Descending buttons are not working correctly.	Before clicking a sort button, be certain that the active cell is in the column you want to sort. You may be sorting the wrong column.
My column headings are being sorted with the rest of the worksheet. It looks terrible.	In the Sort dialog box (select Data ➤ Sort), click the Header Row option button in the My List Has section.
My columns are being sorted, not the rows!	Select Data ➤ Sort, and then click Option. In the Sort Options dialog box, click Sort Top to Bottom in the Orientation section.
I get an error message when I try to apply an AutoFilter.	The active cell must be within the range of cells containing information.
When I click Top 10, I just hear a beep.	The Top 10 option only works with numeric and date information. You may be trying to select it in a column containing text entries.

continued

Wrap Up

Problem	Solution
I'm applying a custom filter but the results look wrong.	Problems with custom filters are usually the result of errors in logic—especially when selecting the *and* or the *or* operator. Try selecting the other option to see if the results are now correct. Also, make sure that your conditions are set correctly.
My worksheet is not outlining properly.	The outline feature needs a worksheet with formulas that operate on groups of cells. If you get the message "Cannot create an outline," then Excel cannot find formulas that indicate the stop and start of the outline levels.

WRAP UP

Time for a rest. Entering all your information into a worksheet may not be enough if you cannot find the information when you need it. Use the techniques that you learned in this chapter to get the most use out of your work:

- Use Edit ➢ Find to quickly locate information in your worksheet.

- Use Edit ➢ Replace to automatically change information. Use the Replace All feature with caution.

- Arrange rows in order with the Sort Ascending and Sort Descending buttons.

- Sort on more than one column at a time with the Data ➢ Sort command.

- Apply an AutoFilter (Data ➢ Filter ➢ AutoFilter) to display rows containing selected information.

- Apply a custom filter to choose rows meeting specific criteria.

- Choose Top 10 to display rows with the highest or lowest values.

Wrap Up ◄

- Use an advanced filter to choose records based on a criteria range.

- Apply an outline to display selected levels of information.

Everyone feels more comfortable in a familiar environment, and it is no different when using Excel. In the next lesson, you'll learn how to customize Excel for the way you like to work so you feel at home.

Customizing Excel

GOALS

In this lesson, you will discover how to customize the way Excel looks and works to suit your own taste. You will learn how to:

■ Change the magnification of the display

■ Select what parts of Excel appear on screen

■ Determine when formulas are calculated

■ Set options for editing cells

■ Select colors

■ Customize Excel's toolbars and menus

■ Create custom toolbars and menus

90 MINUTES

Get Ready

GET READY

Everyone is more comfortable working in a familiar environment, and it's no different when using a computer. To be comfortable, however, you often need to change the way your environment is laid out, the way objects appear and are arranged. In an office, you'd put pictures of your family or pets on your desk, or bring in your favorite plant. You can also change the way Excel looks and works to make it more comfortable for you.

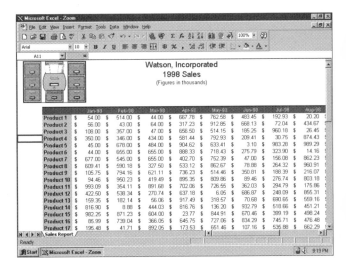

This lesson refers to the following workbooks:

File Name	Location
Zoom	Exercise directory
Zoom Solution	Solution directory
Workout 12	Exercise directory
Solution 12	Solution directory

When you complete this lesson, you'll have customized Excel to create a toolbar and menu, and will have set various Excel options, to create the worksheet shown at right.

CHANGING THE DISPLAY

One of the first things you can do to customize Excel is to change the appearance of the screen. You already know how to hide and unhide rows and columns. You can also hide and display other screen elements, such as the menu bar and toolbars, and you can change the magnification of the display to enlarge or reduce what you see.

▶ Zooming the Display

When you start Excel, your worksheet probably appears at 100% magnification. This means that you'll see the worksheet on the screen about the same size it will appear when printed, give or take the differences in your screen resolution. You can change the magnification, however, to:

- Reduce the display to see more of the worksheet at one time

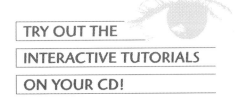

TRY OUT THE
INTERACTIVE TUTORIALS
ON YOUR CD!

- Enlarge the display to make the print easier to read or to or see details in graphics

The easiest way to change the magnification is to pull down the Zoom list in the toolbar.

Select a percentage smaller that 100% to reduce the magnification, or larger than 100% to enlarge the magnification. You can also choose Selection to fill the screen with the currently selected range of cells — up to a 400% magnification. For a custom setting, click the Zoom box in the toolbar, type the desired magnification, and press Enter.

Try it now:

1 Open the Zoom workbook in the Exercise folder. The worksheet extends to cell N69 and contains a graphic.

2 Pull down the Zoom list in the toolbar and select 75%. Excel reduces the magnification so you can see more columns and rows, but the text is still readable.

3 Pull down the Zoom list in the toolbar and select 50%. You can now see all of the columns. At this magnification, however, the columns are too narrow to display the total values in row 69, and the worksheet is getting difficult to decipher.

4 Click the Zoom box.

5 Type **65** and then press Enter. At this custom magnification the text is more readable.

6 Select cells B7 to E18.

7 Pull down the Zoom list and choose Selection. Excel enlarges the selected cells so they fill the window, as shown to the right.

8 Click to deselect the cells. The display remains in the enlarged view.

9 Pull down the Zoom list and choose 100%.

You can also change the magnification by selecting View ➤ Zoom to display the dialog box shown in the following illustration. Choose one of the preset settings, choose Fit Selection to enlarge or shrink the selection to fit on the screen (this is the same as the

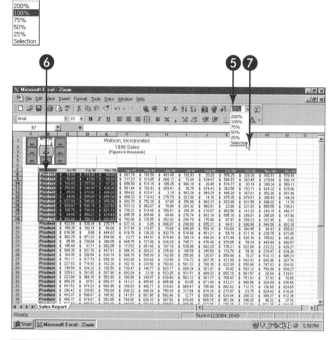

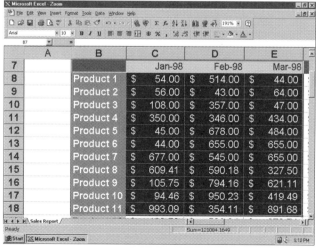

Saving Custom Views

Selection option in the Zoom list), or enter a custom magnification between 10% and 400%.

Saving Custom Views

There is not a single combination of magnification and screen arrangement that's ideal for all occasions. Rather than changing settings each time you want to use a particular combination of settings, you can save the appearance of the screen as a custom view. You can then later restore all of the settings by simply selecting the view from a menu.

A custom view includes the magnification, hidden rows or columns, filter settings, and print settings. For example, suppose you frequently change the worksheet to 75%, hide a column, and set a specific print area. Rather than change to these settings each time, you can save the combination as a view.

TIP *You should always start by creating a custom view using the default screen settings. This way, it is easy to return your document to the original settings.*

In this exercise, you start by saving a view of a worksheet using all of the default Excel options. Then, you change the magnification, hide a column, and set a print area — and at this point save another view. You'll use the first view when you want to quickly return the worksheet to Excel's default view settings:

① Select View ➤ Custom Views. Excel displays the Custom Views dialog box.

② Click Add. Excel displays the Add View dialog box.

③ Type **Original View;** this name clearly identifies the settings in the view.

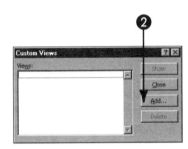

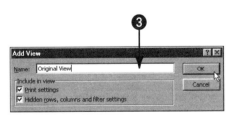

NOTE *The two check boxes in the Add View dialog box determine whether print settings, and hidden rows, columns, and filter settings are also saved with the view.*

4 Click OK to create the view.

5 Now try changing the view. Pull down the Zoom list and select 75%.

6 Right-click the column A header, and select Hide.

7 Select cells B7 to E27.

8 Select File ➤ Print Area ➤ Set Print Area. Leave the cells selected, so the selection will be part of the custom view.

9 Select View ➤ Custom Views. The custom view you already created will be shown and selected in the Custom Views dialog box.

10 Click Add. Excel displays the Add View dialog box.

11 Type **My Custom View**.

12 Click OK.

13 Select View ➤ Custom Views.

14 Click Original View.

15 Click Show. Excel restores the saved view, at 100% magnification, displaying the hidden column, and without the selected cells and print area.

16 Select View ➤ Custom Views.

17 Click My Custom View.

18 Click Show. The reduced worksheet appears, with column A hidden, and the print area set to the selected cells.

19 Select View ➤ Custom Views.

20 Click Original View.

21 Click Show.

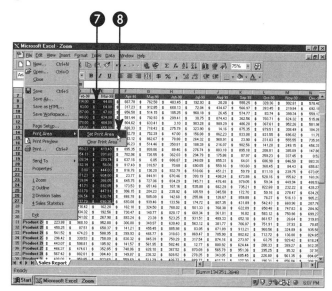

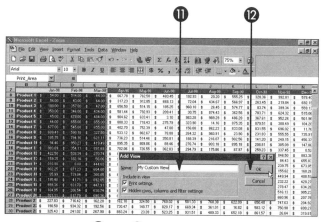

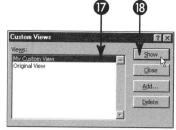

12

Customizing Excel

Saving Custom Views

■ Displaying and Hiding Screen Elements

When you want to display as many cells as possible, zooming the display is not always the solution. If you zoom to see all of the rows or columns in a worksheet, for example, the display may be too small to read.

Using the View menu, however, you can turn off and on the toolbars, formula bar, status bar, and even the title bar, to display additional rows on screen.

For example, select View ➢ Formula Bar to toggle the display of the formula bar on and off; select View ➢ Status Bar to turn the status bar on and off.

To remove all screen elements except for the menu bar, row and column headers, and the sheet tabs, select View ➢ Full Screen. The other elements, including the Windows 95 Taskbar, are removed and Excel displays the button shown here. Click the button when you want to display the removed elements.

You can also turn off and on the toolbars, and display additional toolbars to perform Excel functions. Select View ➢ Toolbars, or right-click any displayed toolbar to display the menu shown to the right.

The toolbars with check marks to their left are already displayed. Click a toolbar with a check mark to remove it from the screen, or click a toolbar without a check mark to display it.

In addition to the Standard and Formatting toolbars, there are toolbars for other Excel features, such as the Web toolbar for communicating with the Internet (see Lesson 9 for the details), and the Drawing toolbar for creating graphics (for more information, check out Lesson 15).

Click here to display
hidden screen elements

When you save a workbook, the zoom settings are saved along with it. When you open the workbook, it appears just as you saved it. Custom views are also saved with the workbook, so you can switch between the different views.

The combination of toolbars that are displayed, and their arrangement on screen, is saved when you exit Excel. The next time you start Excel, you'll see the same toolbars that were on screen at the end of your last session — regardless of which workbook you have open. The options that you'll learn about next are also saved when you exit Excel. The arrangement of toolbars and Excel options are application settings that are not saved with individual workbooks.

SETTING EXCEL OPTIONS

Excel offers eight pages of options that you can set to customize it for the way you work. Some of the options are only for advanced users, and a few are probably hardly ever changed. So as you continue with this lesson, don't worry if some options that you see on the screen seem obtuse. In fact, this lesson concentrates on the options that the average Excel user will need most often. For an additional explanation of any option, click the What's This button (the question mark in the dialog box title bar) then click the option.

To set Excel options, select Tools ➢ Options to display the dialog box shown in the illustration at right. These options affect the default Excel environment, not just the current workbook. You already learned how to use the Custom Lists page of this dialog box (in Lesson 3) to create your own AutoFill series. You'll look at the Chart page of this dialog box in Lesson 13. Now, you'll find out about the other pages of the dialog box.

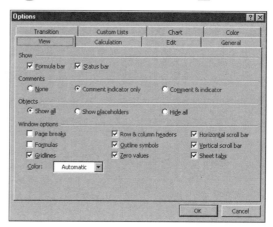

Changing View Options

The options on the View page of the dialog box are most useful because they let you choose what appears on screen. You can choose to display the formula bar and status bar, and how comments and objects appear. Objects include chart and text boxes, buttons, and drawing objects. Charts and text boxes, for example, can slow down scrolling because Excel has to redraw graphic images in the new position. If you select Show Placeholders, these objects appear as gray rectangles that show where you have objects on a worksheet but don't slow scrolling. Selecting Hide All removes objects from the screen and prevents them from printing.

In the Window Options section, select the check boxes for the items that you want to appear, or remove the check mark to clear the item from the display. If you added custom borders to a worksheet, for example, clear the Gridlines check box to remove the default lines from the screen so they don't interfere with your custom borders. If you display grid lines, use the Color list to change the line color.

The Formulas option is very useful. When you select this option, Excel displays the actual formulas in the worksheet rather than the results. Check this option and print a hard copy of a worksheet for a

Changing View Options

record of the formulas that you used. Just widen the columns enough to display the entire formulas. If you accidentally delete the workbook from your disk, you'll have a printed record that you can use for a backup.

Now you'll look at the effects of some of these options:

1. Select Tools ➢ Options.

2. Click the View tab, if that page of the dialog box is not already displayed.

3. Select Hide All.

4. Uncheck Gridlines.

5. Uncheck Row & Column Headers.

6. Click OK. With these elements removed, the worksheet looks like the illustration on the next page.

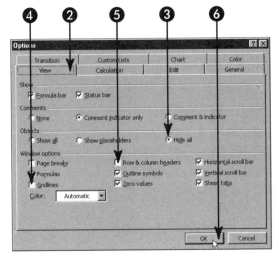

HIDING ZERO VALUES

The Zero Values setting in the Window Options section can be useful. When this box is not checked, cells that contain a zero value will appear blank. Often you want the zero to appear to make it clear that the value of the item is zero. But sometimes you do not want zeros to appear. For example, suppose you create an invoice form that resembles the illustration at right. The zeros in the Total column are the result of the formulas that reference blank cells in the QTY and PRICE columns. Most users do not want the zeros to appear in these rows. In this case, clear the Zero Values check box.

Change the Zero Values setting to clear this column

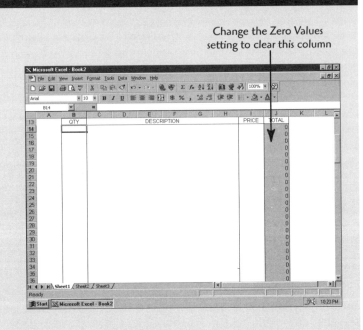

■ Other Useful Excel Options

Although most of the options on the other pages of the Options dialog box are for advanced users, there are several that you should consider:

- The options on the Edit page of the Options dialog box, for example, can make it easier to edit and format the contents of cells. You can choose the direction in which to move when you press the Enter key, or you can choose to have pressing Enter accept a cell entry without moving to another cell, just like pressing the Enter button on the formula bar.

- The General options determine some basic ways that Excel operates. Two of the most useful options are the Recently Used File List and Sheets in New Workbook settings. The Recently Used File List option lets you set the number of recently opened files that appear on the bottom of the File menu. You can enter any value from 0 (to list no files) to 9 if you want to quickly access a larger number of recently used workbooks. The Sheets in New Workbook option lets you change the number of worksheets in new workbooks. If you find yourself normally adding sheets to workbooks, setting this number to a higher value will save you time.

- The Calculation options determine when and how formulas are recalculated.

- The Transition options are strictly for users of other spreadsheet programs, such as Lotus 1-2-3, who are also using Excel.

- The Color options let you choose the color palette from which you can select colors for fonts, borders and grid lines, drawing objects, chart fills, and chart lines.

CUSTOMIZING TOOLBARS

Although Excel's toolbars give you access to most of the features you'll want to use, others that you use frequently may not be provided.

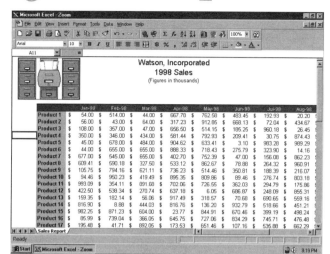

Customizing Toolbars

For example, if you often use custom views, you'll get tired of selecting View ➤ Custom Views, selecting the view from the dialog box, and then clicking Show each time you want to change views. Rather than go through this series of steps each time, you can add the custom view list to the toolbar. Then to change views, just pull down the list from the toolbar.

You can add and delete items from toolbars, create new toolbars, and change the icons on toolbar buttons. Start all of this magic by selecting Tools ➤ Customize to display the dialog box shown to the right.

You customize a toolbar by dragging buttons on and off it, or by changing the appearance of an existing button. Custom toolbars can speed up and simplify your work by making the features that you use just a click away. If you make a mistake while customizing a toolbar, such as deleting a button that you use often, you can always reset the toolbar to its original layout by selecting the toolbar in the Toolbars list of the Customize dialog box, and then clicking Reset.

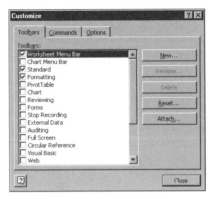

MOVING TOOLBARS

You don't have to leave toolbars where Excel puts them. You can move them anywhere on the screen.

Toolbars can be either docked or floating. A docked toolbar is fixed to one of the edges of the screen. (For example, the Standard and Formatting toolbars are docked to the top of the screen, just under the menu bar, by default.) When you move a toolbar away from any of the edges of the Excel window, it becomes a floating toolbar. (Some toolbars associated with specific features, such as the Chart toolbar, are displayed as floating toolbars by default.) Floating toolbars appear in their own small windows, with a title bar and Close box.

To move a docked toolbar, drag on the double lines at the far left end of the toolbar. To move a floating toolbar,

simply drag on its title bar — this is how you can move any window. When you're moving either type of toolbar, you can dock it by dragging it to any edge of the screen, or you can make it float by dragging it anywhere within the worksheet window. If you drag to the far left, right, or bottom of the screen, however, the toolbar appears with the buttons all on one column or row, called *docked*. If you move the toolbar elsewhere on the screen, it appears in its own small window, with a title bar and close box, called *floating*. You can drag a floating toolbar anywhere on the screen.

To return a toolbar to its previous location, you drag it back where it came from, or you can double-click its title bar (if it's floating) or the double line on its left edge (if it's docked).

Adding Toolbar Buttons

When you want to add a button to the toolbar, you first select the category of the command that you want to add. Then, you select the specific command in that category, and drag it to the toolbar.

NOTE *How many buttons you can add to a toolbar before others disappear depends on the resolution of your screen. If Windows 95 is set at 480 by 640 resolution, the default toolbars fit all of the way across the screen. Adding one new button will cause another to scroll off of the screen and out of view. If your screen is set at a higher resolution, such as 800 by 600, your toolbars will have room for several new buttons. The illustrations in this lesson show Excel at 800 by 600 resolution so you can see the effect of adding new buttons to a toolbar.*

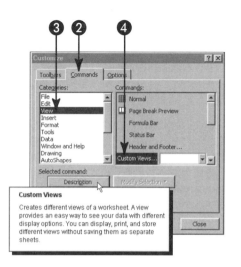

As an example, add the Custom Views pull-down menu to the Formatting toolbar:

❶ Select Tools ➢ Customize.

❷ Click the Commands tab. Excel displays the options shown in the top illustration at right.

❸ Click View in the Categories list. The commands in the View category appear in the Commands list.

❹ Click Custom Views in the Commands list. To read a description of the command, click the Description button. Read the description that appears, and then click away from the description to remove it from view.

❺ Point to the Custom Views item in the commands list.

❻ Drag it to the Formatting toolbar. As you drag over the toolbar, an icon of a button with a plus sign moves with the mouse pointer. The plus sign indicates that you are adding the button to the toolbar. You'll also see an I-beam icon indicating the position of the new toolbar button when you release the mouse.

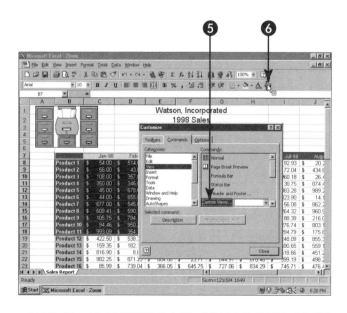

12

Customizing Excel

Changing Toolbar Buttons

7 Move the mouse so the I-beam is to the right of the Font Color button, and then release the mouse button. The Custom Views pull-down list is inserted into the toolbar. If you are using 480 by 640 resolution, so it extends below the edge of the screen, drag the button to the left of the Font Color button.

8 Close the Customize dialog box. The toolbar now includes the custom views list.

Custom views list

Changing Toolbar Buttons

In addition to adding buttons to a toolbar, you can delete buttons, change their position, and change how they appear. You can only do these things, however, when the Customize dialog box is displayed:

- Delete a button by dragging it off the toolbar.

- Change the position of a button by dragging it along the toolbar, or to another toolbar, or to the menu bar.

- Change the appearance of a button by right-clicking it and selecting options from the shortcut menu.

To see how this works, start by deleting one button and moving another. Remember, you can only change a toolbar when the Customize dialog box is open:

1 Select Tools ➤ Customize.

2 Drag the Custom Views button from the toolbar onto the worksheet. When you release the mouse, the button is removed from the toolbar.

3 Drag the Print Preview button to the far left end of the Standard toolbar. As you drag, you'll see the icon of a button and the I-beam. The icon does not include a plus sign, because you are moving, not copying, the object.

4 Release the mouse button when the I-beam is to the left of the New button. The toolbar buttons are now rearranged.

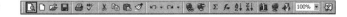

Changing Toolbar Buttons

NOTE

If you change your mind about the new position of a button, just drag it back. If you delete the button by mistake, you can return the toolbar to its default layout by using the Reset button in the Customize dialog box.

⑤ To restore the Standard toolbar to its original condition, first click the Toolbars tab of the Customize dialog box.

⑥ Click Standard in the Toolbars list.

TIP

Click the name Standard, not the check box to its left. If you click the check box, you'll remove the Standard toolbar from display. If this happens, just click the check box again to redisplay the toolbar.

⑦ Click Reset. A message appears asking if you want to reset the changes that you made to the toolbar.

⑧ Click OK.

⑨ Click Close when you're done customizing the toolbar.

For more customization options, make sure the Customize dialog box is open and right-click a toolbar button to see the shortcut menu shown to the right. The options on the shortcut menu let you reset the button to its default settings and change the name that appears in the ScreenTip when you point to the button. To change the ScreenTip, type the text you want to appear in the Name text box of the shortcut menu.

You can select to display the default style (which shows the icon), to display just the name of the button (such as the word New for the New button), or to display both text and the icon. The Begin a Group option inserts a vertical line before the button — or removes the line if it is already there.

Some items in the Commands list in the Customize dialog box do not have an icon along with the text. This means that only the text appears when you add the command to a toolbar. If you want an icon on the button, you have to add one yourself. To do so, right-

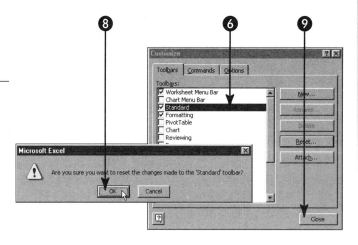

Creating a New Toolbar

click the button, choose Change Button Image from the shortcut menu to see the options shown to the right, and then click the image you want to use.

Creating a New Toolbar

You can only add so many buttons to a toolbar before it looks cluttered. As an alternative to adding buttons to an existing toolbar, you can create a new one. Once you create the toolbar, you add and customize its buttons as you just learned.

As an example, you'll create a custom toolbar now. You'll add buttons for creating diagonal text, displaying the AutoFormat dialog box, and enlarging and reducing the display. The Customize dialog box should still be on screen with the Toolbars tab displayed; if not, select Tools ➢ Customize and click the Toolbars tab if necessary:

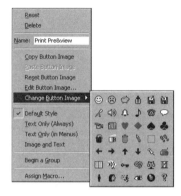

❶ Click New. A dialog box appears in which you enter the toolbar's name. The default suggestion is Custom 1.

❷ Type **MyBar**.

❸ Click OK. A small blank toolbar appears on screen, as shown to the right. (If the bar is obscured, move the dialog box out of the way.)

❹ Click the Commands tab.

❺ Click View in the Categories list.

❻ Scroll the Commands list to see the Zoom In and Zoom Out commands.

❼ Drag the Zoom In command to the blank toolbar.

❽ Drag the Zoom Out command to the right of the Zoom In button in the toolbar. The I-beam should be to the right of the button when you release the mouse.

❾ Click Format in the Categories list.

❿ Scroll to the bottom of the Commands.

⓫ Drag the AutoFormat command to the right end of the new toolbar.

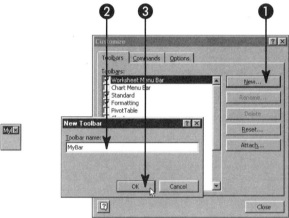

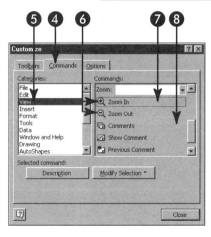

⑫ Scroll up the Commands until you see the commands for vertical and rotated text.

⑬ Drag the Vertical Text button to the right end of the toolbar. Then place Rotate Text Up to its right, and follow that with Rotate Text Down, Angle Text Downward, and Angle Text Upward.

⑭ Right-click the AutoFormat button on the new toolbar. That's the third button from the left.

⑮ Click Begin a Group. Excel inserts a vertical line to the left of the button.

⑯ Right-click the Vertical Text button on the new toolbar.

⑰ Click Begin a Group.

⑱ Click Close to close the Customize dialog box.

This may not be a toolbar that you use often, so you can temporarily remove it from the screen. You'll then display it again and try out the new buttons:

⑲ Click the Close button on the right end of the toolbar.

⑳ Right-click any toolbar. The name of your custom toolbar appears at the bottom of the shortcut menu.

㉑ Click MyBar. Your custom toolbar appears.

㉒ Click Zoom In on the toolbar. Excel magnifies the screen to 200%.

㉓ Click Zoom Out. The screen returns to 100%. If you continue clicking on Zoom Out the magnification changes to 75%, 50%, and then 25%. Click Zoom In until you return the screen to 100%.

㉔ Click cell B8.

㉕ Click Vertical Text. The letters appear one on top of the other in the cell.

㉖ Click Vertical Text again. The text in cell B8 reverts to its original alignment. The particular buttons that you added to the toolbar are toggles, changing the text between the alignment shown on the button and default horizontal text.

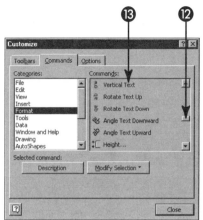

12

Customizing Excel

㉗ Try the other formatting buttons on the new toolbar.

You can close the toolbar and then reopen it at any time. If you do not want to keep this toolbar, select Tools ➢ Customize and click the Toolbars tab if necessary. Click MyBar at the end of the Toolbars list, and then click Delete.

CUSTOMIZING MENUS

You can customize menus, and create new ones, just as easily as you can create and customize toolbars. In fact, you use the same dialog box. You can add new commands to a menu, delete and move commands, and create entirely new menus. You can also add menus to a toolbar, if you don't want to add them to the menu bar. This way, a toolbar can contain custom pull-down menus as well as buttons.

TIP

You can move and dock the menu bar, just as you can toolbars. To move the menu bar, drag it by the double lines on its far left edge.

Adding Menus and Menu Items

You can add an item to a menu, and a menu to a toolbar, by dragging and dropping. When you drag an item from the Customize dialog box to the menu bar, Excel pulls down the menu you point to so you can drop the item where you want. It's that simple.

Take a look at two techniques now. You'll add a command to a menu, and you'll add a built-in menu to the toolbar:

❶ Select Tools ➢ Customize, and then click the Commands tab.

❷ Make sure the File item is selected in the Categories list.

❸ Scroll to the end of the Commands list.

❹ Click Toggle Read Only.

5 Drag Toggle Read Only to the Edit item on the menu bar — do not release the mouse button yet. When you point to Edit, the menu is pulled down. As you drag down the menu, a horizontal line appears.

6 Drag the mouse so the horizontal line is under the Repeat command, and then release the mouse button to place the command there. The icon and text of the command appear in the menu, as shown to the right. (Note that the full names of the Undo and Repeat commands will depend on your last actions.)

Excel contains a number of built-in menus that you'll see when using the menu bar. You can add these menus to the toolbar to access them a little faster. Not only are the main menu items available, such as File and Edit, but the submenus as well, such as Clear and Row.

For example, suppose you use the Clear command from the Edit menu to clear either the formats or contents. Rather than pull down the Edit menu first to access Clear, you can add the menu to the toolbar.

7 In the Commands tab of the Customize dialog box, which should still be on screen, scroll to the bottom of the Categories list.

8 Click Built-in Menus.

9 Drag Clear in the Commands list to between the Cut and Copy buttons in the Standard toolbar. Once you close the Customize dialog box, you'll now be able to access the Clear menu from the toolbar. Remember, depending on the resolution of your screen, adding the button to the toolbar may push others off of the screen.

You can customize menu items just as you customize toolbar buttons. With the Customize dialog box displayed, right-click the menu item to display the shortcut menu. However, only the Reset, Delete, Name, and Begin a Group options are available.

Now you'll restore the menu and toolbar to their default layout:

10 Drag the Clear menu off the Standard toolbar.

11 Pull down the Edit menu.

12 Drag Toggle Read Only off the menu.

12

Customizing Excel

Creating New Menus

You can also quickly reset the menu bar using the Toolbars tab of the Customize dialog box. Select Worksheet Menu Bar in the Toolbars list, click Reset, and then click OK in the message box that appears.

Creating New Menus

Toolbars are useful, but a bar of tools takes up valuable screen real estate. When you want access to a number of functions but don't want to give up a worksheet row, create a menu instead. Menus are easy to create and use, and you can add menus to either the menu bar or a toolbar.

As an example, you'll create a menu of text rotation options:

1 With the Commands tab of the Customize dialog box displayed, scroll to the bottom of the Categories list.

2 Click New Menu. The Commands list now shows one item, New Menu.

3 Drag New Menu from the commands list to the right side of the Formatting toolbar. A menu labeled New Menu appears.

4 Now change the name. First right-click the new menu. The shortcut menu appears.

5 Delete the text in the Name box.

6 Type **My Menu** in the Name box and press Enter.

7 Now, to add items to the menu, drag commands or built-in menus to it. Start by scrolling the Categories list and selecting Format.

8 Scroll through the Commands list until you see the commands for vertical and rotated text.

9 Drag Vertical Text to the My Menu — but do not release the mouse button yet. When you drag the first item to the menu, all that appears when it drops down is a empty box.

10 Drag the command to the empty box — the I-beam will appear within it — and then release the mouse button to add the

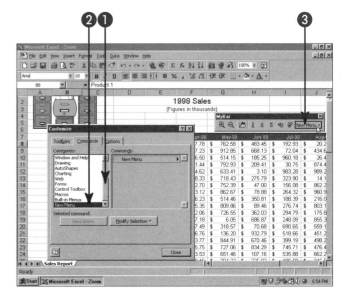

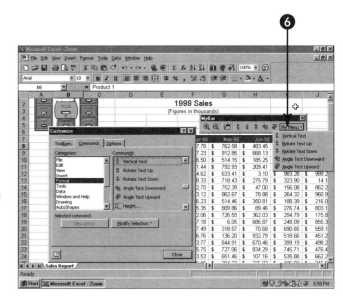

command to the menu. The menu remains pulled down, so you can add items to it easily.

⓫ Drag Rotate Text Up to insert it at the end of the menu. When you drag into the menu, you'll see a horizontal line indicating the command's position. Release the mouse button when the line is below the Vertical Text command.

⓬ Add the following commands to the end of the menu: Rotate Text Down, Angle Text Downward, Angle Text Upward. The completed menu should appear as shown to the right.

⓭ Drag the custom menu off the toolbar to delete it.

⓮ Click Close to close the Customize dialog box.

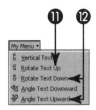

TIP

Remember, to make any changes to the toolbars or menus, you must display the Customize dialog box.

■ Customization Options

The Options tab of the Customize dialog box gives you some final ways to tailor Excel to your taste. You can choose to display large toolbar buttons and determine whether to show the ScreenTips when you point to a button. Large toolbar buttons are easier to see and helpful to the visually impaired, but the bars take up quite a lot of space, as shown in the illustration to the right.

You can also choose a menu animation option to customize the way drop-down menus appear. By default, there is no animation — the menu just appears when you click the menu bar. You can select to have menus unfold open, slide open, or open randomly using one of the two animations.

When a menu slides open, it appears to be pulled straight down like a window shade. When a menu unfolds, it appears diagonally from the upper-left to the lower-right corner.

12

Customizing Excel

Skills Challenge

If you share your computer with other Excel users, especially in an office, you may want to restore all of the default toolbars and menus. It can be disconcerting to find tools missing from a toolbar, or to see new icons and menus.

SKILLS CHALLENGE: CUSTOMIZING YOUR SCREEN

In this exercise, you'll create a number of custom views and design your own toolbars and menus. You will design two views for a workbook — Administration and Employee. The Employee view will have some confidential information hidden. You'll save the workbook with the Employee view on screen, so it automatically appears when the workbook is next opened.

You'll end the exercise, however, by restoring Excel to its default layout. You don't want to face angry coworkers in the morning!

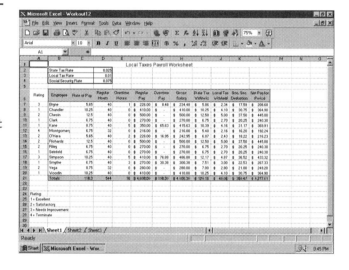

1 Open the Workout 12 workbook.

2 Zoom the display to 75%. The worksheet contains payroll information as well as employee ratings.

3 Save the current view as a custom view with the name Administration.

 What is the purpose of creating and saving custom views?

4 Hide column A to conceal the employee rating information.

5 Zoom the display to 100%.

6 Save the current view as a custom view with the name Employee.

7 Save the workbook with the name Payroll Information.

8 Close and then reopen the workbook.

 What view is displayed when you close and then reopen a workbook that has several views?

TRY OUT THE
INTERACTIVE TUTORIALS
ON YOUR CD!

9 Change to the Administration view. The hidden column reappears, and the screen zooms to 75%.

10 Remove the Formatting toolbar from the screen.

> **3** *What are the ways to remove a toolbar from the screen?*

11 Create a new toolbar, giving it a name of your choice.

 12 Add the following commands to the toolbar, from left to right as listed here. Group the commands from each category: From the Format category, add Font and Font Size. From the Edit category, add Paste Formatting and Paste Values. From the View category, add Custom Views and Full Screen. The toolbar should appear as shown to the right.

> **4** *What is the purpose of grouping buttons on a toolbar?*

 13 Change the image of the Full Screen button so it appears as shown to the right.

14 Create a new menu on the right end of the menu bar, and change its name to Useful Tasks.

> **5** *Do you have to add new menus to the menu bar?*

15 Add the following commands to the menu, top to bottom as listed here. From the File category, add Mail Recipient and Routing Slip. From the Tools category, add Calculate Now. From the Data category, add AutoFilter, Show All, and Advanced Filter. The completed menu will look like the figure at right.

16 Close the Customize dialog box and practice using the custom toolbar and menu.

> **6** *Can you make changes to the toolbars or menu bar when the Customize dialog box is closed?*

 17 If you share your computer with other users, and do not think the custom toolbar and menu will be useful, delete them.

Troubleshooting

TROUBLESHOOTING

You should keep track of changes you make in the Options dialog box; there is no Reset command to automatically restore all of the default settings. If you do run into problems when using the techniques you learned in this lesson, these troubleshooting ideas should help:

Problem	Solution
The toolbars on my screen look nothing like they used to. I can't find the buttons I want to click. What's the story?	Some user probably removed or changed the toolbars. Select Tools ➤ Customize, and click the Toolbars tab. Check the Worksheet Menu Bar, Standard, and Formatting check boxes. Click each of these items, click Reset, and then click OK in the message box that appears. This returns the default toolbars and the menu bar to their original layouts.
I added an item to a toolbar, but all that appears in its place is an empty button.	Some items in the Commands tab of the Customize dialog box do not have an icon. If you add the item to a toolbar, and then choose Default Styles from the shortcut menu, Excel removes the text, leaving a blank button. Add an icon to the button using the Change Button Image option from the shortcut menu.
I'm trying to drag a button off of the toolbar to remove it, but it is not working.	You can only delete, add, and change toolbars when the Customize dialog box is displayed. Select Tools ➤ Customize, and then drag the button off. Don't worry — a lot of beginning users make this mistake.

Problem	Solution
I know that I created a custom toolbar, but it is not on my screen.	Don't panic. A previous user may have closed the toolbar. Right-click any toolbar. The name of your custom toolbar should be at or near the bottom of the shortcut menu. Click the name to display the toolbar. If the toolbar is not listed, someone deleted it. Sorry.

WRAP UP

Customizing Excel to suit your tastes can make your work go more smoothly and effectively. Although things can go wrong, mistakes are easy to correct. In this lesson, you learned how to customize Excel in these ways:

- Zoom the display to enlarge or reduce what you see on screen. Use either the Zoom list in the toolbar, or the View ➢ Zoom command

- Create custom views that contain a specific magnification, hidden rows and columns, and print settings

- Use the View menu, and the toolbars shortcut menu, to hide and display screen elements

- Customize the way Excel looks and works using the Tools ➢ Options command

- Customize and create toolbars and menus

Now that you know how to customize Excel, take some time to set it up for yourself. Work through the pages of the Options dialog box, selecting the settings that you want. Then, scroll through all of the categories and commands using the Tools ➢ Customize command. Create a new toolbar with the commands that you want to access that are not already on an Excel toolbar.

Now that you know how to customize the screen, you'll take a look at a way to customize the way your information appears. In the next lesson, you will learn how to create charts and maps to

PART V

Excel Graphics

This part shows you how to add eye-catching graphics, create charts and maps, insert special effects with WordArt, and create your own custom artwork. It includes the following lessons:

- Lesson 13: Creating Charts and Maps
- Lesson 14: Using Clip Art and WordArt
- Lesson 15: Creating Custom Graphics

Creating Charts and Maps

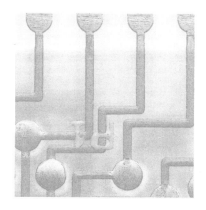

 GOALS

In this lesson, you will learn how to create charts and maps to graphically illustrate your data. You'll learn how to:

■ Create embedded charts and chart sheets

■ Customize charts

■ Map data

■ Customize data maps

60 MINUTES

Get Ready

GET READY

Sometimes the most effective way to get your point across is to illustrate it with a chart or map. Charts and maps can display trends, emphasize important points, and just add life to otherwise humdrum numbers.

This lesson refers to the following workbooks:

File Name	Location
Charts	Exercise directory
Charts Solution	Solution directory
Workout 13	Exercise directory
Solution 13	Solution directory

When you complete this lesson, you'll have created the chart and map shown on this page.

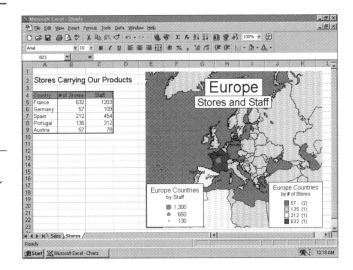

EMPHASIZING DATA IN CHARTS

No matter how much formatting you apply to a worksheet, its numbers are not always easy to interpret. You can only see so many cells at one time, and it's often difficult to detect relationships, see trends, and draw conclusions. Representing data in a chart can solve these problems. A well-organized chart can make numbers come alive, draw attention to the points you want to make, and have the most impact on your audience.

The charts that you learn about in this lesson are often called graphs. Excel uses the term chart to refer to graphic representations of worksheet data.

Before creating a chart, you'll take a look at what charts are made of. The illustration at the top of the next page shows a typical chart and the data used to create it. This particular chart, a two-dimensional column chart, compares the profits of two companies over a three-year period. Column charts are just one type of chart that Excel can create, as you'll soon learn.

Creating a Chart

A chart must have at least one data series. A data series is a set of numbers that are different values of the same component. This chart has two series, one for each of the companies. (You could conceivably also plot this data as three series — one for each year.) The series are indicated in the legend that shows the colors used to represent the areas in each series.

The chart also has category and value axis labels. The category labels explain that the areas represent a span of time over three years, from 1997 to 1999. The value axis shows the value that the areas represent — the dollar amounts between 0 and $1,000,000. The category axis is also called the x axis. The value axis in this chart is also called the y axis.

Every chart must contain at least one data series, but not all charts have the same number of axes. Two-dimensional charts have an x axis and a y axis. Three-dimensional charts also have a z axis. (In three-dimensional charts, the value axis is actually the z axis. The y axis represents the depth of the chart.) Pie charts can only chart a single data series and have no axes at all.

Excel lets you create two general types of charts — embedded charts and chart sheets. An embedded chart is right on a worksheet, although it's not necessarily on the sheet containing the data you used to create the chart. Because the chart is part of a worksheet, you can print it on the same page as other worksheet data. A chart sheet is a special type of sheet in the workbook. Chart sheets contain just the chart itself, with no worksheet cells.

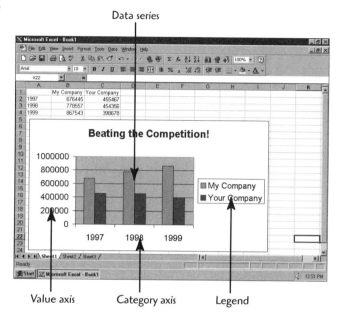

Data series

Value axis   Category axis   Legend

13

Creating Charts and Maps

Creating a Chart

Creating a chart is really easy. Start by selecting the cells that contain the information you want to chart, including the row and column labels, as shown to the right. This isn't really necessary because you'll have a chance to choose the cells later, but it saves a step. The row labels will become the category axis labels; the column labels will identify each series in the legend.

The selected cells don't have to be contiguous. Select the first group of cells that contain the data you want to include, and then hold down the Ctrl key and select any additional cell groups you want to include.

Employee Sales Figures

All figures in Francs		
	1997	1998
Smithers	565468	464565
Watson	369575	453769
Ringhold	653589	764546

Creating a Chart

NOTE *Although there is no "official" limit to the amount of data that can be included in a chart, there is a practical limit. If you try to chart a large number of rows, for example, not all of the labels will fit on the category axis.*

You then use a special feature called the Chart Wizard to create the chart:

1 Open the Charts workbook on the Exercise directory.

2 On the Sales worksheet, select cells B3 to D7.

3 Click the Chart Wizard button on the Standard toolbar. You'll see the first Chart Wizard dialog box, shown in the illustration at right. Here you select the type of the chart. Typically, you choose both a type and a subtype. For example, if you select Pie as the chart type, the dialog box displays several different types of pie charts. At this point you can choose a specific subtype. When you click a subtype, a description of it appears below the subtype list.

NOTE *In the Standard Type page of the first Chart Wizard dialog box, you choose a chart type and subtype. You can also select a chart type from the Custom Types page of the dialog box. The options in the Custom Types tab do not have subtypes.*

4 Make sure the Column chart type is selected, and click the icon for the 3-D column subtype — the last subtype shown.

5 Point to the button labeled *Press and hold to view sample.*

6 Hold down the mouse button. The subtypes will be replaced by a rough sample of the chart.

7 Release the mouse button.

8 Click Next.

TRY OUT THE

INTERACTIVE TUTORIALS

ON YOUR CD!

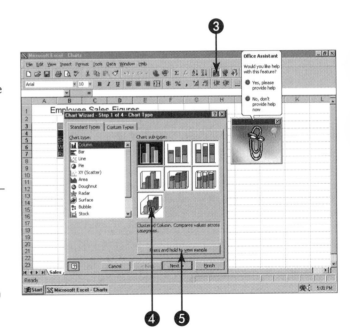

NOTE

In the second Chart Wizard dialog box, you can change the range of cells to use for the chart, and the cells to plot as the data series. If you selected the correct cells before starting the Wizard, you won't need to make any changes here. If you did not select cells first, use the Data Range and Series pages of this dialog box to choose which cells to plot. You can also choose to plot the series shown in the rows rather than in the columns. If you select to plot the rows in this example, there will be three series, one for each employee. The way you plot the chart depends on how you want to illustrate and emphasize the information in the worksheet.

9 Click Next to accept the default settings. The Wizard page that now appears, shown in the illustration at right, lets you set a wide range of chart options. The number of pages in the dialog box depends on the chart type. With a pie chart, for example, there will be just three pages — Titles, Legend, and Data Labels. You'll use the Titles page in this lesson. The other pages are described in Table 13-1, which follows a bit later in this lesson.

10 In the Chart Title box, type **Sales by Employee**. When you stop typing, Excel adds the title to the sample of the chart.

11 In the Category (X) Axis box, type **Employee**. This text appears below the x axis.

12 In the Value (Z) Axis box, type **Francs**.

13 Click Next. In this final Wizard dialog box, you choose whether to place the chart in a separate chart sheet (the As New Sheet option), or to embed it within an existing worksheet (the As Object In option). The default setting is to save the chart in the current sheet. You'll use that setting for this exercise.

14 Click Finish.

15 Make sure the chart is selected. If it's not, click once on it. The sizing handles are displayed. To see what the chart will look like when printed, click the Print Preview button.

16 Print a hard copy of the chart by clicking the the Print button.

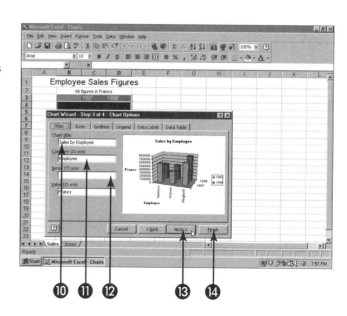

Creating a Chart

Excel displays the chart in the current worksheet, along with the Chart toolbar, as shown at right. Also notice that the Data pull-down menu on the menu bar has been replaced with the Chart menu. Don't worry if the chart seems too small; you'll take care of that later. If it gets in the way, you can move the toolbar out of the way by dragging it by its title bar. (Check Lesson 12 for more details on working with toolbars.)

The small black boxes around the border of the chart are called *handles*. You use the handles to change the size of the chart, and they indicate that the chart is selected. The data used to create the chart is also surrounded by a border. There are separate borders around the column labels, the row labels, and the data being plotted.

If you click outside the chart area, the handles and Chart toolbar disappear and the chart is no longer selected. The chart is linked to the worksheet cells that you selected to create it. If you change any of the text or values in the cells, Excel adjusts the chart automatically to reflect those changes.

When you print or preview your worksheet, Excel also prints or previews any embedded charts in the worksheet or the print area. If the chart is selected or in a separate chart sheet, however, only the chart itself prints or appears in the print preview. If not all of your row labels appear in the chart, try enlarging it (you'll learn how soon), and printing the chart by itself on a page in landscape orientation. If you have a color printer, your chart will print with the same colors that you see on screen; otherwise, Excel selects shades of gray and patterns to represent the colors on a monochrome printer.

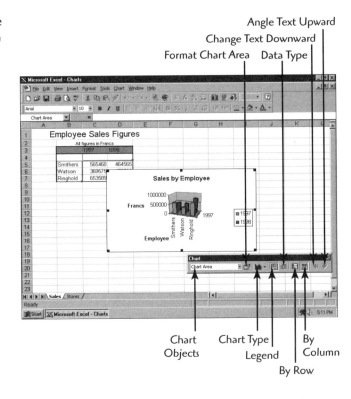

Angle Text Upward
Change Text Downward
Format Chart Area   Data Type

Chart Objects   Chart Type   By Column
Legend   By Row

CREATING A CHART SHEET

You can also create a chart by placing it on a chart sheet. Chart sheets are separate sheets of the workbook that only contain a single chart. You can quickly create a chart sheet by selecting the cells you want to chart and then pressing the F11 key. Excel creates a chart sheet using all the default values, a two-dimensional column chart without any titles. To customize the chart before you create it, use the Chart Wizard, and then select As New Sheet in the final Wizard dialog box. You can customize charts in a chart sheet pretty much the same way that you customize embedded charts, as you will learn in this lesson. However, you cannot change the size or position of the chart on a chart sheet.

In the third Chart Wizard dialog box, you filled out the Titles page. That dialog box will contain a number of pages, which are described in Table 13-1.

TABLE 13-1 PAGES OF THE THIRD CHART WIZARD DIALOG BOX

Page	Description
Axes	Turn off or on the text along the Category, Value, and Series axes, and determine whether the category axis uses a timescale
Gridlines	Turn off or on grid lines at the major and minor intervals along the axes
Legend	Hide or display the legend, and choose a legend position
Data Labels	Choose to display values, labels, or percentages (for pie charts) with the series
Data Table	Select to include a table of the plotted data with the chart, and to include color keys to the legend items with the data

■ Working with Charts

You can select the whole chart to change its size and position, or you can select individual parts of the chart to customize that part. When you point to the chart, a ScreenTip appears showing the name of the part you are pointing to.

To select the entire chart, use either of these techniques:

- Click the border around the chart.

- Point inside the chart near the border so the ScreenTip says Chart Area and click.

You'll know that the entire chart is selected because it will be surrounded by handles, and Chart Area appears in the Chart Objects box in the Chart toolbar. The cells used to create the chart will also be surrounded by a border.

To delete a chart from a worksheet, click it so the entire chart is selected, and then press the Delete key. To delete a chart sheet, right-click its worksheet tab and select Delete from the shortcut menu.

You customize a chart using the Chart toolbar, the menu bar, and the shortcut menu that appears when you right-click a chart. As with all shortcut menus, the options that appear depend on where you are pointing. For example, if you right-click the chart area, the shortcut menu will include the options shown in the illustration at right. The menu will include fewer items when you right-click any other part of the chart.

You can also customize a chart using the menu bar. Use the Format menu, for example, to display a dialog box for formatting the selected area, and use the Chart menu to make more comprehensive changes to the chart.

If you change your mind about your choices in the Chart Wizard, pull down the Chart menu, or right-click the chart area. The first four items in the Chart menu, and the four items in the second section of the Shortcut menu, correspond to the four Wizard dialog boxes. Click Chart Options in either menu, for example, to display the dialog box for entering chart titles and setting the other options mentioned earlier. Use the Chart Type option to change the type and subtype of the chart. Use the Location option in the menu or shortcut menu to move the chart to a chart sheet, or to a worksheet, and use the Source Data option to change the cells being plotted.

Changing the Chart Size and Position

You can quickly change the chart's size by dragging the handles using these techniques:

- Drag a handle on the top or bottom border to change the chart's height.

- Drag a handle on the right or left border to change the chart's width.

- Drag a handle on a corner to change the chart's height and width at the same time.

To move the chart within the worksheet, point to the border anywhere around the chart so the mouse pointer appears like an arrow and then drag. As you drag the chart, a dashed border indicates the new chart position and the mouse pointer turns into a four-directional arrow.

Try changing the size and position of the chart now:

1. Make sure that the entire chart is selected.

2. Point anywhere around the chart so the mouse pointer appears as a four-sided arrow when you click the mouse, and drag the chart so it starts in column A, row 8.

3. Point to the handle in the lower-right corner of the chart so the mouse pointer appears as a two-pointed diagonal arrow.

4. Drag the handle to cell H27. As you drag, you'll see an outline of the chart indicating its new size. When you release the mouse button, the chart now appears as in the illustration at right.

Changing the Chart Type

You can always change the chart type if the chart type and subtype you selected do not adequately portray what you want to get across. In fact, Excel gives you several ways to change the chart type.

Next you'll try various methods to see the other chart types that are available. If the chart is not selected, select it now, and then follow these steps:

1. Pull down the Chart Type list in the Chart toolbar to display the options shown at right. When you point to a chart type, a ScreenTip appears with its name.

2. Click the 3-D Area Chart option, the middle button on the top row. Each series is now shown as a continuous area, rather than as individual columns.

3. Right-click the chart area and choose Chart Type from the shortcut menu to see the Chart Type dialog box. You can also display this dialog box by choosing Chart ➢ Chart Type.

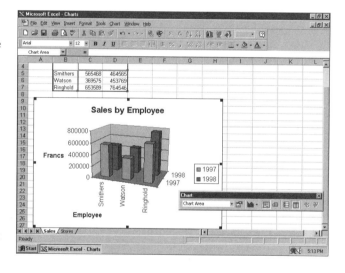

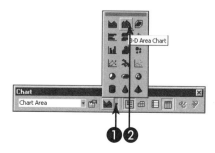

Changing Chart Elements

The Chart Type dialog box is the same as the first Chart Wizard dialog box but with a few additional options. For example, you can choose to use the type and subtype as the default style for all new charts. If you display this dialog box when a particular series is selected, you can also choose to apply the new type to that series alone.

4 Click the Custom Types tab to see the options shown at right.

5 Scroll the Chart Type list and click Tubes. The Sample area displays how the chart will appear. Custom Types also include background color schemes and various arrangements of the axis, legend, and data labels. In this case, Excel removes the title and moves the legend below the chart.

6 Click OK. You'll leave the background as it is but return the chart to a three-dimensional column chart.

7 Pull down the Chart Type list in the Chart toolbar and select 3-D Column Chart, the middle button in the third row. Excel retains the color scheme, legend, and data label arrangement.

Changing Chart Elements

In addition to changing the chart type, you can change the appearance of each part of the chart. To add titles, a legend, grid lines, a data table, or data labels, use the Chart Options command from the Chart menu or shortcut menu. You can also add a legend, data table, and grid lines using the Chart toolbar.

To quickly choose formatting options for a specific chart element, such as an axis or data series, double-click the part of the chart you want to change. Remember, when you point to the chart, the ScreenTip indicates what you are pointing to. So, before you double-click, make sure the ScreenTip shows you are pointing to the correct part.

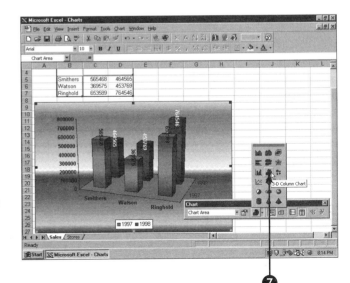

Changing Chart Elements

You can also select the part of the chart first, and then choose options from the shortcut menu or Format menu. Select a chart element using any of these methods:

- Click the part of the chart.

- Right-click the part of the chart to select it and display the shortcut menu.

- Pull down the Chart Objects list in the Chart toolbar and select the part from the list.

You'll know the part is selected when the handles appear around just it — not around the entire chart or some other element of the chart.

EXPLODING PIE CHARTS

If you create a pie chart, you can drag one or more segments so they appear separated from the pie, or exploded. Click the segment so only it is selected — you have to click once to select the pie then again on the slice you want to select — as shown here.

Then drag the segment away from the pie the distance you want. Exploding a segment draws attention to that specific section of the pie, as shown in the illustration below.

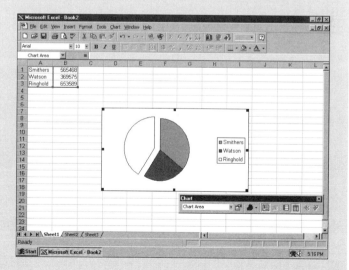

13

Creating Charts and Maps

Changing Chart Elements

Once the part is selected, its name appears after the Format option in the shortcut menu and the Selected option in the Format menu. So customize the part by choosing Format from the shortcut menu, or selecting Format ➢ Selected.

If you double-click the chart element, or use the Format or shortcut menu, Excel displays a dialog box with options for that element. The options in the dialog box depend on the object you selected.

To experiment with this feature, you'll make some changes to the chart now:

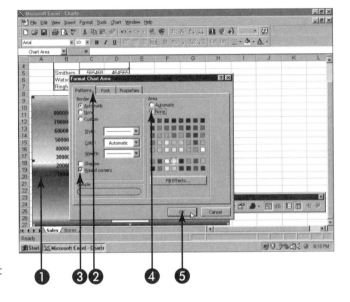

❶ Select the entire chart.

❷ Select Format ➢ Selected Chart Area to display the Format Chart Area dialog box. Click the Patterns tab if that page of the dialog box is not displayed.

❸ Click Round Corners in the Border section.

❹ Click None in the Area section. By the way, you can use the Fill Effects option to display more extensive choices for changing the chart background.

❺ Click OK.

❻ Pull down the Chart Objects list in the Chart toolbar, and select Series "1998."

❼ Select Format ➢ Selected Data Series. In the dialog box that appears, you set the patterns, shape, and other options for the selected series.

❽ Click the Shape tab to see the following options.

❾ Click column shape number 6.

❿ Click OK. The 1998 series is now represented by cone-shaped objects, while the 1997 series still uses columns.

⓫ Select Chart ➢ Chart Options.

⓬ Choose the Data Labels tab if that page of the dialog box is not already displayed.

⓭ Click None. This removes the data labels from the cones and columns.

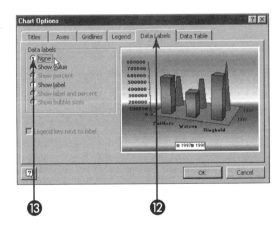

⑭ Click the Titles tab.

⑮ In the Chart Title box, type **Employee Sales**.

⑯ Click OK.

⑰ Double-click the chart title (not the words themselves in the title) to display the options for customizing the title.

⑱ Click the Font tab.

⑲ Scroll the Font list and select Times New Roman.

⑳ Click OK. The chart now appears as shown in the second illustration at right. Refer to the workbook Chart Solution in the Solution folder to check your work.

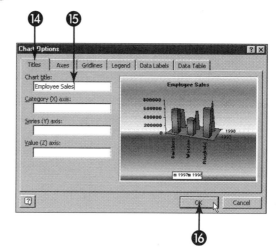

13

Creating Charts and Maps

SETTING THE AXIS SCALE

When you format the value axis, you can set the scale used to represent the minimum and maximum values, and the intermediate tick marks, along the axis. When you create a chart, Excel uses the largest number being plotted for the value at the very top of the axis, and the lowest number for the bottom of the scale. Negative values appear below the zero line. Change the scale to use other values.

For example, suppose you are charting student grades. Even though the highest grade is just 88, you want the maximum value on the axis to be 100. To change the scale, double-click the value axis line, and click the Scale tab. Double-click in the Maximum text box, and type 100.

Mapping Excel Data

Working with Three-Dimensional Charts

To customize the look of three-dimensional charts, select Chart ➣ 3-D View to open the dialog box shown at right. Here you can change the rotation, elevation, and perspective. Either click the buttons to change the settings, or enter new amounts in the appropriate text boxes.

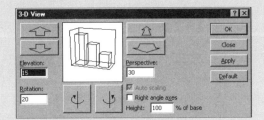

MAPPING EXCEL DATA

If your worksheet is organized by geographic area, you can plot the data on a map. Excel uses colors and patterns to represent the values within their geographic location, as shown in the illustration at right. Before creating a map, check that you've used the names of states or countries as the row labels. For Excel to create a map, it needs state or country names so it can select the map's geographic locations. For states, use either the official Postal abbreviations or the complete names. Use the complete names of countries.

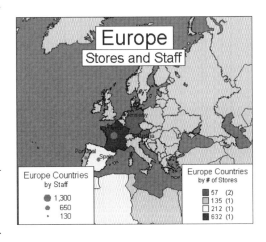

TIP

To create maps, you must have installed the Microsoft Map feature when you installed Excel or the Microsoft Office suite. If you did not install the Map feature, you can easily add it to your setup. See Appendix A for additional information.

Creating a Map

As an example, you'll create the map you saw in the previous illustration. Follow these steps:

1 Click the Stores worksheet tab at the bottom of the screen to display the data for that worksheet.

2 Select cells A4 to C9.

3 Click the Map button in the Standard toolbar. The mouse pointer appears as a crosshair when you move it over the worksheet area.

4 Drag over cells E1 to L23. In most cases, Excel will display the map when you release the mouse button. Sometimes, however, Excel may have more than one way to map the data, or it may not be able to determine the type of map to use. In this case, Excel displays the Multiple Maps Available dialog box.

5 Make sure that the Europe Countries in Europe option is selected.

6 Click OK. Excel displays the map, the Microsoft Map Control, and the Map toolbar, which replaces the Standard and Formatting toolbars, as shown to the right. (You'll learn more about this control and toolbar shortly.)

Even though you initially selected two columns of data (columns B and C), Excel mapped only one of the columns. Notice that the legend divides the values from column B into ranges based on the number of stores. Following the number of stores in each range is the number of countries that fall within the range — the number within parentheses. If the Microsoft Map Control obscures the map, drag it out of the way by its title bar.

Customizing Maps

You use the Microsoft Map Control, the toolbar, and the menu bar to customize the map. Before going on, take a closer look at the Microsoft Map Control.

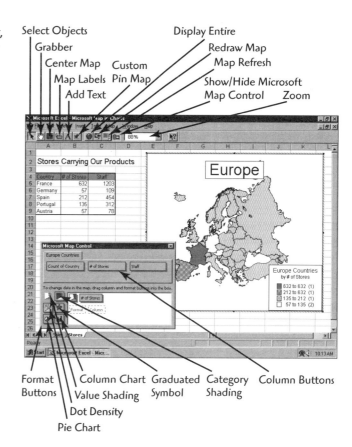

Select Objects
Grabber
Center Map — Custom
Map Labels — Pin Map
Add Text

Display Entire
Redraw Map
Map Refresh
Show/Hide Microsoft
Map Control — Zoom

Format Buttons — Column Chart — Graduated — Category — Column Buttons
Value Shading — Symbol — Shading
Dot Density
Pie Chart

Customizing Maps

You use the format buttons on the left side of the Microsoft Map Control to select the format of the map. You use the column buttons on the top to select the series being plotted. The large box in the control shows the column being plotted and the format applied. Right now, the # of Stores series is plotted, using the Value Shading format.

To change the format, drag a format button into the box, to the column you want to affect. To change the series, drag a column button. For example, to plot the Staff column rather than the # of Stores column, drag the Staff column button to the # of Stores button in the box, and then release the mouse button.

There are two dimmed boxes under the buttons representing the format and column being plotted. Use these boxes to add a series to the map. For instance, to plot the Staff column in addition to # of Stores, drag the Staff button to the dimmed box labeled Column. Then, drag one of the format buttons not currently being used to the column to apply that format. Some combinations of formats cannot be used, but Excel will warn you if you try.

Try making some changes to the map now. You'll start by changing the format of the map and adding a second series and legend:

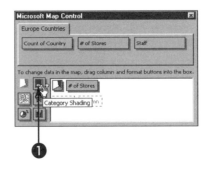

1. Drag the Category Shading button at right. With this format, the legend and map are color-coded, and the legend shows the specific values for the countries from the worksheet.

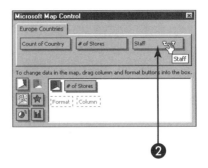

2. Drag the Staff column button from the top of the dialog box to the dimmed box that says Column. Excel adds a second legend to the map using the Dot Density format, as shown here. The dot density format inserts dots on each geographical area in proportion to the value. In this case, each dot represents 30 staff members.

3. Drag the Graduated Symbol format button to the Dot Density button for the Staff column. The Graduated Symbol format inserts bullets on the map and in the legend. The size of the bullet is relative to the value.

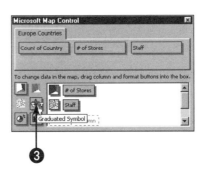

4. Click the legend that says Europe Countries by Staff. It will be surrounded by a frame with handles, and the mouse pointer appears as a four-directional arrow.

5. Drag the legend to the lower-left corner of the map.

If you want to delete a series of data from a map, drag its column button out of the Microsoft Map Control window. Excel removes the legend and the information from the map. To add data to the map, select Insert ➢ Data, and then select the range of cells to add.

Now, you'll add labels to the map to help identify the countries, and position the map differently within the map border. If you like, you can close the Microsoft Map Control by clicking its Close button, or by clicking the Show/Hide Microsoft Map Control button on the toolbar. Click the toolbar button again if you want to redisplay the Map Control.

6 Click the Map Labels button in the Map toolbar. A dialog box appears with options for inserting map feature names (such as country names) or values from the worksheet. Map feature names is the default.

7 Click OK.

8 Point to France in the map. A ScreenTip appears with the name of the country.

9 Click France. Excel inserts the country name on the map.

10 Add the names to Spain, Portugal, Germany, and Austria. Because the name will appear where you click, click in locations so the names do not overlap.

11 Click the Center Map button in the Map toolbar. The area of the map you now click will be centered in the map box.

12 Click Germany in the map. Excel positions the map so Germany is in the center. To instead position the map in the box by dragging, click the Grabber button in the toolbar and then drag the map.

13 Click the Center Map button to turn that feature off.

Adding Map Features

In addition to labels, you can add geographic features to maps, such as country and state capitals, oceans, and major highways. The more

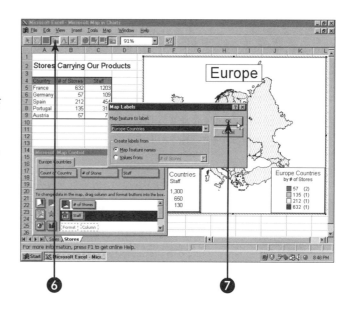

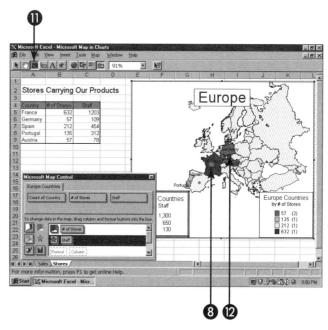

13

Creating Charts and Maps

Adding Map Features

detail you add to a map, however, the more difficult it can be to read, so add features with caution.

In this exercise, you will add the oceans and other continents to give the map some additional perspective:

① Select Map ➤ Add Feature. Excel opens the Add Feature dialog box.

② Scroll the list and select World Oceans.

③ Click OK. Excel adds a blue background to represent the oceans.

④ Select Map ➤ Add Feature.

⑤ Scroll the list and select World Countries.

⑥ Click OK. Excel adds to the map the other countries from the displayed area, as shown in the illustration at right. To display the entire world, by the way, click the Display Entire button on the toolbar.

TIP

The Undo option is not available when working with maps — either from the Standard toolbar or the Edit menu. If you select options and map features and end up with changes you don't want to keep, select View ➤ Previous from the menu bar. Excel will return the map to its previous view.

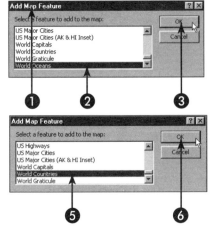

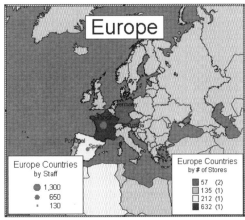

ADDING AND REMOVING OTHER MAP FEATURES

Use the Map ➤ Features command to display the dialog box shown here for adding and removing features from the map. The dialog box lists a standard set of features as well as ones you've applied using the Map ➤ Add Features command. The checked boxes indicate the features applied to the map. You can select and deselect check boxes to add and remove features.

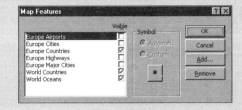

Finally, you'll add and format a subtitle for the map:

7 Select View ➢ Subtitle. Excel inserts a box under the map title with the text *Subtitle*.

8 Double-click the subtitle box.

9 Delete the text in the box, and then type **Stores and Staff**.

10 Click the map outside of the text box.

11 Click the text box again to select it.

12 Drag the text box so it appears centered under the title.

13 Click outside of the map.

To add text anywhere on the map, click the Add Text button on the toolbar, click the map where you want the text to appear, and then type.

The completed map is shown in the illustration at right. Refer to the workbook Chart Solution in the Solution folder to check your work.

If you later want to move the map, just drag it to the new location. When you click the map once, it will be surrounded by handles that you can also use to change its size. Remember, you can drag top, bottom, and side handles to change size of map in one direction at once; you can drag corner handles to change map size in two directions at once. To move the map, point to it so the mouse pointer appears as a four-directional arrow, and then drag the map to its new location. To make more extensive changes to the map, double-click it to display the map toolbar and the Microsoft Map Control.

SKILLS CHALLENGE: CHARTING AND MAPPING WORKSHEET DATA

You conquered the world map in the exercises in this lesson; now it's time to conquer the United States. In this challenge, you'll create both a chart and a map to illustrate the same set of information. Then, you decide which format is most suitable for the data:

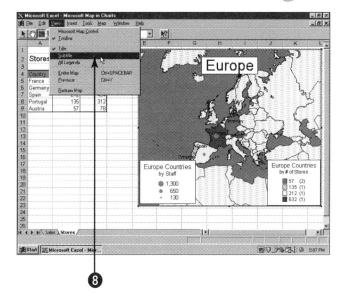

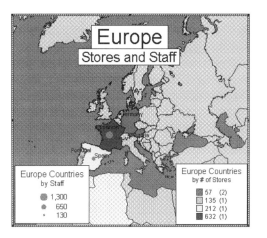

Skills Challenge

1 Open the Workout 13 workbook on the Exercises folder of the CD. The workbook contains two worksheets — Chart and Map — with identical data.

2 On the Chart worksheet, create a chart using the data in cells A3 to C13 using the Columns With Depth chart type in the Custom Types list.

 Can you later change the chart type if you do not like your selections from the Chart Wizard? If so, how?

3 Enlarge the chart just enough that you can see all of the row labels along the Category axis.

 Can you change the size of a chart if you create it in its own chart sheet? If not, what are the benefits of using a separate chart sheet?

4 Format the chart area with a light shade of gray. The final result should resemble the illustration at right.

5 On the Map worksheet of the workbook, create a map using the data in cells A3 to C13 of that sheet.

 How does information have to be entered in a worksheet if it is to be used with a map?

6 Use a map of the United States without the inset of Alaska and Hawaii.

7 Plot both the Inquiries and Sales series.

8 Use the Graduated Symbol format for the Sales series.

9 Use the Category Shading format for the Inquiries series.

 Can you use the same format for both series?

10 Add the U.S. Highways feature to the map. (Hint: You'll find it in the Map Features dialog box.)

TRY OUT THE
INTERACTIVE TUTORIALS
ON YOUR CD!

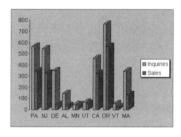

⑪ Position the legend for the Inquiries series in the lower-left corner of the map.

⑫ Change the map title to Inquiries and Sales. The map should appear as in the illustration at right. Refer to the workbook Solution 13 in the Solution folder to check your work.

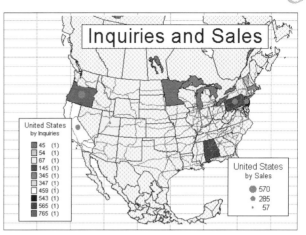

TROUBLESHOOTING

As you can see, creating charts and maps can add some real impact to a workbook, although there are things that can go wrong. If you have problems with these features, check out these troubleshooting tips.

Problem	Solution
I centered the map but it keeps moving.	When you click the Center Map button, the button remains on even after you click to center the map. If you click elsewhere on the map, it will center itself again. Click the Center Map button to turn it off immediately after you've centered the map as desired.
My chart looks strange; some of it is too small to read, and some of the text is too large.	When you add axis titles and legends to the chart, Excel reduces the size of the chart itself. Either enlarge the chart, or remove some of these other elements. You can also try reducing the size of the text.

continued

13

Creating Charts and Maps

Troubleshooting

Problem	Solution
I'm trying to edit my map, but when I double-click it, Excel displays a message that it is having trouble retrieving the data. When I click OK to clear the message, all of the data is gone from the map.	We can't explain why this happens — only that it may occur sometimes after you reopen the workbook. Here's how to get your data back. Once the map is selected, choose Insert ➤ Data. A dialog box appears asking you to specify the range of cells to plot. Either enter the range, or drag over it in the background, and then click OK. Excel will start over and plot the first series. Click the Show/Hide Microsoft Map Control button and complete your map again.
I selected a custom chart type, now my titles and subtitled are gone.	Remember, custom chart type includes a complete chart layout. If the layout does not include a title or subtitle, Excel removes them from your chart when it applies the format. Select Chart ➤ Chart Options, click the Titles tab, and reenter your text.
I'm having trouble selecting the part of the chart I want to format.	Sometimes takes a few tries to select a specific part of a chart. If you continue to have trouble, use the Select Objects list in the Chart toolbar. Pull down the list and select the part of the chart that you want to format.

Troubleshooting

Problem	Solution
I created a chart, but Excel used the wrong information for the axes. I wanted to have the column labels along the *x* axis, not the row labels.	That's easy to do without having to rearrange your worksheet. Click the chart, pull down the Chart menu, and choose Source Data. In the Data Range tab of the dialog box that appears, click the Rows option button and then click OK. This tells Excel to use the information in the rows for the series, which means the information in the columns will become the *x* axis. Generally, your choice of rows or columns for the series and *x* axis depends on how you want to illustrate and emphasize the information in the worksheet.
I was formatting my two-dimensional chart and suddenly the information in the worksheet changed. How did that happen?	When you are working with two-dimensional bar, column, and line charts, you can actually change the data in the worksheet by dragging the bar, column, or line. When you select a series in a column chart, for example, you'll see an extra handle in the center of the top line on the column. Dragging this handle changes the height of the column, and changes the related worksheet cells to match the column height. If this happens to you, click Undo.

13

Creating Charts and Maps

Wrap Up

WRAP UP

Charts and maps let you add some pizzazz to a worksheet, whether you are displaying them on screen or printing them. In this lesson, you learned how to:

- Create a chart by selecting data and then clicking the Chart Wizard toolbar button.

- Select options from the Chart Wizard dialog boxes.

- Create an embedded chart or a chart on its own chart sheet.

- Customize a chart using the Chart toolbar, the menu bar, and the shortcut menus that appear when you right-click various elements of the chart.

- Double-click chart elements to select format options for them.

- Create maps by selecting the data, clicking the Map button in the Standard toolbar, and then dragging to draw the map in the worksheet.

- Format, change, and add series to maps using the Microsoft Map control.

- Add and delete map features using the Map ➢ Add features and Map ➢ Features commands.

Charts and maps are just two types of graphics that you can add to a worksheet. In the next lesson, you'll learn how to add clip art and your own custom artwork to worksheets.

Using Clip Art and WordArt

60 MINUTES

GOALS

In this lesson, you will learn how to add clip art and special text effects to worksheets, including:

- Inserting clip art into worksheets
- Changing the size and position of graphics
- Customizing clip art
- Creating special text effects with WordArt

Get Ready

GET READY

Charts and maps are only two of the graphic elements that you can add to enhance a worksheet. You can also insert clip art and scanned images into a worksheet, and you can create special effects with text using Microsoft WordArt. You'll be amazed how quick and easy it is, even if you're not artistically inclined.

This lesson refers to the following workbooks and files:

File Name	Location
Graphics	Exercise directory
Graphics Solution	Solution directory
Watson.bmp	Exercise directory
MyLogo.bmp	Exercise directory
Solution 14	Solution directory

When you complete this lesson, you'll have created the worksheet shown in the illustration at right.

INSERTING CLIP ART AND PICTURES

The fastest way to add graphics to a worksheet is to insert a piece of clip art that's already been created. Excel includes a number of interesting graphics ready for you to insert, but you're not limited to those. You can insert graphics of all types, including images you download online, those that you purchase on disk, or artwork that you scan into your computer.

You can use graphics to help illustrate important points, or just to add some visual appeal. For example, add a company logo to the top of your worksheet, or insert scanned pictures of your company's products. You should avoid, however, using too many graphics that do not relate to the function of the worksheet. Extraneous clip art, drawings, and special effects can make a worksheet difficult to read, and can make opening and scrolling through workbooks rather slow.

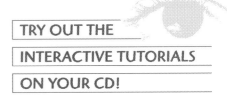

TRY OUT THE

INTERACTIVE TUTORIALS

ON YOUR CD!

Inserting Microsoft Clip Art

The Microsoft Clip Gallery is a collection of graphic images provided with Excel. The graphics in the gallery may vary, depending on whether you installed Excel as part of Microsoft Office or as a stand-alone product.

TIP

If your Clip Gallery does not include a graphic file used in this lesson, select a similar graphic to use in its place.

You'll start this lesson by adding a graphic from the Gallery. Although the upper-right corner of the graphic will begin in the active cell, you can move the graphic and change its size, just as you moved and repositioned charts and maps in the previous lesson:

1 Open the Graphics workbook in the Exercise folder.

2 Click cell E6.

3 Select Insert ➤ Picture ➤ Clip Art to display the Microsoft Clip Gallery shown in the illustration at right. Excel organizes clip art into categories. Select All Categories to list all of the art in the Pictures box, or choose a specific category from the Categories list.

NOTE

Depending on how you installed and set up Excel or Microsoft Office, you may see a dialog box reporting that there's additional clip art on the installation CD-ROM. If you don't want to see additional clip art, click OK. To see the clip art, just put the designated CD in the drive and click OK. If you don't want to see this reminder message the next time you open the Clip Gallery, select the check box labeled Don't Remind Me Again.

4 Click the Academic category.

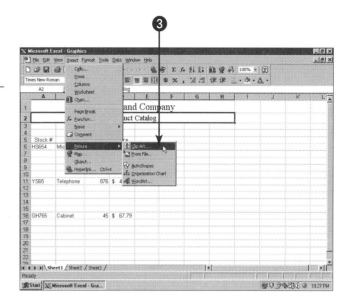

14

Using Clip Art and WordArt

Inserting Microsoft Clip Art

⑤ Double-click the graphic of the microscope. Excel inserts the graphic into the worksheet, surrounded by handles, and opens the Picture toolbar, as shown to the right. The upper-left corner of the graphic is aligned with the active cell. Drag the Picture toolbar out of the way, so you can see the information in the worksheet. You won't be using the toolbar until later in this lesson.

| TIP |

To delete a graphic from the worksheet, click it to select it, and then press the Del key.

Picture
Toolbar

⑤

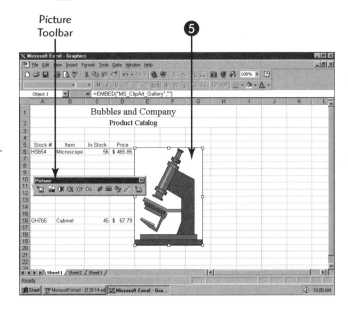

VISUAL BONUS

Using the Picture Toolbar

The Picture toolbar appears whenever a graphic is selected, and disappears if no graphic is selected. You use the toolbar to customize the appearance of a graphic, as you'll learn later in this lesson.

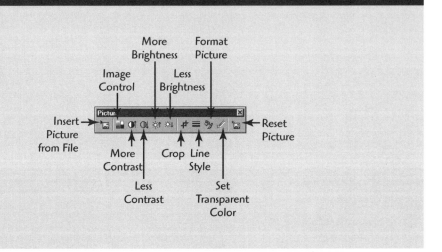

Changing Clip Art Size and Position

Changing the Size and Position of Clip Art

Excel inserts clip art in the size in which it was created. In many cases the graphic will be too big. In this exercise, for example, the microscope is much too large for the worksheet. Because the graphic begins where you want it to (in cell E6), you have to change its size but not its location. By default, Excel lets you change the size of the graphic but not its proportions when you drag a corner handle. As with charts, you drag on graphics' side handles to change their size in one direction only. You drag on a corner handle to change their size in two directions at once — that is, to shrink or enlarge them without changing their proportions. Typically, graphics look better in their original proportions so you're better off changing their size by dragging on a corner handle.

TIP

Depending on the size and position of a graphic, you may have to drag several handles — or drag the same handle several times — to get the correct size and position. Don't worry if you cannot get it right it by dragging just once.

1 Make sure the graphic is selected, and then scroll down to see the handle in the lower-right corner of the graphic.

2 Drag the lower-right handle up to the lower-right border of cell E9. The graphic now fits nicely to the right of the Microscope stock item, as shown to the right.

To move the graphic on the worksheet, select it and then drag it where you want it. You can also use the Cut, Copy, and Paste commands to position the graphic elsewhere on the worksheet, or anywhere in the workbook for that matter.

Now try adding another graphic to the worksheet and changing its position and size:

3 Click cell H11.

4 Select Insert ➢ Picture ➢ Clip Art.

5 Click the Communication category.

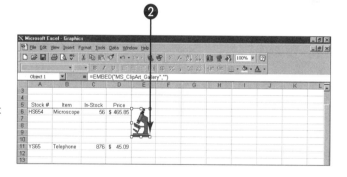

Inserting a Graphic File

NOTE *If your Clip Gallery does not have a Communication category, select any graphic for this part of the exercise.*

6 Double-click the telephone graphic.

7 Drag the lower-right handle up to the lower-right corner of cell I14.

8 Point to the graphic so the mouse pointer is shaped like a four-directional arrow.

9 Drag the graphic so its upper-left corner fits in the upper-left corner of cell E11.

Finally, you'll add the graphic for the last product in the worksheet:

10 Click cell E16.

11 Select Insert ➢ Picture ➢ Clip Art.

12 Click the Business category.

NOTE *If your Clip Gallery does not have a Business category, select any graphic for this part of the exercise.*

13 Double-click the file cabinet graphic.

14 Drag the lower-right handle of the graphic to the lower-right corner of cell F20. Your worksheet should now appear as shown to the right.

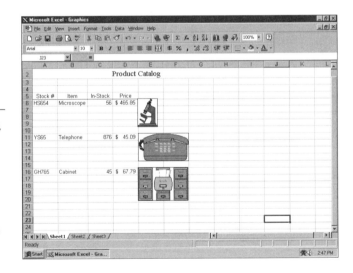

Inserting a Graphic File

You can insert almost any graphic into your worksheet, not just those in the Microsoft Clip Galley. In fact, you can insert graphics in any of

Changing Graphics

these common formats: WMF, JPEG, BMP, PCX, TIF, WPG, PICT, CGM, GIF, CorelDRAW.

So, for example, you can insert GIF and JPEG graphics that you download online, a WPG graphic from WordPerfect, and even a PICT graphic from your friend's Macintosh computer. Now use a graphic file to add a logo to the worksheet:

1 Click cell H9.

2 Select Insert ➤ Picture ➤ From File. The Insert Picture dialog box appears in Preview mode, so you'll see a sample of the selected picture.

3 Pull down the Look In list and click your hard drive.

4 Double-click the Exercises folder.

5 Click MyLogo. In a moment or so you'll see a preview of the graphic to the right of the list of files.

6 Click Insert.

7 Drag the logo to the left of the title, centered in columns A and B, in rows 1 and 2.

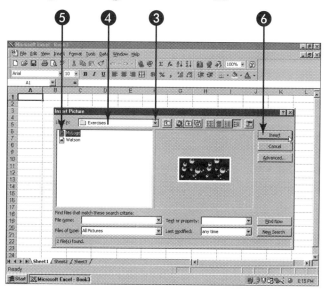

Changing Graphics with the Picture Toolbar

Almost everything about Excel is customizable, and it's no different with clip art and graphics. In fact, Excel offers several ways to change the appearance of graphics. You can even layer multiple graphics on top of one another, and arrange them in order.

As you customize graphics, however, you should save your work at regular intervals. Excel will let you reset the graphic to its original format, but you'll loose all of your changes if you choose to reset the graphic, and you'll have to start over. If you save the workbook, you can always reopen the previous version and pick up again where you left off.

With Excel, you customize a graphic using either the Format Picture dialog box or the Picture toolbar. The Picture toolbar appears automatically whenever a graphic is selected. If the toolbar does not appear, right-click a graphic and choose Show Picture Toolbar from

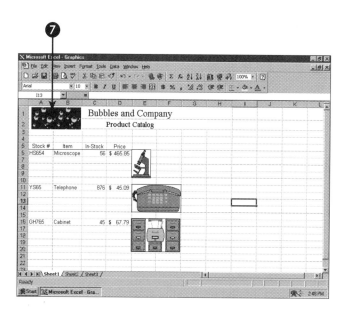

14

Using Clip Art and WordArt

Changing Graphics

the shortcut menu. Now you'll use the Picture toolbar to customize graphics on your worksheet:

1 Click the logo graphic.

2 Click the More Brightness button in the Picture toolbar four times. Each time you click the button, the graphic becomes lighter. If you make unintended changes to the graphic, you can always click the Reset Picture button to restore the graphic to its original format.

3 Click the Set Transparent Color button. The mouse pointer takes on the shape of the icon on the Set Transparent Color button.

NOTE *The Set Transparent Color button will be dimmed when you select a clip art graphic from the Clip Gallery, and some other types of graphic images.*

4 Click the background of the logo, not on any of the bubbles. The background of the graphic becomes transparent.

5 Drag the graphic so it is centered over the two-line title. Because the background is transparent, you can still read the title.

6 Click the telephone graphic.

7 Click the Image Control button on the Picture toolbar to see the options.

8 Click Grayscale. Excel replaces the colors in the graphic with shades of gray. The Black & White options removes all colors and shades of gray, and the Watermark option dims the entire graphic. Choose Automatic if you later want to redisplay the colors.

9 Click the filing cabinet graphic.

10 Click the Crop button on the Picture toolbar. Cropping a picture hides portions of it.

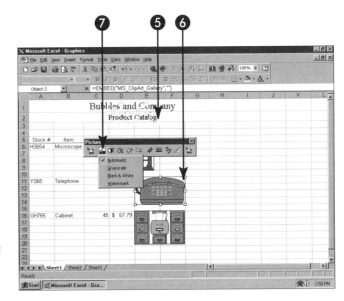

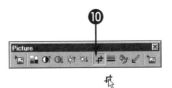

Using the Format Picture Dialog Box ◀

⑪ Point to the center handle on the right side of the graphic. The mouse pointer becomes shaped like the icon on the Crop button, which you saw a moment ago in the "Visual Bonus."

⑫ Drag the handle to the left. As you drag, a dashed line indicates where the cropping will occur.

⑬ Release the mouse button when the dashed line is just to the right of the first cabinet.

NOTE *The cropped part of the image is not deleted from the graphic, it is just not displayed at the moment. You can later use the Crop button to drag the border to the right and redisplay the hidden portion of the image.*

⑭ Click the Crop button to turn off this feature.

⑮ Click the Line Style button on the Picture toolbar. You'll see a list of styles for the border around the graphic.

⑯ Click the 3 pt double-line style to insert a line around the selected graphic.

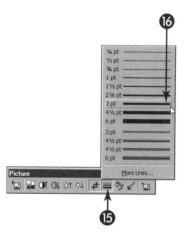

Using the Format Picture Dialog Box

The Format Picture dialog box, shown in the illustration at right, offers many of the same options for customizing a graphic as the Picture toolbar. The disadvantage of using the dialog box is that you cannot see the effects of your changes on the graphic as you make them, as you can when using the toolbar. However, the dialog box does offer some additional options. In addition, it is ideal when you want to make several changes to a graphic at one time, or when you need to make the graphic a precise size.

To display the dialog box, use any of these methods:

■ Right-click the graphic and choose Format Picture from the shortcut menu.

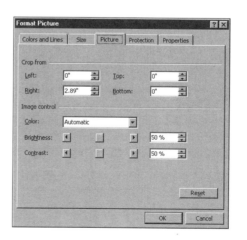

14

Using Clip Art and WordArt

Using the Format Picture Dialog Box

- Click the Format Picture button on the Picture toolbar.

- Select Format ➤ Picture. (The Picture option is only available in the menu when a graphic is selected.)

- Display the Colors and Lines page of the dialog box by choosing More Lines from the Line Style button on the Picture toolbar

Once you open the dialog box, use its options to customize the selected graphic.

As an example, you'll change the lines around one of the clip art graphics and add a color to its background:

❶ Click the microscope graphic.

❷ Click the Line Style button in the Picture toolbar.

❸ Select More Lines to see the dialog box shown in the illustration at right.

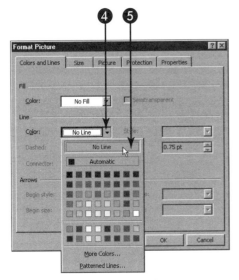

❹ Pull down the Color list in the Line section. The palette that appears lets you choose from preset colors, create custom colors, and choose a line pattern.

❺ Click No Line.

❻ Pull down the Color list in the Fill section. The options are similar to those for changing the chart area color in a chart.

❼ Click the yellow sample color.

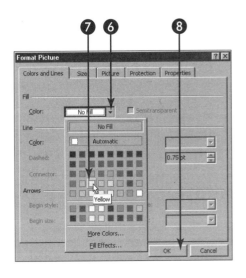

❽ Click OK. The graphic now has a yellow background but no border.

The other pages of the Format Picture dialog box give you additional control over the appearance of the graphic, as described here:

- **Size page**: Use this page to change the graphic's size by entering a specific height and width, or a percentage of the original size. You can also choose not to lock the aspect ratio so you can change the graphic's proportions by dragging. (The aspect ratio is the ratio between the picture's height and width.)

- **Picture page**: Use this page to crop the graphic, select an Image Control option, and adjust its brightness and contrast.

- **Protection page**: Use this page to unlock or lock the graphic when you turn on worksheet protection.

- **Properties page**: Use this page to affect how the graphic moves when you move cells. By default, if you select and move a range of cells that includes the graphic, the graphic moves along with the cells. You can also choose to both move and size the graphic with the cells, or not to move or size the graphic. From this page, you can also select not to print the graphic with the worksheet.

VISUAL BONUS

Changing How Graphics Overlap

The Order option in the graphic shortcut menu affects how overlapping graphics appear, as illustrated here. You'll learn about the Grouping command in Lesson 15. Grouping lets you combine several graphics into one, or separate a graphic into its individual elements.

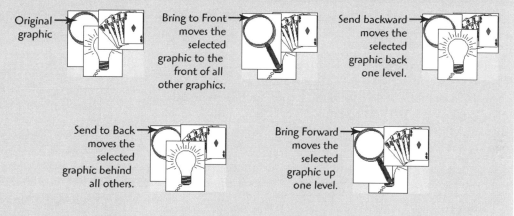

Original graphic

Bring to Front moves the selected graphic to the front of all other graphics.

Send backward moves the selected graphic back one level.

Send to Back moves the selected graphic behind all others.

Bring Forward moves the selected graphic up one level.

Creating a WordArt Effect

USING WORDART

WordArt is a special Microsoft program that lets you create special effects with text directly from within your Excel workbook or other Microsoft Office application. Use WordArt to create eye-catching headlines, logos, graphics, and other effects, such as those shown to the right.

Once you create and insert a WordArt effect in your worksheet, you can move it around, change its size, and customize it.

Creating a WordArt Effect

WordArt gives you an almost unlimited combination of formatting and effects to choose from. To get started easily, you can choose from 30 preset combinations. Choosing a preset design doesn't lock you in, however, because you can change all of the design elements at any time.

Next you'll use WordArt to add a special heading to the Graphics workbook. Once you create a WordArt graphic, you move it where you want it on your worksheet. You do not have to select a cell to position the WordArt ahead of time. In fact, in this exercise, you create the WordArt graphic on Sheet2 of the workbook, and then copy it to Sheet1:

1 Click the Sheet2 worksheet tab.

2 Select Insert ➤ Picture ➤ WordArt. You'll see the preset WordArt options shown here. Each of the options includes a shape and color for your own text — the word *WordArt* is only shown as example text.

3 Select the leftmost design in the fourth row of options.

4 Click OK. Excel displays the Edit WordArt Text dialog box, as shown in the illustration at right.

5 Type **Bubbles are the Best**.

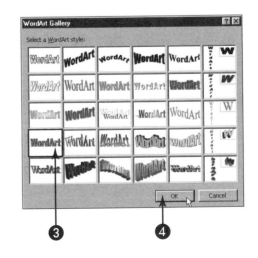

Customizing WordArt

NOTE *In the Edit WordArt Text dialog box, you can also choose the Font to use, the size of characters, and boldface and/or italic. Long text will wrap to the next line in the dialog box, but it will still appear as one line in the graphic. To enter multiple lines, press Enter where you want the lines to break.*

6 Click OK.

Excel displays the WordArt graphic, selected and surrounded by handles, and the WordArt toolbar, as shown to the right.

NOTE *Your WordArt toolbar may be docked at the top of the screen, or in some location other than that shown in the illustration.*

If you're satisfied with the design of your WordArt image, click elsewhere on the worksheet to deselect it and remove the WordArt toolbar. You can then change the size and position of the WordArt graphic as you'll learn next. To redisplay the WordArt toolbar, just click the WordArt image, or double-click the WordArt itself to display the Edit WordArt Text dialog box.

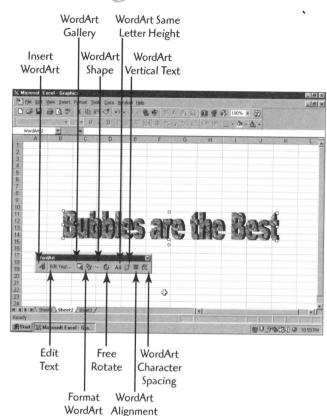

Customizing WordArt

As with clip art, you can move WordArt by dragging, and you can change the size and proportions of WordArt by dragging its handles.

Notice that the WordArt graphic has an extra diamond-shaped handle. The position of the handle depends on the shape you selected. You can use that handle to adjust the shape. Try it now:

1 Point to the diamond-shaped handle on the WordArt graphic. The mouse pointer turns into an arrowhead.

2 Drag the diamond handle slightly to the right. When you release the mouse button, the WordArt takes the new shape shown here. If you move the handle too far, just drag it back.

14

Using Clip Art and WordArt

Customizing WordArt

You use the WordArt toolbar to customize the graphic's text and appearance. For example, click the WordArt Gallery button if you want to select from another of the preset combinations, or click the WordArt Shape button to choose another shape for the text from the options shown at right.

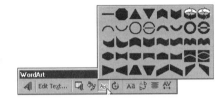

The Format WordArt button displays a dialog box for changing the colors and lines, size, protection, and properties of the graphic, much like the options in the Format Picture dialog box. If you want to change the text in the WordArt, click the Edit Text button to display the Edit WordArt Text dialog box, edit the text, and then click OK.

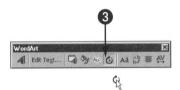

The other buttons on the toolbar create some interesting effects, so take a look at them now:

❸ Click the Free Rotate button. Excel replaces the square handles around the graphic with four round ones, and changes the mouse pointer to the icon shown in the second figure at right. To rotate a graphic, drag one of the round handles.

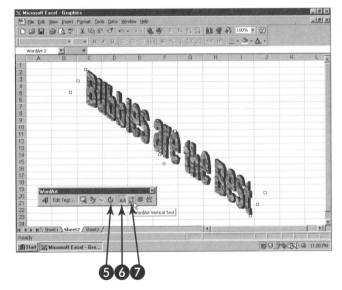

❹ Drag the handle in the lower-right corner down so the graphic is at a 45-degree angle.

❺ Click the Free Rotate button to turn off this option.

❻ Click the WordArt Same Letter Heights button. Excel makes all of the letters the same size, regardless of their case.

❼ Click the WordArt Vertical Text button. The characters are now positioned vertically down the page.

❽ Click the WordArt Vertical Text button again to restore the text to its previous shape.

❾ Click the WordArt Character Spacing button to see the options shown at right. Use these options to adjust the spacing between characters.

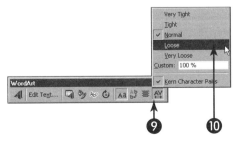

❿ Click Loose. The characters become a little narrower, and extra space is added between them.

⓫ Click the Edit Text button to access the WordArt Text dialog box.

⓬ Pull down the Size list and select 18.

⑬ Click OK.

⑭ Click the Cut button in the Standard toolbar.

⑮ Click the Sheet1 worksheet tab.

⑯ Click the Paste button in the Standard toolbar.

⑰ Drag the WordArt graphic so it starts in cell G1.

⑱ Click outside the graphic.

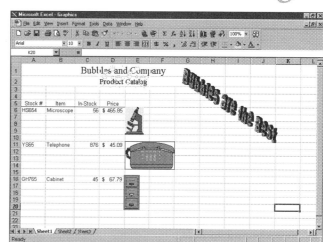

The completed worksheet should look like the figure shown at right. If any of your graphics look differently, take some time to change their size or position. You'll find a copy of the completed workbook in the file Graphics Solution in the Solution folder.

You can create WordArt graphics of more than one line of text by simply pressing Enter after each line in the Edit WordArt Text dialog box. To adjust the alignment of the lines, click the WordArt Alignment button. You can choose to left align, center, and right align text, justify the lines by adding spaces between words or letters, or justify text by stretching the characters.

You can also format the lines in a "button" shape by choosing one of the three-line circle shapes from the WordArt Shape button, as shown in the example at right.

SKILLS CHALLENGE: INSERTING CLIP ART AND WORDART

Graphics can be eye-catching and effective, and they can also be fun. So have a little fun and create the worksheet shown on the next page. The worksheet includes two clip art images and two WordArt graphics:

❶ Start a new workbook.

❷ Insert the clip art graphic of the stop sign, from the Signs category.

What is the difference between the Insert ➤ Picture ➤ Clip Art command and the Insert ➤ Picture ➤ From File command?

TRY OUT THE

INTERACTIVE TUTORIALS

ON YOUR CD!

Skills Challenge

3 Crop out the pole under the stop sign.

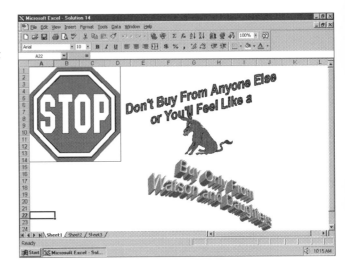

2 *What is the difference between cropping a graphic and changing its size?*

4 Create the WordArt graphic with the preset design that is second from the left in the top row of options, using these two lines of text in 20-point Arial bold:

Don't Buy From Anyone Else

or You'll Feel Like a

5 Format the WordArt so it appears in a red fill color. (Hint: Use the Format WordArt button to access the dialog box for setting fill color and line options.)

6 Format the WordArt with a line weight of 1.5 points.

7 Position the WordArt next to the stop sign, as shown in the illustration.

8 Insert the clip art of the donkey from the Animals category.

3 *How can you locate a graphic in the Clip Gallery if you do not want to select a specific category?*

9 Scale and position the graphic as shown in the illustration.

10 Format the graphic so it has no line around it.

11 Use the Order command from the shortcut menu to position the graphic behind the text.

4 *What is the difference between the Send to Back and Send Backward Order options?*

12 Insert the graphic file named Watson in the Exercise.

13 Change the Watson graphic to a grayscale.

14 Scale and position the graphic so it appears as in the illustration.

⑮ Without moving or resizing, position the Watson graphic so it does not obscure the donkey graphic. (Hint: Use the Order command.)

⑯ Remove the grid lines from the display.

You'll find a copy of this workbook under the name Solution 14 in the Solution.

TROUBLESHOOTING

Graphics and WordArt can be fun and effective, but they can be frustrating when things don't go quite as you planned. Make sure you save your workbook before adding graphics, and don't be afraid to delete a graphic and start over when something goes terribly awry. These tips might also help you when you run into trouble.

Problem	Solution
I can't select my WordArt graphic.	To select a WordArt graphic, point to it so the mouse appears as a four-directional arrow, and then click. If the mouse is shaped like a white plus sign, you'll select a worksheet cell rather than the graphic.
I'm trying to crop a graphic, but I'm just changing its size.	Remember, to crop a graphic by dragging, you must first click the Crop button in the Picture toolbar.
I can't drag the corner of my graphic where I want it.	Because Excel keeps graphics in their original proportions when you drag a corner handle, it is sometimes difficult to get the graphic to fit in the desired area. You may have to drag back and forth until you get the hang of it. If you still can't do it, display the Size page of the Format Picture dialog box, and clear the Lock Aspect Ration dialog box.

continued

► Troubleshooting

Problem	Solution
I made some changes to my graphic but it looks terrible. Now I can't get it to look good again.	To remove all of the formats that you've applied, make sure the graphic is selected and click the Reset Picture button on the Picture toolbar.
It is difficult to read the words in my WordArt graphic.	There are combinations of formats and shapes that are just difficult to read. You may have selected the wrong combination. Start by trying a different design, either by choosing another of the preset formats or a WordArt shape. If you have to use the selected shape, try a different font size, or a different font or color combination.
Excel won't use the graphic that I'm trying to insert from a file.	Excel can use a wide selection of the most popular graphic formats. However, there are some formats that it cannot use, and some graphics may just be too complicated for it to use. If Excel can't use one of the common formats described in this lesson, you may have to install the graphic filters. Run the Setup program that you used to install Excel, and choose the option to install all of the Converters and Filters. Converters and filters allow Excel to open workbooks and graphic files in a variety of formats. You need a filter, for example, for each type of graphic that you want to use. Some filters are installed automatically when you install Excel; others are installed only if you perform a Custom installation.

WRAP UP

In this lesson, you learned how to insert graphics and special text effects into worksheets. Among other things, you learned how to:

- Use the Insert ➢ Picture ➢ Clip Art command to insert Microsoft clip art into the worksheet

- Use the Insert ➢ Picture ➢ From File command to insert other graphic images

- Change the size and position of clip art, graphics, and WordArt by dragging

- Use the Picture toolbar and Format Picture dialog box to customize the appearance of graphics

- Use the Insert ➢ Picture ➢ WordArt command to create special effects with text

- Select a WordArt preset design as a starting point, and then customize the design with the WordArt toolbar

- Use the Order option from the shortcut menu to layer overlapping graphics

In Lesson 15, you'll learn even more ways to add special effects to a worksheet, by designing and creating custom graphics.

14

Using Clip Art and WordArt

Creating Custom Graphics

90 MINUTES

GOALS

In this lesson, you will learn how to create and customize graphic objects, including:

- Drawing lines, ovals, and rectangles
- Creating text boxes and text objects
- Drawing AutoShapes
- Formatting graphic objects
- Rotating and flipping objects
- Adding shadows and 3-D effects
- Working with groups and layers

Get Ready

GET READY

You can create your own artwork to add your personal design to a worksheet, or when you cannot find a piece of clip art to use. Use the Paint application in the Windows 95 Accessories menu or another drawing program to create the graphic, and then insert it into the worksheet just as you learned how to insert clip art in Lesson 14. You can also create simple drawings, even if you're not artistically inclined, directly from within Excel.

This lesson refers to the following workbooks:

File Name	Location
Artwork	Exercise directory
Artwork Solution	Solution directory
Workout 15	Exercise directory
Solution 15	Solution directory

When you complete this lesson, you'll have created the workbook shown in the illustration at right. Compare your work with the workbook Artwork Solution in the Solution folder.

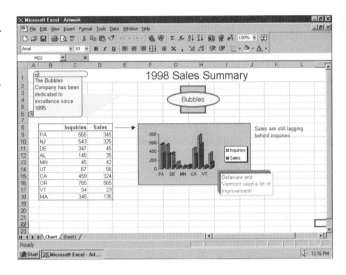

DRAWING CUSTOM GRAPHICS

Excel's drawing tools let you create lines, rectangles, ovals, text boxes, and all sorts of basic shapes. You can even use the drawing tools to customize graphics from the Microsoft Clip Gallery.

Displaying the Drawing Toolbar

To gain access to Excel's drawing tools, you have to display the Drawing toolbar. It' simple — here's how:

1 Open the Artwork workbook in the Exercise folder.

2 Click the Drawing button in the Standard toolbar. Excel displays the toolbar shown at right. By default, the toolbar is docked at the bottom of the window.

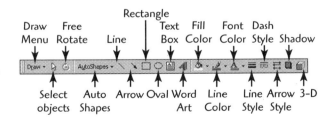

You can also display the Drawing toolbar by right-clicking any other toolbar and selecting Drawing from the shortcut menu that appears. To remove the toolbar, again click the Drawing button in the Standard toolbar or click Drawing on the shortcut menu.

Drawing Basic Shapes

The Drawing toolbar offers a variety of methods for creating and customizing shapes. Use the Line, Arrow, Rectangle, Oval, and Text Box tools to create basic objects and shapes. As a general rule, click the tool and then drag to create the object in the worksheet using these methods:

- Drag without holding down any keys to draw freehand.

- Hold down the Shift key and drag to constrain the drawing to a straight line or arrow, a square, or a circle.

- Hold down the Ctrl key and drag to create the object around a center point.

- Hold down the Alt key to align the shape with cell grid lines. You can also set Excel to automatically align objects to the cell grid lines. To do so, pull down the Draw menu on the Drawing toolbar, point to Snap, and click To Grid.

TIP

For these techniques to work, you must release the mouse button before releasing the Shift, Ctrl, or Alt key. If you release the key by mistake before you release the mouse button, just hold down the key again and continue dragging.

When you draw, Excel uses a method known as "rubber-banding." This means that the shape of the objects gets larger or smaller, and changes size and direction as you drag. When you release the mouse button the object's size is finalized, although you can always move and resize the object by dragging, using the techniques that you've already learned for moving and resizing clip art and charts.

After you draw an object, it appears selected with handles. Drag the handles to change the size or position of the object. To move an object, first point to it and then drag when the mouse pointer turns

TRY OUT THE

INTERACTIVE TUTORIALS

ON YOUR CD!

15

Creating Custom Graphics

Creating AutoShapes

into a four-directional arrow. Click away from the object to deselect it. Select the object again by pointing to it so the four-directional arrow appears and clicking. Try these techniques now:

❶ Click the arrow button on the drawing toolbar.

❷ Hold down the Shift key, click at the left end of cell E8 and drag across to the right end of the cell, over toward the chart, to draw the arrow. When drawing an arrow, drag toward the object you want to point to. (Remember, you use the Shift key to draw a straight line.)

❸ Release the mouse button and then the Shift key.

❹ Click the Rectangle button.

❺ Hold down the Alt key, point to the line between cells K2 and K3, and then drag down to cell K6. The upper-left corner of the rectangle will be inserted where you started to drag.

❻ Release the mouse button, and then the Alt key. Because you held down the Alt key when you drew the rectangle, it aligned with the cell grid lines.

❼ Click the Oval button. You now want to draw an oval centered over the rectangle.

❽ Hold down the Ctrl key, point to the center of the rectangle, and drag to the right and down to draw the object shown at right. When you use the Ctrl key, the object you create is centered around the position where you start to drag.

❾ Release the mouse button, and then the Ctrl key.

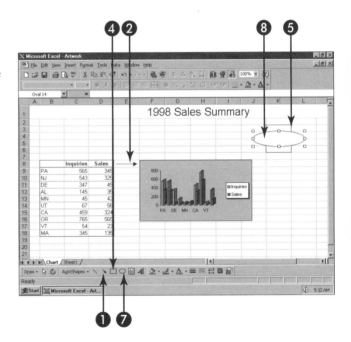

▶ Creating AutoShapes

Lines, arrows, rectangles, and ovals are just a few of the shapes you can create using Excel. You can also drag to create many more decorative and complex shapes. To gain access to these shapes, click the AutoShapes button on the Drawing toolbar to see a list of categories. Each category has as a submenu of shapes that you can draw. The Lines submenu shown here, for example, lets you draw lines and arrows, arcs and curves, and even freehand doodles. (You may want to look at the other submenus to see what types of shapes are available.)

Creating AutoShapes

You create most of the shapes using the same basic technique — select the object and drag to create it in the size and position desired. With most of the shapes, you can also just click once to insert an object of a default size, and then later change its size and position by dragging. Two of the tools work slightly differently, however:

- The Freeform tool in the Lines menu lets you create an object composed of any number of connected lines. After selecting the tool, click once to start drawing, and then release the mouse button if you want to draw a line segment. (Hold down the mouse button and drag to doodle freehand.) When you get to the end of one line segment, click the mouse again. Double-click to stop drawing.

- The Curve tool in the Line menu lets you draw a curve. You can also create an object composed of several curved line segments. Click once to start the objects, and then release the mouse button. Drag the mouse to draw a line the desired length. To start the curve, click and then drag back to curve the line in the direction you want. Double-click to end the drawing, or click once and draw another curved line segment.

Follow these steps to draw an AutoShape:

① Click AutoShapes ➢ Stars and Banners.

② Click the Vertical Scroll shape — on the left side of the bottom row.

③ Hold down the Alt key and drag from the upper-left corner of cell A1 to the bottom of cell C6.

When selected, most AutoShapes — except for simple lines, rectangles, and ovals — have one or more diamond-shaped yellow handles, just like the handle on WordArt graphics. You use the handles to change the shape of the graphic. By the way, the vertical scroll that you just created also has the diamond-shaped handle, but it is off the left edge of the window. If you dragged the scroll to the right, that handle would appear.

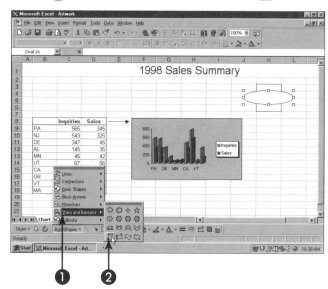

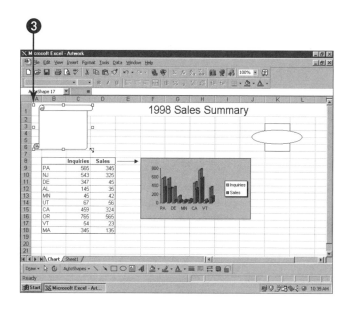

Adding Text to an Object

Callouts are a special type of AutoShape. Each callout consists of a pointer and a text box. Some of the boxes are rectangular, others are graphic shapes, and some just have a single line. Once you draw a callout, you can position both the box and the pointer. As an example, look at the illustration here. On the left is a callout just after it was created. In the center is the callout after the box was moved down. Notice that the end of the pointer remained at the original position so the callout line is at a different angle. On the right is the same callout after the end of the pointer was moved. By moving the box and the pointer, you can create a callout that points in almost any direction.

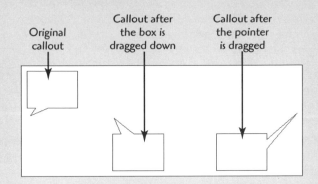

Original callout

Callout after the box is dragged down

Callout after the pointer is dragged

CREATING TEXT BOXES

You use the Text Box tool to add text anywhere on the worksheet. Text you add using this tool is not contained within a specific cell, but is instead contained in a graphic box much like a piece of clip art. You can use the Text Box button two ways: to add text within another object, such as an oval or AutoShape object, or as a separate object itself. The text object can be enclosed in a box or superimposed directly over worksheet cells.

Adding Text to an Object

You'll start by adding text to the scroll and oval shapes that you just created. As you type text, you can format it using the Formatting toolbar. The font, font size, bold, italic, underline, and alignment functions work the same as when you're typing text in a cell. Select options for the text you are about to type, or drag over existing text to select it and then apply a format:

❶ Click the Text Box button. When you move the mouse pointer over the worksheet, it appears like an upside down cross.

Creating Text Objects

2 Click within the scroll. Excel surrounds the scroll in a border of diagonal lines and a set of handles, and places an insertion point in the upper-left corner. The diagonal lines indicate that the object is a text box and that it is selected.

3 Type this: **The Bubbles Company has been dedicated to excellence since 1895.**

4 Click the Text Box button. You have to click the Text Box tool each time you want to create text.

5 Click the oval object that you created.

6 Click the Center button on the Formatting toolbar. The insertion point is centered in the oval.

7 Select 12 from the Font Size list in the Formatting toolbar.

8 Type **Bubbles**, the company name. Don't worry for now if the text does not appear centered vertically within the oval. You'll take care of that later.

9 Click elsewhere in the worksheet.

To edit or format the text once you've moved out of the box, point to it so the mouse appears like an I-beam and then click.

Creating Text Objects

Now you'll use the Text Box button to create a separate text object. There are, however, two types of objects you can create, and it all depends on how you use the mouse. After you click the Text Box tool, use one of these techniques:

- Drag in the worksheet to create an opaque box of a fixed size.
- Click in the worksheet to create a transparent box that expands to fit the text you enter.

Try both methods now to see the differences between them:

1 Click the Text Box tool.

2 Click the chart, about at the start of cell I8. Excel inserts a small frame with handles. As you type, the frame will expand to fit the

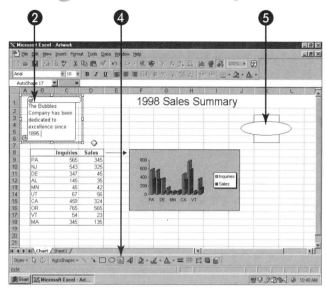
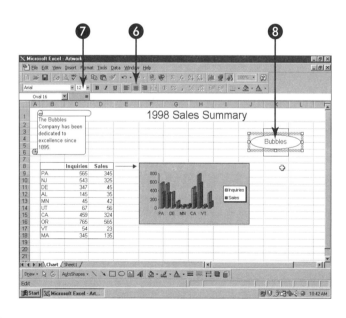

Formatting Text Objects

amount of text. However, you must press Enter to end one line of text and start the other.

❸ Type **Sales are still lagging**, and then press Enter.

❹ Type **behind inquiries.**

❺ Click elsewhere in the worksheet. The text appears superimposed over the chart and the grid lines on the worksheet.

❻ Click the Text Box tool.

❼ Drag to create a rectangle about two columns wide and three rows high at the lower-right corner of the chart. When you release the mouse button, a white opaque box, with a border, appears selected as shown to the right.

❽ Type **Delaware and Vermont need a lot of improvement!** As you type, Excel *wraps* the lines so they fit within the width of the box. If you type more lines that can fit, the text will scroll up and out of sight. To display the text, you can or reduce the font size or enlarge the box by dragging its handles.

❾ Click outside of the text box.

Formatting Text Objects

When the insertion point is within text in a text box or object, you can add, delete, edit, and format text just as you can work with text in a cell using the Formatting toolbar. You can also use a dialog box to format text — the number of pages in the dialog box depends on how you display it.

If the insertion point is within a text box, select Format ➢ Text Box, or right-click the text and choose Format Text Box. When working with text in a graphic object, even one that you did not create with the AutoShapes menu, select Format ➢ AutoShapes, or right-click and choose AutoShapes from the shortcut menu. The dialog box will be called either Format Text Box or Format AutoShape, and it will have just one page, called Font.

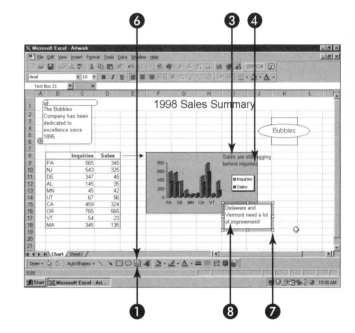

Formatting Text Objects ◀

For a wider range of options, you can display a dialog box of seven tabs, as shown in the following illustration. Point to the frame around the selected text box and double-click. You can also click the frame and choose Format ➤ AutoShape (or Format ➤ Text Box), or right-click and choose Format AutoShape (or Format Text Box). Options you select in this dialog box affect all of the text in the object.

You'll use the Alignment tab now to center the text within the oval:

1 Click the oval object.

2 Point to the frame around the graphic so the mouse appears as a four-directional arrow, and then double-click.

3 Click the Alignment tab. The Horizontal option is already set at Center because you clicked the Center button of the Formatting toolbar. You now have to center the text vertically.

4 Pull down the Vertical list and select Center.

5 Click OK. The text is now centered within the oval.

The options in the Orientation section of the dialog box let you display the text vertically within the text box or object. Checking the Automatic Size option lets Excel expand the object automatically to fit the text within it.

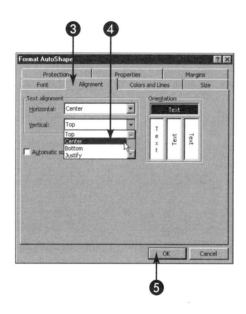

CHANGING THE COLOR, LINE STYLE, AND POSITION OF GRAPHICS

Once you create an object, you can customize it in a number of ways. Using the Drawing toolbar, for example, you can select a line and text color, and add a background color or fill effect, change the type of line or arrow, and modify the type of line around a rectangle or oval. You can also align multiple objects in relation to each other, and flip and rotate objects.

In this lesson, you'll use the Drawing toolbar to select format options.

15

Creating Custom Graphics

Moving Graphic Objects

TIP

The Format AutoShape dialog box described earlier offers other ways to format a graphic. To display this dialog box, double-click the object, or select Format ➤ AutoShape, or chose Format AutoShape from the shortcut menu. The options in the dialog box are similar to those in the Format Picture dialog box you used in Lesson 14, although the pages and options in the dialog box depend on the type of object you have selected.

Moving Graphic Objects

You can change the position of a graphic object by dragging it. When you are working with text boxes and objects that you've added text to, however, keep in mind that there are two ways to select them. If you click the object so the insertion point is within the text and the border around it appears as diagonal lines, you can format the text within the box. To format the box or object itself, click the border so the border itself appears as small dots rather than diagonal lines.

As an example, you'll move the text that that now appears to overlap with the chart:

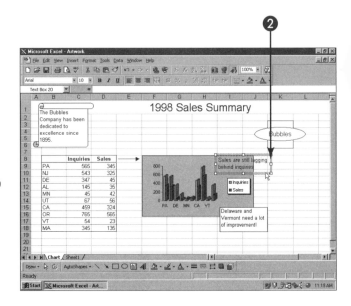

❶ Click the text that you entered in the upper-right corner of the chart. The text will be surrounded by a diagonal-line frame and the insertion point will appear in the text where you clicked.

❷ Click anywhere on the diagonal-line frame. The frame now appears to be made up of small dots. This indicates that the entire text box is selected.

❸ Point to the frame so the mouse pointer appears as a four-directional arrow.

❹ Drag to the right. As you drag, a dashed outline of the box shows its location.

❺ Release the mouse button when the outline is just to the right of the chart, so the box, and the text within it, no longer overlaps with the chart.

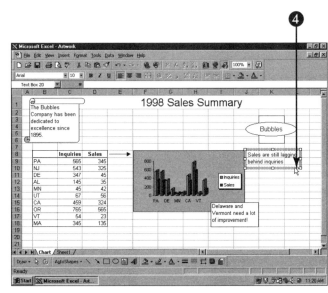

MOVING GRAPHICS BY NUDGING

Although it is easy to move a graphic by dragging it, it is often difficult to move it small amounts this way. That's when you should just *nudge* the graphic. There are two ways to nudge: by using the Nudge command in the Draw menu, or by pressing the arrow keys.

To use the Nudge command, select the object, pull down the Draw menu in the Drawing toolbar, point to Nudge, and select the direction in which you want to move the

object — either up, down, left, or right. To use the arrow keys, select the object and press the arrow key to move the graphic in the direction of the arrow.

Each time you nudge it, the object moves a small amount, so you can control its precise location. You can only nudge a text box or object that you've added text to when the border around it appears as small dots, not diagonal lines.

TIP

You can click the diagonal-line frame and drag the mouse in one step. As soon as you click, the object is selected and the frame appears as small dots. You do not have to release the mouse button and then click the frame again.

Choosing Colors

Changing the color of objects is easy. Select the object you want to format, and then choose an option from the Fill Color, Line Color, or Font Color buttons on the Drawing toolbar. To quickly apply the color shown on the face of the button, just click it. To choose another color, pull down the list associated with the button and choose from the palette that appears:

1 Click the rectangle that you created starting in cell K3. To select the rectangle and not the oval, make sure the mouse pointer is within the rectangle when you click.

2 Pull down the Fill Color list in the Drawing toolbar. You can select from a palette of colors, choose No Fill to clear fills from the selected object, choose More Fill Colors to choose from a much wider range of colors, or choose Fill Effects to create a custom background pattern.

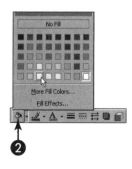

Choosing Colors

3 Click pale blue — it's the third color from the right on the bottom row.

4 Click the oval to select it. You won't be able to change the fill color if the insertion point it in the oval. Click the border of the object so it appears to be small dots rather than diagonal lines. At this point you can add a fill color or pattern.

5 Pull down the Fill Color list and select light yellow — the third color from the left on the bottom row. Because you drew the oval over the rectangle, the oval is in the foreground.

6 Click the scroll shape to select it.

7 Click the border of the box.

8 Click the Fill Color button to add a light yellow background to the scroll.

9 Click the text box that you drew over the chart.

10 Pull down the Line Color list in the Drawing toolbar. You can select from a palette of colors, choose No Line, Automatic, More Line Colors, or Patterned Lines.

11 Click red.

12 Drag over the text in the box to select it.

13 Pull down the Font Color list in the Drawing toolbar and click red.

You can format a text box using the Format Text Box dialog box. Right-click the frame around the selected box and choose Format Text Box from the shortcut menu.

■ Changing Line and Arrow Styles

By default, Excel draws lines, arrows, and the lines around objects in $3/4$-point solid lines. You can customize the line style by using the Line Style and Dash Style buttons on the Drawing toolbar, or by using the Format AutoShape dialog box.

To change the direction and type of arrowhead on an arrow, click the Arrow Style button and select from these options.

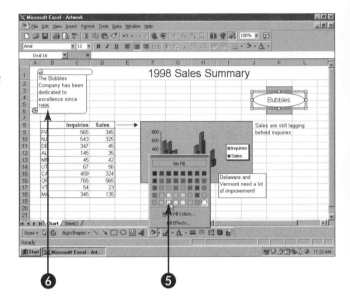

Selecting More Lines or More Arrows from either list displays the Format AutoShape dialog box with additional choices.

Flipping and Rotating Objects

The Rotate or Flip option on the Draw menu lets you free rotate an object by dragging it, or rotate it left (counterclockwise) or right (clockwise) in 90-degree increments. You can also flip an object horizontally (from left to right) or vertically (from top to bottom).

When you click the Free Rotate button on the Drawing toolbar, or select Free Rotate from the Rotate or Flip menu, Excel displays the round handles that you learned about in Lesson 14. Drag one of the round handles to rotate the object.

Try using the Rotate or Flip command now:

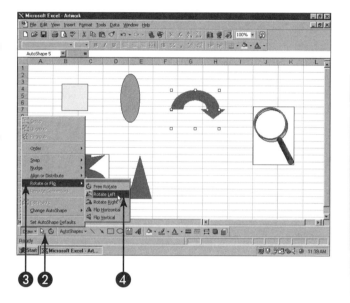

❶ Click the Sheet1 worksheet tab. This worksheet contains several objects that you'll use to practice working with drawing features, as shown to the right.

❷ Click the arrow object.

❸ Pull down the Draw menu on the Drawing toolbar and point to Rotate or Flip.

❹ Click Rotate Left. The arrow rotates 90 degrees counterclockwise.

❺ Pull down the Draw menu on the Drawing toolbar and point to Rotate and Flip.

❻ Click Flip Horizontal.

NOTE

If you use the Free Rotate command to rotate a graphic object to which you've added text, only the graphic rotates, not the text around it. The rotate and flip options will be dimmed when you select a text box.

15

Creating Custom Graphics

Aligning and Distributing Objects

▶ Aligning and Distributing Objects

Aligning objects means positioning them in relation to one another. For example, you may want several objects to be aligned at the top, or centered over each other.

You can also *distribute* objects horizontally or vertically, which spaces them out evenly between the first and last object in the group. Suppose, for instance, you want to space a series of objects evenly between the left and right side of the page. You would move the first object to the left, the last object to the right, select all the objects, and choose the Distribute Horizontally command from the Align or Distribute option in the Draw menu. In fact, you'll try using that option now to evenly space three objects, and then to align them on the center:

❶ Click the square object.

❷ Hold down Shift and click the oval and arrow objects to select them also.

❸ Click the Draw menu in the Drawing toolbar, and click Align or Distribute to see the options shown at right. The graphic next to each item illustrates the resulting position of the objects. For example, to align objects so they are exactly centered with respect to each other, choose both the Align Center and Align Middle options.

❹ Click Distribute Horizontally. Excel moves the graphic in the center so the three are evenly spaced.

❺ Click the Draw menu in the Drawing toolbar, choose Align and Distribute, and choose Align Middle. The centers of each object are now aligned.

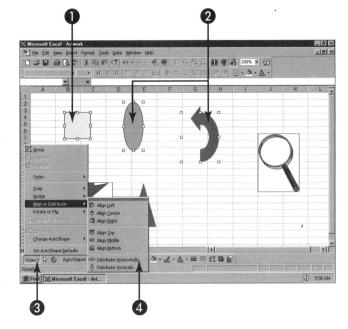

NOTE *Another way to position objects is to move one so one of its handles is aligned with a handle on the other, such as aligning two objects on their corners. Rather than try this manually by dragging, you can set Excel so it automatically snaps the handles together for you. Pull down the*

Draw menu on the Drawing toolbar, point to Snap, and then select To Shape. Now when you drag and drop one graphic onto another, Excel will snap together the two closest handles.

WORKING WITH GROUPS

You can create some sophisticated graphics using the Drawing toolbar, such as logos and pictures. However, each object that you add to the graphic is treated as a separate entity. Each time you want to change the graphic — for example, if you want to move it — you have to select all of the objects. Although there are easy ways to select multiple objects, it can be time-consuming. There is also the risk that you'll miss one of the objects and not modify it with the group.

To avoid this problem, you can group individual objects into one composite object. You can then select the entire set of objects by clicking once, or apply standard formats to the entire group. When you want to format a specific object in the group, you can ungroup the objects, dividing the composite into its individual pieces.

Grouping Multiple Objects

To combine a number of objects into one, you have to start by selecting them all. You can do this by holding down the Shift key while you click, or you can use the selection tool in the Drawing toolbar. As an example, you'll combine the rectangle and oval object on the Chart sheet of the Artwork workbook to create a single object:

1 Click the Chart worksheet tab.

WORKING WITH LAYERS

In Lesson 14, you learned how to work with layers by changing the arrangement of overlapping graphics. You can use the same techniques to adjust the position of drawn objects. To gain access to the layering options, right-click a graphic and choose Order from the shortcut menu, or pull down the Draw list in the Drawing toolbar and select Order.

15

Creating Custom Graphics

Ungrouping Clip Art

❷ Click the Select Objects button on the Drawing toolbar so it appears pressed down.

❸ Drag around the rectangle and the oval objects. As you drag, a dashed line indicates which objects will be selected; objects must be completely within this rectangle to be selected. When you release the mouse button, all of the objects within the rectangle are selected. You could move all of the objects now at one time by dragging, but you'd have to reselect them each time you wanted to move them together again.

❹ Right-click the selected objects, choose Grouping in the shortcut menu, and then choose Group. (You can also select Group from the Draw menu in the Drawing toolbar.) Only one set of handles remain on the object, indicating that it is now one composite item.

❺ Drag the composite object so it is centered underneath the worksheet title.

❻ With the objects still selected, click the Line Style button in the Drawing toolbar and select the 3 pt double-line style from the options that appear. Notice that all of the lines in the graphic are affected.

❼ Right-click the object, choose Grouping from the shortcut menu, and choose Ungroup.

If you later want to group the objects again, select any one of them and choose Regroup from the shortcut menu, or choose Grouping and then Regroup from the Draw menu.

Ungrouping Clip Art

Clip art from the Microsoft Clip Gallery is made up of a series of individual objects that have been grouped together. By ungrouping a clip art graphic, you can change its color, size, and position, and otherwise customize its individual parts.

Try it now. Ungroup a piece of clip art so you can modify some of its parts, and then regroup the parts so you can move the graphic as one object again:

❶ Click the Sheet1 tab of the workbook.

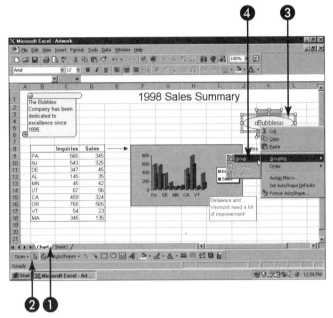

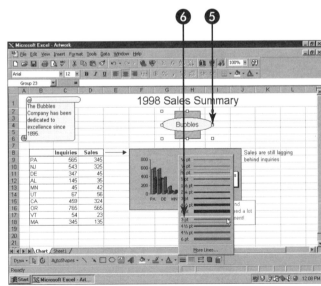

2 Right-click the magnifying glass graphic.

3 Choose Grouping from the shortcut menu, and choose Ungroup. A message warns you that ungrouping the object will loose embedded data or linking information. This means that the resulting graphic will no longer be associated with the Clip Gallery — although the original graphic will still be in the gallery.

4 Click Yes. All of the individual objects will now be surrounded by handles — quite a few for a simple-looking object such as the one shown just below. Because there are so many small objects, it is often difficult to select the one you want the first time.

5 Click outside the graphic.

6 Click the top of the frame around the "lens" of the graphic to select it.

7 Pull down the Fill Color list in the Drawing toolbar and click yellow. The "lens" is now yellow.

8 Click the circle at the very bottom of the handle.

9 Click the Fill Color button. The circle is now yellow as well.

10 Now press the Delete key to delete that part of the graphic. You can delete, move, or resize the individual parts within the graphic.

11 Using the Select Objects tool, drag to form a rectangle around the entire graphic.

12 Right-click the object, choose Grouping from the shortcut menu, and choose Group. The graphic is now treated as one object.

Now that you've regrouped the parts of the graphic it is treated as a single object. However, it is no longer considered a clip art graphic, but is rather a drawing object much like the shapes and AutoShapes that you draw yourself. As you'll learn, this means that you can apply three-dimensional effects to the object to create some unusual and appealing results.

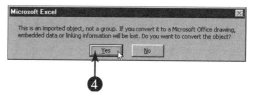

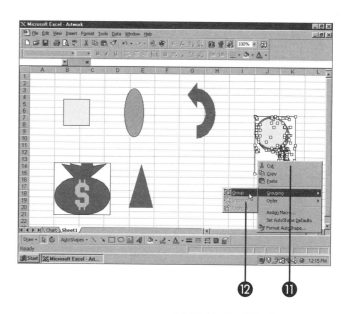

Adding Shadows

ADDING SHADOWS AND
THREE-DIMENSIONAL EFFECTS

Of all of the ways you can customize graphic objects, adding shadows and three-dimensional effects can have the most impact. These two formatting methods pack a lot of punch in creating eye-catching graphics.

You can add shadows to drawings you create with the Drawing toolbar as well as clip art from the Microsoft Clip Gallery, with some limitations, as you will learn in the following exercise.

Adding Shadows

Shadows can be quite effective for adding depth to a graphic, and, as with most Excel features, you have many options to choose from. A shadow consists of three main elements — the position of the shadow, its depth, and its color. Using the Shadow list in the Drawing toolbar, you select a basic shadow style, including the direction of the shadow and the depth.

Next you'll add a shadow to several of the graphics on your workbook:

1 Click the square object on the Sheet1 page of the workbook.

2 Click the Shadow button in the Drawing toolbar to see these options. Here you select the shadow to apply. Each shadow style has a number, and when you point to an option a ScreenTip displays its style number.

3 Click Shadow Style 5 — the first option in the second row. A shadow appears behind the selected rectangle.

4 Click the money bag graphic.

5 Click the Shadow button in the Drawing toolbar. Because this is a Clip Gallery graphic, a number of the shadow options are dimmed.

6 Choose Shadow Style 14. The shadow is just applied to the graphic box, not to the money bag or the dollar symbol.

7 Click the magnifying glass.

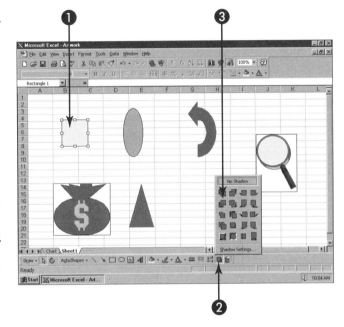

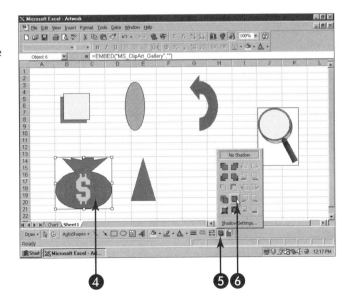

8 Click the Shadow button in the Drawing toolbar and choose
Shadow Style 3. All of the shadow options are available, and the
shadow is applied to the entire graphic because it was converted
to a drawing object when you ungrouped it. The shadows look
like the ones shown at right.

You can always choose a different style to apply, or you can
select No Shadow to remove the shadow.

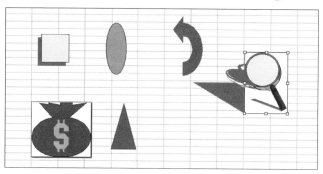

Customizing Shadow Settings

The 20 default shadow styles cover a wide range of effects, including
two styles that make the object appear like a button. For even more
control over the effect, however, you can use the Shadow Settings
toolbar to adjust the position, depth, and color of the shadow. Try
it now:

1 Click the square graphic.

2 Click the Shadow button in the Drawing toolbar.

3 Click Shadow Settings to see the toolbar shown at right. Use the
nudge buttons to change the position of the shadow, affecting
its location and depth. Use the Shadow Color button to change
the shadow's color, and click Shadow On/Off to toggle the
shadow on and off.

4 Click the Nudge Shadow Left button three times. Only the
shadow moves, not the rectangle.

5 Click the Nudge Shadow Down button three times. The shadow
now appears deeper.

Now try adding and customizing a shadow on the Chart sheet of
the workbook:

6 Click the Chart worksheet tab. The Shadow Settings toolbar
remains on screen.

7 Click the scroll graphic.

8 Click the Shadow button in the Drawing toolbar and choose
Shadow Style 4.

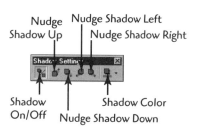

Nudge Shadow Up — Nudge Shadow Left — Nudge Shadow Right — Shadow On/Off — Nudge Shadow Down — Shadow Color

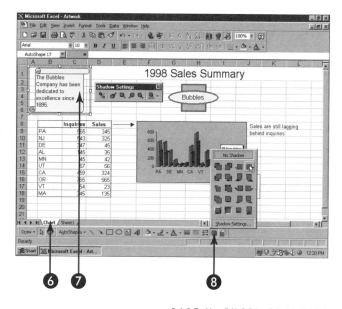

15

Creating Custom Graphics

Creating 3-D Effects

9 Pull down the Shadow Color list in the Shadow Settings toolbar and select yellow.

10 Click the Nudge Shadow Right button 10 times.

11 Click the text box below the chart.

12 Click the Shadow button in the Drawing toolbar and choose Shadow Style 13. This style insert two shadows of different densities.

13 Pull down the Shadow Color list in the Shadow Settings toolbar and select red.

14 Click the Close box on the Shadow Settings toolbar.

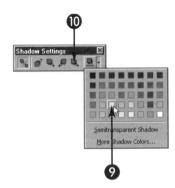

Creating 3-D Effects with Graphic Objects

You add three-dimensional effects to an object much as you add shadows. Although you cannot apply three-dimensional effects to clip art, you can add them to most AutoShapes. The only exceptions are callouts and a few other AutoShapes.

TIP

An object cannot have both a shadow and 3-D effect. If you apply a 3-D effect to the rectangle with the shadow, for example, the shadow will be removed.

1 Click the Sheet1 worksheet tab.

2 Click the oval graphic.

3 Click the 3-D button on the Drawing toolbar to display the options shown here. Pointing to an option displays a ScreenTip with its style number.

4 Click 3-D Style 10.

5 Click the triangle graphic.

6 Click the 3-D button on the Drawing toolbar and select 3-D Style 4. The object now appears to have transparent surfaces — this is called a *wire-frame* image.

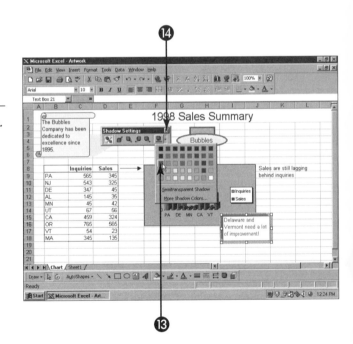

7 Click the magnifying glass.

8 Click the 3-D button on the Drawing toolbar and select 3-D Style 9. The graphics now look like the ones in the illustration at right.

Customizing 3-D Objects

The three-dimensional illusion is created by a combination of these features:

- Depth
- Color
- Rotation
- Angle
- Direction of lighting
- Surface texture

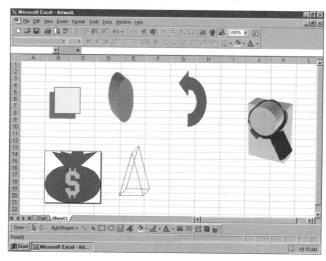

When you select an option from the 3-D list in the Drawing toolbar, Excel applies a default set of these elements to create the effect of three dimensions. If you like, you can customize all of the elements of the design to create your own special effect.

There are hundreds of combinations from which you can choose, and each object looks different with the same combination. For example, the four surface 3-D options (wire frame, matte, plastic, and metal) look different even on the same object based on the lighting, direction, and shadow color. The best way to choose the correct design is just to experiment, selecting options until the image look good to you.

As an example, you'll customize several three-dimensional objects:

1 Point to the triangle object. When the mouse looks like a four-directional arrow, click the triangle to select it.

2 Click the 3-D button on the Drawing toolbar and select 3-D Settings. Excel opens the 3-D Settings toolbar shown in the illustration at right.

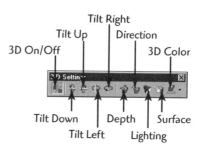

15

Creating Custom Graphics

Customizing 3-D Objects

3 Click the Tilt Down button three times. Each time you click, the image appears to tilt over, as if someone were pushing the top of the triangle forward from the back.

4 Click the Tilt Right button 7 times. The triangle rotates to the right.

5 Click the Oval object.

6 Click the Depth button on the 3-D Settings toolbar to see the options shown at right. The depth setting controls the length of the three-dimensional object — the default is 36 points. You can choose one of the standard depths shown here, or enter your own measurement in the Custom text box.

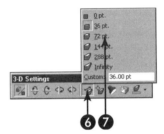

7 Click 72 pt. to double the depth of the oval.

8 With the oval still selected, click the Direction button to see the options shown at right. You can select one of the directional options, and you can choose to have the effect appear in perspective or with parallel planes. The Perspective option makes the image appear more three-dimensional. Leave the direction as is.

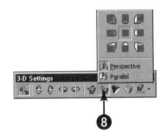

9 Click the magnifying glass.

10 Click the Lighting button to see the options shown at right. The lighting options simulate a light source shining on the object in terms of its direction and intensity. When you point to a lighting option, the small graphic in the center changes to illustrate its effects. The center graphic, by the way, is also a choice — a light source that casts no shadow.

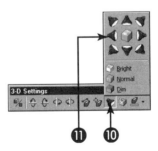

11 Click the light source on the center left.

12 Click the arrow graphic. You can apply a three-dimensional effect and customize it directly from the 3-D Settings toolbar.

13 Click the 3-D On/Off button. Excel applies the most recently used effect to the selected object.

14 Pull down the 3-D Color list in the 3-D Settings toolbar.

15 Click yellow.

16 Click the Close box of the 3-D Settings toolbar.

Lighting and Texture Options

Because there are so many possible combinations of three–dimensional effects, it is just not practical — or even possible — to show them all. However, the illustration at right includes examples of the four surface textures, and illustrations of the nine different lighting directions. Keep in mind that the subtle variations of texture and light may not be as apparent on this printed page as they are on screen.

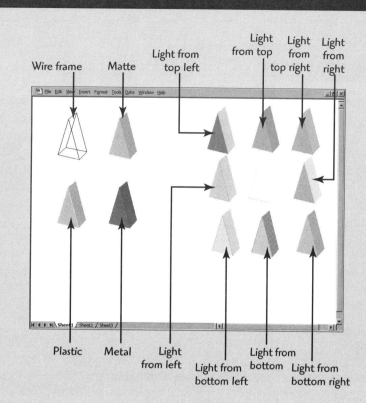

Wire frame Matte Light from top left Light from top Light from top right Light from right

Plastic Metal Light from left Light from bottom left Light from bottom Light from bottom right

15

Creating Custom Graphics

Skills Challenge

The graphics now appear as shown to the right.

SKILLS CHALLENGE: CREATING AND CUSTOMIZING GRAPHICS

In this challenge, you'll practice your graphic skills by creating a variety of objects. Take your time, following the steps to create and format each of the objects. When you're done, your worksheet will look like the one in the bottom illustration at right.

1 Open the Workout 15 workbook in the Exercise directory.

2 Draw the Rounded Rectangular Callout.

> **1** *Does it matter if you draw a callout in the exact position where you want it?*

3 Add the text within the callout, in a 14 point font.

> **2** *Do you have to click the Text Box tool?*

4 Format the callout object so the text is centered horizontally and vertically.

> **3** *How do you select the object so you can change the alignment of text?*

5 Adjust the callout box and pointer so it appears as in the illustration.

6 Draw a 32-point star AutoShape about the size of the one in the illustration.

> **4** *How can you tell which AutoShape object is the 32-point star?*

7 Insert the name Wilson within the star, in a 14 point font.

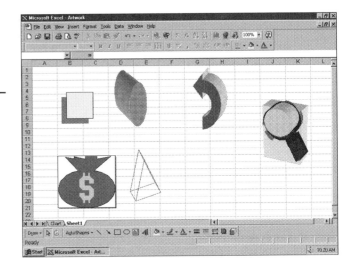

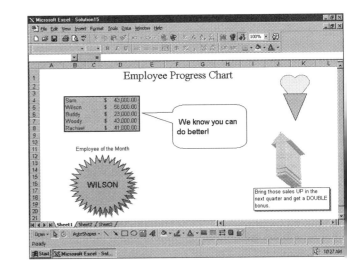

8 Apply shadow style 6 to the star.

9 Fill the star with the sky blue fill color.

10 Draw and position the heart and triangle shapes. (Hint: Both are in the Basic Shapes category. You'll have to draw and rotate the triangle to get it the shape shown in the illustration.)

11 Set the order of the two shapes so the heart is behind the triangle as shown.

12 Add fill colors of your choice to the two shapes.

13 Create the text box, and add the text to it using a 10-point font.

14 Apply shadow style 14 to the text box.

15 Create the three-dimensional arrow. (Hint: You have to draw and then rotate the Striped Right Arrow AutoShape, and then apply 3-D style 13.)

16 Adjust the sizes and position of the objects so they appear as in the illustration.

Compare your work with the workbook Solution 15 in the Solution folder.

TRY OUT THE

INTERACTIVE TUTORIALS

ON YOUR CD!

TROUBLESHOOTING

Excel's drawing features make it easy to personalize worksheets, and create unique designs. Problems can arise, however, so review these troubleshooting tips even before things go wrong.

Problem	Solution
I'm trying to draw a line between the corners of two cells, but I just cannot get it right.	That's easy. Pull down the Draw menu on the Drawing toolbar, choose Snap, and choose To Grid. Now click near the corner of one cell and drag near the corner of the other cell. Your lines will snap into place.

continued

Troubleshooting

Problem	Solution
I'm trying to draw and move a shape but I can't get it in the exact position; it seems to jump around.	Turn off the To Grid and To Shape snap features. With these on you won't be able to move the graphic in small increments.
I can't select a graphic.	Make sure you point to the graphic so the mouse pointer is shaped like a four-directional arrow.
I'm trying to draw a callout so it's pointing at a certain spot, but I can't do it.	Honestly, don't even try to draw the callout so it points where you want it. Just select the callout you want and draw it close to the place where you want to point. Then drag the callout box and pointer so they are where you want them.
I can't draw or move two objects exactly centered on each other.	Use the Align or Distribute option from the Draw menu instead. Select both objects, and choose Align Center and Align Middle from the Align or Distribute submenu.
I drew an object and added text to it; now it won't rotate.	You cannot use Free Rotate to rotate a text box, or the text within another object. You can rotate an AutoShape that you added text to, but only the shape rotates. To display the text vertically, use the Alignment page of the Format AutoShape or Format Text Box dialog box. To draw text at any angle, use WordArt.
I can't get my text to fit in the box.	Either make the text smaller or the box bigger.

Problem	Solution
I'm trying to change the alignment of text in the Format AutoShapes or Format Text dialog boxes, but it only contains the Font tab.	That's because you displayed the Format AutoShape or Format Text Box dialog box when the insertion point was within a text box. Double-click the object when the mouse pointer appears as a four-directional arrow to open the Format AutoShape or Format Text dialog box.

WRAP UP

If you are artistically inclined, you can create some exciting and eye-grabbing graphics. But even if art is not your forte, you can use the drawing features, especially AutoShapes, to add a real flair to your worksheet. Here's a recap of the features you learned in this lesson:

- Display the Drawing toolbar

- Create lines, ovals, rectangles, and AutoShapes by dragging

- Create text boxes and add text to objects

- Format objects and text using the Formatting toolbar or a dialog box

- Add shadows and three-dimensional effects to objects

- Customize shadows and three-dimensional effects

Well, you made it. You've learned techniques for creating, formatting, and customizing worksheets. Take a look at Appendix B in this book to get some ideas for your own work.

15

Creating Custom Graphics

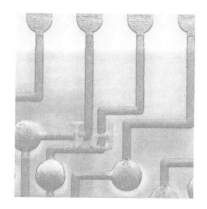

Installing Excel

Installing Excel

In this appendix, you'll learn how to install Excel, and how to later add or remove parts of it. Installing Excel is easy. You just make a few simple choices, and the Setup program does the rest.

INSTALLING EXCEL

You can purchase Excel by itself or as part of the Microsoft Office suite, but the installation procedure is about the same. If you use the Office suite, you just have to go through one additional dialog box that lets you select options for other Office programs. You can also buy Excel either on CD-ROM or on floppy disks. Again, the installation process is about the same — you'll just have to swap disks often if you're not using a CD. By the way, a CD-ROM drive is an excellent investment, if you do not have one. Not only will you be able to install programs faster, you'll be able to use the CD that accompanies this book!

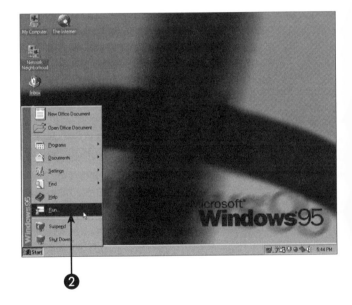

■ Starting the Setup Program

It is best to quit all programs before starting the installation process, especially any programs that are part of the Office suite. Then follow these steps:

❶ Insert the Excel 97 CD in your CD drive. The drive may spin a moment or so until Windows 95 recognizes the CD.

❷ Click Start and point to Run to see the dialog box shown at right.

❸ Type **D:\Setup** and then click OK.

TIP *If your CD-ROM is designated as a drive other then D, use that letter instead.*

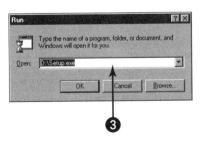

❹ In a moment, a Welcome dialog box appears. Click the Continue button to display a dialog box asking for your name and organization.

⑤ Depending on your setup, there may already be information in the dialog box when it appears. If necessary, add to or edit the information in the dialog box, and then click OK.

⑥ Next you'll see a dialog box asking you to confirm your name and organization. Click OK if the information is correct or click Change if you have to correct it.

⑦ When the name and organization information is correct, a dialog box in which you enter the CD key appears. This is a long number that you'll find on a sticker on the back of the CD box. Type the number in the box and then click OK.

⑧ Now you'll see a dialog box with the Product ID number of your software. Copy the number, store it in a safe location, and then click OK.

⑨ The next dialog box lets you designate the folder in which your program files will be stored. It is usually best to accept the default location by clicking OK. If you must use a different location, however, click Change Folder and then enter or browse to the location.

The Setup program now provides a number of options. If you are using the Excel 97 CD, the options are Typical and Custom. If you are using the Microsoft Office CD, the dialog box also includes the Run from CD option. To perform all the exercises in this book, you can select either option from the Excel CD, but use the Custom selection from the Microsoft Office CD.

- The *Typical* option installs the parts of the program that most people use. Some advanced features of the software are not installed, but this installation uses the minimum amount of disk space.

- The *Custom* option lets you select from all of the features in Excel or the Office suite. Choose this option to pick and choose the elements of Excel or Office that you want to install.

- The *Run from CD* option for the Suite installation installs the minimum amount of software on your hard disk, getting most of the program information from the CD. If you go this route, you'll be able to use all of the program's features but you must

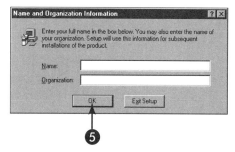

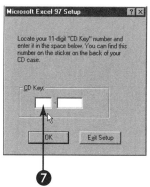

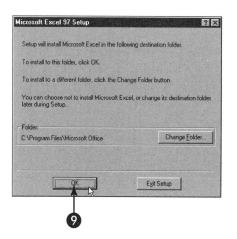

A

Installing Excel

Adding and Removing Components

have the CD in the drive to do so, and some features of Excel may run a little slower than usual.

■ Selecting Excel Installation Options

If you choose the Typical option from the Excel CD, you'll see the top dialog box shown in the illustration. The series of check boxes let you choose which Excel components you want to install.

For example, to use all of the techniques covered in this book, check the Microsoft Map and Internet Assistant Wizard check boxes. To install all of the typical parts of Excel, click Select All. Once you've chosen the components you want to install, click Continue. If you selected the Custom option, that dialog box offers a wider variety of choices, as shown in the second dialog box. Many of these choices consist of several individual components. If a check box is selected but gray, some of the components are not included.

For example, the Spreadsheet Templates box is gray, indicating that not all of the available templates will be installed. To add or remove components from an option, select it in the Options list, and then click the Change Option button. An additional dialog box appears listing the specific items in that part of Excel. Select items from that dialog box and then click OK.

When you've selected the parts of Excel that you want to install, click Continue. The Setup program will install the files onto your hard disk, update the Windows 95 system information, and then display a message that the installation process was completed successfully. Click OK — you're ready to run Excel.

If you are setting up Excel from the Microsoft Office suite CD, choosing Typical or Custom will display similar dialog boxes but with slightly different options.

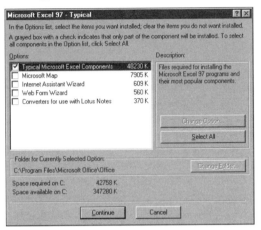

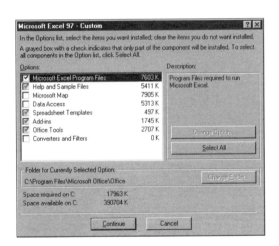

ADDING AND REMOVING PROGRAM COMPONENTS

Even after you install Excel, it is never too late to change your setup decisions. You can add components that you later find you need, or delete components that you do not use.

Adding and Removing Components

Just start the Setup program as you did when you installed the program originally. Setup will detect that it has already been installed, and will display the dialog box shown in the illustration at right.

Click Add/Remove to display a dialog box listing Excel components. Use the dialog box just as you did when you selected components to install. To remove a component, however, deselect its check box, and then click Continue.

Use the Reinstall option to repeat the last installation that you performed. Sometimes, important files become corrupted or erased. This option restores any files that have been deleted or made unusable.

The Remove All option deletes Excel from your computer.

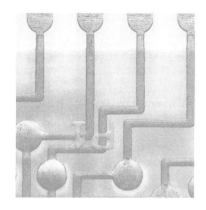

Practice Projects

Project 1: Your Family Budget

Congratulations! You've completed this book and now have the skills needed to create workbooks of all types using Excel 97. By completing the Skill Challenges, you've proved that you can work independently, but to keep your skills sharp, you should continue to practice them. The more you use Excel, the better at it you will become. You will get faster at developing workbooks, and your work will become more sophisticated. You will also pick up additional skills and learn more about Excel.

This appendix suggests some projects you might use to continuing practicing your skills. It includes a variety of projects, including those for the homeowner, consultant, business executive, and hobbyist.

Although you should develop the projects on your own, several of them are illustrated here, and the workbooks are included in the Solution folder. Use the workbooks only to confirm your own work, or to help out if you run into difficulty with a formula or format.

PROJECT 1: YOUR FAMILY BUDGET

Every family can use a budget to keep track of income and expenses. By preparing a family budget, you can see where your money is going, and perhaps improve your financial decisions. The accompanying illustration shows a typical budget worksheet.

You can use the worksheet to keep a weekly or monthly budget, depending on when you get paid and how you organize your finances. Just be consistent. If you use your weekly income, for example, enter your weekly expenses. Many of your recurring items will be monthly, so that's usually a good place to start.

If you get paid weekly or biweekly, however, you'll have to convert your income to monthly. Don't just multiply weekly income by four, or biweekly income by two. There are really more than four weeks in most months. The best approach is to calculate your total annual income and then divide by 12. If you don't earn a consistent amount each month, you may choose to insert several income categories on the worksheet, and then total their sums.

Lesson 5 can help you format the budget so it looks attractive, with custom borders and fill colors.

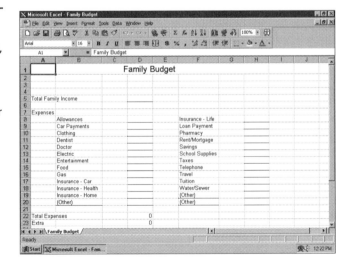

Project 2: Your Household Inventory

TIP

You will find this workbook under the name Family Budget in the Solution folder.

PROJECT 2: YOUR HOUSEHOLD INVENTORY

Create a workbook to keep track of your household possessions. Use the workbook to make sure you have enough insurance, or just so you know where everything is located. You'll find the workbook invaluable in the event of some loss or damage. Make a copy of the workbook and store it in a safe deposit box in a bank or at a friend's house. If your only copy of the workbook was damaged or stolen along with your other property, you wouldn't have the record to report to the insurance company.

Divide the workbook into multiple sheets, using each sheet for the contents of a different room. Use the room name on the worksheet tab, and have separate columns for the name of each item, the date you purchased it, and its cost. Also consider recording where you purchased each item and the expiration date of its warranty.

Total the value of the items in each room, and then create a grand total for the entire house.

Check out Lesson 6 for help working with multiple worksheets.

TIP

You can use a similar worksheet to keep track of a stamp, trading card, or other collection.

PROJECT 3: YOUR PERSONAL ADDRESS BOOK

Keeping track of names, addresses, and phone numbers in a telephone book is easy, but it is even easier with Excel. Create a worksheet listing the names and telephone numbers of friends, along with their birthdays, anniversaries, and other important dates to remember. Then at the end of each month, you can sort the database by birthday, for example, as a reminder to send cards or

Project 4: Your Company's Sales

make birthday phone calls. You can even use a filter to display your friends whose birthday or anniversary is that month.

Refer to Lesson 11 to refresh your memory about sorting and filtering information in a worksheet.

PROJECT 4: YOUR COMPANY'S SALES

Create a worksheet to check your company's sales efforts. A basic worksheet should record your sales goals, estimated sales, and actual sales, for each month, with quarterly subtotals. The worksheet shown in the accompanying illustration also includes ratios comparing the actual sales against your goals and estimates.

Create charts comparing your quarterly and annual goals, estimates, and actual sales. Check out Lesson 13 for help creating the charts.

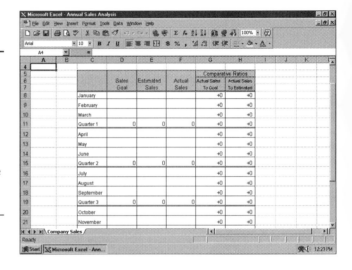

TIP

You will find this workbook under the name Annual Sales Analysis in the Solution folder.

PROJECT 5: YOUR BILLABLE TIME

If you are a consultant, lawyer, or other professional who charges clients by the hour, create a worksheet to record your billable time, as shown in the accompanying illustration.

Use the Time Started and Time Ended columns to record when you worked for a client. Calculate the amount of time by subtracting the start time from the ending time. (You'll have to choose the time format 13:30 to display the calculation in hours and minutes format.) Calculate the chargeable cost of the time using a formula such as =24*D9*E9. (You need to multiply the time spent by 24 to convert the time into a decimal number.) A time of 2:30 (two hours and thirty minutes) becomes 2.5 (two and one half hours), which is then multiplied by the hourly rate.

For help working with formulas and functions, refer to Lesson 8.

PROJECT 6: YOUR COMPANY'S TIME SHEET

If you manage a company with employees, create a worksheet to record each employee's regular and overtime hours. A sample worksheet is shown in the accompanying illustration.

This type of worksheet uses time calculations to determine the number of regular and working hours. The formula to calculate regular hours is 24*((C9–B9)+(E9–D9)); the formula for overtime is 24*(G9–F9).

If you're letting employees complete the time sheet, protect and hide the cells containing formulas, and protect the cell containing the hourly wage.

Check out Lesson 7 for help protecting cells and hiding formulas.

PROJECT 7: YOUR LETTERHEAD

Create a worksheet using a piece of clip art, a WordArt design, or your own custom artwork to print letterhead paper. The letterhead will come in handy if you do not have Microsoft Word or another sophisticated word processing program. You can print the letterhead in Excel, and then use a program such as WordPad that comes with Windows 95 to type and print your letters.

Refer to Lessons 14 and 15 for help creating graphics, and to Lesson 10 for help setting up the printed page.

Project 8: Your Web Page

PROJECT 8: YOUR WEB PAGE

If you are connected to the Internet, use Excel's Internet Assistant to create your personal page for the World Wide Web. Start by designing a worksheet that contains information about yourself, and add links to your favorite Web sites. Then find out from your Internet service provider or your network administrator how to publish your page to the Web.

For help creating Web pages, check out Lesson 9.

Answers to Questions

Lesson 1

This appendix includes all answers to the Skills Challenge exercises from the end of each lesson. If you did not know the correct answer, go back and quickly scan through the lesson again, particularly to the section relation to the question. If the question involves an Excel procedure that you are having problems with, review the Troubleshooting section at the end of the lesson.

LESSON 1

Question 1: What is another way to start a new workbook?

You can choose New from the File menu. When you select File ➢ New, Excel displays the New dialog box. Click the General tab of the dialog box, and then double-click the icon labeled Workbook.

Question 2: If you typed 20.00 in the cell, what would have appeared before you applied the Currency style?

Excel displays values without trailing zeros, so 20.00 would have appeared as 20 in the cell. When you click the Currency Style button, Excel displays a preceding dollar sign and two decimal places.

Question 3: Why should you use cell references in the formula rather than the values within the cells?

You should use cell references whenever possible so Excel will automatically recalculate the result of a formula if the value in a referenced cell changes.

Question 4: When you type 22 in the cell, why does is appear in Currency format?

Excel displays $22.00 in the cell because the Currency style has already been applied to the cell. When you apply a format to a cell, the format affects whatever you type in that cell, until you apply another format or remove all formats.

Question 5: How long can a file name be in Windows 95?

File names can be up to 255 characters long, including spaces.

Question 6: Does closing the workbook delete it from your disk?

No. Closing a workbook just clears it from the screen. As long as you previously saved the workbook, it is on your disk. If you close a workbook before you save it, Excel displays a message asking whether you want to save the changes you've made to the workbook.

LESSON 2

Question 1: How do you select more than one cell?

You can select more than one cell by dragging. Point to the first or last cell of the group that you want to select so the mouse pointer appears as a large white plus sign. Hold down the right mouse button and drag to the cell at the opposite end of the range.

Question 2: What other ways are there to change the column width?

You can drag the column boundary to widen or narrow a column. As you drag, a ScreenTip shows the resulting width of the column. To set a specific width, choose Format ➢ Column ➢ Width. Enter the width of the column in characters, and then click OK.

Question 3: What is the difference between deleting and clearing cells, rows, and columns?

Clearing a cell, row, or column removes the information, formats, or both, but leaves the cells in the worksheet. It does not affect the position, row number, or column letter of other information. Deleting a cell, row, or column actually removes those cells from the worksheet. If you delete a row, for example, rows below it move up to take its place, and their row numbers change accordingly.

Question 4: How do you choose to edit in the cell or in the formula bar?

To edit within the cell itself, activate the cell and press F2, or double-click the cell. To edit within the formula bar, activate the cell and then click in the formula bar. No matter where you edit, the changes are reflected in both the cell and the formula bar.

Lesson 3

LESSON 3

Question 1: How do you complete a series, other than entering all of the values yourself?

In most cases, enter the first value of the series, and then drag the Fill handle of the cell to the other cells you want to fill. If Excel does not complete the series for you, if you want values that are not consecutive, enter the first two values in the series, select those two cells, and then drag the fill handle of the last cell to complete the series.

Question 2: What is the fastest way to use AutoSum?

The fastest method is to select the range of cells C3 to G7, and then click the AutoSum button.

Question 3: What is the average displayed in the status bar?

The average commission is $41,833. Display the average by selecting cells F12 to F17, right-clicking the status bar, and selecting Average from the shortcut menu.

Question 4: Who has earned the largest commission and what is the amount?

The largest commission is $56,000, earned by Wison. Display the largest commission by selecting cells F12 to F17, right-clicking the status bar, and selecting Max from the shortcut menu.

Question 5: Who has the smallest commission and what is the amount?

The smallest commission is $23,000, earned by Buddy. Display the smallest commission by selecting cells F12 to F17, right-clicking the status bar, and selecting Min from the shortcut menu.

LESSON 4

Question 1: What are the ways to copy information?

To copy information using drag and drop, select the cell or cells that you want to copy, point to the cells, and drag, holding down the Ctrl key when you release the mouse button. You can also select

---

the cells or cells, and click the Copy button in the Standard toolbar or select Edit ➢ Copy. Then click where you want the information to be inserted, and click the Paste button or select Edit ➢ Paste.

Question 2: Can you also transpose cells from a column into rows?

Yes. If you select and copy cells that are in a row, the Transpose command pastes them into a column. If you select and copy cells that are in a column, the Transpose command pastes them into a row.

Question 3: When you insert a row, where is it inserted and what happens to the current row?

When you insert a row, it appears above the current row, and assumes the current row's number. The current row and rows beneath it are renumbered accordingly. When you insert a column, it is inserted to the left of the current column, and it assumes the current column's letter. The current column and all columns to the right of it are "relettered" accordingly.

Question 4: Do you have to delete the rows one at a time?

No. You can delete multiple rows by selecting them first. Drag over the row headers of the rows you want to delete, and then right-click and choose Delete from the shortcut menu. You can also choose Edit ➢ Delete. Another way to delete rows is to select cells with the rows, and then choose Edit ➢ Delete. In the dialog box that appears, click Entire Row, and then click OK.

LESSON 5

Question 1: What effect does merging have on cell grid lines?

Merging cells removes all of the grid lines and borders between the cells. It does not affect the grid lines or borders around the selected cells.

Lesson 6

Question 2: What are the two ways to change the horizontal alignment?

The quickest way to change the horizontal alignment of text in a cell is to click the Align Left, Center, Align Right, or Merge and Center buttons on the Formatting toolbar. You can also select Format ➢ Cells, click the Alignment tab in the dialog box that appears, and then select an option from the Horizontal list: General, Left, Center, Right, Fill, Justify, and Center Across Selection.

Question 3: What are the two ways to add double bottom lines?

One way is to pull down the Borders list in the Formatting toolbar and choose the border style. You can also select Format ➢ Cells and click the Border tab. In the dialog box that appears, select the line style and then the border position.

Question 4: Can you set the two adjacent columns to the same width by dragging?

Yes. First select the columns. Then drag the right boundary of either column header. As you drag, a ScreenTip shows the resulting column width. Release the mouse button when the column is the desired width.

LESSON 6

Question 1: What are the two ways to rename a worksheet?

Double-click the worksheet tab, or right-click the tab and choose Rename from the shortcut menu. Then type the new name and press Enter or click away from the tab.

Question 2: What are the two ways to move a worksheet?

You can drag and drop the worksheet tab to a new position among the other tabs. You can also right-click the tab and choose Move or Copy from the shortcut menu. In the dialog box that appears, use the To Book list to choose to move the sheet to another open workbook or to a new workbook that Excel creates for you. Then choose the position for the sheet from the Before Sheet list — either one of the existing sheets or to the end of the sheets.

Question 3: Does clearing cells on one worksheet affect the contents of the other worksheets in the workbook?

Typically it doesn't. However, if the active worksheet is grouped with other sheets, clearing cells clears the same cells in all worksheets in the group. If the sheets are grouped, the notation Group appears in the title bar, and the tabs of the sheets in the group are selected. To ungroup the sheets, click the worksheet tab of a worksheet that's not in the group.

Question 4: Can you use panes to display two worksheets from one workbook at the same time?

No. You can only use panes to display different sections of the same worksheet. Use windows to display more than one worksheet, or workbook, at a time.

Question 5: Can you drag and drop between worksheets when they are not displayed at the same time? If so, how do you do this?

Yes. Point to the cell or selected cells you want to drag (so the pointer appears as an arrow), hold down the Alt key, and then drag the cells to the tab of the worksheet you want to move or copy them to. Excel opens the sheet, at which point you can release the Alt key (don't release the mouse button yet). Drag to the location where you want to place the cells, and then release the mouse button. Hold down the Ctrl key when you release the mouse to copy the cells to the new location.

Question 6: Does closing the window also close the workbook?

No. When a workbook is displayed in more than one window, closing just one of the windows does not close the workbook.

LESSON 7

Question 1: What does the formula =B7*C7 calculate?

This formula multiplies the hourly pay rate by the number of regular hours worked for the person named Bryne. You can enter the formula in this cell and copy it down the column.

Lesson 7

Question 2: Why can you use relative addresses in columns E, F, and G?

You use a relative address because you want Excel to change the cell reference to the appropriate row when you copy the formulas down the column.

Question 3: Why do you need an absolute address in the formula =G7*$C$2?

You use an absolute reference to cell C2 because you want the reference to remain constant when you copy the formula down the column. The reference to cell G7 is relative because you want Excel to change the reference in each copied cell.

Question 4: Why should you set a data validation rule for these cells?

You set a validation rule to prevent users from entering values less than 0 and greater than 15. This way, a user cannot enter a negative value for an employee's work rate, or a value higher than the company limit of $15. You set data validation rules in other cells as well to avoid the entry of improper data.

Question 5: What other ways are there for you to protect this workbook?

In addition to turning on worksheet protection, you can protect a workbook by setting a password that is required to open the workbook. You can also protect the workbook structure from being changed, and prevent users from changing the size and position of worksheets.

Question 6: What happens when you change the state tax rate?

Cell C2 is a locked cell. As soon as you start typing in the cell, Excel displays a message reporting that the cell is protected and is read-only. To change the value in the cell, you have to turn off worksheet protection.

LESSON 8

Question 1: What cells do you have to select to assign these cell names?

To name the cells using their corresponding labels, you have to select cells D4 to F5 — both the labels and the cells you wish to name.

Question 2: How many required and optional arguments does the DB function have?

The DB function has the syntax DB(*cost,salvage,life,period, month*). The first four arguments are required; the month argument is optional.

Question 3: How does Excel treat the spaces between words when it creates a cell name?

When you use the Insert ➣ Name ➣ Create command, Excel assigns names to cells using labels that you designated. Spaces between words in labels are changed to underscore characters. For example, the label Salvage Value is converted to the cell name Salvage_Value.

Question 4: Can you use either a name or cell address for the reference?

Yes, you can. You can use either a cell's address or name in a formula. Using names makes it easier to read and interpret a formula, but takes longer to type.

LESSON 9

Question 1: What start page is used by your system, and will everyone's start page be the same?

The start page will depend on your Internet service provider, and the way your Web browser was set up.

Question 2: Do you have to type the http:// designation for a URL when creating a hyperlink?

No. Excel will automatically add the designation for you. However, if you want to create a link to an ftp site or another type of site, you must enter the designation (such as **ftp://**) yourself.

Lesson 10

Question 3: How do you find an address if you do not know what it is?

In the Insert Hyperlink dialog box, click the Browse button to display the Link to File dialog box. Then click the Search the Web button to launch your Web browser. Once you're connected, use a search engine or surf the Web to locate the site you want to use for the link. Copy the address, and then return to Excel and add the address to the Link to File or URL text box.

Question 4: What is the address of Corel Corporation's main site?

The site is www.corel.com.

Question 5: What value appears in cell G16 and what address appears in the formula bar?

Because of the data link between that cell and cell D8 of the Schedule workbook, the date 18–May appears in the cell, and the reference to [Schedule.xls]Sheet1!$D$8 appears in the formula bar.

Question 6: Was the change reflected in Workout 9 and, if so, why?

The new value that you entered in cell D8 of the Schedule workbook also appears in cell G16 of the Workout 10 workbook. That's because there is a data link between the two cells.

LESSON 10

Question 1: What are two methods that you can use to change page breaks?

You can insert a page break by clicking in the cell that you want to start the new page, and then selecting Insert ➢ Page Break. You can also choose View ➢ Page Break Preview, and then drag the page break line to the desired location.

Question 2: How would you reduce the worksheet to fit on a specific number of pages?

Select File ➢ Page Setup, and click the Page tab. Select the Fit To option button, and then enter the number of pages wide and tall that you want the printout to be.

Question 3: Does creating print titles affect the number of pages, or the page break positions?

It can. Because print titles appear on every page of the worksheet, they add additional rows and/or columns to the printed page.

Question 4: How would you use a standard header as the basis for a custom header?

Select the standard header before clicking the Custom Header button to create the custom header.

LESSON 11

Question 1: What conditions have to be met before you can apply an AutoFilter?

The information in the worksheet must be arranged like a database. There must be column labels, and the active cell must be within the data. The database must be separated from other information in the worksheet by at least one row and column.

Question 2: What happens to the rows that do not meet the filter conditions?

Rows that do not meet filter conditions are temporarily hidden from view, but they are not deleted.

Question 3: Do you have to first remove the previously applied filters? If so, why?

It depends on what you want to accomplish. If you want to apply an entirely new filter condition, remove all of the other filters first. If a filter is already in place, a new filter only applies to the currently displayed rows.

Question 4: How does Excel know where to separate the rows of the worksheet into outline levels?

Excel creates outline levels using SUM formulas to divide the rows or columns into groups. The SUM formulas are treated as subtotals for each outline group.

Lesson 12

Question 5: What is the purpose of creating, expanding, and collapsing outlines?

Creating an outline enables you to select the range of information to display. You collapse an outline to remove various levels of detail, displaying subtotals and totals for an overall look at the information. You expand an outline to display as much detail as desired.

LESSON 12

Question 1: What is the purpose of creating and saving custom views?

Creating and saving custom views lets you quickly restore a combination of settings, such as the magnification, hidden columns and rows, and a print area. Rather than select individual settings each time you want to use the combination, you just select the custom view that you previously created.

Question 2: What view is displayed when you close and then reopen a workbook that has several views?

When you open a workbook, you'll see the custom view that was in effect when the file was last saved.

Question 3: What are the ways to remove a toolbar from the screen?

If the toolbar is floating (appears in a window within the worksheet), click the Close box in its title bar. For all toolbars, right-click any toolbar to display a shortcut menu, or select View ➢ Toolbars, and then click the name of the toolbar that you want to close.

Question 4: What is the purpose of grouping buttons on a toolbar?

You group buttons to illustrate some relationship between them. For example, you might group buttons that offer alternative formats, or that relate to the same command category.

Question 5: Do you have to add new menus to the menu bar?

No. You can add menus to a toolbar as well as a menu bar.

Question 6: Can you make changes to the toolbars or menu bar when the Customize dialog box is closed?

No. For you to make any changes to a toolbar or menu bar, the Customize dialog box must be displayed. To open the dialog box, select Tools ➢ Customize, or right-click a toolbar or menu bar and choose Customize from the shortcut menu.

LESSON 13

Question 1: Can you later change the chart type if you do not like your selections from the Chart Wizard? If so, how?

Yes. After you create a chart, you can always change the chart type. There are several ways to do so: Select the chart, and then choose Chart ➢ Chart Type; select from the Chart Type list in the Chart toolbar; or right-click most areas of the chart and choose Chart Type from the shortcut menu.

Question 2: Can you change the size of a chart if you create it in its own chart sheet? If not, what are the benefits of using a separate chart sheet?

You cannot change the size of a chart when it is in a chart sheet, although you can change the size of the page on which the chart is printed. Create a chart on a chart sheet when you want the chart to appear by itself on screen and when printed.

Question 3: How does information have to be entered in a worksheet for use with a map?

You must enter information using the names of states or countries as row labels. Enter the complete state name or use the official two-character postal abbreviations.

Question 4: Can you use the same format for both series?

No. When you create a map with more than one series, each must use a different format.

Lesson 14

LESSON 14

Question 1: What is the difference between the Insert ➢ Picture ➢ Clip Art command and the Insert ➢ Picture ➢ From File command?

Use the Clip Art command to insert a graphic image from the Microsoft Clip Gallery. Use the From File command to insert a graphic that is stored on a file on your disk.

Question 2: What is the difference between cropping a graphic and changing its size?

Cropping a graphic hides or redisplays portions of it. Changing the size of a graphic reduces or enlarges it without changing its contents.

Question 3: How can you locate a graphic in the Clip Gallery if you do not want to select a specific category?

You can choose (All Categories) from the list of categories, and then scroll through the thumbnail sketches to locate the graphic. You can also click Find in the Microsoft Clip Gallery window, and then enter a key word, file name, or clip type to search for clip art files.

Question 4: What is the difference between the Send to Back and Send Backward Order options?

The Send to Back option moves the selected graphic object behind all other overlapping objects. If a graphic is in the foreground, on top of five other graphics, the Send to Back command moves the graphic to the very bottom of the stack, so the remaining four are above it. The Send Backward option moves the selected graphic back one layer — from the topmost to the second position in the stack, for example.

LESSON 15

Question 1: Does it matter if you draw a callout in the exact position where you want it?

No. After you create a callout, you can change its position by dragging the callout box and line.

Question 2: Do you have to click the Text Box tool to insert text into a callout?

No. The Callout object includes its own text box.

Question 3: How do you select the object so you can change the alignment of text?

You must select the object so the insertion point does not appear in the text. Click the object so it is surrounded by a border of diagonal lines, and then click the border again so it appears as small dots.

Question 4: How can you tell which AutoShape object is the 32-point star?

The star shapes are in the Stars and Banners category of the AutoShapes list. The 32-pont star is indicated by the number 32 within it.

What's on the CD-ROM?

Using the Software

The CD-ROM in the back of the book includes all the exercise files and the exclusive *One Step at a Time On-Demand* software. This interactive software coaches you through the exercises in the book's lessons while you work on the computer at your own pace.

USING THE ONE STEP AT A TIME ON-DEMAND INTERACTIVE SOFTWARE

The *One Step at a Time On-Demand* interactive software includes all the exercises in the book so that you can search for information about how to perform a function or complete a task. You can run the software alone or in combination with the book. The software consists of three modes: Demo, Teacher, and Concurrent. In addition, the concept option provides an overview of each exercise.

- **Demo** mode provides a movie-style demonstration of the same steps that are presented in the book's exercises, and works with the completed exercise files that are included on the CD-ROM in the Exercise folder.

- **Teacher** mode simulates the software environment and permits you to follow the exercises in the book's lessons interactively.

- **Concurrent** mode enables you to use the *One Step at a Time On-Demand* features while you work within the actual Microsoft Excel 97 environment. This unique interactive mode provides audio instructions, and directs you to take the correct actions as you work through the exercises. (Concurrent mode may not be available for all exercises.)

■ Installing the software

The *One Step at a Time On-Demand* software can be installed on Windows 95 and Windows NT 4.0. To install the interactive software on your computer, follow these steps:

❶ Launch Windows (if you haven't already).

❷ Place the *Excel 97 One Step at a Time* CD-ROM in your CD-ROM drive.

3 Click the Start menu.

4 Select Run. The Run dialog box appears.

5 Type **D:\Setup.exe** (where D is your CD-ROM drive) in the Run dialog box.

6 Click OK to run the setup procedure. The On-Demand Installation dialog box appears.

7 Click Continue. The On-Demand Installation Options dialog box appears.

8 Click the Full/Network radio button (if this option is not already selected).

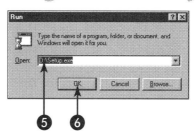

NOTE

Full/Network installation requires approximately 150MB of hard disk space. If you don't have enough hard disk space, click the Standard radio button to choose Standard installation. If you choose standard installation, you should always insert the CD-ROM when you start the software to hear sound.

9 Click Next. The Determine Installation Drive and Directory dialog box appears.

10 Choose the default drive and directory that appears, or click Change to choose a different drive and directory.

11 Click Next. The Product Selection dialog box appears, which enables you to verify the software you want to install.

12 Click Finish to complete the installation. The On-Demand Installation dialog box displays the progress of the installation. After the installation, the Multiuser Pack Registration dialog box appears.

13 Enter information in the dialog box.

14 Click OK. The On-Demand Installation dialog box appears.

15 Click OK to confirm the installation has been successfully completed.

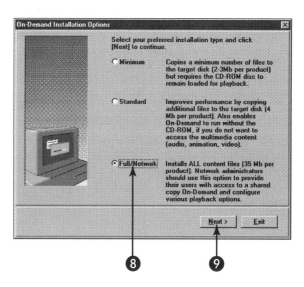

D

What's on the CD-ROM?

Using the Software

■ Running Demo, Teacher, or Concurrent mode

NOTE

If you run the One Step at a Time On–Demand software in Windows 98, we recommend that you don't work in Teacher or Concurrent modes unless you turn off the Active Desktop feature. However, Teacher mode or Concurrent mode may not work properly at all in Windows 98. At the time of the writing of this book, the final release of Windows 98 wasn't available, so we couldn't test all the topics in Teacher mode or Concurrent mode.

Once you've installed the software, you can view the text of the book and follow interactively the steps in each exercise. To run Demo, Teacher, or Concurrent mode, follow these steps:

1 From the Windows desktop, click the Start menu.

2 Select Programs ➤ IDG Books Worldwide ➤ Excel 97 One Step at a Time. A small On-Demand toolbar appears in the upper-right corner of your screen.

3 Launch Excel 97.

4 The On-Demand Reminder dialog box appears, telling you that the On-Demand software is active. If you don't want to display the dialog box, deselect the Show Reminder check box. Then click OK.

5 Click the icon of the professor. The Interactive Training — Lesson Selection dialog box appears.

6 Select the Contents tab, if it isn't selected already. The contents appear, divided into five parts.

7 Click the plus icon next to the part you want to explore. A list of lessons appears, corresponding to the lessons in the book.

8 Click the plus icon next to the lesson you want to explore. A list of topics appears. If you work in Concurrent mode, it's important to begin with the first topic of any lesson, because the software will direct you to open a specific file as you complete all the steps in that lesson.

9 Double-click a topic of your choice. A menu appears.

10 Select Demo, Teacher, or Concurrent (if available).

11 Follow the onscreen prompts to use the interactive software and work through the steps.

In Demo mode, you only need to perform actions that appear in red. Otherwise, the software automatically demonstrates the actions for you. All you need to do is read the information that appears onscreen. (Holding down the Shift key pauses the program; releasing the Shift key activates the program.) In Teacher mode, you need to follow the directions and perform the actions that appear onscreen.

■ Getting the most out of using the One Step at a Time software

We strongly recommend that you read the topics in the book as you use the software, especially while working in Concurrent mode. In those instances where the onscreen instructions do not match the book's instructions exactly, or when the software appears to stop before completing a task, the book will provide the instructions necessary for you to continue.

■ Stopping the program

To stop running the program at any time, press Esc to return to the Interactive Training—Lesson Selection dialog box. (To restart the software, double-click a topic of your choice and select a mode.)

■ Exiting the program

Press Esc when the Interactive Training—Lesson Selection dialog box appears to exit the program. The On-Demand toolbar appears in the upper-right corner of your screen. Click the icon that displays the lightning bolt image. A menu appears. Choose Exit. The On-Demand—Exit dialog box appears. Click Yes to exit On-Demand.

D

What's on the CD-ROM?

Using the Software

■ Installing the exercise files

To allow the *One Step at a Time On-Demand* software to access the exercise files for the lessons in this book, you need to set up a folder for the exercise files on your hard drive. Follow these steps:

1 Double-click the My Computer icon on your desktop.

2 In the My Computer window, double-click the hard drive (C) to open a window for that drive.

3 Open the File menu.

4 Choose the New command.

5 Choose Folder from the submenu. A new folder appears at the end of the list with the name "New Folder."

6 Type **Excel 97 One Step** to name the folder, and press Enter.

7 Click the Close (X) button in the upper-right corner of the window to close it.

8 Place the book's CD-ROM in the CD-ROM drive.

9 Double-click the My Computer icon on your desktop and double-click the CD-ROM icon, usually labeled D:, to open a window for the drive in which you placed the CD-ROM.

10 In the CD-ROM (D:) window, click the folder named Exercise to select it.

11 Select Edit ➤ Copy.

12 Close the CD-ROM window.

13 Double-click the My Computer icon on your desktop, and double-click the hard drive icon.

14 Double-click the Excel 97 One Step folder to open it.

15 Select Edit ➤ Paste to copy the contents of the Exercise folder from the CD-ROM to the hard drive.

16 Double-click the Exercise folder to open it. All the exercise files are now located within this folder.

17 Select Edit ➤ Select All to select all files within the folder.

⑱ Select File ➣ Properties to open the Properties dialog box.

⑲ Remove the check mark from the Read Only check box at the bottom of the dialog box. This allows you to make changes to the files as you work with them in the book's exercises.

⑳ Click OK to close the dialog box.

㉑ Close all the open windows on your desktop.

NOTE
Follow steps 9 through 20 above for the Solution folder to copy it to your hard drive as well.

■ Running the demo program

You may install additional modules of On–Demand Interactive Learning and find out more about PTS Learning Systems, the company behind the software, by using a file on the CD-ROM included with this book. Follow these steps:

❶ Start your browser.

❷ Select File from the menu.

❸ Select Open.

❹ Type **D:\info\welcome.htm**, where D is your CD-ROM drive.

❺ Click OK to view the contents.

USING THE EXERCISE FILES

The files are in two folders — Exercise and Solution:

- In the Exercise folder, you'll find the workbooks that you need to complete the exercises and Skills Challenge.

- In the Solution folder, you'll find all of the completed exercises and Skills Challenge workbooks.

Using the Exercise Files

When an instruction says to open a workbook from the Exercise folder, use the Open button from the Standard toolbar, or the File ➢ Open command. Pull down the Look In list in the Open dialog box and click the listing for your hard drive — it will usually be drive C, but it could be D or some other letter. Then double-click the folder labeled Exercise to display the workbooks in that folder. Locate the workbook you want to open, and then double-click it.

To find a workbook that you need to complete a Skills Challenge, look in the Exercise folder. The workbook will be named "Workout" followed by the lesson number, as in "Workout 5."

When you've completed an exercise or Skills Challenge, you can compare your work with the appropriate workbook in the Solution folder. The workbooks normally have the same name as the one used for the exercise, but with the word "Solution" appended. For example, if you used the workbook Sales Analysis for the exercise, the completed file in the Solution folder is called "Sales Analysis Solution." The completed workbook for each Skills Challenge is called "Solution," followed by the lesson number. For instance, the solution for the Skills Challenge in Lesson 12 is called "Solution 12."

You should save your own work, either at regular intervals or when you've completed an exercise or Skills Challenge. When the Save As dialog box appears, pull down the Look In list and choose the letter of your hard disk, or of a floppy disk if that's where you intend to save the workbook.

C – D

continued

F – G

Index

K – M

K

keyboard shortcuts
    activating worksheets, 135
    copying cells, 91
    copying to the Clipboard, 91
    cutting to the Clipboard, 91
    moving around worksheets, 23
    pasting from the Clipboard, 91
    selecting cells, 49
    switching between windows, 151–152
    switching between worksheets, 135

L

label ranges, defining by pointing, 191-192
labels, defined, 2
landscape orientation, 246
LEFT function, 206
legends, 319, 322
letterhead, practice project, 395
line styles, 368-369
lines, drawing, 359
locked cells, troubleshooting, 184
locking
    cells, 172
    graphic images, 347

worksheets, 171
logical functions, 206-207
lookup functions, 205-207
Lotus 1-2-3, help for, 62

M

macros, virus protection, 46
magnifying the display. *See* **zooming**
maps
    See also charts
    adding features, 329-331
    creating, 327
    customizing, 327-329
    plotting charts on, 326
    removing features, 329-331
    troubleshooting, 333-335
    undoing changes to, 330
margins, setting, 247-248
Margins tab, Page Setup dialog box, 247-249
math functions, 204
MAX function, 205
maximum values, finding, 205
mean, calculating, 204-205
median, calculating, 204-205
menu bars
    defined, 20
    resetting, 304

menu items
    adding, 302-303
    customizing, 303
menus
    animation, 305
    creating, 304
merged cells
    splitting, 118-119
    troubleshooting, 131
merging cells, 118
Microsoft Clip Gallery
    defined, 339-340
    ungrouping clip art, 372-373
Microsoft Internet Explorer, 215
Microsoft's IntelliMouse, 23
MIN function, 205
minimum values, finding, 205
mouse, Microsoft's IntelliMouse, 23
mouse pointers
    arrow, 5
    arrow and question mark, 62
    black plus sign, 5
    four-directional arrow, 360
    two-directional arrow, 140
    white plus sign, 5
moving borders
    copied cells, 91
    and formulas, 31
    ranges to be totaled, 6
moving columns, 93-94

P – R

T

Index

Index

Now it's easy to remember what you just learned and more...

With *On-Demand*, you'll never rely on the help function again – or your money back.

cing *On-Demand Interactive Learning*™ — the remark-
ftware that actually makes corrections to your documents
. Unlike the standard help function that merely provides
d" responses to your requests for help or makes
ite down a list of complicated instructions, *On-
d* lets you learn while you work.

rrent Mode — makes the ***changes for you***
your document.

r Mode — ***guides you*** step-by-step to
changes safely outside your document.

Mode — ***shows you*** how the changes are
safely outside your document.

-Demand take care of the software commands for you.
llow the on-screen pointer and fill in the information, and
learn in the fastest and easiest way possible — without
aving your document.

In fact, *On-Demand* makes your work so easy, it's
guaranteed to help you finish complicated
documents neatly and on time. With over
eleven years in software education and
a development staff that's logged
more than 5,000 hours of
classroom teaching time, it's
no wonder that Fortune 500
corporations around the world use
On-Demand to make learning for their employees
quicker and more effective.

"On-Demand Interactive Learning for Word 97. The best training title of this group..." —*PC World*

The Concurrent Mode Difference
Concurrent Mode guides you through learning new functions without having to stop for directions. Right before your
eyes, a moving pointer clicks on the right buttons and icons for you
and then lets you fill in the information.

*"On-Demand lets me get my work done and learn without
slowing me down."*   —*Rosemarie Hasson, Quad Micro*

ES AVAILABLE FOR: Windows® 3.1, 95, NT, Microsoft® Word, Microsoft Excel, Microsoft PowerPoint, Microsoft Access,
soft Internet Explorer, Lotus® SmartSuite, Lotus Notes, and more! Call for additional titles.

AY GUARANTEE:
-Demand at the introductory price of **$32**⁹⁵ (U.S. dollars) for one title or pay **$29**⁹⁵ (U.S. dollars) each for two titles. That's a
s of almost 10%. Use *On-Demand* for 30 days. If you don't learn more in a shorter period of time, simply return the software
Learning Systems with your receipt for a full refund (this guarantee is good only for purchases made directly from PTS).

all PTS at 800-387-8878 ext. 3053 or 610-337-8878 ext. 3053 outside the U.S.

PTS Learning Systems   IDG103197

IDG BOOKS WORLDWIDE, INC.
END-USER LICENSE AGREEMENT

my2cents.idgbooks.com

Register This Book — And Win!

Visit **http://my2cents.idgbooks.com** to register this book and we'll automatically enter you in our monthly prize giveaway. It's also your opportunity to give us feedback: let us know what you thought of this book and how you would like to see other topics covered.

Not on the Web yet? It's easy to get started with *Discover the Internet,* at local retailers everywhere (see our retailer list at IDG Books Online).

Discover IDG Books Online!

The IDG Books Online Web site is your online resource for tackling technology — at home and at the office.

Ten Productive and Career-Enhancing Things You Can Do at www.idgbooks.com

1. Nab source code for your own programming projects.

2. Download software.

3. Read Web exclusives: special articles and book excerpts by IDG Books Worldwide authors.

4. Take advantage of resources to help you advance your career as a Novell or Microsoft professional.

5. Buy IDG Books Worldwide titles or find a convenient bookstore that carries them.

6. Register your book and win a prize.

7. Chat live online with authors.

8. Sign up for regular e-mail updates about our latest books.

9. Suggest a book you'd like to read or write.

10. Give us your 2¢ about our books and about our Web site.

CD-ROM Installation Instructions

Installing the Software

The CD-ROM includes the interactive *One Step at a Time On-Demand* software. This software coaches you through the exercises in the book while you work on a computer at your own pace.

INSTALLING THE ONE STEP AT A TIME ON-DEMAND INTERACTIVE SOFTWARE

The *One Step at a Time On-Demand* software can be installed on Windows 95 and Windows NT 4.0. To install the interactive software on your computer, follow these steps:

1 Launch Windows (*if you haven't already*).

2 Place the *Excel 97 One Step at a Time* CD-ROM in your CD-ROM drive.

3 Click the Start menu.

4 Select Run. The Run dialog box appears.

5 Type **D:\Setup.exe** (where D is your CD-ROM drive) in the Run dialog box.

6 Click OK to run the setup procedure. The On-Demand Installation dialog box appears.

7 Click Continue. The On-Demand Installation Options dialog box appears.

8 Click the Full/Network radio button (if this option is not already selected).

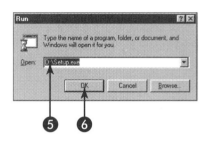

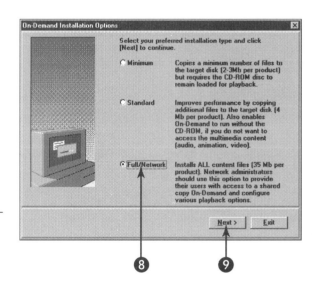

NOTE *Full/Network installation requires approximately 150MB of hard disk space. If you don't have enough hard disk space, click the Standard radio button to choose Standard installation. If you choose standard installation, you should always insert the CD-ROM when you start the software to hear sound.*

9 Click Next. The Determine Installation Drive and Directory dialog box appears.

10 Choose the default drive and directory that appears, or click Change to choose a different drive and directory.

11 Click Next. The Product Selection dialog box appears, which enables you to verify the software you want to install.

12 Click Finish to complete the installation. The On-Demand Installation dialog box displays the progress of the installation. After the installation, the Multuser Pack Registration dialog box appears.

13 Enter information in the dialog box.

14 Click OK. The On-Demand Installation dialog box appears.

15 Click OK to confirm the installation has been successfully completed.

Please see Appendix D, "What's on the CD-ROM?", for more information about running the *One Step at a Time On-Demand* interactive software.

INSTALLING THE EXERCISE FILES

To access the exercise files for the lessons in this book, you'll need to set up a folder for the exercise files on your hard drive. Follow these steps:

1 Double-click the My Computer icon on your desktop.

2 In the My Computer window, double-click the hard drive (C) to open a window for that drive.

3 Open the File menu.

4 Choose the New command.

5 Choose Folder from the submenu. A new folder appears at the end of the list with the name "New Folder."

6 Type **Excel 97 One Step** to name the folder, and press Enter.

7 Click the Close (X) button in the upper-right corner of the window to close it.

8 Place the book's CD-ROM in the CD-ROM drive.

9 Double-click the My Computer icon on your desktop and double-click the CD-ROM icon, usually labeled D:, to open a window for the drive in which you placed the CD-ROM.

10 In the CD-ROM (D:) window, click the folder named Exercise to select it.

11 Select Edit ➢ Copy.

12 Close the CD-ROM window.

13 Double-click the My Computer icon on your desktop, and double-click the hard drive icon.

14 Double-click the Excel 97 One Step folder to open it.

15 Select Edit ➢ Paste to copy the contents of the Exercise folder from the CD-ROM to the hard drive.

16 Double-click the Exercise folder to open it. All the exercise files are now located within this folder.

17 Select Edit ➢ Select All to select all files within the folder.

18 Select File ➢ Properties to open the Properties dialog box.

19 Remove the check mark from the Read Only check box at the bottom of the dialog box. This allows you to make changes to the files as you work with them in the book's exercises.

20 Click OK to close the dialog box.

21 Close all the open windows on your desktop.

NOTE

Follow steps 9 through 20 above for the Solution folder to copy it to your hard drive as well.